PATENT LAW FUNDAMENTALS

by

Peter D. Rosenberg
B.A., B.Ch.E., J.D., LL.M.(Patent & Trade Reg. Law)

Member, New York Bar
Examiner, U.S. Patent Office

1975

Clark Boardman Company, Ltd.
New York, New York

Any opinions expressed in this work are those of the author and do not necessarily represent those of the U.S.Patent Office.

Library of Congress Catalog No. 74-15799

ISBN 0-87632-098-1

This work is affectionately dedicated to my parents, whose constant encouragement and unfaltering confidence in me—even during the darkest hours—were in no small measure responsible for making it a reality.

About the Author

Peter D. Rosenberg holds Bachelor of Arts and Bachelor of Chemical Engineering degrees from New York University. He received his Juris Doctor degree from New York Law School, and his Master of Laws in Patent and Trade Regulation Law from The George Washington University. Mr. Rosenberg is a member of the New York Bar, the American Bar Association, and the American Patent Law Association. He presently is a patent examiner in the U.S. Patent Office.

PREFACE

> Next came the patent laws. These began in England in 1624, and in this country with the adoption of our Constitution. Before then any man might instantly use what another man had invented, so that the inventor had no special advantage from his invention. The patent system changed this, secured to the inventor for a limited time exclusive use of his inventions, and thereby added the fuel of interest to the fire of genius in discovery and production of new and useful things.*
>
> Abraham Lincoln
> Lecture on 'Discoveries, Inventions and Improvements' (February 22, 1860)

From the very beginning, invention has been an integral part of the American scene. The pioneering instinct of the early settlers had many manifestations. Though surrounded by a new and untamed environment, they were determined to progress beyond what had been left behind–to make two ears of corn grow where only one grew before. They did not despair, buoyed by faith, they believed the promise: 'Seek and ye shall find.'

Convinced that innovation contributed the the amelioration of society, the enlightened framers of the Constitution enshrined this conviction in that noble instrument, providing an appropriate reward for the followers of their creed, promising that one would not be suffered to reap where he had not sown. They envisioned an aristocracy founded, not upon birth or social position, but upon one's own merit. The contributions of authors and inventors were, in their minds, worthy of special recognition.

The founding fathers builded better than they knew. Innovation did not fade with the passing of the colonial era. It flourished to an extent that the framers of the Constitution could never have dreamed. America's hospitable climate not only nurtured indigenous inventors, but attracted many from less enlightened lands. Ericsson, Bell, Berliner, Pupin, and Tesla are but a few of the many who sought and found fame and fortune on this fecund soil. Some began inventing only after arriving here. Some had no formal scientific training. For these with imagination and initiative, invention and the patent system have been the epitone of the American dream, providing a road from rags to riches.

But it is the public at large which has reaped the greatest benefits. Convenience and comforts formerly unavailable even to monarchs and millionaires are now accessible to the very humblest. Invention has wrought greater, more fundamental, and more enduring social change than has war and revolution. The observation that James Watt made more law than all the judges of England is perhaps an understatement. Nor has our own generation remained immune from patented innovations. The transistor of Shockley, Bardeen, and Brattain not only freed electronics from dependence upon vacuum tubes, but made feasible such exotic things as space travel, satellite communication, and the cardiac pacemaker. The Xerox of Chester Carlson, himself a patent attorney, made copying on ordinary paper a reality.

It is the patent system, by creating property in invention, which has stimulated the rapid, continuous, and steady technological progress, the fruits of which we enjoy today. And although the system directly rewards only applied science, patent profits do patronize pure scientific research, a dramatic example being the Nobel Prizes, made possible by the fortune derived by Alfred Nobel from his patents on dynamite. It should be remembered too that Albert Einstein, during some of his most fruitful years, supported himself by working as an examiner in the Swiss patent office.

Despite all the demonstrable benefits generated by the patent system there are those who cry it down, who label it an anachronism, who see it as begetting excessive economic concentration, as erecting barriers to market entry, and as condoning monopoly pricing.

Such hostile attitudes, while disheartening, are not surprising in view of the general lack of appreciation of just what the patent system really protects; for many who malign the system do so out of ignorance. Some who presume to speak with authority fail to grasp just how the patent system works. They are deceived because they think in terms of the generalities of the social sciences, when, in fact, the patent law demands a specificity peculiar to the physical sciences. Indeed, the level of appreciation of the patent laws among nonpatent lawyers today is perhaps comparable to the lay public's understanding of the laws of England before Blackstone. Contributing to the confusion is the fact that for nearly the past two decades there has not been extant even a single book on the subject of patent law, simple enough to be comprehensible, fundamental enough to be meaningful, and yet complete enough to be of value to the uninitiated.

It was the realization of this condition that motivated this author to embark upon the project of synthesizing the instant tome. The text is designed primarily for those with a general education who seek a fundamental understanding and a working knowledge of the subject. It is fervently hoped that members of both the general legal and scientific communities will glean from this work a genuine appreciation of the problems involved in translating a scientific conception into legally enforceable property rights and that members of the patent bar will find here a coherent and meaningful exposition of the patent law. Although instruction in patent law has been sorely neglected in our universities, I think that all will agree that it is truly an intellectual discipline, involving a unique blend of logic, law, and physical science.

An attempt has been made to avoid the legalisms that are so frustrating to the layman. Where, however, these were found to promote clarity and precision, rather than obscure it, they were not disturbed. The emphasis, particularly in the early chapters, is upon the more abstract and immutable aspects of patent law. As the work progresses, more frequent references are made to specific statutory implementation. While subject to change, the concreteness of the statute should reinforce the reader's grasp of the underlying principles.

Although the author does not wish to be cast as an apologist for the status quo, he must confess that a conscious effort has been made to refrain from indulging in a discourse on what the law *should be,* the author being content to expose the law for what it is. No doubt, however, some of his own opinions have slipped into the text and he would, therefore, like to make it clear that this work is entirely his own doing and in no way represents the position of his employer. Hopefully, it will in some small measure serve to prevent letters patent from sharing the fate of letters of marque and reprisal and to keep the flow of technological improvements coming.

Peter D. Rosenberg

Arlington, Virginia
September 1974

* Lincoln was himself a patentee. U.S. Patent No. 6,469 was granted to him in 1849.

TABLE OF CONTENTS

PART I: CONCEPTUAL FOUNDATIONS

PART II: THE SUBSTANTIVE REQUISITES OF A VALID PATENT

Chapter 5

Chapter 6

Chapter 7

Chapter 8

PART IV: OBTAINING PATENT PROTECTION

Chapter 12

Chapter 13

PART V: EXPLOITING PATENT RIGHTS

Chapter 14

Chapter 15

PART VI: PATENTS IN GLOBAL CONTEXT: OBTAINING AND MAINTAINING RIGHTS ABROAD

Chapter 16

Chapter 17

The Congress shall have Power . . .

To promote the Progress of Science and useful Arts, by securing for limited Times to Authors and Inventors the exclusive Right to their respective Writings and Discoveries. . . .

U.S. Constitution
Article I, Section 8, Clause 8 (1789)

–Part I–

CONCEPTUAL FOUNDATIONS

> [A]nd it cannot be doubted that the settled purpose of the United States has ever been, and continues to be, to confer on the authors of useful inventions an exclusive right in their inventions for the time mentioned in their patent. It is the reward stipulated for the advantages derived by the public from the exertions of the individual, and is intended as a stimulus to those exertions.
>
> J. Marshall, Ch. J.
> *Grant v. Raymond*,
> 31 U.S. (6 Pet.) 218, 241 (1832)

Underlying every intellectual discipline there are but a limited number of elements and unifying concepts. Thus, in chemistry there are the chemical elements and the laws of simple and of multiple proportions; in grammar, the parts of speech and the rules of syntax; and, in mechanics, the notions of mass, time, length, and Newton's laws of motion. These can be arranged, combined, and applied in an infinite variety of ways, so as to give an almost frightful appearance of unfathomable complexity. Patent law is no exception.

Accordingly, the purpose of Part I is to dissect the patent system, leaving exposed to view only those principles which are not readily divisible into more fundamental components. It is felt that those presented here are indispensibly necessary for acquiring an understanding and appreciation of how the patent system functions: its objectives, its modus operandi, and its limitations and shortcomings.

Chapter 1

WHAT A PATENT IS

SYNOPSIS

§ 1. Letters Patent; Letters Close
§ 2. A Patent as a Grant; As a Contract
§ 3. Patents as Monopolies and as (Intellectual) Property
§ 4. Inventions and Discoveries
§ 5. Patents are to Trade Secrets as a Right in Rem is to a Right in Personam

> Inventions secured by letters patent are property in the holder of the patent, and as such are as much entitled to protection as any other property.... Letters patent are not to be regarded as monopolies, created by the executive authority at the expense and to the prejudice of all the community...but as public franchises granted to the inventors of new and useful improvements...as tending to promote the progress of science and the useful arts, and as matter of compensation to the inventors for their labor, toil, and expense in making the inventions, and reducing the same to practice for the public benefit, as contemplated by the Constitution and sanctioned by the laws of Congress.
>
> Nathan Clifford, J.
> *Seymour v. Osborne*,
> 78 U.S. (11 Wall.) 516, 533-534 (1870)

§ 1. Letters Patent; Letters Close

The word "patent" is derived from the Latin *patere* to be open. Indeed, as employed in common parlance "patent" [pronounced păt′ent] signifies that which is open to view or open to public scrutiny. A written instrument which bears the seal of its author upon its face is known as an open letter, or as letters patent (from the Latin *literae patentes*), because such can be read without breaking the seal.[1] Formerly, in England, royal letters patent bore an actual wax imprint of the great seal, which being so large, was pendant from the parchment document by a silk cord.[2] Documents which are first folded and then sealed, so that their contents cannot be read without breaking the seal, are known as letters close. The latter format is appropriate for private or secret correspondence. The infamous *lettres de cachet,* an instrument of oppression of the *ancien regime,* were a species of letters close.[3] The salutation of letters patent is usually some variant of the Latin rubric: *Pateat universis per praesentes*—"To all to whom these presents shall come." Such a format is appropriate for documents which affect the public; as those which evidence the bestowal by a sovereign authority of special rights, as for example, the creation of a body corporate, a title of nobility, a franchise, or rights in land or in an invention. Hereinafter, letters patent, unless otherwise noted, will refer to those granted for inventions.

A person upon whom the rights mentioned in letters patent are conferred, or his successors in interest, is known as the patentee or as the holder or owner of the patent.

While letters patent derive their name from the fact that the documents officially evidencing such aforementioned rights were open to view, because of the manner in which the seal was affixed thereto, with respect to letters patent for inventions, it has been the practice ever since the enactment of the Statute of Monopolies in 1623 for an official description of the invention to accompany the recitation of patent rights; thereby making both the details of the invention and the legal rights associated with it matters of public record. Every patent is thus both a scientific and legal document.

"Letters patent," often shortened to just "patent," may refer to the instrument evidencing[4] patent rights or to the underlying rights themselves. However, the word "patent," standing alone, often refers to a copy of just the official description of the invention. Such official description is more properly referred to as the (patent) specification. It will be pointed out here that every United States patent specification concludes with one or more claims, which, while possessing a degree of descriptiveness, are intended primarily as a definition of the precise scope of the legal rights of the patentee.[5]

In the United States and most other countries, the actual letters patent consist of a copy of the patent specification and a covering sheet which formally recites, in general terms, the patent rights of the holder of the patent. The two are permanently attached to each other by a ribbon whose strands are fastened to the covering sheet by a gummed facsimile of the patent office seal, so that the components cannot be separated without either destroying the seal or cutting the ribbon. Such document is competent legal evidence of the patentee's rights in his invention.

§ 2. A Patent as a Grant; As a Contract

The rights recited in letters patent are often spoken of as a grant. "To grant," literally means to give, bestow, or confer. Consistent with the foregoing definition, letters patent do give and confer upon the patentee certain legal rights. While a grant merely recites rights passing from the party who does the giving (called the grantor) to the party who receives the grant (called the grantee), the recipient-grantee, unless the grant is a gift, gives the grantor something in exhange for and in consideration of the grant. It is true that prior to the Statute of Monopolies, the English sovereigns all too frequently granted to their favorites, by royal letters patent, monopolies on industries to which such subjects had made no contribution.[6] In the United Kingdom, a grant by letters patent was, and, at least in theory, still is deemed an exercise of the royal prerogative–an act of the sovereign's special grace and favor, which may be withheld at the pleasure of the Crown, even from one who has made a meritorious invention. However, in England ever since the enactment of the Statute of Monopolies, and always in the United States, whenever letters patent are granted, consideration must pass from the patentee to the public.[7] The consideration or quid pro quo[8] which is given to the public is the disclosure of a theretofore unknown invention. The inventor makes a truly Faustian bargain with the sovereign, exhanging secrecy, of indefinite and of possibly perpetual duration, for ephemeral patent rights!

Although one court has attempted to distinguish the grant recited by letters patent from a contract,[9] the great weight of authority is that a patent is very much a contract. While the words contained within the four corners of letters patent do not themselves explicitly recite the terms of a contract between the sovereign and the patentee, such is implicit from the provisions of the patent statute.[10]

It should be emphasized that no patent rights come into being until the actual grant of letters patent occurs. In United States practice, the life of a patent is measured from the day on which such letters issue.[11] There can be no infringement prior to such date.[12] Note that in the United States, a patent is more often spoken of as being "issued," than as being "granted." Perhaps this is because the United States is a more impersonal sovereign than is a king or queen.

By way of contrast, the inception of a copyright (or rights in a trademark) does not depend upon any administrative act of the government. A copyright (or rights in a trademark) arises spontaneously upon the fulfillment of certain statutory requirements. Copyrights[13] and trademarks[14] may be registered with the appropriate administrative agency of the government, but such registrations merely involve official recognition of preexisting rights.

§ 3. Patents as Monopolies and as (Intellectual) Property

Up to this point, the term "patent rights" has been employed without specifying the nature of these rights. An inventor, assuming that his invention is neither illegal nor immoral, would possess the right, independently of the Constitution and the patent laws promulgated pursuant thereto, to make, use, sell, and otherwise enjoy his invention.[15] These rights are sometimes spoken of as an inventor's common-law rights, because they are recognized and protected by the common law independently of the Constitution and federal patent statutes. More will be said about an inventor's common-law rights in Section 5 of this chapter.

However, without the protection of the patent laws, anyone who learns, by fair means, of another's invention would be free to copy that invention and, thenceforth, to enjoy that invention to the same extent as its inventor. In fact, those who would merely copy another's invention, are likely to reap greater economic benefits therefrom than the inventor, since the copier would not be burdened with the costs incidental to the development of the invention.

The Constitution, Article I, Section 8, Clause 8, confers upon the Congress power to secure to authors and inventors, for periods of limited duration, the *exclusive* right to their respective writings and discoveries. Ever since the first Congress met in 1790, this power has been continuously implemented by appropriate legislation. The patent laws do, in effect, vest an inventor with an inchoate right to the exclusive use of his invention, but this inchoate right can be perfected only by proceeding in the manner which the patent law requires.[16]

All of the other "rights" associated with letters patent flow from the fundamental right of exclusivity in the subject matter of the invention. By making his right exclusive, the patent laws give to the inventor (and to his successors in interest) a legal monopoly in the subject matter of his invention.

The word "monopoly" denotes the right of exclusive sale (from the Greek μονος = alone, πολειν = to sell). Because of the potential economic impact of such right upon the public, the word "monopoly" often carries an unpleasant connotation. The opprobrium associated with "monopoly" is at least in part attributable to a consequence of monopolies other than patent monopolies, namely, that by fiat the public at large is deprived of engaging in a business or occupation the necessary knowledge for which was not the contribution of those enjoying the monopoly, but rather was in the public domain,[17] that is, was available to all, prior to the monopoly grant. A patentee is granted no such privilege. His patent covers not what was previously known to the public, but rather what had been unknown to the public prior to the publication of the specification which accompanied his patent grant. Although the term "franchise" has been applied to the exclusive right conferred by letters patent, it will in this text be used to signify monopoly rights in a business the knowledge needed for which already resides in the public domain. Such rights exist in the regulated industries (as for example, public utilities), for supposed reasons of "public convenience and necessity."[18]

Unlike a franchise, a patent deprives the public of nothing that it freely enjoyed prior to the grant of the patent. A patent takes nothing from the people. Rather, by adding to the sum of human knowledge, patents actually give something to the public.[19] Moreover, the scope or extent of no patent is nearly so broad as that of the typical franchise. The scope of patents is narrowly and very carefully circumscribed by what are known as "claims."

Ownership of any form of property carries with it the exclusive right to its enjoyment. That is the essence of property![20] And because *exclusivity* is an incident of every patent, patents have the dignity of property[21] —a status that is explicitly recognized in the Patent Act.[22] But a monopoly does differ from other, more traditional, forms of property in a very significant way: a monopoly "reads on," or covers, an indefinitely large number of articles—even articles which were not in being at the time the monopoly came into effect.[23] Thus, a monopoly carries with it the power to control an indefinitely large class of things; not merely existing items.

Patents, copyrights, and trademarks are frequently spoken of collectively as intellectual or information property. "Industrial property" is usually reserved for patents and trademarks, collectively.

A fundamental principle common to all genres of intellectual property is that they do not carry any exclusive right in mere abstract ideas. Rather, their exclusivity touches only the concrete, tangible, or physical embodiment of an abstraction. In the case of a patent, the specification, upon the issuance of letters patent, becomes a matter of public record. Immediately thereafter anyone is free to think and to write about what is covered by the patent without trespassing upon the exclusive right of the patentee. However, none but the patentee or his licensees may lawfully embody what is covered by that patent, as by constructing the claimed device or by carrying out the steps of the claimed process. Similarly, the ideas and facts underlying a copyrighted manuscript—even during the subsistence of the copyright—belong to the public.[24] Copyright protects only the author's verbal and graphic embodiment of ideas and facts. That is to say, copyright protects only the particular expression and format selected by the author to convey facts and ideas. It is thus that copyrights do not encroach upon, at least in no substantial way, and indeed may be reconciled with, the freedoms of speech and of the press that are guaranteed to all the people by the First Amendment.[25] Trademarks and service marks are only subject to exclusive appropriation when applied to or used in connection with particular goods or services, respectively.[26] Hence, the subject matter or res of the patentee's, copyright proprietor's and trademark owner's property is truly intangible and incorporeal.[27]

Although the Constitution speaks of the "exclusive right" of inventors, an inventor—even by obtaining a valid patent upon his invention—will not necessarily have the right to make, use, or sell his own invention! The exclusivity flowing from a patent is but a negative right, "the right to exclude others. . . ."[28] As was mentioned in Section 2 of this chapter, an inventor would have the affirmative right to make, use, and sell his own invention independent of the Constitution and the patent laws.

But now consider the following facts. *A* discovers that an evacuated container having two electrodes (a diode) can rectify an alternating current and he obtains a patent on the structure of such tube, the claims of which call for "two electrodes." Subsequently, *B* discovers that an evacuated container having three electrodes (a triode) can not only rectify but can amplify as well. *B* obtains a patent on the structure of his triode, the claims of which call for "three electrodes." Since every three-electrode vacuum tube, must necessarily contain two electrodes, it is impossible for *B*, or indeed anyone, to make, use, or sell a triode without in so doing trespassing upon, that is, infringing, the claims drawn to *A's* diode. Should *A* invoke his patent rights, *B* could not lawfully make, use, or sell his own invention for the life of *A's* patent, albeit the same is patented and *B* is the patentee.

Because every three-electrode structure must necessarily have two electrodes, a claim calling for (at least) two electrodes, in a sense, encompasses or, to use the term of art, "reads on" what is recited in a claim calling for three electrodes, since it is necessary to have two plus one electrodes to meet or satisfy that for which the claim calls. A claim calling for at least two electrodes may be said to dominate a claim calling for at least three electrodes. A claim calling for at least three electrodes may be said to be subservient to a claim calling for at least two electrodes.[29]

Normally, the invention corresponding to the dominant patent must have been made earlier than that corresponding to the subservient one; for otherwise the more specific disclosure corresponding to the claims of the subservient patent would anticipate, and thus render invalid, the more general claims of the later patent. A dominant patent is in some contexts referred to as a blocking patent, because its holder can prevent others, including those who hold subservient patents, from practicing their inventions.[30] At this point it is appropriate to introduce other terminology related to, but not synonomous with the dominant-subservient relationship. The claims of dominant patents are, in a sense, broader than those subservient thereto; the claims of a subservient patent are, in a sense, narrower than those of a patent whose claims dominate. The average patent contains several claims, which differ from one another by their breadth. As will be seen in Chapter 3 the term "breadth" may refer to two entirely distinct properties of a claim. It will also be demonstrated in Chapter 3 that a claim may be so phrased as to read on either (1) only the elements actually recited in that claim and no others (closed language) or (2) at least those elements actually recited in the claim plus any additional elements which may accompany those recited (open language). A claim couched in closed language and reciting "two electrodes" would not read on a device having three electrodes.

Both dominant and subservient patents may represent truly basic or pioneer inventions, such as those covering the diode and triode.

The characterization of a patent as an improvement is often meaningless and even misleading. Some of the most basic inventions were improvements. James Watt's steam engine was but an improvement upon the steam engine of Newcomen. Similarly, Newcomen's steam engine was but an improvement upon earlier models. Alexander Graham Bell characterized his telephone an "An Improvement in Telegraphy."[31] The term "paper patent" signifies a patent for an invention which either is incapable of being put into practice, or, if put into practice, proved not to be commercially feasible.[32]

Where there are subsisting dominant and subservient patents, it is more precise to speak of the right of each patentee as "the right to exclude others" from the subject matter of his invention, rather than as "the exclusive right" to his invention, since the latter suggests that the patentee has positive rights in his invention.[33] As a consequence of the right of each patentee to exclude others, each can prevent the other from embodying that which is recited in the claims of his own patent. Thus, *B* could prevent *A* from embodying specifically what is recited in *B's* claims, namely, a vacuum tube having three electrodes. This is actually what happened, at least for a time. In the situation above, *A* and *B* correspond to real people, namely, Sir Ambrose Fleming and his assignee, the Marconi Wireless Company, and Dr. Lee DeForest, respectively. Both the patent covering Fleming's diode and the patents covering DeForest's triode—or "audion" as DeForest himself called it—were held valid and each device was held to infringe the claims of the other's patent.[34] In most instances wherein there are such overlapping claims owned by different parties, each licenses the other, so that each party can exploit his own invention as well as that of the other party. Such a mutual arrangement is often referred to as a "cross license."[35]

A patentee is under no obligation to exploit his invention or to allow others to do so. It is well-settled that a court will not decline to enjoin an infringement merely because the patentee has not used his invention.[36]

§ 4. Inventions and Discoveries

The term "author" is generally associated with writings and "inventor," with inventions, although an inventor may be described as the author of his invention.[37] While the Constitution speaks of "Authors and Inventors" and of "their respective Writings and Discoveries," the term "invention" is not mentioned. From the Constitution, one might conclude that "invention" and "discovery" are synonyms. Indeed, a provision of the Patent Act presently in force declares: "When used in this title unless the context otherwise indicates – The term 'invention' means invention or discovery."[38]

Notwithstanding the foregoing statutory provision and the fact that these terms are frequently used interchangeably in common usage, they have each acquired, since the framing of the Constitution, at least in technical usage, different and distinctive meanings. So fundamental is this technical distinction between "inventions" and "discoveries," that only inventions are patentable – naked discoveries are not![39] The term "invention" properly signifies that which was created or contrived by man. According to Webster: "Invention is applied to the contrivance and production of something that did not before exist. Discovery brings to light that which existed before, but which was not known."[40]

An example of such a discovery was Newton's formulation of the law of universal gravitation, relating the force of attraction between two bodies, F, to their masses, m and m', and the square of the distance, d, between their centers, according to the equation $F = mm'/d^2$. But this relationship always existed–even before Newton announced his celebrated law. Such "mere" recognition of a theretofore existing phenomenon or relationship carries with it no rights to exclude others from its enjoyment. *A patent system must be related to the realm of commerce rather than to the realm of philosophy.*[42] Patentable subject matter must be new (novel); not merely heretofore unknown. There is a very compelling reason for this rule. The reason is founded upon the proposition that in granting patent rights, the public must not be deprived of any rights that it theretofore freely enjoyed. Moreover, another consequence that would attach to patents granted upon naked discoveries, as that term is defined by Webster, would be that their scope would not be commensurate with the discoverer's contribution. A patent upon a principle or law of nature would encompass every illustration and application of that principle or law. Consider, again, Newton's law of universal gravitation. It would, indeed, be a vain and foolish gesture to grant a mortal the right to exclude others from enjoying the benefits derived from the operation of that law. In attempting to assert that right, one would have to do, in effect, what King Canute did–command the tide not to come in! Patents, however, may issue, and in fact have issued, upon a myriad of inventions inspired by an appreciation of Newton's law of universal gravitation. Such involve the contrivance of novel combination of physical means of manipulative steps[43] —as the plumb line and the centrifuge and methods of using the same. Most inventions do involve one or more underlying discoveries. For example, Edison's incandescent lamp, comprising a carbonized filament disposed in an evacuated glass chamber, involved the discovery that the ability of a material to glow or incandesce without being rapidly dissipated depends upon its fineness, its resistivity, and the degree of evacuation of the environment in which the filament of high resistivity is placed.[44]

The discoverer of a heretofore unknown or unappreciated property of a known substance may not patent that substance, since such substance lacks novelty. The classic example of this rule is Dr. Morton's discovery of the anesthetic properties of ether.[45] However, one may now obtain a patent upon a new use for a known substance, provided that the new use is expressed as a novel process or method.[46]

Another consequence of the rule that the physical object or embodiment to be protected by a patent must itself be truly new is that naturally occuring products or products of nature—substances inherently produced by natural processes—have been held to lack novelty. Thus, synthetic alizarin was held to be unpatentable, since it was substantially the same as naturally occurring alizarin.[47] However, the isolation of a substance which heretofore existed only in such impure form that a desirable property of that substance went unnoticed, may entitle the one who first isolated the substance and recognized that property to a patent upon the purer product.[48] The rationale of granting such a patent is that a material having precisely the refined composition is new—it never before existed.

Still another consequence which should flow from the requirement that the physical object to be protected by a patent must be new is that an existing but unknown substance, such as the penicillin mold, would be per se unpatentable—even by the one who first recognized it as possessing theretofore wholly unknown and unappreciated properties.[49]

Finally, it should be mentioned here that a so-called "plant patent" is not strictly upon the plant per se, but rather only upon asexually reproducing such plant.[50] See Chapter 5.

§ 5. Patents Are to Trade Secrets, as a Right in Rem Is to a Right In Personam

It was noted at the outset of Section 3 that an inventor would possess the right to practice his own invention, independently of the patent laws. This common-law right, however, is not exclusive. Anyone who either invents it independently, albeit subsequently, or who learns of the invention from another, by fair means, may from that moment onward copy it and practice it to the same extent as its first inventor. Notwithstanding the absence of de jure exclusivity, an inventor who keeps his invention secret may enjoy de facto exclusivity. That is to say, that exclusivity exists merely by virtue of the fact that no one but the inventor knows how to practice the invention.

Public disclosure of how to make and use the invention is mandated by the patent law as a condition precedent to obtaining patent rights; public disclosure is not a condition precedent to the enjoyment of one's common-law rights. Rather, the latter spontaneously and automatically come into being, upon the making of an invention, and the inventor incurs no correlative obligation to disclose it. In fact, the practical value of one's common-law rights resides in the fact that how to make the invention is secret and that, therefore, the inventor may enjoy de facto exclusivity.

For those inventions which are capable of being practiced and yet maintained secret, the common-law rights offer the inventor a realistic alternative to patent rights. Examples of such are processes and complex compositions, which defy chemical analysis, as Coca Cola. No costs are involved in obtaining common-law rights. An inventor need not satisfy the Patent Office or a court that his invention meets the rigorous standards of patentability mandated by the patent laws; he is not obliged to educate potential competition by public disclosure. Moreover, unlike patent rights, which are limited to a single term of seventeen years from the date of issue, common-law rights are of indefinite, and possibly of perpetual, duration. De facto exclusivity lasts as long as the invention remains a secret, which, of course, may be forever.

An inventor who does not apply for a patent, but rather practices his invention relying upon his comon-law rights, runs the risk that others, working independently of him, may stumble upon his invention. Such independent invention, albeit later in time, will necessarily terminate the de facto exclusivity enjoyed by the first inventor. An inventor who does not apply for a patent within one year from the time the invention is first put into public use or offered for sale forever thereafter waives his right to a patent.[51] And even though the steps comprising a process or the formula of a composition are not publicly known, if the product made according to that secret process or formula was in public use or was offered for sale for a period of more than one year prior to the date of application for patent, the first inventor would be barred from obtaining a patent thereon, as the physical result of his invention was in the public domain for more than one year.[52] Patents may issue only for new, and not merely heretofore unknow, contrivances.[53] It is an open question whether a subsequent inventor who made the invention entirely independently of the first inventor would be entitled to a patent thereon, where he is the first to teach the public how to make or use the invention.[54]

One who wrongfully appropriates the invention of another is liable to the inventor for his wrong. This brings up a fundamental distinction between the patent and the common-law rights of an inventor. The common-law rights of an inventor are said to be only rights in personam, that is, they are rights which may be asserted only against the very person or persons who wrongfully appropriate the invention.

An inventor has, of course, the right to disclose his invention to the public. He also has the right to suppress it, that is, the right not to disclose it to anyone, and the right to disclose it in confidence to a limited number of people, for a limited purpose. It is the latter alternative which may enable an inventor to reap substantial profits from his invention, without securing a patent thereon. Thus, an inventor may confide the secret of his invention in his employees, so that they can assist him in practicing the invention. He may confide in others, who will practice the invention and pay him a royalty therefor. Disclosure by the inventor, under these circumstances, is made only for a limited purpose–not for the benefit of the public at large. As a general rule, the common law will recognize and will protect the confidence,[55] to the extent that should those in whom the inventor has confided breach the confidence, the inventor may sue them, but only them, for damages and/or an injunction. If contrary to their agreement, those in whom the secret has been confided should publicly disclose the invention, the inventor has but a right in personam – a right of legal action against the very parties that breached the the confidence. He has no rights against members of the public, who, as a result of another's wrongdoing, innocently learn of the invention. The public at large may thenceforth freely practice the invention, without paying tribute to the inventor. Public acquisition of what had been secret is deemed to be by "fair means" whether the public disclosure was inadvertent or deliberate. From the instant that an invention is publicly disclosed, a mere (trade) secret and all rights associated therewith vanish forever.[56] The invention irretrievably passes into the public domain and, thus, beyond the control of its author. It may never be recalled from the public domain, either by its author or by anyone else.

A patent is essentially a right in rem[57] —a right as against the world. A right in rem follows, that is, it is an incident of its physical object. Regardless of who or how others learn of a patented invention, the patentee's right to exclude them from making, using, and selling that invention attaches.

It should be noted here that in a significant respect, a patent is not strictly a right in rem, for its very validity may be called into question independently and repeatedly, by everyone who is sued for its infringement or who is entitled to sue for a declaratory judgement of invalidity. Thus, even after the Patent Office has issued a patent and several courts have upheld its validity, it is possible for a party, not a privy to the earlier determinations, and therefore not bound thereby, to challenge the patent's validity and, thus, to demonstrate to the satisfaction of the court that the patent, in fact, should not have ever issued. Hence, any determination of validity is necessarily on in personam. A holding of invalidity, on the contrary, would, except in exceptional circumstances,[58] be in rem—a bar to subsequent attempts to enforce the patent against others.[59]

To encourage inventors to exchange their common-law right, to practice their inventions in secret, for patent rights, the Patent Act[60] provides that pending applications shall be kept in confidence by the Patent Office. This provision, in effect, directs the Patent Office not to destroy, by publication, an inventor's common-law rights and, thus, encourages the submission to the Patent Office of inventions for its consideration. The inventor is promised that merely by soliciting, before the Patent Office, he is not giving up his common-law rights. Though the Patent Office may refuse to issue a patent, it must do nothing to jeopardize even an unsuccessful applicant's common-law rights. On these he may fall back, if unsuccessful before the Patent Office. It should be noted, however, that an applicant who is refused a patent by the Patent Office and then avails himself of his right to appeal the adverse decision of the Patent Office to a court, loses his common-law rights, by reason of the fact that court proceedings are a matter of public record, any member of the public having access thereto.[61]

In recent years, on the theory that federal patent law has pre-empted state trade secret law, some courts questioned the enforceability of contracts providing for the payment of royalties for access to secret, unpatented information.[62] Doubt even as to the enforceability of agreements to pay for secret information incorporated in applications for patent pending before the Patent Office had been raised.[63] Fortunately, the Supreme Court has resolved these uncertainties, ruling that State trade secret law has not been pre-empted by federal patent law.[64] Thus, trade secrets remain a viable supplement (and in some instances even an alternative) to patent protection. Finally, it should be borne in mind that the Supreme Court has questioned the thesis that one, even by contract, may be compelled to continue to pay royalties for an invention after the patent thereon has been declared invalid.[65]

Notes

[1] See G. Ramsey, "The Historical Background of Patent," 18 J. Pat. Off. Soc'y 6 (1936).

[2] See C. Dickens, "A Poor Man's Tale of a Patent."

[3] *Bouvier's Law Dictionary*, 8th ed., Vol. III (West Publishing Co. 1914), p. 2514.

[4] United States v. Stone, 69 U.S. (2 Wall.) 525, 535 (1864).

[5] 35 U.S.C. 112.

[6] See Sears, Roebuck Co. v. Stiffel Co., 376 U.S. 225, 229, 140 U.S.P.Q. 524, 527 (1964).

[7] *In re* Tenney, 254 F.2d 619, 624, 117 U.S.P.Q. 348, 352 (C.C.P.A. 1958).

[8] See for example, Flick-Reedy Corp. v. Hydro-Line Mfg. Co., 351 F.2d 546, 551, 146 U.S.P.Q. 694, 697 (7th Cir. 1965).

[9] Krantz v. Olin, 356 F.2d 1016, 1020, 148 U.S.P.Q. 659, 662-63 (C.C.P.A. 1966) (Rich, J.).

[10] Grant v. Raymond, 31 U.S. (6 Pet.) 218, 241-42 (1832).

[11] 35 U.S.C. 154.

[12] Gaylor v. Wilder, 51 U.S. (10 How.) 477, 493 (1850).

[13] 17 U.S.C. 11.

[14] 15 U.S.C. 1051 §1.

[15] Patterson v. Kentucky, 97 U.S. (7 Otto) 501, 507 (1878).

[16] Gaylor v. Wilder, 51 U.S. (10 How.) 477, 493 (1850).

[17] See Stimpson v. Woodman, 77 U.S. (10 Wall.) 117, 123 (1869) (Clifford, J., dissenting). Compare, Comm'r v. Deutsche Gold-und-Silber Scheideanstalt, 397 F.2d 656, 663, 157 U.S.P.Q. 549, 555 (D.D.C. 1968).

[18] See generally, Pacific States Co. v. White, 296 U.S. 176, 184 (1935).

[19] United States v. Dubilier Condenser Corp., 289 U.S. 178, 186, 17 U.S.P.Q. 154, 157 (1933); United States v. Bell Telephone Co., 167 U.S. 224, 238-239 (1896); Seymour v. Osborne, 78 U.S. (11 Wall.) 516, 533-534 (1870). Compare, Henry v. Dick Co., 224 U.S. 2, 27 (1912); Continental Paper Bag Co. v. Eastern Paper Bag Co., 210 U.S. 405, 424 (1908).

[20] See generally, Picard v. United Aircraft Corp., 128 F.2d 632, 643, 53 U.S.P.Q. 563, 573 (2d Cir. 1942) (Frank, J., concurring).

[21] Wilson v. Rousseau, 45 U.S. (4 How.) 646 (1846).

[22] 35 U.S.C. 261.

[23] See Blake & Pitofsky, *Cases and Materials on Antitrust Laws* (Foundation Press, 1967), p. 258.

[24] See generally Sheldon v. Metro-Goldwyn Pictures Corp., 81 F.2d 49, 28 U.S.P.Q. 330 (2d Cir.), *cert. denied* 298 U.S. 669 (1936). Compare, Nichols v. Universal Pictures Corp., 45 F.2d 119, 7 U.S.P.Q. 84 (2d Cir. 1930), *cert. denied* 282 U.S. 902 (1931).

[25] See Lee v. Runge, 404 U.S. 887, 171 U.S.P.Q. 322 (1971) (Douglas, J., dissenting). See also, Nimmer, "Does Copyright Abridge the First Amendment Guarantees of Free Speech and Press?," 17 U. Calif. L.A. 1180 (1970).

[26] United Drug v. Theodore Rectanus Co., 248 U.S. 90, 97 (1918); Avon Shoe Co. v. David Crystal, Inc., 171 F. Supp. 293, 300, 121 U.S.P.Q. 397, 402 (S.D.N.Y. 1959).

[27] McClaskey v. Harbison-Walker Refractories Co., 46 F. Supp. 937, 938, 54 U.S.P.Q. 488, 489, *rev'd on other grounds* 138 F.2d 493, 59 U.S.P.Q. 252 (3d Cir. 1943).

[28] United Shoe Machinery Co. v. United States, 258 U.S. 451, 463 (1921); Motion Picture Co. v. United Film Co., 243 U.S. 502, 510 (1916); Bloomer v. Quewam, 55 U.S. (14 How.) 539, 549 (1852).

[29] DeForest Telegraph & Telephone Co. v. Marconi Wireless & Telegraph Co., 236 Fed. 942 (S.D.N.Y. 1916), *aff'd* 243 Fed. 560 (2d Cir. 1917). See also, Marconi Wireless Telegraph Co. v. United States, 320 U.S. 1, 57 U.S.P.Q. 471 (1943).

[30] See generally, Special Equip. Co. v. Coe, 324 U.S. 370, 382, 64 U.S.P.Q. 525, 531 (1945) (Douglas, J., dissenting); Hartford-Empire Co. v. United States, 323 U.S. 386, 431-432, 64 U.S.P.Q. 18, 38 (1945).

31 See specifications of U.S. Pat. Nos. 161,793, 174,465, and 186,787.

32 See generally, Frank B. Killian & Co. v. Allied Latex Corp., 188 F.2d 940, 942, 89 U.S.P.Q. 219, 221 (2d Cir. 1951); Morton v. Ladd, 218 F. Supp. 824, 825, 138 U.S.P.Q. 285, 286 (D.D.C. 1963).

33 See Smith v. Nichols, 88 U.S. (21 Wall.) 112, 118-119 (1874); *In re* Heinle, 342 F.2d 1001, 1005, 145 U.S.P.Q. 131, 135 (C.C.P.A. 1965); Union Stone Co. v. Allen, 14 F. 353 (C.C.E.D. Pa. 1882).

34 No 29 *supra.*

35 United States v. Line Material Co., 333 U.S. 287, 76 U.S.P.Q. 399 (1948).

36 Continental Paper Bag Co. v. Eastern Paper Bag Co., 210 U.S. 405 (1908).

37 Grant v. Raymond, 31 U.S. (6 Pet.) 218, 241 (1832).

38 35 U.S.C. 100(a).

39 *In re* Kemper, 14 Fed. Cas. 286 (No. 7,687)(C.C.D.C. 1841).

40 See also, *Black's Law Dictionary* (4th ed. 1934), p. 959. Compare, A.O. Smith Corp. v. Petroleum Iron Works Co., 73 F.2d 531, 24 U.S.P.Q. 183, 189 (6th Cir. 1934).

41 *In re* Fear, 136 F.2d 908, 909, 58 U.S.P.Q. 403, 404 (C.C.P.A. 1943); Georgia-Pacific Plywood Co. v. United States Ply Corp., 148 F. Supp. 846, 851, 112 U.S.P.Q. 26, 29 (S.D.N.Y. 1956).

42 Brenner v. Manson, 383 U.S. 519, 536, 148 U.S.P.Q. 689, 696 (1966).

43 DeForest Radio Co. v. General Elec. Co., 283 U.S. 664, 684-685, 9 U.S.P.Q. 297, 303 (1930). See also, United States v. Dubilier Condenser Corp., 289 U.S. 178, 188, 17 U.S.P.Q. 154, 158 (1933). Jennings v. Brenner, 255 F. Supp. 410, 412, 150 U.S.P.Q. 167, 169 (D.D.C. 1966).

44 See The Incandescent Lamp Patent, 159 U.S. 465 (1895).

45 Morton v. New York Eye Infirmary, 17 Fed. Cas. 879 (No. 9,865) (C.C.S.D.N.Y. 1862).

46 35 U.S.C. 100(b).

47 Cochrane v. Badische, 111 U.S. 293 (1883).

48 Merck v. Chase, 273 F.2d 68, 155 U.S.P.Q. 139 (D.N.J. 1967) (Vitamin B_{12}); Farbenfabriken v. Kuehmsted, 171 Fed. 887 (N.D. Ill. 1909) (aspirin).

49 General Elec. Co. v. Jewel Incandescent Lamp. Co., 326 U.S. 242, 247-48, 67 U.S.P.Q. 155, 157-158 (1945); De Forest Radio Co. v. General Elec. Co., 283 U.S. 664, 684-685, 9 U.S.P.Q. 297, 303 (1931); LeRoy v. Tatham, 55 U.S. (14 How.) 155, 174-176 (1812).

50 35 U.S.C. 163.

51 35 U.S.C. 102(b).

52 Metallizing Engineering Co. v. Kenyon Bearing & A.P. Co., 153 F.2d 516, 68 U.S.P.Q. 54 (2d Cir. 1946).

53 See Ex parte Frohardt, 139 U.S.P.Q. 377 (P.O. Bd. App. 1962).

54 See Gillman v. Stern, 114 F.2d 28, 46 U.S.P.Q. 430 (2d Cir. 1940).

55 Dupont Powder Co. v. Masland, 244 U.S. 100 (1917).

56 Smith v. Dravo Corp., 203 F.2d 369, 373, 97 U.S.P.Q. 98, 101 (7th Cir. 1953).

57 Mercoid Corp. v. Mid-Continent Co., 320 U.S. 661, 678, 60 U.S.P.Q. 21, 29 (1943) (Jackson, J., dissenting).

58 See Kaiser Indus. Corp. v. Jones & Laughlin Steel Corp., 181 U.S.P.Q. 193 (W.D.Pa. 1974).

59 Blonder-Tongue Laboratories, Inc. v. University of Illinois Foundation, 402 U.S. 313, 169 U.S.P.Q. 513 (1971).

60 35 U.S.C. 122.

61 See *In re* Sackett, 136 F.2d 248, 57 U.S.P.Q. 541, 542 (C.C.P.A. 1943). But see, C.C.P.A. Rules of Practice, Rule 5.13(g) providing for in camera proceeding.

62 Painton & Co. v. Bourns, Inc., 309 F. Supp. 271, 164 U.S.P.Q. 595 (S.D.N.Y. 1970), *rev'd* 442 F.2d 216, 169 U.S.P.Q. 529 (2d Cir. 1971).

[63] See Lear v. Atkins, Inc., 395 U.S. 653, 674-675, 162 U.S.P.Q. 1, 10 (1969).

[64] Kewanee Oil Co. v. Bicron Corp., 416 U.S. 470, 181 U.S.P.Q. 673 (1974), *rev'g* 478 F.2d 1074, 178 U.S.P.Q. 3 (6th Cir. 1971).

[65] See Lear v. Atkins, Inc., 395 U.S. 653, 673-674, 162 U.S.P.Q. 1, 9 (1969).

Chapter 2

PATENTS, COPYRIGHTS, AND TRADEMARKS: SIGNIFICANT POINTS OF COMPARISON AND CONTRAST

> The ordinary trade-mark has no necessary relation to invention or discovery. The trade-mark recognized by the common law is generally the growth of a considerable period of use, rather than design, and when under the act of Congress it is sought to establish it by registration, neither originality, invention, discovery, science, nor art is in any way essential to the right conferred by that act. If we should endeavor to classify it under the head of writings of authors, the objections are equally strong.
>
> Miller, J.
> Trade-mark Cases, 100 U.S. (10 Otto) 82, 94 (1879)

Notwithstanding the frequent grouping together of patents, copyrights, and trademarks under a single heading, such as intellectual property, the law associated with one diverges on many crucial points from that associated with the other two. For example, as noted in Chapter 1, §2, a patent does not come into existence unless and until it is formally granted by the government, after an official search and examination on the merits have been conducted by the Patent Office. Federal copyright arises spontaneously upon compliance with certain formalities. The function of the Copyright Office is to register copyrights. This involves merely the recognition of preexisting rights. The Copyright Office conducts no search or examination on the merits; it merely scans applications to see whether they comply with certain formal requirements. The Patent Office does search and examine on the merits trademark applications, but the federal government does little more than to recognize, by its trademark registrations, rights which already exist at common law.[1] Such registrations do confer certain valuable advantages, largely procedural in nature, as access to the federal courts.[2]

Hinted at in the preceding paragraph is the fact that a difference among the three genres of intellectual property is the extent to which the states and their common law retain or share jurisdiction with the federal government. In this regard, it must first be noted that the power to promote the progress of science and the useful arts, expressed in Article I, Section 8, Clause 8 of the Constitution, has been construed as applying only to patents and copyrights; not to trademarks.[3] The power of the federal government to legislate with respect to trademarks is derived solely from the Commerce Clause, Article I, Section 8, Clause 3. Accordingly, a federal statute relating to trademarks which was not expressly circumscribed by the limitations imposed by the Commerce Clause, in that it was not confined to interstate commerce, international commerce, and/or commerce with the Indian tribes, was held to be unconstitutional.[4]

As was discussed in the preceding chapter, an inventor does have a common-law cause of action in state court against those who breach his confidential disclosure of how to practice an invention. Similarly, unless it has been registered with the Copyright Office,[5] state law controls the wrongful appropriation of an unpublished work, and an author's rights in such unpublished work are sometimes referred to as his common-law copyright. In a sense, an unpublished writing is analogous to an undisclosed or secret invention – neither is freely available to the general public, which is to say that neither is in the public domain. But publication in reference to copyright law is a word of art, having a significantly different, and in fact more restrictive, meaning than when that word is used in other contexts, as for example, when used in connection with the law of libel. Generally, a work is not deemed to have been published, in the copyright sense, until it has been reduced to graphic form, authorized copies of which have been made available to the public at large. For example, a speech which has been merely *orally* delivered, albeit to thousands and even millions of people is not deemed to have been published.[6] State law alone governs the wrongful appropriation of such unpublished works, unless these have been registered with the Copyright Office.[7] Moreover, the Supreme Court has expressly sanctioned the right of the states to legislate in regard to copyright. Specifically, the Court upheld a California penal statute which made the unauthorized transfer of a performance from tapes or records onto other tapes or records with the intention of selling the copied performance a crime.[8] Even though the statute in question, in effect, barred such copying *in perpetuity*, the Court was of the opinion that no compelling federal interest had been violated. Hence, the common law plays a more significant role in protecting some genres of writings than does federal statutory copyright, in that the practical value of such genres as speeches and plays resides in their oral and/or visual presentation, rather than in their presentation in written form. For such works, the common law provides meaningful protection, since their economic value can continue to be exploited while remaining unpublished.

A trademark may be any word, name, symbol or device, or any combination thereof adopted and used by a manufacturer or merchant to identify his goods and distinguish them from those manufactured or sold by others.[9] That different goods bear the same trademark is notice to the public that they emanate from a common source. Since a word or symbol has no trademark significance in gross, that is, when it is divorced or disassociated from goods, there can be no such thing as a secret or unpublished trademark. Indeed, trademark rights are acquired through the use in commerce of the mark in association with and appurtenant to goods.

While there is no such thing as a secret or unpublished trademark, which would correspond to a trade secret for an invention and to a common-law copyright for a writing, trademark rights arise and exist by virtue of state common law. Federal law only provides for registration, where a trademark has been used in interstate commerce.[10] Such registration carries with it little more than the federal recognition of preexisting, state based, common-law rights. Moreover, the acquisition of a federal registration does not preclude the registrant from suing in a state court to redress the wrongful appropriation of his registered mark. Rather, federal registration merely establishes a right of access to the federal court system and to certain other incidental advantages—largely procedural in nature. The concurrent jurisdiction of state and federal courts over federally registered marks is in contrast to both federally registered copyright in published works and to patents. Upon public disclosure of an invention,[11] or publication of a writing, only federal rights may exist, and then only if these were secured as provided by statute. It is possible to federally register certain forms of unpublished works,[12] and it is doubtful whether a common-law cause of action survives such registration.[13]

From the foregoing discussion it should be apparent that both state and federal law play a role in protecting intellectual property rights. Indeed, Congress' very power to promote the progress of science and the useful arts and to regulate interstate commerce is not made exclusive by the express wording of the Constitution. Nevertheless, by a process of judicial interpretation, the doctrine of federal preemption has been engrafted upon these powers. In essence, this doctrine requires that, where the Constitution explicitly recognizes

Congress' power to regulate, but is silent about denying such a power to the states, the states must so limit their regulation as not to conflict with the scheme or policy of federal regulation. This doctrine had its genesis in *Gibbons v. Ogden,*[14] a case so celebrated that the reader will undoubtedly recall it from his high school course in American History. It was presented there, as in courses in constitutional law, for its landmark interpretation of the Commerce Clause. That, indeed, was the point on which the Court's decision turned. However, the reader may be unaware of the fact that in issue in that case were the steamboat "patent" rights granted by the New York State Legislature to Robert Fulton and Robert Livingston, giving to them, for a period of years, the exclusive right to navigate in the waters of the state by boats propelled by steam.[15] Aaron Ogden had secured, by assignment, a portion of those rights, namely, the right to steam navigation between New York City and places in New Jersey. Robert Fulton never bothered obtaining a United States patent, but chose instead to secure what was, at that time, considered to be the equivalent, i.e., separate monopolies within the territories of the several states from the respective legislatures. Until Chief Justice Marshall handed down his opinion in *Gibbons v. Ogden,* inventors felt as secure with state granted monopolies upon their inventions as with federally granted ones. These had existed in Colonial times, even before the Revolution.[16] The Constitution, in empowering the Congress to secure to inventors the exclusive rights to their discoveries, did not expressly say that the states could not continue to do likewise. However, interest in obtaining formal grants of monopoly for inventions from state legislatures rapidly waned in favor of federal patent rights, after Marshall held that what purported to be a right to exclude all others from navigating by boats propelled by steam was ineffective against those who held licenses issued pursuant to an act of Congress authorizing the holders to engage in costal trade. Such act of Congress, like other laws of the United States enacted pursuant to constitutional authority, is the supreme law of the land. When a state law touches upon an area covered by a federal statue, the federal policy implicit therein may not be set at naught, or its benefits denied by the state law.[17]

Nevertheless, protection by the several states of secret or unpublished works has survived to this day. That such protection has remained viable is attributable in large part to the dearth of federal legislation in this area – federal copyright in certain genres of unpublished works being the principal exception.[18] Also, the inherently inconspicuous nature of rights in unpublished and secret works has sheltered these from the likelihood of their interfering, even incidentally, with federal legislation not directly touching such rights. As in other fields where the Constitution appears to allow for a concurrent state-federal power, the states, by an application of the Supremacy Clause, have been relegated to a subsidiary and supplementary role, being suffered but to fill the interstices or voids in the federal scheme of regulation.

Rights in undisclosed inventions, in unpublished writings, and in trademarks are the intellectual property rights which arise from and are protected by the laws of the several states. These laws are to be gleaned largely from court decisions, that is, from the common law, although some of the rules have been formalized and codified, in some states, by legislative enactments. Some of the resulting statutes are wholly declaratory of preexisting case law. Others alter or add to the case law. The generic name by which this body of law is known is unfair competition, unfair trade practices, or business torts.

In the offing are further federal encroachments upon the already narrowly circumscribed sphere in which the states have been left virtually free to recognize and protect rights of their own creation in intellectual property. It should be recalled that a trademark may consist of any word, name, symbol, or device adopted by a merchant to identify his goods and to distinguish them from those of others. "Device" is included in the foregoing definition because the very shape or configuration—the physical appearance—of goods may constitute a trademark. To perform a trademark function, not only must the configuration be distinctive, it must be nonfunctional as well, that is, it must not be essential to the use of the article. Notwithstanding these limitations, the Supreme Court in *Sears, Roebuck & Co. v. Stiffel Co.*[19] and *Compco Corp. v. Day-Brite Lighting, Inc.*[20] left in doubt the continued viability of configurations as protectable trademarks. While apparently recognizing the right of the states to provide for the labeling of goods in order to indicate their source of origin, the Court refused to allow a state to prohibit or otherwise impose liability for acts of copying and imitating, regardless of the copier's motives, where the original article was protected neither by a valid federal patent or copyright and was in the public domain. Although the Court did not elaborate upon in what "labeling" may consist—whether it may reside in the configuration of the article—the Court made it abundantly clear that it would not sanction the imposition of any liability by a state for simulating the article per se.

In *Lear, Inc. v. Atkins*,[21] the Supreme Court seemed to suggest that State Law might not protect inventions for indefinite or perpetual periods of time, as such protection would be contrary to the "limited times" proviso of Article I, Section 8, Clause 8. The Court, however, in more recent decisions has sanctioned protection of such duration in regard to both trade secrets and "writings."[22]

It should be borne in mind that Congress, by private act, may extend the duration of a federal copyright or patent beyond that provided for by statute. Private laws extending the term of a patent or copyright have been enacted only on the rarest of occasions. To date, there is but a single instance of Congress, by private act, extending the life of a patent beyond its seventeen-year term.[23] That act was passed to rectify a horrendous injustice. The patent in question had previously been declared to be invalid by a United States Circuit Court of Appeals, but it was learned later that one of the judges in so holding had been influenced by a bribe.[24] That judge was subsequently defrocked, indicted, and convicted, and he served a term in federal penitentiary. Recently, Congress acted to extend the term of the copyright on the writings of Mary Baker Eddy which form the basis of Christian Science.[25]

The Patent Act provides for a single, nonrenewable term of seventeen years, which begins to run from the day on which patent rights are granted.[26] This event coincides with the release by the Patent Office to the public of the inventor's disclosure of how to make and use his invention.

Statutory copyright subsists for an initial term of twenty-eight years, renewable for one additional twenty-eight year term.[27] For published works, the initial term is reckoned from the day of first publication; for unpublished works, from the day of registration in the Copyright Office.

ascribed to a trademark. The vitality of any word, symbol, or device as a trademark depends upon its continued use in commerce. Moreover, exclusive rights in a mark will cease to exist if, notwithstanding such continuous use, it, in fact, becomes commonly accepted as the generic name for the goods the origin of which it was intended to identify.[28] However, the federal registration of a trademark, to remain in effect, must be renewed every twenty years, and, at approximately five-year intervals, an affidavit must be filed with the Patent Office, demonstrating that the trademark is still in use or that its nonuse is due to special, mitigating circumstances.[29]

Not only does the procedure differ for bringing into being patents, copyrights, and trademarks, but the substantive criteria for the validity of each are totally dissimilar. Patentable subject matter must be new, useful, and unobvious.[30] Copyrightable subject matter need only be original.[31] A trademark need be neither novel nor original; all that is required is priority of appropriation in trade.[32] As used in the law of intellectual property, the terms "novelty" and "originality" are words of art, having special significance. "Novelty" is applied to matter which never before existed. "Originality" means only independent creation. Two identical photographs of the same subject would both be copyrightable, provided that one was not derived or copied from the other.[33] If one independently arrived at an invention, such creation would involve originality, but unless no one had made that invention before, it would lack novelty and for that reason be unpatentable. The quality of unobviousness or invention, characteristic of patentable subject matter, is, in essence, a requirement that there be present a certain quantum of novelty.

Common to patents, copyrights, and trademarks are monopoly rights: the right to exclude others—but from what? How much or how many different things are covered by each? How much variation need there be to avoid a charge of infringement? The answer to these questions cannot be fully appreciated without an understanding of verbal patent claims. It must suffice here to say that a patent (excepting design or plant patents) takes within its purview whatever can be read on its verbal claims and functional equivalents thereof. Copyright protects only against literal copying and colorable variations. Trademark infringement occurs where there is an unauthorized use of the same or of a confusingly similar mark on like goods.

From the foregoing discussion, it should be apparent that the latitude of protection accompanying a patent is potentially more extensive than that incidental to a copyright or trademark. The extremely limited sphere in which a copyright or a trademark is operative will be brought into sharper focus by the following illustrations. Architectural plans may be copyrighted, but such copyright protects only against the copying of those plans and not against copying or embodying in three-dimensional form the design represented by those plans[34] A known word may be adopted as one's exclusive trademark, provided that word is not descriptive of the article to which it is applied. But one may not appropriate to his own, exclusive use such word for all purposes. Rather, exclusivity exists only in connection with particular goods. Ordinarily, a trademark owner has no exclusive rights in a mark when such is divorced from goods or articles of commerce. Trademark rights are thus said to be rights appurtenant and not in gross.[35]

Although a patent has the potential of encompassing a relatively wider field of variations than either a copyright or a trademark, the scope of a patent and of the accompanying rights are far more limited in other respects. Already mentioned is the significantly shorter duration of patents. The possible remedies available against an infringer serve as another example of the more limited nature of many aspects of the rights incidental to patents. While injunction and damages are available for patent, copyright, and trademark infringements, the copyright law further provides for recovery of the infringer's profits,[36] and for the alternative of statutory damages[37] and for the punishment of deliberate infringement for profit as a misdemeanor.[38] Both the patent and copyright laws also allow a court to assess reasonable attorneys fees against an infringer.[39]

Still another aspect of the more liberal treatment accorded copyrights is the variety of works which come under the aegis of copyright protection. Although the Copyright Act does enumerate several different, specific classes of copyrightable subject matter,[40] the Act further declares that all the "writings" of an author shall be copyrightable.[41] Patentable subject matter, in contradistinction to copyrightable subject, matter must clearly fall within one of the rigid, distinct, and inflexible classes set forth in the Patent Act. A good example of the inflexibility of the classes of patentable subject matter, relative to the classes of copyrightable subject matter, is furnished by computer programs. The Patent Office has consistently resisted granting patents for naked computer programs, largely on the ground that these do not fall within one of the enumerated classes of patentable subject matter.[42] While the Copyright Act does not specify computer programs as a specific class of copyrightable subject matter, the Copyright Office has expressed a willingness to register copyrights on computer programs.[43] The Trademark Act provides for a classification of goods and services.[44] One must specify in his application for registration the classes in which he intends to use his mark.

As discussed in Chapter 1, §3, the holders of an improvement patent would be unable lawfully to exploit such patent where its claims are subservient to claims of an earlier patent without the consent of the holder of such dominant patent. Similarly, a copyright proprietor has the exclusive right to derivative works, such as an arrangement, adaptation, translation, new edition, dramatization, or other version of his earlier work.[45]

One noteworthy instance in which preferential treatment is accorded to patents is furnished by the tax laws. The sale and certain other transfers of patent rights may be eligible for capital gains treatment.[46] The Internal Revenue Code specifically excepts the transfer of copyrights from the possibility of enjoying capital gains treatment.[47]

While other topics also present opportunities to compare, contrast, and analogize patents, copyrights, and trademarks, these interrelationships and parallels are more appropriately treated elsewhere in this text. Let it suffice for the present to draw attention to two other sets of parallel relationships: the fair use doctrine in copyright law and the experimental use doctrine in patent law; repair versus reconstruction of patented articles and the re-use of articles bearing a trademark.

Notes

[1] Georator Corp. v. United States, 485 F.2d 283, 179 U.S.P.Q. 450 (4th Cir. 1973).

[2] *Ibid.*

[3] Trademark Cases, 100 U.S. (10 Otto) 82 (1879).

[4] *Ibid.*

[5] See Wheaton v. Peters, 33 U.S. (8 Pet.) 591 (1834).

[6] See for example, King v. Maestro, 224 F. Supp. 101, 140 U.S.P.Q. 366 (S.D.N.Y. 1963).

[7] 17 U.S.C. 2.

[8] Goldstein v. California, 412 U.S. 546, 178 U.S.P.Q. 129 (1973).

[9] 15 U.S.C. 1127 (Lanham Act, §45).

[10] See Dawn Donut Co. v. Hart's Food Stores, Inc., 267 F.2d 358, 121 U.S.P.Q. 430 (2d Cir. 1959).

[11] See for example O'Brien v. Westinghouse Elec. Co., 293 F.2d 1, 130 U.S.P.Q. 79 (3d Cir. 1961).

[12] Photo-Drama Motion Pictures Co. v. Social Uplift Film Corp., 213 Fed. 374, 378 (S.D.N.Y. 1914), *aff'd* 220 Fed. 448, 450 (2d Cir. 1915). Compare, Loew's Inc. v. Superior Court, 115 P.2d 983 (Cal. Sup. Ct. 1941).

[13] 17 U.S.C. 12.

[14] Gibbons v. Ogden, 22 U.S. (9 Wheat.) 1 (1824).

[15] Livingston v. Van Ingen, 9 Johns. Rep. 568 (N.Y. Ct. Err. 1812).

[16] See generally, B.W. Bugbee, *The Genesis of American Patent and Copyright Law* (Public Affairs Press, 1967).

[17] Sears, Roebuck & Co. v. Stiffel Co., 376 U.S. 225, 231, 140 U.S.P.Q. 524, 527-528 (1964).

[18] 17 U.S.C. 12.

[19] 376 U.S. 234, 140 U.S.P.Q. 225 (1964).

[20] 376 U.S. 234, 140 U.S.P.Q. 528 (1964).

[21] 395 U.S. 653, 162 U.S.P.Q. 1 (1969).

[22] See Kewanee Oil Co. v. Bicron Corp., 416 U.S. 470, 181 U.S.P.Q. 673 (1974) (trade secrets); Goldstein v. California, 412 U.S. 546, 178 U.S.P.Q. 129 (1973) (copyright).

[23] 58 Stat. 1095 (Dec. 23, 1944).

[24] See Ronson Patents Corp. v. Sparklets Devices, Inc., 103 F. Supp. 726, 93 U.S.P.Q. 296 (E.D. Mo. 1952), *aff'd* 202 F.2d 87, 96 U.S.P.Q. 201 (8th Cir. 1953). See also Manton v. United States, 107 F.2d 834 (2d Cir. 1938), *cert. denied* 309 U.S. 664 (1940).

[25] Pri. L. 92-60 (Dec. 15, 1971).

[26] 35 U.S.C. 154.

[27] 17 U.S.C. 24.

[28] See for example, DuPont Cellophane Co. v. Waxed Prod. Co., 85 F.2d 75, 30 U.S.P.Q. 332 (2d Cir.), *cert. denied* 299 U.S. 601 (1936) ("cellophane"); Bayer Co. v. United Drug Co., 272 Fed. 505 (S.D.N.Y. 1921) ("aspirin").

[29] 15 U.S.C. 1059 (Lanham Act, §9). See also, 15 U.S.C. 1058a (Lanham Act, §8(a)) requiring affidavit of use at the end of six years.

[30] 35 U.S.C. 101, 102, 103.

[31] See generally, Mazer v. Stein, 347 U.S. 201, 218, 100 U.S.P.Q. 325, 333 (1954).

[32] Trademark Cases, 100 U.S. (10 Otto) 82, 94 (1879).

[33] See Schwarz v. Universal Pictures Co., 85 F. Supp. 270, 83 U.S.P.Q. 153 (S.D. Cal. 1945).

[34] Muller v. Triborough Bridge Authority, 43 F. Supp. 298, 52 U.S.P.Q. 227 (S.D.N.Y. 1942).

[35] See Katz Drug Co. v. Katz, 188 F.2d 696, 699, 89 U.S.P.Q. 303, 306 (8th Cir. 1951).

[36] 17 U.S.C. 101(b).
[37] 17 U.S.C. 101(b).
[38] 17 U.S.C. 104.
[39] 17 U.S.C. 1(e), 116 (copyrights); 35 U.S.C. 285 (patents).
[40] 17 U.S.C. 5.
[41] 17 U.S.C. 4.
[42] See Gottschalk v. Benson, 409 U.S. 63, 175 U.S.P.Q. 673, 676 (1972).
[43] Copyright Office, The Library of Congress, Cir. 31D, *Computer Programs* (Apr. 1967).
[44] 15 U.S.C. 1112 (Lanham Act, § 30). Trademark Rules 2.85-2.88.
[45] 17 U.S.C. 1(a)-(e).
[46] I.R.C. 1201-1223, 1235. See Chapter 14.
[47] I.R.C. 1221(3).

Chapter 3

PATENT CLAIMS: BASIC RULES OF CONSTRUCTION AND DRAFTING

SYNOPSIS

Some persons seem to suppose that a claim in a patent is like a nose of wax which may be turned and twisted in any direction, by merely referring to the specification, so as to make it include something more than, or something different from, what its words express. The context may undoubtedly be resorted to, and often is resorted to, for the purpose of better understanding the meaning of the claim; but not for the purpose of changing it and making it different from what it is. The claim is a statutory requirement, prescribed for the very purpose of making the patentee define precisely what his invention is; and it is unjust to the public, as well as an evasion of the law, to construe it in a manner different from the plain import of its terms.

Bradley, J.
White v. Dunbar,
119 U.S. 47, 51-52 (1886)

A patentee makes his own bargain; he demands what he thinks to be the just measure of his contribution; and he abandons to the public all that he does not reserve in his claims.

Per Curiam
Ajello v. Pan-American Airways Corp.,
128 F.2d 196, 197, 53 U.S.P.Q. 530, 531 (2d Cir. 1943)

It was stated in Chapter 2 that a patent has the *potential* of covering a relatively wider or broader range of variations than either a copyright or a trademark. This potential, however, can be realized only where a patent contains effective verbal claims.

In the literature, patent claims are frequently analogized to the metes and bounds of a deed to real property or to the fence enclosing such property. Both the metes and bounds of a deed and the claims of a patent define the physical extent of the property. One who enters upon the realty of another, without the consent of its owner, commits a trespass. Similarly, one who, without the consent of the patent owner, constructs a device or carries out a process which is covered by a claim of a subsisting patent, commits a trespass,[1] more commonly referred to as an infringement of the patent, and, more precisely, of the patent claim.[2]

It cannot be emphasized too strenuously that the claims are the only definitive statement of the invention represented by the patent. The patentee is legally bound by and limited to the recitations contained in the claims of his patent. Claiming has been characterized by the Supreme Court as a patentee's "most solemn act."[3]

Although the more technical rules of patent claim drafting will be treated elsewhere in this text (Chapter 12), enough of the basic principles will now be outlined to enable the reader to grasp the gist of the subject. Over the years, a series of extremely intricate–albeit on the whole eminently logical–rules have evolved from Patent Office and judicial experience with the millions of patents processed during that period.

Throughout the law there runs a dichotomy between matters of substance and matters of procedure or form; between rights and obligations, on one hand, and the means by which these may be secured and enforced, on the other. Patent law is no exception. In fact, as will be presently demonstrated, an extension of the concept underlying this dichotomy takes on particular significance in regard to patent claims. Not only are there rules of substance and rules of form applicable to the construction and interpretation of patent claims, but the very words making up a claim fall into two classes: (1) structural language, which is substantive in nature, and (2) functional language, which is analogous to a formal matter in that it does not limit, but is only explanatory of, structural language.

Few of the rules relating to form are specifically stated in the Patent Act. In fact, the only section of the Act which specifically addresses itself to patent claims, and there only inter alia, is Section 112. The most pertinent portion of Section 112 merely requires that *the specification shall conclude with one or more claims particularly pointing out and distinctly claiming the subject matter which the applicant regards as his invention.*[3] While just what is required by the foregoing provision is itself rather hazy, it does form the basis for a system of patent claiming which is distinct from that prevalent in many other countries. In such countries, the outer reaches or periphery of an invention are not explicitly claimed, but rather only its essence—the inventive concept. Under such a system it is difficult to assess, with any degree of certainty, whether there has been an infringement. That must await a judicial determination, the court having a wide degree of discretion. In the United States, the literal language of the claim, somewhat tempered by the doctrine of equivalents,[4] is controlling.

The Commissioner of Patents has authority to promulgate *Rules of Practice*, which are not inconsistent with the specific provisions of the Patent Act.[5] A number of rules relating to the drafting of patent claims have been "codified" as *Rules of Practice*. A source of many of the rules of claiming are court decisions, decisions of the Patent Office Board of Appeals, and decisions of the Commissioner of Patents. Still other "rules" have no official sanction, but are nonetheless adhered to, with surprising regularity, by the Examining Corps with the cooperation of the Patent Bar, because they represent logical or convenient solutions to recurrent problems. To encourage uniformity in practice within the Examining Corps, a *Manual of Patent Examining Procedure* (M.P.E.P.) has been made available by the Patent Office. It sets forth the "authorized" approach to a myriad of problems, including some bearing upon the interpretation and construction of patent claims. Most of its content is merely a restatement of rules gleaned from more authoritative sources.

The objective of what follows is to develop, logically and rigorously, the basic rules of patent claim construction. An understanding of these rules should enable one to formulate effective claims, as well as to comprehend the scope of existing claims. To accomplish this, three fundamental rules will first be presented, then auxiliary principles will be progressively introduced, largely in the abstract, until the point is reached where the reader should be possessed of enough information to be able to apply these principles to realistic situations.

The following are the three cardinal rules:

(1) Each claim must be expressed in a single sentence, beginning with "What I (We) claim is . . . " or other words of equivalent import.

(2) The object of each claim must "read on" the unique combination of features which are distinctive of and which characterize the invention.

(3) The object of each claim must *not* read on a combination of features found united in the same manner in the prior art.

It should be noted that the first of the above rules relates to a matter of form and is neither a provision of the Patent Act nor one of the *Rules of Practice*. Rather, it is merely set forth as "present Office practice" in the *Manual of Patent Examining Procedure*.[6] The second and third rules are substantive in nature and are necessitated by Section 102 of the Patent Act. This section does not directly relate to claim construction, but to novelty and its antithesis—anticipation. In essence, all that rule 2 says is that a claim must claim what is new; all that rule 3 says is that a claim must not claim what is old.

§ 1. Uniqueness of Claim

It will be recalled from Chapter 1 that a claim reads on subject matter if there is a correspondence of features between those effectively recited in the claims and those possessed by that subject matter. That is to say, the unique combination of distinguishing features must appear as effective recitations in a claim for such claim to read on the invention. A claim which reads on an invention, in effect, fences off that invention from the public domain.

A claim is said to read on a device, a process, or on another claim or, indeed, on any written (verbal or graphic) representation of an invention. Any written representation of an invention may be spoken of as reading on its physical object. However, the physical object which corresponds to a claim is *not* properly spoken of as reading on such claim. Rather, a physical object or embodiment, the features of which correspond to a claim, is said to infringe such claim. The reader may have already realized that reading on is what a writing is capable of doing to another writing or to a physical object; infringement is what a physical object is capable of doing to a claim. In a sense, one is the reciprocal or correlative of the other.

While an inventor may point to a constructed device and say "Here is my invention," what he really means is that here is a concrete entity which is illustrative of and which embodies my invention. Any specific physical entity can amount to no more than a working model of an invention. Thus, an invention or its representation in the form of patent claims and its physical object are entirely distinct entities! A claim is an abstraction and generalization of an indefinitely large number of concrete, physical objects.

It should also be recalled from Chapter 1 that a claim may be so couched as to read not only upon the unique combination of features which characterize an invention and which are explicitly recited in a claim, but also upon any additional and nonessential features associated in context with those explicitly recited. Such a claim is said to be couched in "open language." This is the usual mode of claiming. Alternatively, a claim may be couched in "closed language." Such a claim will only read on physical entities which possess the *very* features explicitly recited and no others. That is to say, a claim couched in closed language will not read on an entity which contains features in addition to those explicitly recited. There must be a complete identity of features between what is recited in closed language and its physical object for such a claim to infringe the physical object. All the features possessed by the physical object must be recited in the claim. It should be apparent that, at least for (mechanical) devices, infringement of claims couched in closed language may be readily avoided by merely adding thereto superfluous features. Closed language is frequently of value in claiming compositions of matter.

§ 2. Structural and Functional Language

Of significance almost equal to the rule that the claims are the only definitive statement of the invention set forth in the patent is the distinction between structural and functional language.

Structure is here used as a generic term which encompasses both physical bodies and physical operations. A horizontal member, a vertical member, a beam, a box, and a bridge are all examples of physical bodies. Washing, drying, hydrogenating, and oxidizing are all examples of physical operations.

"Physical" is here used as a generic term which encompasses both physical and chemical changes. It is employed to distinguish the manipulative from the mental. The reader is cautioned, however, that in other works the term "structure" is often give a more restrictive meaning, being confined to and synonymous with physical bodies, and being exclusive of physical operations.

Function is here used as a generic term which encompasses the inherent and inevitable effects which accompany a given structure. It may be (1) a result flowing from the use of a given structure; (2) an inherent property possessed and exhibited by a structure; and/or (3) an advantage to be derived from a given structure.

As will be discussed more fully in Chapter 6, the physical object or embodiment of that which is sought to be protected by a patent must itself be new. Hence, *only structural language is determinative of the metes and bounds of a patent claim.* Functional recitations, standing alone, while helpful in understanding the meaning of a claim and the invention that it represents, cannot be relied upon to distinguish over the prior art.

There is another reason for the rule that only structural language is determinative of the metes and bounds of a patent claim: A claim which merely recites a desired property or result is generic to and so necessarily encompasses every possible way of achieving the stated result, while not even setting forth just how such property or result may be attained. It must be noted, however, that a recitation of certain inherent properties may be the only way to express a complex chemical composition. Claims directed to such compositions have been referred to as "finger-print" claims.[7] They may be permissible, but only where there is no more precise manner of fully characterizing what has been invented.

One who merely recites a desired result has made no contribution to the useful arts. Progress is possible only where there is revealed a mechanism or feature-by-feature description of just how the desired result may be attained. While within the four corners of the patent specification the invention must be described with such blow-by-blow particularity as to enable one skilled in the art to which it most nearly relates to be able to practice it without resort to undue further experimentation, the claims need only recite that unique combination of structural features and the manner in which these are related to one another which enables them to cooperate to produce the unitary result characteristic of the invention. Whatever gives an invention its distinctive character must be stated in the claims; nonessential features, the exclusion of that which would not destroy its character, need not be recited in the claims. It is only necessary that claims point out the invention; then need not describe it.[8] A particular feature upon which an applicant predicates patentability, however, must be recited in the claims; it is not sufficient merely to disclose it in the specification.[9] While reciting a list of ingredients may suffice as a definition of a composition of matter, a mere list of parts cannot adequately define a mechanical device, even though such parts cannot be found together in the prior art. A claim should somehow bring out how the recited structure, having its own distinctive properties, functions as a unity. There are an infinite number of ways of arranging or permutating known structures; only those arrangements possessing some particular virtue, something distinct and apart from that of its separated, individual components, are patentable. The claims should bring this out. Claims addressed to mechanical devices which omit mention of the cooperative relationship between the recited parts are said to constitute an unpatentable aggregation, rather than a patentable combination. There must be some efficacy to the co-action of parts, and this should be expressed in the claims.

A refusal by the Patent Office to issue a patent because the claims were characterized by the examiner as being aggregative, was overruled by an appellate tribunal.[10] That court's reasoning appears to be that the examiner rejected the claims without setting forth a statutory basis therefor, the Patent Act not in haec verba proscribing aggregations. That a claim merely enumerates a list of parts, without articulating how these are related, clearly seems not to comply with the requirement of Section 112 that the claims particularly point out and distinctly claim the invention.

It has been noted that there is a distinction between the description of the invention as this is set forth in the specificaton and as is recited in the claims. This distinction can be best summed up by reversing a rule of thumb that has been sometimes applied as a gauge of patentability itself: The discrepancy between the specification description and the claim description should be viewed as a difference merely in degree (or detail), not as a difference in kind.[11] While the fundamental and underlying relationship between the critical structural elements which constitute the invention must be expressed in the claims, the claims may omit mention of nonessential features and they may employ generic terms in lieu of specific ones to characterize essential structural elements of the inventive combination, provided that where a generic term is employed in a claim, all members of the recited genus are capable of performing the function performed in the combination by the species described in the specification.

The motivation for generalizing the description of a structural element or for omitting entirely its mention is to broaden the claim's scope. The Supreme Court long ago recognized that if an inventor were required to confine his claims to the detailed examples and illustrations set forth in his specification, most patents would be of little worth.[12]

The scope of a claim may be viewed as having two dimensions or aspects: (1) breadth or extension and (2) depth or intensity. Breadth or extension signifies the possible number of physical objects upon which a claim is capable of reading. Depth or intensity signifies the degree of particularity or detail with which each structural element is described. The breadth of a claim is quite obviously of crucial importance, for it represents the physical extent of the patent property. If a patent be analogized to real estate, the breadth of a claim would correspond to the area or number of acres of that property.

The breadth of a claim may be affected by altering the genus-species recitation of each structural element and/or by changing the number (combination-subcombination) of structural elements recited.[13] A claim may be broadened by generalizing the description of structure; a claim may be narrowed by particularizing the description of structure.

A generic expression necessarily encompasses a greater number and wider variety of physical objects than would the expression representing any of its constituent species. Hence, use of generalized or generic terms to describe structure yields claims of relatively greater breadth than would use of more specific terms.

As an example, consider the incandescent lamp. Thomas A. Edison discovered that a filament of high resistance is capable of giving light by incandescence, "Filament of high resistance" is a generalized expression of specific materials having the recited properties of (1) ductility (which is the capacity for being drawn into a filament or fine diameter), and (2) high resistance. One material having these properties is carbon. "Filament of *carbon* of high resistance" is a species of the genus "filament of high resistance." The recitation of "carbon" narrows the claim, making it more specific. Carbon, in fact, was the only substance which Edison's specification disclosed as possessing the necessary properties. Consequently, the claims of his patent were restricted to "filament of carbon of high resistance."[14] Subsequently it was discovered by others that tungsten also possessed the desired properties. Not only can tungsten be made into filaments of high resistance, but such filaments are capable of lasting for much longer periods of time than are those made of carbon.

Abbreviated notation, employing the letters of the alphabet, may be used to symbolize structural elements, each letter representing a different structural element. For example, *A* may be used to represent *a filament of high resistance.* A numerical subscript may be employed to signify a structural element expressed as a species. Thus, A = filament of high resistance; A_1 = filament of carbon of high resistance; A_2 = filament of tungsten of high resistance.

If the letters *A, B, C* represent the different structural elements possessed by an invention, a claim calling for *A B,* and *C* would, of course, read on that invention. But, if couched in open language, so too would a claim calling for any and only a subcombination of the foregoing elements (*A, B, C, AB, AC,* or *BC*). The term "subcombination" signifies a combination having fewer structural elements than that possessed by the entire or complete combination (*A, B, C*).

To further illustrate the combination-subcombination relationship, consider again the incandescent lamp. The essential structure of such a lamp consists not only of its filament of high resistance, but also of a glass bulb or receiver from which air has been exhausted and of conductors passing through the glass bulb connecting the filament to a source of electric current.

Let *A* = filament of high resistance; *B* = "receiver" or bulb made entirely of glass; *C* = evacuated atmosphere of the glass bulb; *D* = conductors passing through the glass bulb.

Each and every subcombination of structural elements, which itself corresponds to a novel physical entity, may be separately claimed. Thus, the first claim of Edison's incandescent lamp patent, after reciting, "An electric lamp for giving light" calls for only "a filament of carbon of high resistance secured to metallic wires." No mention was made of the glass bulb, or of its evacuated atmosphere, or of conductors passing through the bulb.[15]

Claims drawn to a subcombination are highly desirable because they may make liable as a direct infringer one who would merely manufacture a component of the entire combination.[16] Of course, such would be the case only where the claim calling for the subcombination of elements reads on the component.

Applying the technique of broadening a claim by omitting therefrom a recitation of structure involves the risk that such claim will be held not to satisfy the requirement of Section 112, that the claims particularly point out and distinctly claim the invention. Nevertheless, the Supreme Court has sanctioned the practice of omitting from the claims structure which, though necessary for the operation of the claimed device, does not affect the unique or peculiar qualities and characteristics of the recited structure. It held valid claims drawn to a battery, which claims recited a unique combination of electrode materials, but which omitted mention of electrolyte—a component which is well known by those skilled in the battery art to be necessary for the operation of all batteries.[17] The specification, moreover, described the manner of assembling and using the claimed structure, including the addition of electrolyte. A peculiar advantage of the claimed structure, which was clearly recognized in the specification, was its ability to become active immediately upon the addition of water-electrolyte.

§ 3. Phraseology of Claim

Up to this point, the underlying principles governing the formulation of patent claims have been presented one-by-one and largely in the abstract. The time has now come to demonstrate how these fundamental considerations may be applied to organize and to express verbally an inventive concept. The reader is cautioned against regarding the concrete examples which follow as being exhaustive; they are merely illustrative.

A claim's phraseology may be broken down into three major parts: (1) preamble or introductory phrase; (2) transitional phrase; and (3) body of the claim.

[1] The Preamble or Introductory phrase

This phrase sets the stage for the recitations which follow, either by summarizing the invention expressed by the claims and/or by placing it in the perspective of the prior art. A preamble which merely summarizes the invention is, in essence, a title for that invention. It may state no more than the generic class into which the invention falls. This may be coupled with a statement of intended use, or the overall or ultimate object or purpose, or motivation for the invention, its salient properties or characteristics.

> The method of treating the liquid portions of the paraffin series of petroleum distillation having a boiling point upward of 500° F. to obtain therefrom low-boiling point products of the same samples. . . . [18]

> Apparatus for modulating the amplitude of oscillations derived from a microwave source. . . . [19]

> An electric lamp for giving light by incandescence. . . . [20]

> A flux composition . . . .

A claim may be worded such that the prior art is segregated from the features which are entirely new to or modified by the instant invention, the recitation of the prior art being relegated to the preamble. The detail with which the prior art is set out in the claims varies widely from case to case, as this format is not mandatory in American practice. A claim so phrased is often referred to as a "Jepson-type" claim.[21] The recitations contained in the preamble of a Jepson-type claim are deemed to limit the structure recited in the body of the claim. The original Jepson claim was:

> In an electrical system of distribution of the class wherein a variable speed generator charges a storage battery and when the battery becomes sufficiently charged a voltage becomes effective to regulate the generator for constant potential [*preamble*]

> the combination with said voltage coil of [*transition*]

> a coil traversed by current flowing to the battery which is acted upon by decreasing battery current to reduce the potential maintained constant by the voltage cell. [*body*]

While the question is not entirely settled, the weight of authority appears to support the position that the recitations of the preamble are to be ignored in construing the scope of a claim, unless words in the preamble are repeated, or at least referrable to words, in the body of the claim.[22] A statement of intended use, which is merely recited in the preamble (as, for example, "a *flux* composition" or "a process of *brewing*"), would not limit the recitations of structure which follow the preamble to the indicated use.[23] Similarly, a claim addressed to old structure, which in its preamble recites a new use or application for that structure, is considered to be anticipated by the prior art disclosing the existence of that structure. A new use for old structure may, nevertheless, be patentable, if claimed as a new process or method of using that structure.[24] See Chapter 5.

[2] Transitional Phrase

This phrase indicates, in an abbreviated way, whether the recitations of structure which follow it are left open or are closed to additional structural elements.

"Comprising" (or, less commonly, "including" or "containing") characterize a claim as being open. As such, they denote that the invention includes the structure which is explicitly recited in the claim but does not exclude the presence of additional structure not recited in the claim.[25]

"Consisting of" (or, less commonly, "composed of") characterize a claim as being closed. As has already been noted, because of the ease with which infringement thereof may be avoided, claims couched in closed language are generally of practical value only for compositions of matter. Even for such, closed language is far less desirable than open language, since the presence of even a minor amount of an additional ingredient, save for naturally occurring impurities, would avoid infringement of the claim. The severity of closed language may be mollified somewhat by inserting, as a modifier, "essentially" immediately after "consisting" (as, for example, "consisting essentially of"). Such a transitional expression is construed as "reading on" not only the recited ingredients, but also upon the recited ingredients plus minor amounts of additional, unspecified substances, the presence of which would not affect the efficacious properties of those ingredients expressly recited.[26]

The position of the transitional phrase in a claim is between its preamble and its body. It immediately follows the preamble and immediately precedes the body.

A comma (,) is usually employed to separate the preamble from the transitional phrase, the comma clearly setting the preamble apart from the rest of the claim.

[3] Body of Claim

The body of a claim, which is all the language coming after the transitional phrase, states, as a series of phrases, the structural elements (be they the steps or operations of a process, the component parts of a mechanical device, or the ingredients of a composition of matter) which make up and form the inventive entity. Where the invention involves a cooperation among elements (as in a machine), such must also be recited in the body of the claim. The function, operation, purpose, or relevant properties of an element may also be included to explain or further characterize and qualify such element.[27]

> Apparatus for modulating the amplitude of oscillations derived from a microwave source, which comprises *a gas at low pressure characterized by sharp resonance lines of selective absorption of incident microwave energy of the frequency of said source in an amount dependent on the numbers of the molecules of said gas in the various possible energy levels, means for guiding waves of said source through said gas, whereby energy of said source is absorbed by said gas, an auxiliary source of electromagnetic waves of a higher frequency, means for subjecting said gas to the field of said auxiliary source to alter the said numbers and so the amount of said absorption, and means for varying the strength of said auxiliary source field under control of a modulating signal.*

§ 4. The Means Clause

The reader should study with care the use of the word "means" in the above claim. Thus:

> means for guiding waves of said source through said gas . . . .

> means for subjecting said gas to the field of said auxiliary source to alter the said numbers . . . .

> means for varying the strength of said auxiliary source field . . . .

In each instance, the word "means" is immediately followed by, coupled with, and qualified by the function which it performs. Each of the above clauses, in effect, calls for structure—more precisely—for apparatus or, indeed, for any physical body or bodies having the capacity to perform the function recited after the words "means for." Such a clause is completely devoid of the details of apparatus capable of satisfying the recitation of function. Indeed, a "means clause" (consisting of the words *means for* and a statement of the function which such means is supposed to perform) is to be construed as calling for ANY means capable of performing the indicated function. It should be apparent that a "means clause" is the broadest, most generalized mode possible of expressing an element and that such an expression endows a claim with relatively great breadth. Such mode of claiming is usually reserved for pioneer invention. (The foregoing example is a claim from one of the basic patents on the laser.)

In fact, there was a time when it was not permissible to characterize an element of a combination claim by the use of a means clause.[28] However, Section 112 of the Patent Act presently in force, while requiring that patents conclude with claims which particularly point out and distinctly claim the invention, further expressly sanctions the practice of expressing an element in a claim for a combination:

> as a means or step for performing a specified function without the recital of structure, material, or acts in support thereof, and such claim shall be construed to cover the corresponding structure, material or acts described in the specification and equivalents thereof.

As the foregoing provision indicates, under appropriate circumstances, it is likewise permissible to generalize the operations making up a method or process, characterizing one or more of its operations, as steps for performing an indicated function, without reciting in the claim any further details of such operation.

It may have occurred to the reader that a "means clause" stripped of the words "means for" not only states a function, but recites an operation as well. For example:

> (means for) guiding waves of said source through said gas . . ..

> (means for) subjecting said gas to the field of said auxiliary source to alter the said numbers . . .

Why then would any one claiming a process want to introduce into such claim the words "steps for"? Would not the presence of the words "steps for" introduce a redundancy? Every process has an ultimate object or overall effect. Such may be set out in a claim's preamble. However, to attain the ultimate result, one or more distinct operations may be necessary. If a group of these operations can be generalized in terms of an intermediate result or effect, such may be recited as "steps for" + the result. The breadth of such a recitation parallels that calling for "means for" + a function (or result).

To tie together the concepts of structure and function, clarification of one other point now seems to be in order. The reader may be puzzled by an apparent contradiction, namely, that at the outset of this section, physical operations and physical objects were subsumed under the heading of structural language, which it was said was to be distinguished from functional language. If, as was indicated in the immediately preceding paragraph, a statement of function expresses a physical operation, how then can a distinction be drawn between a physical operation (which this author has classified under "structure") and a statement of function. The answer is that it depends upon how and in what context the statement is made. If the recitation of a physical operation is so detailed that one of ordinary skill in the art to which it relates would be capable of carrying it out, it should be deemed as much a statement of structure as that calling for a physical object. Such differs from a recitation so disposed in a claim (often at the precise point of novelty) as to mask or obscure the route by which that claim's ultimate objective is to be attained.[29] The following is an example of a claim that makes improper use of functional language, in that it relies upon a functional statement (which appears in italics) to distinguish over the prior art:[30]

> A filament for electric incandescent lamps or other devices, composed substantially of tungsten and made up mainly of a number of comparatively large grains of such size and contour as *to prevent substantial sagging and offsetting* during a normal or commercially useful life for such a lamp or other device.

However, the reader is again alerted to the fact that most writers confine "structure" to physical objects, excluding therefrom physical operations. Moreover, recitations relating to physical operations are given no weight in construing apparatus or product claims. The foregoing rule may be expressed as follows: A claim addressed to structure must distinguish over the prior art by structural recitations. [31] Here, of course, "structure" does not include physical operations; it is rather confined to physical bodies or instrumentalities capable of yielding the indicated function. A complementary rule applies to process claims: A claim addressed to a method must distinguish over the prior art by its steps; no weight can be given to apparatus or product recitations in method claims.[32] The statutory classes of invention and their significance in claim construction will be discussed more fully in Chapter 5.

§ 5. "Single Means" Claims

While the usual process claim involves a series or sequence of physical operations, which operations mark out the route and path by which the process' goal is to be attained, it must be noted that claims addressed to a method or process may properly call for but a single operation or step. For example:[33]

> A single-step process for converting the molybdenum values of ore material containing sulfides of molybdenum to water-soluble molydate which comprises reacting a mixture of said material, and at least stoichiometric amounts based on the amount of said sulfides of molybdenum of an alkali metal nitrate and an alkali metal carbonate.

Such a single-step process claim is to be distinguished from a claim which merely calls for "a step (or steps) for" performing a stated function. In the single-step process claims above, the details of the single step are spelled out and the context or stage at which it is to be performed is indicated—here in the preamble. On the contrary, a claim which merely calls for "a step (or steps) for" performing a stated function necessarily encompasses all possible modes of arriving at the stated function and result inherent therein. No particular mode of accomplishing the indicated result is spelled out in the claim. Such a claim corresponds in scope to one calling for a single "means for" performing a stated result. Whether the word "step(s)" or "means" is used, the claim is known as a single means claims. Such is not sanctioned by Section 112,[34] since that section contains a proviso that the claim be directed to a *combination* (of means or steps). A claim for a combination of means or steps is known as a means-combination claim.

Before leaving the subject of claim construction and interpretation, a word of caution already given will be reiterated: The foregoing presentation was merely illustrative and by no means exhaustive of the subject. There are an infinite number of variations. Some of the principles set forth are not applicable to some types of inventions. For example, although, of course, in the larger sense, there is "cooperation" between the subatomic particles (protons, electrons, neutrons, etc.) comprising an atom, the aspect of cooperation, stressed in the preceding discussion, is not really a pertinent consideration in formulating claims to a chemical element. Such a claim need only recite enough information to identify that element, its atomic number and/or atomic mass sufficing.[35] Similarly, to claim a chemical compound, it may suffice merely to call for a specific configuration of atoms or the product of a specified chemical reaction.

Essential though less significant aspects of claim construction (e.g., multiple claims, antecedent basis) were not mentioned. Treatment of these rules has been deferred to Chapter 12.

Notes

[1] Continental Paper Bag Co. v. Eastern Paper Bag Co., 210 U.S. 405, 430 (1908). Straussler v. United States, 290 F.2d 827, 831, 129 U.S.P.Q. 480, 483 (Ct. Cl. 1961).

[2] Fulton Co. v. Powers Regulator Co., 263 Fed. 578, 580 (2d Cir. 1920).

[3] See Mahn v. Harwood, 112 U.S. 354, 360-361 (1884).

[4] See Tigrett Indus., Inc. v. Standard Indus., Inc., 397 U.S. 586, 165 U.S.P.Q. 289 (1970); Graver Tank Co. v. Linde Air Prod. Co., 339 U.S. 605, 85 U.S.P.Q. 328 (1950).

[5] 35 U.S.C. 6.

[6] M.P.E.P. 608.01(m).

[7] See Benger Laboratories, Ltd. v. R.K. Laros Co., 209 F. Supp. 639, 135 U.S.P.Q. 11 (E.D. Pa. 1962).

[8] *In re* Lindberg, 194 F.2d 732, 93 U.S.P.Q. 23, 26 (C.C.P.A. 1952); Sid W. Richardson, Inc. v. Bryan, 144 F. Supp. 916, 110 U.S.P.Q. 424, 427 (S.D. Tex. 1956). See also, Shaw v. E.B. & A.C. Whiting Co., 417 F.2d 1097, 1106, 163 U.S.P.Q. 580, 587 (2d Cir. 1969), *cert. denied* 398 U.S. 954 (1970); Ex parte Levine, 159 U.S.P.Q. 252 (P.O. Bd. App. 1967).

[9] *In re* Thomson, 336 F.2d 604, 607, 143 U.S.P.Q. 21, 23 (C.C.P.A. 1964).

[10] See *In re* Gustafson, 331 F.2d 905, 141 U.S.P.Q. 585 (C.C.P.A. 1964). But see, Nugey v. Oliver Mfg. Supply Co., 321 F.2d 118, 121-122, 138 U.S.P.Q. 98, 100 (3d Cir. 1963).

[11] See for example, *In re* Budde, 319 F.2d 242, 246, 138 U.S.P.Q. 71, 73-74 (C.C.P.A. 1963). *In re* Fields, 304 F.2d 691, 695, 134 U.S.P.Q. 242, 245 (C.C.P.A. 1962). See also, *In re* Chandler, 254 F.2d 396, 399, 117 U.S.P.Q. 361, 363 (C.C.P.A. 1958).

[12] Continental Paper Bag Co. v. Eastern Paper Bag Co., 210 U.S. 405, 418 (1908).

[13] See generally, Special Equip. Co. v. Coe, 324 U.S. 370, 376-377, 64 U.S.P.Q. 525, 529 (1945).

[14] U.S. Pat. No. 223,898.

[15] The Incandescent Lamp Patent, 159 U.S. 465 (1895).

[16] See generally, Aro Mfg. Co. v. Convertible Top Replacement Co., 377 U.S. 476, 141 U.S.P.Q. 681 (1964); 365 U.S. 336, 128 U.S.P.Q. 364 (1961). See also, Chapter 15.

[17] United States v. Adams, 383 U.S. 39, 148 U.S.P.Q. 479 (1966).

[18] U.S. Pat. No. 1,049,667, claim 1 (to Burton).

[19] U.S. Pat. No. 2,819,450, claim 1 (to Townes).

[20] U.S. Pat. No. 223,898, claim 1 (to Edison).

[21] Ex parte Jepson, 1917 C.D. 62, 243 O.G. 525 (Comm. Pat. 1925).

[22] Kropa v. Robie, 187 F.2d 150, 88 U.S.P.Q. 478 (C.C.P.A. 1951); Ex parte Feissel, 131 U.S.P.Q. 252, 254 (P.O. Bd. App. 1958).

[23] *In re* Thuau, 135 F.2d 344, 57 U.S.P.Q. 324 (C.C.P.A. 1943).

[24] 35 U.S.C. 100(b).

[25] Ex parte Davis, 80 U.S.P.Q. 448 (P.O. Bd. App. 1948).

[26] *In re* Garnero, 412 F.2d 276, 162 U.S.P.Q. 221, 223 (C.C.P.A. 1969). See also U.S. Pat. No. 3,442,644 at col. 1, lines 55-59.

[27] U.S. Pat. No. 2,819,450, claim 1.

[28] Halliburton Oil Well Cementation Co. v. Walker, 329 U.S. 1, 71 U.S.P.Q. 1 (1946).

[29] See Chicopee Mfg. Corp. v. Kendall Co., 288 F.2d 719, 722, 129 U.S.P.Q. 90, 91 (4th Cir. 1961); Ex parte Ball and Hair, 99 U.S.P.Q. 146, 150 (P.O. Bd. App. 1953). Compare, *In re* Chandler, 254 F.2d 396, 117 U.S.P.Q. 361 (C.C.P.A. 1958); Ex parte Mayer, 111 U.S.P.Q. 109 (P.O. Bd. App. 1956).

[30] General Elec. Co. v. Wabash Appliance Corp., 304 U.S. 364, 37 U.S.P.Q. 466 (1938).

[31] See for example, *In re* Attwood, 354 F.2d 365, 148 U.S.P.Q. 203 (C.C.P.A. 1966).

[32] Ex parte Seavy, 125 U.S.P.Q. 454, 459 (P.O. Bd. App. 1960).

[33] Ex parte Macy, 132 U.S.P.Q. 545 (P.O. Bd. App. 1960); Ex parte Brian, 118 U.S.P.Q. 242 (P.O. Bd. App. 1958). See U.S. Pat. No. 2,796,344, claim 4.

[34] Ex parte Bullock, 1907 C.D. 93, 127 O.G. 1580 (Comm. Pat. 1907). See also, M.P.E.P. 706.03(c).

[35] See U.S. Pat. Nos. 3,161,463 and 3,161,463 (to Seaborg). *In re* Seaborg, 328 F.2d 993, 140 U.S.P.Q. 659 (C.C.P.A. 1964).

Chapter 4

SOME POPULARLY HELD MISCONCEPTIONS ABOUT PATENTS

SYNOPSIS

> An idea of itself is not patentable, but a new device by which it may be made practically useful is.
>
> Waite, Ch. J.
> *Rubber-Tip Pencil Co. v. Howard*,
> 87 U.S. (20 Wall.) 498, 507 (1874)

Patent law, like no other aspect of the law, is rife with popularly held misconceptions about so many of its fundamental notions. This lack of understanding is, of course, attributable in part to the fact that patent law requires an intimate familiarity with basic concepts of physical science and acquaintance with abstruse technologies. But another and perhaps even more significant reason for these misunderstandings is the fact that patent law has been built up around a nucleus of highly sophisticated, abstract, and seemingly peculiar rules. The word "peculiar" has been applied advisedly, because certain tenets of patent law run contrary, indeed, diametrically opposite, to what common experience has taught the layman.

Some of the notions to be examined here have been discussed earlier in Part I. There, however, they were introduced as pristine legal concepts, the state of the popular mind having been largely ignored. In what follows, special effort has been made to relate these and other concepts indigenous to patent law to common experience, hopefully thereby facilitating the dissipation of misconceptions surrounding them. The author, however, has no illusions about the efficacy of this presentation. He appreciates the fact that these misconceptions are so deeply ingrained that only with the conscious, constant, and concerted efforts of the readers can they be dispelled and relapse prevented.

§ 1. Patentability of Ideas

Perhaps the deepest rooted misconception about patents pertains to "the patentability of ideas." Thus, not infrequently, a certain idea will be spoken of as being "patentable," another idea, as being "unpatentable." Even the Supreme Court, on occasion, has spoken in these terms.[1] Ideas nurture the patent system; they are its pabulum. Strictly speaking, however, naked *ideas are not patentable.*

Those acquainted with the mysteries of patent law often employ the word "idea" as a shorthanded substitute for "invention" or for the physical exploitation or embodiment of an idea. When a patent attorney speaks of the patentability of an idea, he means the patentability of an invention and its exploitation in tangible form. To the uninitiated, however, this causes confusion and misunderstanding. It projects an erroneous image, tending to leave laymen with the impression that patents somehow interfere with the freedom of thought.

As was brought out in Chapter 1, no patent confers a right to exclude others from the underlying idea which gave rise to the invention. The monopoly conferred by a patent attaches only to the embodiment of an idea in tangible form. Patent rights and rights in physical objects which possess the physical attributes called for by the claims of a patent are entirely distinct.

The very motivation for having a patent system is to enlarge the fund of knowledge freely accessible to the public. The patent system fulfills this objective by offering monopolies, for limited times, upon the exploitation, in tangible form, of ideas in exhange for public disclosure. Immediately upon the granting of a patent, the ideas disclosed in the patent specification become available to the public. Everyone is free to think about any patented invention, even during its ephemeral life. The patent system imposes no constraints upon thought; it certainly encourages the free exchange of ideas.

§ 2. Mathematics and the Patent Attorney

Closely associated with the misconception about "the patentability of ideas" is the widely held belief that mathematical ability is necessary to perform the day-to-day work of a patent attorney.[2] The fact of the matter is that the practice of patent law is one of the very few occupations which, while requiring familiarity with principles of physical science, does not require mathematical skill. As will be discussed in § 4, quantitative relationships are normally not patentable. A pure mathematical formula is in the nature of a naked idea. Of course, in patent law, it is necessary to be able to compare the prior art with the invention sought to be patented. Such may necessitate some incidental mathematical calculations. But, as will presently be discussed much more fully, as a general rule, a mere change in degree—a mere linear extrapolation or projection—of the prior art does not rise to the dignity of a patentable invention.

§ 3. "One Picture is Worth a Thousand Words"

Another misconception about patents is generated by the application to this subject of a maxim, the origin of which is commonly ascribed to the ancient Chinese philosopher Confucius, namely, that "One picture is worth a thousand words." This aphorism, while of almost universal application, is not valid for patent claims. In fact, the inverse approaches much nearer to the truth: *One word may be worth ten thousand pictures.*

To understand why this is so, the reader should recall what was said earlier about how a change in a claim's breadth may be effected. In short, the greater the detail with which the invention is set forth in a claim, the narrower is the scope of that claim. To infringe a claim it would be necessary for a physical object to possess *all* the features called for by the claim.

The layman, having been conditioned by common experience to revere detail, particularly when such contains unfamiliar technical jargon, is impressed by lengthy claims, even if such merely recite the insignificant and incidental nuts and bolts that are possessed by one particular embodiment of the invention. Little does the layman realize that the inclusion in the claims of such unimportant features would make it easy for a competitor to design around those claims, thereby avoiding infringing them. Each structural feature expressly recited in a claim qualifies the invention, having the effect of narrowing its scope. For this reason, the recitation of a structural feature (previously characterized as an element) is frequently referred to as a limitation. Each limitation limits or restricts the claim to the element of structure which it describes, making it necessary for the patentee to find each such limitation in an alleged infringing device. An exception should be noted: A claim calling for a composition of matter, which contains an ingredient recited as a Markush Group ("a member selected from the group consisting of . . .") would be broadened by increasing the number of members of such group.[3] And, of course, a claim's breadth would be unaffected, though its actual length increased, by the inclusion of functional language—that is, language which merely recites properties or effects which inherently flow from recited structure. Such language is mere padding and surplusage; it does not possess any limitations in addition to those implicit in the recited elements of structure.

What does the foregoing discussion have to do with picture? Just this: An ordinary picture (not a block diagram) of a device, by its very nature, is far more detailed than a verbal description is likely to be. Words tend to be generic. One must try hard to capture in a sentence all the qualities present in a visual image. For example, suppose that a screw is a significant element of a device. A picture of the device would reveal, not only the presence of that screw, but whether its head were round, square, etc. Verbal representation is more flexible as a medium for expressing physical elements. Verbal expression gives the inventor a degree of latitude in circumscribing his invention not possible with a diagram. An inventor need recite only those elements which are essential. The ordinary diagram cannot differentiate between essential and nonessential features, for it shows all. Thus, while an inventor may properly claim as his invention what is shown in an appended diagram, most inventors shun such "picture claims,"[4] for the reason that it is usually a very simple matter to avoid infringing such a claim—only one element need be altered or eliminated.

§ 4. "The Whole Must Equal the Sum of Its Parts"

Patent law deviates from common experience in still another significant way. The reader will recall, no doubt from his high school course in plane geometry, the axiom "The whole must equal the sum of its parts." As eminently logical as this maxim sounds, it is not valid for so-called patents for a combination of old elements. To this effect the Supreme Court has actually stated:[5]

> [O]nly when the whole in some way *exceeds* the sum of its parts is the accumulation of old devices patentable. [Emphasis added.]

The foregoing proposition is one formulation of a substantive requisite of a patentable invention. The other requisites are novelty and utility. In addition, the subject matter must fall within one of the statutory classes of invention.

The requirement that the whole exceed the sum of its parts is but a specific application to combinations of old elements of a more general requirement that is applicable to all patentable inventions. Nevertheless, couching this requirement in terms of a geometric impossiblity is representative of the generally prevalent attitude of the judiciary toward invention and the Herculean burden that courts have imposed upon those who seek patent protection for their innovations. So exigeat is this requirement that noncompliance has been found even for novel compositions of matter capable of producing demonstrably synergistic effects.[6] The general rule is set forth in Section 103 of the Patent Act presently in force:

> A patent may not be obtained though the invention is not identically disclosed or described as set forth in section 102 of this title, if the differences between the subject matter sought to be patented would have been *obvious* at the time the invention was made to a person having ordinary skill in the art to which said subject matter pertains. [Emphasis added.]

Prior to the present Act the word "obvious" did not appear in the statute. The word "invention" itself was used instead, and the requirement that a contribution exhibit this illusive quality was purely a judge-made rule. That a novel and useful contribution to be patentable must exhibit unobviousness or invention had its inception in a mid-nineteenth century case, wherein the Supreme Court held that the mere substitution of a porcelain door knob handle for the wooden door knob handle of the prior art did not amount to a patentable invention.[7] That Court then went on to draw a line of distinction between mechanical skill and invention, indicating that only contributions evidencing invention would be worthy of patent protection. Neither that nor subsequent courts ever spelled out, in general terms, what would consititute a (patentable) invention. Rather, there evolved, through case-by-case adjudication, what have been called the negative rules of invention. If the innovation present in a particular case fell within one of these a priori rules, the contribution could be summarily denied the benefits of patent protection as lacking invention, without regard to the state of the art at the time the contribution was made. For example, innovation which could be characterized as a change in degree (and not a change in kind) was deemed to be devoid of invention.

The hostility of the judiciary to patents grew with the passage of time. And in what appeared to be an attempt by the Supreme Court to cut the flow of patents to a trickle and to preclude corporations from securing patent protection for their systematic research, that Court, in 1941, held invalid a patent on the ground that the innovative step did not come about by a "flash of creative genius."[8] It should be recalled that Thomas A. Edison had admitted that his inventions were not nearly so much a result of his genius as of his "perspiration."[9] The absurdity of inquiring into the mental state of the inventor was recognized by Congress, which in enacting the second sentence of Section 103 repudiated a flash-of-genius as a requirement. It declares:

> Patentability shall not be negatived by the manner in which the invention was made.

While the Supreme Court has respected this mandate of Congress and disavowed a flash of genius as a requirement for patentability,[10] the very same Court insists that the line of cases embracing the other "Negative Rules of Invention" was not overruled by the first sentence of Section 103. Rather that statutory requirement, said the Court, is but a codification of those earlier precedents.[11] It should be noted that the requirement that patentable invention be nonobvious or unobvious first appeared in a Supreme Court opinion[12] and is in its effect a negative rule of invention; indeed, in many respects, the most generalized of those rules.

Before leaving the subject of unobviousness, a few observations are in order. There is a distinction, albeit a sometimes subtle and hazy one, between mechanical skill, on one hand, and invention or unobviousness, on the other: *Perfection of workmanship, however much it may increase the convenience, extend the use or diminish expense, is not patentable.*[13] The mere carrying forward of an old idea is not patentable.[14] These are but a few of the expressions of the dichotomy of mechanical skill and invention. Implicit in formulations of what is or what is not invention is a hypothetical person—a person having ordinary skill in the art to which the subject matter of the invention pertains.[15] He is not too unlike the reasonable man of negligence law. The capacity of these hypothetical "men" gauge the necessary degree of innovation or care, as the case may be. In fact, unobviousness may be looked upon as a requirement that there be a certain degree, quantum, or level of novelty. There must be a difference between what is sought to be patented and the prior art, and *the difference the difference makes* is of critical significance. If the difference would not have been obvious to a person of ordinary skill in the art to which the invention relates, at the time the invention was made, the invention possesses a quantum of novelty sufficient to support a patent. While there must be some difference in structure, between what is sought to be patented and the prior art (in order that the combination be novel), in judging unobviousness, the subject matter *as a whole* must be considered. Though the structural difference between the prior art and the claims under consideration be minor, yet if to that difference there can be attributed a truly unexpected, surprising, or unusual result—an "impalpable something"[16] —the contribution may be said to have been unobvious. That which one skilled in the calling could produce as a spontaneous response to need, by the mere routine application of known principles, cannot be the subject of a valid patent. This, however, is not to say that obvious and "obvious to try" are synonymous.[17] For example, the prior art may attribute a certain efficacy to a certain general class of combinations of known elements. Though a specific combination falling within such class were never before known, it would, without more, be prima facie obvious to make that combination for the purpose taught by the prior art. But if one discovered lurking concealed within that class a specific combination possessing a truly unexpected result—a new function—neither taught by the prior art nor possessed by the other members of the class, the prima facie obviousness of the combination *as a whole* would be rebutted.

There is another subtle distinction incidental to the application of the foregoing principles, to which, at this point, attention should be called. Inventions—once made—can usually be explained by resort to previously known scientific principles. In fact, it can be said with reasonable certainty that, in the entire history of mankind, there has not been a single invention made which does not obey some law of nature, or, indeed, which violates any law of nature! This fact, however, is not to be equated with the rule that a patentable invention must not have been logically deducible from the prior art. The difference between the two propositions is, at one level, the difference between foresight and hindsight. Fundamentally, it is due to the very real difference between physical and empirical results and theoretical explanations for the same. The patent laws are concerned only with tangible results and with specific physical means or pathways by which such results may be obtained. An inventor need not indulge in speculation. Ordinarily, he is not required to offer an explanation of why he obtains his results; he need only reveal how others may reproduce the same.[18] A dramatic example of the difference between theoretical and inventive contributions is furnished by comparing the work of von Helmholtz and Thomas A. Edison in acoustics. The former studied, in minute detail, the mechanisms by which sounds are produced and perceived, publishing these studies in a celebrated treatise. Yet nowhere in that treatise is there a hint or suggestion, no less a teaching, that it might be possible to preserve for posterity a record of those ephemeral undulations which account for what is perceived as sound. It remained for Thomas Edison to take that step with his phonograph.[19] I leave it to the reader to decide who made the greater contribution to civilization.

§ 5. Patent Pending; Patent Medicine

Perhaps the most widely held misconceptions about patents relate to the use of the very word "patent" in "patent pending" and in "patent medicine." The word "constructive" when applied as a modifier to the word "contract" or to the word "trust" does violence to the legal concepts inherent in a true contract or trust. A commensurate distortion occurs when patent is used in conjunction with "pending" or "medicine".

At the point in time when an article is stamped "patent pending" the invention to which that marking refers is unpatented and perhaps even unpatentable! "Patent Pending" properly signifies merely that a patent *application* is pending before the Patent Office; not that a patent is then in force. Therefore, the article to which this language is affixed is technically not, at the time of its marking, subject to a subsisting patent covering the invention to which the marking refers.

Patent protection in the United States commences on the day letters patent are issued and lasts for seventeen years. No infringement can occur before the issuance of the patent. Copying or otherwise simulating an article marked merely "patent pending" during only the pendency of the corresponding patent application(s) before the Patent Office would not, by itself, be unlawful or otherwise constitute an invasion of any of the patentee's rights. However, any unauthorized making, using, or selling of articles from the time of issuance of letters patent would constitute infringement. Anyone engaged in the unauthorized manufacture of patentee's invention before the issuance of letter patent would have to close down such operations upon the issuance of the patent, lest he be subject to liability as an infringer. Marking articles "patent pending" indicates that a patent has been applied for and that a patent application is pending before the Patent Office. This serves as notice to would-be competitors that the marked articles may not be in the public domain and may be subject to an inchoate right to patent protection. The Patent Act expressly sanctions the marking of articles with the words "patent applied for," "patent pending," or with any words of like import, where an application for patent has in fact been made.[20] The same section of the Act imposes a penalty for employing such language, either affixed to an article or in connection with advertising, for the purpose of deceiving the public when no application for patent has in been made, or if made, is not pending. Any person may sue for the penalty, one half going to the person suing and the other to the United States.

Where an article is actually covered by a subsisting United States patent, the patentee and persons authorized by him to make or sell any patented article may give notice to the public that the same is patented, either by fixing thereon the word "patent" or the abbreviation "pat.", together with the number of the patent, or when, from the character of the article, this can not be done, by fixing to it, or to the package wherein one or more of them is contained, a label containing a like notice. In the event of failure so to mark, no damage shall be recovered by the patentee in any action for infringement, except on proof that the infringer was notified of the infringement and continued to infringe thereafter, in which event damages may be recovered only for infringement occurring after such notice. Filing of an action for infringement shall constitute such notice.[21] The penalty which the Patent Act imposes for falsely indicating that a patent has been applied for also applies to falsely indicating that an article is subject to a subsisting patent.

Although the primary value of a patent resides in the exclusivity which it commands, because, in the popular mind, there is associated with patents a certain governmental imprimatur,[22] the fact that an article embodies one or more United States patents is of value in advertising and sales promotions. Of course, the fact of the matter is that the Patent Office, in granting patents does not employ as a criterion the potential economic worth or lack thereof of the inventions presented to it. Rather, it merely certifies that it *appears* that claimed subject matter is new, unobvious, and has some degree of practical utility and that the claims are sufficiently definite to reasonably apprize the public of the metes and bounds of the patent property.

While patent medicines have gone the way of the minstrel show, many people still employ this terminology as a synonym for nonprescription drugs. However, "patent medicine" has been judicially construed as signifying a secret, and thus necessarily unpatented medicine.[23] A condition precedent to obtaining a United States patent is public disclosure of how to make and use the invention. The Federal Food and Drug Administration imposes even more rigorous requirements, including clinical testing prior to marketing of anything that is to be sold as a drug or medicine. When a drug is marketed, its contents must be listed on the label.[24] Thus, since the advent of these regulations, there can be no such thing as a patent medicine, in the accepted meaning of this term. It is interesting to note that "patent" has also been applied, in the vernacular of the storage battery art, to electrolytes whose compositions are secret![25] Of course, such "patent electrolytes" are necessarily unpatented.

One final point deserves emphasis here, namely, that the Patent Office has no power to police patents. It cannot recall a patent once issued. Its jurisdiction is confined to patent applications, except for certain relatively minor and essentially ministerial functions, as the recordation of assignments,[26] the entering of disclaimers,[27] and the issuance of certificates of correction.[28] The Patent Office does, however, have power to affect indirectly rights in subsisting patents, as through its power to grant or refuse to reissue,[29] or to award a patent to an applicant, as the prior inventor, though it had previously issued a patent on the same invention to another.[30]

Notes

1 Gottschalk v. Benson, 409 U.S. 63, 71, 175 U.S.P.Q. 673, 676 (1972); Rubber-Tip Pencil Co. v. Howard, 87 U.S. (20 Wall.) 498, 507 (1874).

2 See for example, M. Mayer, *The Lawyers* (Dell Publishing Co. 1966) p.375.

3 See Ex parte Markush, 1925 C.D. 126, 340 O.G. 839 (Comm. Pat. 1925).

4 See for example, Ex parte Squires, 133 U.S.P.Q. 598 (P.O. Bd. App. 1961); *In re* Tanczyn, 202 F.2d 785, 97 U.S.P.Q. 150 (C.C.P.A. 1953).

5 Great Atlantic & Pacific Tea Co. v. Supermarket Equip. Co., 340 U.S. 147, 152, 87 U.S.P.Q. 303, 305 (1950); Lage v. Caldwell Mfg. Co., 221 F. Supp. 802, 806, 138 U.S.P.Q. 497, 501 (D. Neb. 1963).

6 *In re* Szumski, 302 F.2d 753, 133 U.S.P.Q. 551, (C.C.P.A. 1962). Sterling Drug, Inc. v. Brenner, 256 F. Supp. 1000, 150 U.S.P.Q. 584 (D.D.C. 1966); Ethyl Corp. v. Ladd, 221 F. Supp. 751, 138 U.S.P.Q. 663 (D.D.C. 1963).

7 Hotchkiss v. Greenwood, 52 U.S. (11 How.) 248 (1850).

8 Cuno Engineering Corp. v. Automatic Devices Corp., 314 U.S. 84, 51 U.S.P.Q. 272 (1941).

9 Newspaper Interview: LIFE, ch. 24 (1932).

10 Graham v. John Deere Co., 383 U.S. 1, 15, 148 U.S.P.Q. 459, 466 (1966).

11 *Ibid*

12 Pearce v. Mulford, 102 U.S. (12 Otto) 112, 117-118 (1880).

13 Reckendorfer v. Faber, 92 U.S. (2 Otto) 347, 356, 357 (1875).

14 Smith v. Nichols, 88 U.S. (21 Wall.) 112, 119 (1875).

15 35 U.S.C 103.

16 Harvey v. Levine, 322 F.2d 481, 138 U.S.P.Q. 659 (6th Cir. 1963).

17 *In re* Lindell, 385 F.2d 453, 155 U.S.P.Q. 521 (C.C.P.A. 1967); *In re* Tomlinson, 363 F.2d 928, 150 U.S.P.Q. 623 (C.C.P.A. 1966).

18 *In re* Libby, 255 F.2d 412, 414, 118 U.S.P.Q. 94, 96 (C.C.P.A. 1958).

19 See Edison Bell Phonograph Co. v. Smith & Young, 11 R.P.C. 389, 398 (1894).

20 35 U.S.C. 292.

21 35 U.S.C. 287.

22 Isenstead v. Watson, 157 F. Supp. 7, 115 U.S.P.Q. 408 (D.D.C. 1957).

23 See Jacobs v. Beecham, 221 U.S. 263, 272-273 (1910).

24 Federal Food Drug & Cosmetic Act of 1938, §502(c). See also, §505 (new drugs).

25 G. W. Vinal, *Storage Batteries* (John Wiley & Sons 1940), p. 145.

26 35 U.S.C. 261.

27 35 U.S.C. 253.

28 35 U.S.C. 254, 255.

29 35 U.S.C. 251.

30 35 U.S.C. 135, 291.

–Part II–

THE SUBSTANTIVE REQUISITES OF A VALID PATENT

> Nor does it detract from its merit that it is the result of experiment, and not the instant and perfect product of inventive power. A patentee may be baldly empirical, seeing nothing beyond his experiments and the result; yet if he has added a new and valuable article to the world's utilities he is entitled to the rank and protection of an inventor.
>
> McKenna, J.
> *Diamond Rubber Co. v. Consolidated Tire Co.*,
> 220 U.S. 428, 435-436 (1911)

The power to reward authors and inventors by protecting their work product against piracy emanates directly from Article I, Section 8, Clause 8 of the Constitution. This clause, however, does little more than express, in the most general of terms, the firm conviction of the enlightened framers of the Constitution that those whose exertions so directly and demonstrably ameliorate civilization should enjoy the fruits of their labors.

To Congress was delegated the task of filling in the myriad of details necessary for the establishment and maintenance of an orderly system of recognizing and protecting rights in intellectual property. These "details" fall into two broad categories: (1) substantive, those which affect a substantial or ultimate right; and (2) procedural, those which are merely incidental to the recognition of substantive rights.

Part II is devoted to an analysis of the substantive requisites of a valid patent. The procedural requisites for obtaining a patent form the subject matter of Part IV.

Chapter 5

STATUTORY SUBJECT MATTER

SYNOPSIS

> A process is a mode of treatment of certain materials to produce a given result. It is an art, or a series of acts, performed upon the subject-matter to be transformed and reduced to a different state or thing. If new and useful, it is just as patentable as a piece of machinery. In the language of the patent law, it is an art. The machinery pointed out as suitable to perform the process may or may not be new or patentable; whilst the process itself may be altogether new and produce an entirely new result. The process requires that certain things should be done with certain substances, and in a certain order; but the tools to be used in doing this may be of secondary consequence.
>
> Bradley, J.
> *Cochrane v. Deener*,
> 94 U.S. 780, 788 (1877)

Other than indicating that the motivation for granting to Congress the power to secure to inventors the exclusive rights to their "discoveries" is to promote the progress of science and the useful arts, the Constitution does not spell out the subject matter of inventions amenable to patent protection. Since the exercise of this power is permissive, and not mandatory, Congress may withhold some, and, indeed, even all of it.[1] One manner in which Congress may restrict the granting of patents is to limit that protection only to certain enumerated categories of invention, these specified categories of patentable or statutory subject matter being less extensive, even collectively, than the realm of inventive subject matter.

This chapter has three divisions: the first delineates the categories or classes of invention patent protection for which, Congress has declared, is possible. Therein is also considered the overlap and conflict between these classes. The second division explores the domain of nonstatutory subject matter. The third division examines the relationships between patentable subject matter and subject matter entitled protection under other federal statutes or the common law.

§ 1. Statutory Subject Matter

In marking off the realm of patentable or statutory subject matter, the approach which Congress has consistently followed, from its very first enactment in 1790, is to list categories or classes of patentable subject matter. Section 1 of the Act of 1790 declared amenable to patent protection: "any useful art, manufacture, engine, machine, or device, or any improvement therein not before known or used . . . . " Subsequent enactments have retained this format largely intact. The redundancy in "engine, machine, or device" was recognized, the verbiage removed, machine being retained and engine and device removed. Until the present Act, the word "process" did not appear; the "art" in "useful art" was construed, at an early date, to encompass a process or method.[2] Indeed, the very first patent issued by the United States, and signed by President Washington, Secretary of State Jefferson, and Attorney General Randolph, was for apparatus and process for making potash and pearlash. As will presently be seen, of all the classes of statutory subject matter, the one which has presented, and which continues to present, the most numerous problems is the "process" or "art," an "art" being, indeed, a word of art.

In 1842 Congress expanded the horizons of statutory subject matter to include (ornamental) designs. The realm of statutory subject matter was further enlarged in 1930 to include plants. However, the act extends patent protection only to asexual reproduction and it specifically exempts from its purview all tuber propagated plants and plants found in an uncultivated state.[3] In 1970 there was enacted the Plant Variety Protection Act.[4] It provides patent-like protection for sexual reproduction of new varieties of plants. Unlike the Plant Patent Act of 1930, the Plant Variety Protection Act 1970 is not administered by the Patent Office. Rather, the Plant Variety Protection Act creates a new office, within the Department of Agriculture, known as the Plant Variety Protection Office. It is vested with power to issue Certificates of Plant Variety Protection, which certificates carry rights of exclusivity analogous to those embraced in letters patent.

In contemplation of law, a design or a plant patent is as much a patent as is one for a process, machine, manufacture, or composition of matter. Nevertheless, the literature applies such terms as "invention patent," "utility patent," and "patents proper" to patents for processes, machines, manufactures, and compositions of matter collectively, to distinguish this group from design and/or plant patents. The reader should bear in mind, however, that nonobviousness or invention is as necessary for the validity of a design patent as it is for a so-called invention patent.[5] By virtue of the Constitution, it would appear that Congress has the power to extend patent protection to all subject matter falling within what can fairly be construed as "the useful arts." In specifying classes or categories of statutory subject matter, Section 101 declares amenable to patent protection "*any* new and useful process, machine, manufacture, or compositions of matter [emphasis added] . . . . " The word "any" is also applied to new, original and ornamental designs in Section 171 and to distinct and new varieties of plants in Section 161, although Section 161 qualifies "any" by excepting tuber propagated plants and plants found in an uncultivated state. Moreover, it has recently been held that all that is necessary to make a sequence of operational steps a statutory "process" within 35 U.S.C. 101 is that it be in the technological arts.[6] Congress may, of course, carve out particular exceptions from the enumerated statutory classes. One such exception is contained within the Patent Act itself, namely, that for tuber propagated plants and plants found in an uncultivated state. The Atomic Energy Act of 1954 excepts from patent protection inventions useful solely in the utilization of special nuclear material or atomic energy in an atomic weapon.[7]

The reader may be puzzled by the fact that Section 1 of the Act of 1790, in enumerating categories of subject matter amenable to patent protection, contains the phrase "or any *improvement* therein not before known or used [emphasis added] . . . . " Section 101 of the present Act retains the substance of that recitation. Some consider the phrase as raising improvements to the dignity and status of separate and distinct statutory classes of invention. Such an interpretation, however, makes little sense, particularly in view of the fact that nearly all inventions can be characterized as an improvement on or of something old. Nearly every mechanical device is, in a sense, an improvement on the wheel. Patents on such pioneer inventions as Bell's telephone and Edison's phonograph were entitled improvements.[8] Samuel Hopkins, the first patentee of the United States, referred to his invention as an improvement. It should be borne in mind that nothing was more abhorrent to the strict-constructionist orientation of the common-law legal mind than the failure to spell out, in a legal document or statute, every possible variation, however slight. The framers of the Act of 1790 found it necessary to enumerate "engine, machine, or device," where "machine" suffices today. Accordingly, it is submitted that the recitation of improvment in the present Act is mere surplusage, adding nothing to the preceding categories. Its presence is a mere vestige of the idiom of a bygone era.

Although the Patent Act distinguishes between a process, machine, manufacture, and composition of matter, these four statutory classes, from the standpoint of logic, more conveniently fall into but two categories: one embraces physical objects or instrumentalities and thus comprehends all machines, manufactures, and compositions of matter; the other embraces all physical operations and thus comprehends all processes. The term product is properly used to signify that which is produced by a machine or process. Its meaning, however, may be stretched to comprehend machines. In such sense, it may be employed as a generic term for machine, manufacture, and composition of matter, being in this sense commensurate with physical object or instrumentality. The term "article" is actually shorthand for (article of) manufacture. However, its meaning, like that of product, is sometimes expanded to include all physical objects and instrumentalities.

From the standpoint of the claim drafter, the statutory class to which an invention belongs is a material consideration; for it will, to a significant degree, dictate claim format. The influence of this parameter upon claim construction and interpretation was largely disregarded up to this point, because the object of the discussion heretofore was only to bring out, in general terms, the major factors, common to all inventions, which affect the scope of patent claims. A concerted effort, moreover, has been made to introduce complicating factors one at a time. Of course, deference must be paid to the statutory class to which an invention belongs in organizing a claim and in arriving at the precise language in which it is to be cast. The following precepts should be added to the basic rules of claim drafting set out in Chapter 3:

(1) Each claim should be drawn to but a single statutory class of invention. A claim which is drawn to more than one statutory class is sometimes referred to as a hybrid claim.[9]

(2) All the limitations of a claim upon which patentability turns should belong to the same statutory class. The line of demarcation is rather strictly observed with respect to the process-apparatus dichotomy. Thus, process limitations are given no weight in construing claims drawn to a machine;[10] machine limitations are given no weight in construing claims drawn to a process.[11]

Stated in other words: the patentability of a process claim must turn upon process limitations; the patentability of machine claims must turn upon machine limitations. The line of demarcation between machine, manufacture, and composition of matter claims is not nearly so sharp.

[1] Process

As the terms are used in patent law, process is synonymous with art, method, and mode of treatment.[12]

A process consists of an act, operation, or step, or of a series thereof, performed upon specified subject matter to produce a physical result.

Where a process consists of more than a single step, the arrangement, order, or sequence in which these component steps are to be performed may itself be of patentable significance. Thus, the patentability of a multi-step process may reside solely in the arrangement of its constituent steps—each of the individual steps being old and the particular order constituting a new combination. It should be noted that many of the so called one-step processes actually involve several steps, the single step being performed at a particular stage in a conventional series of steps.

Formerly, the nature of the steps themselves was of significance in determining whether a process fell within the realm of statutory subject matter. At an early date, the courts distinguished between processes involving the use of machines and those involving the application of more fundamental forces, holding that only processes involving the latter type of forces fell within the purview of an art.[13] That processes involving chemical action constituted statutory subject matter was early recognized.[14] With the coming of the Electrical Age, processes based upon transformations of electromagnetic energy became numerous, and these also were deemed to constitute an art.[15]

The rationale for denying that processes involving the use of machines constituted an art was that in such instances the invention resided, not in the process of using the machine, but rather in the machine itself.[16] After a time, the courts mitigated the extreme harshness of this position. A distinction was drawn between (1) processes which amounted to no more than the inherent and necessary function of a machine, the steps of the processing being part and parcel of the peculiar operation of the particular machine; and (2) processes which might be performed by hand or by any of several different mechanisms or machines and thus not inextricably tied to a particular machine. Only the former category of processes was still deemed to lie outside the pale of an act as contemplated by the patent statute.[17] A caveat, however, is in order. Where a patent application contains both machine claims and claims drawn to the method of using such machine, the Patent Office may require restriction between the machine and method claims, if either or both of the following can be shown: (1) the process as claimed can be practiced by another materially different machine or by hand; or (2) the machine as claimed can be used to practice another and materially different process.[18] A consequence of a requirement for restriction is that the applicant will have to elect whether to prosecute in the instant application the machine or method claims. A separate application, known as a divisional, may be filed upon the nonelected group of claims. The subject of restrictions will be treated at length in Chapter 13. Recently, it has been held that even processes which involve no more than the inherent and necessary function of a machine may not be rejected solely on such ground.[19] Restriction may not be required between such method and machine claims, as these do not correspond to separate and distinct inventions!

The law is now fairly well settled: a statutory process may be composed of any combination of physical or manipulative steps. Thus, it has been held that a surgical procedure or technique, which was properly claimed, constituted a statutory process.[20]

The controversy over what constitutes a statutory process still rages, however, with the lines now drawn around what are known as "mental" or "nonphysical" steps. A mental act or step is one which may be performed by the human mind without the need or intervention of a physical instrumentality. Such acts are broadly divisible into: (1) those which merely involve the application of logic or deduction; and (2) those which involved aesthetic thoughts or other value judgements. Examples of mental acts involving simple logic include computing, measuring, determining, counting, dividing, etc. Such acts may also be performed by a machine, according to a predetermined and predeterminable criteria. Where the performance of such acts effects a physical result, it is not seen why such process should be unpatentable.[21] However, where the entire process is purely mental, all of the steps capable of being performed in one's head, as, for example, a technique for computing square roots, it can be argued that a patent on such a process would invade the freedom of thought, and so would violate the First Amendment. Note that the result of such process is not physical, but rather consists of merely the production of numerical values.

It must be emphasized that in regard to processes involving mental steps, particular care must be exercised in determining whether the process is defined with sufficient particularity as to be capable of being carried out. Thus, where a process calls for determining values of a certain parameter, the criteria for ascertaining values of that parameter must be disclosed. A patent specification which lacks this information would be insufficient, though the process itself constitute statutory subject matter. One who would attempt to patent a process in which there is a step involving the making of a value judgment might have difficulty in defining that step with sufficient particularity as to enable others to practice it.

The patentablity of a process may reside in a particular step or in the order in which the constituent steps are performed. Another parameter is the material upon which the steps of the process act. While there are cases which state that one is not entitled to claim a process which differs from the prior art merely in the nature of the starting materials, it is submitted that the materials subjected to treatment by the operations of the process are as much a part of a process as are the physical operations and chemical reactions. Moreover, it is conceivable that sufficient novelty and obviousness may reside in such materials as to sustain the patentability of a process claim, the steps themselves being old. Where a process differs from the prior art solely in that a different but related or analogous starting material is employed, that process, though novel, would be prima facie obvious. The novelty of such a process resides in the fact that the materials are not identical with those employed by the prior art. Failure of the prior art to teach the analogy between the materials would tend to establish unobviousness, as would the existence of a different and unexpected result. In chemical cases, the starting materials are often spoken of as reactants or reagents; and in mechanical cases as the workpiece.

The materials subjected to treatment by the steps of a process and the steps themselves are the parameters which define a process. The nature and composition of the product is defined by and necessarily flows from the foregoing parameters. Two processes which treat the same starting material in the same manner are identical and must of necessity give rise to the same product.

Two interesting problems have arisen in connection with process claims and their relation to the corresponding product. One involves the product and the manner of using it, the so-called new use for an old product; the other involves the product and the process of making it, the so-called product-by-process claim. Does the discovery of a new use for a known substance entitle the discoverer of such new use to a patent on the old substance? The answer is that it does not.[22] Dr. Morton was the first to demonstrate the anaesthetic properties of ether. However, the compound ether was known before. Dr. Morton applied it to surgery. Dr. Morton obtained a patent on the use of ether in anaesthetic surgery.[23] The patent was held invalid.[24] Nevertheless, under present law, one who discovers a new use for a known substance may patent the use itself, provided that the new use is claimed as a process.[25] A composition of matter which cannot be described other than by reference to the process of making it may be claimed as a process.[26] Such a claim is called a product-by-process claim, and is deemed a product claim and not a process claim.[27]

[2] Machine

As the terms are used in patent law, "machine" is virtually interchangeable with apparatus, mechanism, device, or engine. Although the Patent Act employs the word "machine," in practice, the term "apparatus" is much preferred, particularly in the chemical arts. The term "machine" includes tools and other implements intended for use by hand. There is no requirement that a machine to be patentable must be automatic.

A machine is an instrument, that is to say a physical entity, consisting of parts, components, or elements, which are so arranged and organized as to cooperate, when set in motion, to produce a definite, predetermined, and unitary result.[28]

The particular way in which the components are arranged, as well as the nature of the components themselves, are the parameters which define and distinguish a machine. Thus, the patentability of a machine may reside entirely in the manner in which the components are arranged, all of the components being old.[29] Similarly, patentability may reside both in the manner of combining the components and in one or more of the components. An old or exhausted combination which contains a new component, however, is not patentable, although such new component may be patentable by itself.[30] A patentable machine may consist of (1) an entire or integral working entity; or (2) but a component or subcombination of some larger machine.

The material or workpiece upon which a machine is capable operating is not considered to be a component thereof and, thus, is to be ignored in determining the patentability of a machine.

Every different combination of components gives rise to a distinct and inherent rule or law or principle of action, according to which that combination will necessarily operate. This is sometimes referred to as the inherent function of the machine or as its mode of operation. Claims directed thereto may be patentable as a process.[31] The operation of a machine may involve a transmittal, transformation, or any other utilization of energy.

While the novelty of machine claims will turn upon its components and their arrangement, in determining the unobviousness and scope of such claims, a court will also consider the mode of operation and result obtained.[32]

[3] Manufacture

The term "manufacture" is actually shorthand for "article of manufacture," and is derived from the English Statute of Monopolies, which speaks of "any manner of new manufactures." In fact, to this day, in the United Kingdom, patentable subject matter is limited to "any manner of new manufactures." Consequently, British law has given this language a very broad construction, so broad, in fact, that it is almost commensurate with the aggregate of the several classes of subject matter set forth in the United States Patent Act. United States law has given a more restrictive construction upon the term "manufacture." Thus, it has been construed as excluding what is comprehended by the other statutory classes of inventive subject matter.

Also excluded from the class manufacture are articles whose appearance, properties, function, form, shape, and/or size has been only slightly or negligibly altered by a manufacturing process, the essential character of such articles remaining a product of nature. For example, fresh fruit impregnated with a solution of borax was held not a manufacture, even though the borax imparted to the fruit fungicidal properties which made it resistant to decay.[33] In the words of the Supreme Court: "To obtain a patent for a product made from raw material, it must possess a new or distinctive form, quality, or property."

It should be noted that building structures, made as houses and bridges, have been generally regarded as manufactures.[34]

[4] Composition of Matter

As used in patent law, "composition of matter" or "composition" includes chemical compounds and physical mixtures. A transuranic chemical element has been held patentable as a composition of matter.[35]

As the term suggests, "composition of matter" covers materials or substances themselves, and such are wholly independent of and distinct from the particular extrinsic and macroscopic configurations in which they may appear. The latter are manufactures.

A machine is a combination of parts; a composition of matter is a combination, union, or association of ingredients. A chemical element is, in effect, a combination of subatomic particles—protons, electrons, and neutrons. As the patentability of a machine may turn, not only upon the novelty of its components but, on the manner in which these are combined, so too the patentability of a composition of matter may turn, not only upon the novelty of its ingredients, but on the manner in which these are combined. The mode of combination may be (1) chemical, as in the case of compounds; or (2) physical, as in the case of mixtures. A new crystalline form of an old compound has been held patentable as a composition of matter.[36]

Like the components of a patentable machine, the components or ingredients of a patentable composition of matter must cooperate to produce a unitary result—that is, they must, in association, exhibit a set of properties distinct from those possessed by the separated constituents.[37]

[5] Designs

The patentability of a design resides in its appearance.[38] Accordingly, a design that would be hidden from view when the objects embodying it are in their normal use is not the proper subject for a design patent.[39] This principle is in contrast to that applied to patents on processes, machines, manufactures, and compositions of matter, the motivation for which is some utility or function. Moreover, to the extent that appearance is dictated solely by functional or utilitarian consideration, appearance is not patentable as a design.[40] However, the same physical object may have aspects which are patentable as a manufacture and others which are patentable as a design.[41]

While the Patent Act ties patents for designs to articles of manufacture,[42] this wording has been liberally construed as requiring only that the design be in the form of a tangible object, even if that object be as ephemeral as that created by a water fountain.[43] To this end, a design patent application must depict the complete appearance of the article of manufacture in which the design is embodied.[44]

A patentable design, like a patentable process, machine, manufacture, and composition of matter, must be new and unobvious. The Patent Act further requires of a patentable design that it be original and ornamental.[45]

In the opinion of the author, the originality requirement is embraced in the novelty requirement, as originality in the law of copyright is construed as requiring something less than novelty.[46] Others have related the word "original," as this appears in the design patent statute, to unobviousness.[47] This statute further provides that the general provisions of the Patent Act shall apply to patents for design, except as otherwise provided.

One significant difference is that a patentable design must be ornamental. The ornamentality requirement is to designs is what the utility requirement is to processes, machines, manufactures, and compositions of matter. It should be noted that until the Patent Act of 1902, the patent statute employed the word "useful" in regard to all the statutory classes, including design.[48] The act substituted "ornamental" for "useful," with respect to designs.

The ornamentality requirement has made the appearance, attractiveness, and decorativeness of a design a material consideration. It has invited courts to impose upon the law their own subjective notions of aesthetics.[49] It should be noted that in no other species of intellectual property is the aesthetic value of a contribution a consideration. Consequently, design patents have not fared well in the courts.

While ornamentality and unobviousness are virtually inseparable considerations, courts have found the presence of ornamentality, yet found that the design wanting in unobviousness.[50] In evaluating the ornamental and unobvious qualities of a design, it is the overall or total impression that is controlling, not the dissected individual elements.[51] It is the eye of the ordinary purchaser[52] or the taste and fancy of the average man[53] by which these standards are to be gauges.

Another difference between design and the so-called utility patents is their duration. Patents for designs may be granted for the term of three years and six months, or for the term of seven years, or for the term of fourteen years, as the applicant, in his application, elects.[54] The filing fee varies with the duration of the term. Since an applicant may, after allowance of his design patent application, opt for a longer term by amending his application and paying the additional sum, it is advisable to initially request the shortest term.

For design patents, only a single claims, in formal terms is permitted,[55] even though more than one embodiment is disclosed. The claims merely claims the figure(s) depicted in the drawing. No specific description other than a reference to the drawing is ordinarily required or permitted.

[6] Plants

Most new varieties of living plants are amenable to patent or patent-like protection. Such protection is keyed to the reproduction of the protected variety. At least in this respect, this subject matter is more analogous to method-claim protection than to article-claim protection.

Patents for plants confer upon the patentee the right to exclude others from asexually reproducing the plant and from selling and using any plants so reproduced.[56] Tuber propagated plants (such as potatoes) and plants found in an uncultivated state are specifically excluded from plant patent protection.[57] The plant patented may be a cultivated sport, a mutant, a hybrid, or a new found seedling.

A separate act, known as the Plant Variety Protection Act, provides for patent-like protection on new varieties of plants reproduced by sexual means (that is, any production of a variety of seed).[58] This statute is not administered by the Patent Office, but rather by the Office of Plant Variety Protection, a bureau within the Department of Agriculture.[59] The language and provisions of the Plant Variety Protection Act, to a large extent, parallel those set out in the Patent Act. Grants of protection under the Plant Variety Protection Act are not called patents, but rather are styled Certificates of Plant Variety Protection. They confer upon the breeder, who is to be equated with the inventor of utility patents, and his successors in interest the right to exclude others from selling the protected variety or offering it for sale, or reproducing it, or importing it, or exporting it, or using it in producing (as distinguished from developing) a hybrid or different variety therefrom.[60] The use and reproduction of a protected variety in research is expressly exempted from action for infringement.[61] Multiplying a protected variety, even by asexual means, constitutes infringement, unless in pursuance of a valid United States plant patent.[62] A Certificate of Plant Variety Protection would thus seem to preclude the subsequent obtaining of a plant patent. Okra, celery, peppers, tomatoes, carrots, and cucumbers are specifically excluded from plant variety protection.[63]

Unlike the Patent Act, the Plant Variety Protection Act makes provision for what is, in effect, compulsory licensing[64] and for reexamination after issue.[65]

Although the Plant Patent Act states that the provisions of the Act relating to patents for inventions shall apply to patents for plants, except as otherwise provided, the fact that the subject matter and the subject matter of Certificates of Plant Variety Protection involve living matter introduces a fundamental difference with respect to disclosure.

From a written and/or pictorial description of the usual[66] utility or design patent, one skilled in the relevant art can make and use the invention. This is not true of living matter. A mere description is incapable of placing the plant in the hands of the public. Consequently, the paper application is not deemed an enabling disclosure. For the foregoing reason, it has been held that the mere description in a printed publication of a new plant variety, even though such description had been published more than a year prior to the filing date of a plant patent application, did not constitute a statutory bar (under 35 U.S.C. § 102b) to a patent thereon.[67] Accordingly, plant patents, like design patents, may contain but a single claim, in formal terms, which may, however, recite its distinguishing characteristics.[68] Furthermore, a plant patentee to establish infringement must prove access to his stock, that is, a plant, to infringe a plant patent, must have been derived from the very stock of the patentee.[69] In this respect, plant patent infringement is akin to copyright infringement.[70] The mere existence of a patented variety, unappreciated for many years before its discovery, does not invalidate the patent.[71]

The Plant Patent Act requires not only the discovery or recognition of the new plant variety but its asexual reproduction as well.[72] The act of discovery or recognition may be analogized to the conception of a utility or design invention and its asexual reproduction to reduction to practice. The purpose for requiring asexual reproduction is to demonstrate that the plant is in fact a new and distinct variety. Although the Plant Patent Act uses both the terms "invests" and "discovers" in connection with new plant varieties, patentees thereof are properly styled discoverers, as they have contrived nothing—nature has done that. The essence of their contribution is the recognition of the new variety. Perhaps an even more appropriate designation is that employed by the Plant Variety Protection Act, namely, "breeder."

§ 2. Nonstatutory Subject Matter

If invention is whatever is new, useful, and unobvious, then there are categories of invention which are not subject to patent or patent-like protection.

One major category comprises subject matter explicitly excluded by statute. This category may in turn be divided into two: (1) Subject matter excepted from within a single statutory class. These exceptions all relate to plants, and have been enumerated in the immediately preceding section; and (2) Subject matter which might otherwise fall into any of the statutory classes of utility inventions. Thus, the Atomic Energy Act contains a blanket exception, excluding from patent protection any invention or discovery which is useful solely in the utilization of special nuclear material or atomic energy in any atomic weapon.[73] ,

Often considered as constituting a class of unpatentable subject matter is that which is so broad as to be incapable, as a practical matter, of adequate definition and/or is not really new (but merely previously unknown or unappreciated). Such inventions are more appropriately styled discoveries. These have already been discussed at length. They include:

(1) Principles or laws of nature;

(2) Naturally occurring articles.

A third group of subject matter has been excluded by judicial construction. It includes:

(1) Printed matter;

(2) Methods of doing business;

(3) Mental processes.

Printed matter and mere arrangements thereof are seemingly manufactures. Nevertheless, the rationale for denying patent protection to inventions addressed to this subject matter is that the essence of its novelty does not reside in physical structure or extension, but rather in concepts conveyed by the arrangement of words and/or other symbols.[74] The novel aspects of printed matter may be protectible under the copyright laws.[75]

Though seemingly within the class of a process or method, the *Manual of Patent Examining Procedure* declares that "the law is settled" that a method of doing business can be rejected as not being within the statutory classes.[76] It is worthy to note, however, that trademark protection may effectively secure the economic value of a system of doing business. Thus, "Christmas Club" is a federally registered service mark, and the use of these words in connection with that system of doing business is the exclusive right of the trademark owner.[77]

Mental processes have already been mentioned. Recently, the Supreme Court was called upon to decide a case involving the patentability of a digital computer program for carrying out a mathematical operation, to wit, converting binary code to pure binary. The Court found that, in practical effect, the claimed method amounted to a mere mathematical formula and was, therefore, not statutory subject matter. The Court, however, noted that its decision should not be construed as precluding a patent for any program servicing a computer.[78]

§ 3. Multiple and Alternative Protection: Successive and Simultaneous

Of more than academic interest is the possibility of obtaining multiple property rights in the embodiment of a common nucleus of creative ideas.

It is black letter law that but a single patent may be obtained for one invention.[79] However, it must be borne in mind that invention, in its technical, legal sense, is so restrictive that the foregoing rule does not preclude the possibility of several patentable inventions being present in a single nucleus of ideas. For example, it is not unlikely that a new machine will engender a new process of using the same. A new manufacture may stimulate the creation of a new machine to make the same. All would be patentable separately, provided that each one, independently of the others, is new, useful, and unobvious.

Accordingly, a device patentable as a manufacture may also give rise to a patentable design.[80]

Copyright protection is available for three-dimensional artistic works, and it has been held that the incorporation of an artistic article (statuette) in a useful article (lamp base) did not vitiate copyright protection thereon.[81] A copyrightable work of art continues to be protected by copyright even after it has been incorporated in a useful article. The copyrightability of a work of art is not affected by the potential availability of a design patent.

Moreover, a design patent may be secured in an ornamental design even after the same has been copyrighted as a work of art.[82] Accordingly, copyright and a design patent can subsist simultaneously in the same subject matter.

It is the avowed policy of the Copyright Office to refuse to register a copyright claim in patented designs or the drawings or photographs in a patent application after the patent has issued.[83] It is of interest to note that the specifications of at least one United States patent bears a notice of copyright.[84] The effect thereof was never adjudicated.

The shape, form, or configuration of a three-dimensional article may be capable of performing a trademark function.[85] Does the fact that an article is covered by a United States patent preclude its recognition as a trademark? The Supreme Court stated that on the expiration of a patent the monopoly granted by it ceases to exist, and the right to make the thing formerly covered by the patent becomes public property.[86] That case involved pillow-shaped biscuits, to which the patentee had given the name "Shredded Wheat." A utility patent covered both the pillow-shaped product and the process of fabricating it. The biscuit itself had also been the subject of a design patent, which had been held invalid in a collateral suit. The patentee sought to enjoin a competitor from manufacturing pillow-shaped biscuits on the theory that their pillow shape was distinctive, constituting a valid trademark. The suit also sought to enjoin the use of the words "Shredded Wheat" in connection with its competitor's product. In declining to protect the pillow shape as a trademark the Court alluded to testimony which tended to establish that the pillow shape was not purely arbitrary, being, at least in part, dictated by functional considerations—that the cost of the biscuits would be increased and their quality lessened if some form, other than the pillow shape, were substituted. The Court also found that "Shredded Wheat" was not entitled to protection as a trademark, in that, during the life of the patent, these words had become accepted as the generic or common name for pillow-shaped, whole-wheat biscuits. Therefore, they passed into public domain with the cessation of the monopoly which the patent had created.[87]

In a later case, the Supreme Court precluded from trademark protection any matter, albeit distinctive, appearing in the specifications, drawings, or claims of a patent whether or not such matter describes the essential elements of the invention or claims.[88] As that suit involved a utility patent, it has been construed as not barring trademark protection for design patent subject matter. The position of the Court of Customs and Patent Appeals apparently is that the existence of a design patent upon a purely arbitrary and nonfunctional configuration does not preclude protection of that configuration as a trademark.[89]

Notes

1 See McClurg v. Kingsland, 42 U.S. (1 How.) 202, 206 (1843).

2 Corning v. Burden, 56 U.S. (15 How.) 252, 267 (1853).

3 35 U.S.C. 161.

4 P.L. 91-577.

5 See for example, *In re* Laverne, 356 F.2d 1003, 148 U.S.P.Q. 674 (C.C.P.A. 1966); Sel-O-Rak v. The Henry Hanger & Display Fixture Corp., 232 F.2d 176, 109 U.S.P.Q. 179 (5th Cir. 1956).

6 *In re* Musgrave, 431 F.2d 882, 893, 167 U.S.P.Q. 280, 289-290 (C.C.P.A. 1970).

7 42 U.S.C. 2181.

8 See specifications of U.S. Pat. Nos. 161,793, 174,456, and 186,787 to Bell; U.S. Pat. No. 200,521 to Edison.

9 See generally, Ex parte Commet, 98 U.S.P.Q. 15 (P.O. Bd. App. 1953).

10 *In re* Jacoby, 309 F.2d 509, 135 U.S.P.Q. 319 (C.C.P.A. 1962). See *In re* Dilnot, 300 F.2d 945, 133 U.S.P.Q. 289 (C.C.P.A. 1962) for the proposition that a method step cannot impart patentability to a product claim.

11 Ex parte Foreman, 1924 C.D. 47, 326 O.G. 47 (Comm. Pat. 1924).

12 35 U.S.C. 100(b).

13 O'Reilly v. Morse, 56 U.S. (15 How.) 62 (1853).

14 Corning v. Burden, 56 U.S. (15 How.) 252 (1853).

15 The Telephone Cases, 126 U.S. 1 (1888).

16 Risdon Iron Works v. Medart, 158 U.S. 68, 79 (1895); Westinghouse v. Boyden Power Brake Co., 170 U.S. 537, 553 (1898).

17 The Expanded Metal Case, 214 U.S. 366 (1909). See also, *In re* McKee, 79 F.2d 905, 27 U.S.P.Q. 353 (C.C.P.A. 1936); *In re* Parker, 79 F.2d 908, 27 U.S.P.Q. 340 (C.C.P.A. 1936).

18 M.P.E.P. 806.05(e).

19 *In re* Tarczy-Hornoch, 397 F.2d 856, 158 U.S.P.Q. 141 (C.C.P.A. 1968).

20 Ex parte Scherer, 103 U.S.P.Q. 107 (P.O. Bd. App. 1954).

21 See Gottschalk v. Benson, 409 U.S. 63, 175 U.S.P.Q. 673 (1972).

22 See for example, Magic Fingers, Inc. v. Auger, 232 F. Supp. 372, 377, 142 U.S.P.Q. 207, 211 (D. Me. 1964).

23 U.S. Patent No. 4848.

24 Morton v. New York Eye Infirmary, 17 Fed. Cas. 879 (No. 9865) (C.C.S.D.N.Y. 1862).

25 35 U.S.C. 100(b).

26 M.P.E.P. 706.03(e).

27 *In re* Lyons, 364 F.2d 1005, 150 U.S.P.Q. 741 (C.C.P.A. 1966); *In re* Taylor, 360 F.2d 232, 149 U.S.P.Q. 615 (C.C.P.A. 1966). *Contra*, *In re* Freeman, 166 F.2d 178, 76 U.S.P.Q. 585 (C.C.P.A. 1948).

28 Burr v. Duryee, 68 U.S. (1 Wall.) 531, 570-571 (1863).

29 Seymour v. Osborne, 78 U.S. (11 Wall.) 516 (1870).

30 *In re* Hall, 208 F.2d 370, 100 U.S.P.Q. 46 (C.C.P.A. 1953); Ex parte Silverstein, 125 U.S.P.Q. 238 (P.O. Bd. App. 1959). See also Lincoln Engineering Co. v. Steward-Warner Corp., 303 U.S. 545, 37 U.S.P.Q. 1 (1938).

31 *In re* Tarczy-Hornoch, 397 F.2d 856, 158 U.S.P.Q. 141 (C.C.P.A. 1968).

32 See generally, Traitel Marbel Co. v. Hungerford Brass & Co., 18 F.2d 66 (2d Cir. 1927).

33 American Fruit Growers, Inc. v. Brodex Co., 283 U.S. 1 8 U.S.P.Q. 131 (1931).

34 Riter-Conley Mfg. Co. v. Aiken, 203 F. 699 (3d Cir.), *cert. denied* 229 U.S. 617 (1913). Compare, Jacobs v. Baker, 74 U.S. (7 Wall.) 297 (1868).

35 *In re* Seaborg, 328 F.2d 993, 140 U.S.P.Q. 659 (C.C.P.A. 1964).

36 Union Carbide Co. v. American Carbolite Co., 188 Fed. 334 (N.D. Ill. 1911). See also, Union Carbide Co. v. American Carbide Co., 181 Fed. 104 (2d Cir. 1910).

37 Ex parte Macy, 132 U.S.P.Q. 545, 546 (P.O. Bd. App. 1960). See also, Lincoln Engineering Co. v. Stewart-Warner Corp., 303 U.S. 545, 549, 37 U.S.P.Q. 1, 3 (1938); Richard v. Chase Elevator Co., 159 U.S. 477, 487 (1895).

38 Day-Brite Lighting, Inc. v. Compco Corp., 311 F.2d 26, 136 U.S.P.Q. 17 (7th Cir. 1962), *rev'd on other grounds* 376 U.S. 234, 140 U.S.P.Q. 528 (1964). See also, *In re* Halden, 20 F.2d 275 (D.D.C. 1927).

39 *In re* Stevens, 173 F.2d 1015, 81 U.S.P.Q. 362 (C.C.P.A. 1949).

40 Hygenic Specialties Co. v. H.G. Salzman, Inc., 320 F.2d 614, 133 U.S.P.Q. 96 (2d Cir. 1962); *In re* Garbo, 287 F.2d 192, 129 U.S.P.Q. 72 (C.C.P.A. 1961).

41 Robert W. Brown & Co. v. DeBell, 243 F.2d 200, 113 U.S.P.Q. 172 (9th Cir. 1957); Ex parte Gibson, 135 U.S.P.Q. 128 (P.O. Bd. App. 1962); Ex parte Levinn, 136 U.S.P.Q. 63 (P.O. Bd. App. 1962); Ex parte Henck, 131 U.S.P.Q. 33 (P.O. Bd. App. 1961).

42 35 U.S.C. 171.

43 *In re* Hruby, 373 F.2d 997, 153 U.S.P.Q. 61 (C.C.P.A. 1967).

44 Ex parte France, 132 U.S.P.Q. 211 (P.O. Bd. App. 1961).

45 35 U.S.C. 171.

46 See Mazer v. Stein, 347 U.S. 201, 218, 100 U.S.P.Q. 325, 333 (1954).

47 Trojan Textile Corp. v. Crown Fabrics Corp., 143 F. Supp. 48, 110 U.S.P.Q. 231 (S.D.N.Y. 1956).

48 See Ex parte Knothe, 1903 C.D. 42 (Comm. Pat. 1903).

49 Blisscraft of Hollywood v. United Plastics Co., 294 F.2d 694, 131 U.S.P.Q. 55 (2d Cir. 1961).

50 Day-Brite Lighting, Inc. v. Sandee Mfg. Co., 286 F.2d 596, 128 U.S.P.Q. 416 (7th Cir. 1960), *cert. denied* 366 U.S. 963 (1961); Campbell v. Watson, 275 F.2d 166, 124 U.S.P.Q. 164 (D.C.C.), *cert. denied* 362 U.S. 903 (1960); *In re* Rubinfeld, 270 F.2d 391, 123 U.S.P.Q. 210 (C.C.P.A. 1959).

51 Philco Corp. v. Admiral Corp., 199 F. Supp. 797, 131 U.S.P.Q. 413 (D. Del. 1961); *In re* Balmer, 276 F.2d 405, 125 U.S.P.Q. 339 (C.C.P.A. 1960); R-Way Furniture Co. v. Duo Bed Corp., 216 F. Supp. 862, 134 U.S.P.Q. 113 (N.D. Ill. 1962).

52 Aileen Mills Co. v. Ojay Mills Co., 188 F. Supp. 138, 127 U.S.P.Q. 370 (S.D.N.Y. 1960).

53 *In re* Grigsby, 145 F.2d 117 (D.C.C. 1925).

54 35 U.S.C. 173.

55 Rule 153.

56 35 U.S.C. 163.

57 35 U.S.C. 161.

58 P.L. 91-577, §41(f).

59 P.L. 91-577, §1.

60 P.L. 91-577, §83(a).

61 P.L. 91-577, §114.

62 P.L. 91-577, §111(7).

63 P.L. 91-577, §144.

64 P.L. 91-577, §44.

65 P.L. 91-577, §91.

66 See *In re* Argoudelis, 434 F.2d 211, 168 U.S.P.Q. 99 (C.C.P.A. 1970).

67 *In re* LeGrice, 301 F.2d 929, 133 U.S.P.Q. 365 (C.C.P.A. 1962).

68 35 U.S.C. 162.

69 Kim Bros. v. Hagler, 276 F.2d 259, 125 U.S.P.Q. 44 (9th Cir. 1960), *aff'g* 167 F. Supp. 665, 120 U.S.P.Q. 210 (S.D. Cal. 1958); Armstrong Nurseries, Inc. v. Smith, 170 F. Supp. 519, 120 U.S.P.Q. 220 (E. D. Tex. 1958).

70 See for example, Schwarz v. Universal Pictures Co., 85 F. Supp. 270, 83 U.S.P.Q. 153 (S.D. Cal. 1945).

[71] Nicholson v. Bailey, 182 F. Supp. 509, 125 U.S.P.Q. 157 (S.D. Fla. 1960).

[72] Ex parte Moore, 115 U.S.P.Q. 145 (P.O. Bd. App. 1957).

[73] 42 U.S.C. 2181.

[74] Ex parte Des Granges, 142 U.S.P.Q. 41 (P.O. Bd. App. 1962).

[75] But see, Baker v. Selden, 101 U.S. (11 Otto) 99 (1879).

[76] M.P.E.P. 706.03(a). Hotel Security Checking Co. v. Lorraine Co., 160 Fed. 467 (2d Cir. 1908).

[77] See Rand McNally Corp. v. Christmas Club, Inc., 105 U.S.P.Q. 499 (T.T.A. Bd. 1955), *aff'd* 242 F.2d 776, 113 U.S.P.Q. 287 (C.C.P.A. 1957). Compare, Oxenhandler v. Dime Sav. Bank of Brooklyn, 133 U.S.P.Q. 293 (N.Y. Sup. Ct. 1962) (Chanukah Savings Plan).

[78] Gottschalk v. Benson, 409 U.S. 63, 71, 175 U.S.P.Q. 673, 676 (1972).

[79] See Suffold Co. v. Hayden, 70 U.S. (3 Wall.) 315 (1865); Odiorne v. Amesbury, 18 Fed. Cas. 578 (No. 10,430) (C.C.D. Mass. 1819).

[80] *In re* DuBois, 262 F.2d 88, 120 U.S.P.Q. 198 (C.C.P.A. 1958). Compare *In re* Barber, 81 F.2d 231, 28 U.S.P.Q. 187 (C.C.P.A. 1936). See also, Ex parte Schliembolm, 94 U.S.P.Q. 393 (P.O. Bd. App. 1952).

[81] Mazer v. Stein, 347 U.S. 201, 100 U.S.P.Q. 325 (1954).

[82] *In re* Yardley, 493 F.2d 1389, 181 U.S.P.Q. 331 (C.C.P.A. 1974). But see, Korzybski v. Underwood & Underwood, Inc., 36 F.2d 727, 3 U.S.P.Q. 242 (2d Cir. 1929); *In re* Blood, 23 F.2d 772 (D.C.C. 1927).

[84] See specification of U.S. Pat. No. 1,087,186 (1914).

[85] Ex parte Haig & Haig, Ltd., 118 U.S.P.Q. 229 (Comm. Pat. 1958). But see, *In re* Duro-Test Corp., 134 U.S.P.Q. 137 (T.T. App. Bd. 1962); *In re* McIlhenney Co., 278 F.2d 953, 126 U.S.P.Q. 138 (C.C.P.A. 1960).

[86] Scott Paper Co. v. Marcalus Mfg. Co., 326 U.S. 249, 256, 67 U.S.P.Q. 193, 196-197 (1945).

[87] Singer Mfg. Co. v. June Mfg. Co., 163 U.S. 169 (1896).

[88] Kellogg Co. v. National Biscuit Co., 305 U.S. 111, 39 U.S.P.Q. 296 (1938).

[89] *In re* Mogen David Wine Corp., 372 F.2d 539, 152 U.S.P.Q. 593 (C.C.P.A. 1967).

Chapter 6

NOVELTY

SYNOPSIS

> America is a land of wonders, in which everything is in constant motion and every change seems an improvement. The idea of novelty is there indissolubly connected with the idea of amelioration. No natural boundary seems to be set to the efforts of man; and in his eyes what is not yet done is only what he has not yet attempted to do.
>
> A. de Tocqueville,
> *Democracy in America*, Pt. I, Ch. 18.

Novelty or newness is the sine qua non of every invention. The word "invention" is derived from the French verb *invenire*, to find out. That "found out," to be an invention, must be new.

But "novelty" is an ambiguous term, embracing several overlapping and interrelated concepts, which have both subjective and objective aspects. Novelty is relative. Columbus is said to have discovered America, but, it was known to its native Indians for thousands of years prior to his arrival, and had been in existence for millions of years. Implicit in every novelty determination is a frame of reference. One must ask the question: New to whom? This is the subjective aspect of novelty. It has great significance in patent law. Also highly developed in patent law is the objective aspect of novelty. This is embraced in the question: How much and what kinds of differences make a thing new?

Section 101 of the Patent Act expresses the novelty requirement in general terms. Section 102 of the Patent Act attempts to spell out just what is *not* to be considered novel in the patent law sense. It declares:

§ 102. Conditions for patentability; novelty and loss of right to patent

A person shall be entitled to a patent unless—
(a) the invention was known or used by others in this country, or patented or described in a printed publication in this or a foreign country, before the invention thereof by the applicant for patent, or
(b) the invention was patented or described in a printed publication in this or a foreign country or in public use or on sale in this country, more than one year prior to the date of the application for patent in the United States, or
(c) he has abandoned the invention, or
(d) the invention was first patented or caused to be patented, or was the subject of an inventor's certificate, by the applicant or his legal representatives or assigns in a foreign country prior to the date of the application for patent or inventor's certificate filed more than twelve months before the filing of the application in the United States, or
(e) the invention was described in a patent granted on an application for patent by another filed in the United States before the invention thereof by the applicant for patent, or
(f) he did not himself invent the subject matter sought to be patented, or
(g) before the applicant's invention thereof the invention was made in this country by another who had not abandoned, suppressed, or concealed it. In determining priority of invention there shall be considered not only the respective dates of conception and reduction to practice of the invention, but also the reasonable diligence of one who was first to conceive and last to reduce to practice, from a time prior to conception by the other.

The import of the several provisos comprising Section 102 cannot be intelligently evaluated without some perspective. Helpful in gaining that perspective is the dichotomy between, on one hand, the subjective or what is extrinsic, and, on the other, the objective or what is intrinsic. But even before these separate aspects can be explored, a few explanatory words regarding terminology are necessary.

By subjective or extrinsic is meant those qualities or attributes which may vary from observer to observer depending upon their prior experience. The judgment that something is old or that it is new is subjective in the sense that it is made relative to and thus dependent upon one's prior experience. By objective or intrinsic is meant those qualities or attributes which are absolute and do not vary from observer to observer. The judgment that one object differs from another is independent of the prior experience of those making the comparison.

§ 1. The Prior Art

Novelty connotes change or innovation: a difference between that which is sought to be patented and that which went before (the prior art). That which went before lacks novelty and is said to be old.

If there is a physical identity between the prior art and that sought to be patented, that which is sought to be patented is said to be anticipated by the prior art. The words "physical identity" have special significance.

In determining whether there has been an anticipation, only physical differences are considered. Accordingly, if an article was in use or a process had been carried out prior to the point in time when it was first made by the party seeking a patent, that article or process is literally anticipated by the earlier use, even though those who had earlier used the article or had carried out the process were totally unaware of or failed to appreciate its advantages. Even under the foregoing circumstances, the article or process is deemed to have been "known," within the meaning of Section 102(a). Stated in other words, mere existence in use generally suffices to constitute an anticipation. The principles underlying the foregoing results constitute what is sometimes referred to as the doctrine of inherency.

The physical object or embodiment of that which is sought to be protected by a patent must itself be new, and not merely previously unknown. Although one may be the first to observe and recognize a previously unknown, unappreciated, and important property of an existing substance, he has not, for such contribution, earned the right to exclude others from making, using, and selling that substance. Similarly, one who learns of an advantage to be derived from the operation, in a known manner, of an existing machine or of an existing process would not be entitled to a patent either upon the structure of that machine or upon the manner of operating the same.[1]

The foregoing result is derived from and, indeed, is necessitated by the simultaneous application of two fundamental principles, which are that: (1) once subject matter enters the public domain, it remains there forever after;[2] and (2) patentable subject matter must distinguish over that already in the public domain by more than a mere advantage, that is, there must be a physical difference between what already is in the public domain and what is sought to be patented. The reader will observe that the second principle is closely related to the principle that mere ideas are not patentable, in that the recognition of a naked advantage amounts to no more than a mental result—an idea—having as its physical object that which already lies in the public domain. Moreover, the second principle is, in effect, a corollary of the first, in that all advantages are *inherent* in and are incidents of the physical embodiment. It is axiomatic that one who performs the steps of a process must, in so doing, necessarily produce all its advantages, for these naturally flow from it and, indeed, are an inseparable part of it. To grant a patent for the mere recognition of even a previously wholly unknown advantage would involve the removal of the physical means needed to produce that advantage from the public domain.

§ 2. The Doctrine of Inherency

To illustrate how the application of the doctrine of inherency may preclude one who has made a valuable discovery from obtaining patent protection for his contribution, consider the following hypothetical situation: *X* observes that trace amounts of certain rare-earth metal oxides significantly enhance the life of the silica-brick lining of electric arc furnaces when such oxides are incorporated into the silica brick. However, such quantities of these oxides as are effective are inherently present as impurities in the silica brick used to line some prior art arc furnaces, although no one before *X* realized that the presence of these oxides has the effect of prolonging the life of a silica-brick lining. *X* may not patent a silica-brick lining containing rare-earth metal oxides, because such is in fact anticipated by those prior art arc furnaces which happen to contain the same. Of course, if the concentration of the rare-earth metal oxides in the linings of prior art arc furnaces differs from that found efficacious by *X*, then the structure of *X's* furnace lining would not be anticipated by the prior art and *X* could obtain a patent covering such structure. It should be noted here that relatively slight or minor physical modifications of prior art structures have, on occasion, produced wholly new and unexpected results.[3]

Now suppose that *Y* discovers that the same rare-earth metal oxides, when present in the silica-brick lining of a plasma arc furnace, tend to stabilize the plasma arc. Assume that the prior art does not explicitly disclose the combination of a plasma-arc furnace lined with silica brick, but that the prior art does teach the use of such materials to line the interior walls of conventional arc furnaces and that these rare-earth metal oxides have no effect on the stability of the conventional electric arc. Technically, *Y's* combination of a plasma arc in a chamber lined with silica brick which contains rare-earth metal oxides is not anticipated by the aforementioned prior art. Moreover, that prior art does not teach that this combination would have the advantage discovered by *Y*. Nevertheless, one of ordinary skill in the art of constructing arc furnaces who wanted to build a plasma arc furnace, and who looked to the prior art for guidance, would very likely select a lining composed of silica brick (in which there would inherently be present amounts of rare-earth metal oxides effective for stabilizing the plasma arc)—albeit for reasons different from that taught by *Y*. It is an open question whether under such circumstances *Y's* combination of structure would or should be patentable.

The doctrine of inherency frequently comes into play where a mathematical equation or quantitative relationship is claimed. For example: Suppose that *Z* discovers that in the electro-thermic reduction of pyritic copper ores, electric power will most efficiently be expended when there is present a 25 percent by weight excess ore to carbonaceous material. Now assume that the prior art discloses a process for smelting copper ores, which happens to employ 25 percent by weight excess copper pyrites to carbonaceous material. Although that prior art disclosure does not teach that the called for proportions will make the most efficient use of electric power, it would anticipate *Z*'s claims, in that it does call for a 25 percent weight excess ore to carbonaceous material.

The unpatentability of physical laws and their quantitative formulations may be predicated upon the doctrine of inherency. The relations underlying every physical law existed from time immemorial and they are inherently present in and accompany every application and illustration thereof. It is, indeed, safe to say that there has not been an invention made yet that either does not obey some law of nature or violates any law of nature. Patent law, however, is concerned neither with speculations nor theoretical explanations, but rather only with the concrete means or steps by which physical results are obtained. Accordingly, it is ordinarily not incumbent upon an applicant for a patent to advance a theory as to why his invention works. Rather, he need only articulate how it works, that is, how another may reproduce the result he obtained. A theoretical explanation of the mechanism by which a physical result is achieved may, however, in some contexts, help distinguish the instant contribution from the prior art. A physical difference must, nevertheless, be present.

To avoid anticipation and satisfy the novelty requirement, it has been generally held that the degree of physical difference which must exist between that which is sought to be patented and the prior art need be only slight. So long as the physical structure of the invention sought to be patented is not "identically disclosed,"[4] novelty very likely is present. By this standard, even mere colorable or trivial variations of prior art structures would literally possess novelty. It must be noted, however, that such variations, without more, would be unpatentable, as failing to satisfy the unobviousness standard.

§ 3. Novelty and Anticipation

Since physical identity is the test of novelty and anticipation, it should follow that the mere existence, anywhere in the prior art, of physical structure identical in description to that claimed would constitute an anticipation. Indeed, with respect to applications pending before the Patent Office, the courts have sanctioned the application of the broadest interpretation which the claims may reasonably support.[5] Accordingly, a broadly worded claim directed to a picture frame might be deemed anticipated by a water closet seat. Claims of issued patents tend to be treated less harshly, the courts going behind their literal wording and considering the inventive thought that underlies and which motivated the claims.[6] Thus, a court may discount as an anticipation, structure from an art totally unrelated to that to which the invention under consideration is directed, even though such happens to read literally upon one or more of the claims. Similarly, an incidental anticipation which is temporary and transitory may be deemed not to negate novelty.[7]

Determinations of anticipation and novelty are made in light of the prior art. Speaking in general terms, prior art is that fund of information which is available or accessible to the public.

The law conclusively presumes that all are familiar with the entire body of prior art. Even though one may have made an original invention, in that he thought it up by himself, independently and in ignorance of the prior art, if that invention is in fact taught by the prior art, it has been anticipated. That an inventor was unaware of the state of the prior art is immaterial.[8] To be entitled to patent protection, one must not only be the inventor, but the first inventor. The courts, however, have carved out a very narrow exception to this rule where knowledge of how to make and use an invention, though at one time definitely known, has become lost. Such lost art will not constitute an anticipation.[9]

To determine precisely what the law regards as being prior in prior art, one must return to the requirements imposed by Section 102.

Section 102(a) says that an applicant is not entitled to a patent if *at any time* prior to the point at which that applicant made his invention, it was "known or used *by others* in this country, or patented or described in a printed publication in this or a foreign country." (Emphasis added.) The distinction drawn between the source of the prior art, that is, between the manner by which the invention is manifested, should be noted. A dichotomy exists between information which, on one hand, was merely "known or used by others" (personal knowledge) and, on the other hand, information which "was patented or described in a printed publication" (written knowledge). Mere knowledge or use of an invention abroad prior to the point in time at which the applicant made his invention is insufficient to defeat his right to a United States patent. There are at least two sound reasons for disregarding, as an anticipation, that which was merely known or used outside of the United States: (1) such information is not sufficiently accessible to United States industry; (2) proving its very existence would be difficult. By contrast, there will exist some permanent record of that which has been patented or described in a printed publication, and this is so whether the patenting or publication occurred in this or a foreign country.

Because relative to the entire world, even an invention which had been known or used by others only abroad would lack novelty, the United States is said to require only relative novelty. This is in contrast to the absolute or worldwide novelty standard which is mandated by the laws of some countries.

§ 4. Patents and Printed Publications

One may be wondering why the statute bothers to mention separately patents and printed publications. After all is not the distinction immaterial? The specifications of all United States patents are, speaking literally, printed publications. The printing of patent specifications, however, is not a universal practice. In some countries, the contents of patent specifications are merely made available for public inspection, their governments not undertaking to multiply copies of them.

There is quite a bit of uncertainty as to just what constitutes a printed publication within the meaning of Section 102. Before discussing the various judicial interpretations of printed publication, some of the different contexts in which "publication" is used should be mentioned. In the law of defamation, publication signifies communication to a third person. While just what constitutes publication in the context of copyright law depends upon the nature of the work. As a general rule, a work is deemed published when it has been reduced to tangible and permanent form and copies in such form have been offered for sale. Thus, "publication" carries with it the notion that the subject matter in question is available or accessible to the public.

The commonly accepted meaning of the word "printed" should be equally as clear, namely, that copies of the subject matter have been multiplied in ink from set type. However, some tribunals have gone far beyond the denotation of printed, having generalized the phrase "printed publication" so as to include within its purview a microfilm or a photocopy of a typewritten manuscript,[10] or even the original typewritten manuscript itself.[11] As the law now stands, whether or not the information has been reproduced by means other than a conventional printing press is immaterial. However the information was reduced to tangible and permanent form, if that information has been reproduced or duplicated and has been disseminated or otherwise made available to the extent that persons interested and ordinarily skilled in the subject matter or art, exercising reasonable diligence, can locate it and recognize and comprehend therefrom the essentials of the claimed invention without need of further research or experimentation, it might be said that that information exists in a printed publication as that term was contemplated by Congress in Section 102.[12]

The knowledge contemplated by Section 102(a) must be accessible to the public.[13]

Perhaps the most perplexing problem posed by the language of Section 102 is the effect of a prior secret use. To illustrate, consider the following situation:

A makes an invention, about which he tells his wife, *W*. She convinces him to forget about it. *B*, working independently and without knowledge of what *A* has accomplished, makes the very same invention some time later.

(1) But for the fact that another, namely *B*, entered the field, *A* would not be barred from obtaining a patent at some indefinite time in the future.[14]

(2) *A's* invention does not constitute an anticipation of *B's* invention. Although *B's* invention was literally known by others, namely *A* and *W*, Section 102(a) has been construed as requiring *public* knowledge or use.[15]

(3) *B* is entitled, not only to make and use his invention, but to a patent therefor and, thus, to exclude *A* from practicing it.[16] A subsequent inventor who has diligently pursued his labors to the procurement of a patent in good faith and without any knowledge of the preceding discoveries of another, shall, as against that other, who has deliberately concealed the knowledge of his invention from the public, be regarded as the real inventor and as such is entitled to a patent.[17]

If *A* had not "forgotten" about or otherwise concealed or suppressed his invention, but had instead diligently continued to perfect it, albeit in secret, *A* would be deemed the first inventor. See Chapter 9.

§ 5. Secret Use

To illustrate how intricate and interwoven are the provisos comprising Section 102, consider the following situations:

Suppose further that *A* had invented a process and had decided (1) to carry out the practice of that process in secret; and (2) to sell the product so produced. Even though, from an examination of the product, it would not be possible to discern the process by which it was made, the sale of the product for more than one year would bar anyone, including *B*, from patenting either the product or the process.[18] Accordingly, if *A* had sold the product for a period of more than one year before *B* filed an application for a patent, *B's* patent would be invalid, as barred by Section 102(b).

A would not, under any of the circumstances set forth above, be entitled to a patent for his invention, as his conduct amounted to a suppression and concealment, and thus, in contemplation of law, to an abandonment of his invention and of a right to a patent therefor.[19] Section 102(c) says that an applicant is not entitled to a patent if he has abandoned his invention.

Now consider the following situation: *X* applies for a patent, but the Examiner rejects all the claims as unpatentable over the cited prior art. *X* abandons his application. *Y* makes the very same invention independently of and subsequently to *X*. Some time after *X* abandons his application, *Y* files an application disclosing and claiming the very same invention. *Y's* application is allowed and he receives a patent. What are the rights of *X* and *Y*? Mere abandonment of a patent application disclosing and claiming an invention does not constitute an abandonment of the underlying invention.[20] Communication of an invention to the Patent Office in the form of a filed patent application does not constitute public knowledge.[21] Accordingly, *X* could still assert his right to a patent as the prior inventor.

The activities recited in Section 102(b) (public use, sale, patenting, etc.), unlike those enumerated in Section 102(a) (knowledge, use, patenting, etc.) will bar a patent regardless of who commits them. The activities recited in Section 102(a), as negating novelty, clearly do not apply to the applicant himself, as this proviso states that they must have been committed by "*others* . . . *before* the invention by the applicant for patent . . . ." Section 102(b) draws no such distinction: patenting is barred if *anyone* (including the applicant himself) has engaged in any of the proscribed activities for a period of more than one year prior to the day on which the applicant files a patent application. The pivotal event in Section 102(b) is the applicant's filing date; the pivotal event in Section 102(a) is the date of applicant's invention. For both Sections 102(a) and 102(b), the enumerated activities only militate against novelty for the applicable period prior to the occurrence of the pivotal event. The occurrence of the pivotal event (the act of invention by the applicant, for Section 102(a); and the act of filing by the applicant, for Section 102(b)) tolls the statute in the sense that what activities transpire after the occurrence of the pivotal event is immaterial–none can thereafter negate novelty. It must be borne in mind, too, that once an invention becomes publicly known, it is impossible to restore it to secrecy–the act of disclosure is irreversible. Accordingly, though the public use last for but a few days, if it occurred more than one year prior to filing, the invention would lack novelty.

§ 6. Public Use

In Section 102(a) the period is *any time* before the invention by the applicant. This is merely a more formal way of saying that the applicant must be the first inventor, that none preceded him. In Section 102(b) the period is the one year prior to the date application for patent is made. This length of time is a grace period which allows the inventor to file an application for patent up to a year after he has made public his invention. During the grace period the inventor may engage in any activity without prejudicing his right to a patent. It should be noted that in some countries a grace period exists only for certain specified activities, as, for example, disclosure to a learned society or at an exhibition of a scientific nature. United States law imposes no such narrow limitations or restrictions during the one year grace period. The patent act which preceded the one presently in force provided for a grace period of two years.

The language "patented or described in a printed publication in this or a foreign country . . . " appears in both Sections 102(a) and 102(b). However, in Section 102(b) "in public use or on sale in this country . . ." replaces the "known or used . . . in this country . . ." phrase of Section 102(a). It has already been noted that, by judicial construction, the knowledge or use alluded to in Section 102(a) must be public knowledge or use. The judiciary has also placed a gloss on the phrase "in public use or on sale." It has drawn a distinction between a "public use" and an "experimental use." The latter does not come within the proscription of Section 102(b). Some writers speak of experimental use as an exception to Section 102(b).[22]

§ 7. Experimental Use

A use is experimental if its *motive* is truly the testing and/or perfection of the invention. The law recognizes that the inventor may wish to perfect his idea before applying for a patent. After reduction to practice has occurred, however, unreasonable delay in applying for a patent may be construed to be an abandonment with the consequence that the public is entitled to rights in the invention.[23] Whether a use will be held to be experimental or public, is affected by two factors: (1) the intent of the inventor, that is, whether his use was motivated by a desire to experiment or by a desire to profit from his invention; and (2) whether and at what point in time the invention was actually reduced to practice.

The law assigns no fixed, arbitrary period of time after which a use can no longer be experimental. The one year period mentioned in Section 102(b) only commences running when the use has ceased being experimental and becomes a public use. It has been held that a use for as long as six years was experimental and not public use.[24] The dominant motive will control. Thus, a sale which is primarily for the purpose of experiment will not bar patentability.[25] On the other hand, a public use was found where the inventor of a corset stay gave one to a lady friend who wore the same hidden from public view.[26] Thus, the fact that there has been but a single user, or that the invention is given without profit or that it is hidden from the general public's eye would seem not to be determinative of the issue of whether a use has been public or experimental.[27]

Although the absence of profit does not conclusively negate a public use, it is an important consideration.[28] Public use is not synonymous with commercial use.

To constitute a public use, the user need not even realize that he is using the invention. It is immaterial that the use was without the inventor's consent or that the use was due to factors not his fault and beyond his control,[29] unless the invention was gained surreptitiously from the inventor.[30] It may be fair to conclude that public use exists where the invention is used by, or exposed to, anybody other than the inventor or persons under an obligation of secrecy to the inventor.[31]

Experimental use is not to be equated with secret use. Testing, checking, experimentation, and/or evaluation of an invention may be carried out in a manner open to public view. While the invention is in its experimental stage, the public may be incidentally deriving benefits therefrom.[32] However, the parting by the inventor of control over embodiments of his invention, whether by sale or gift, may be taken as evidence of the fact that the experimental period has ended.[33]

A completed sale is not required to come within the "on sale" proviso of Section 102(b). An offer to sell, or possibly even an invitation to make an offer, as through a newspaper advertisement, may suffice.[34]

Comparison of Section 102(a) & (b)

Activity	*Where Engaged In*	*By Whom*	*For How Long*	*Pivotal Event*
Section 102(a)				
known or used	in this country	others	any time	before invention by applicant
patented or described in a printed publication	in this or a foreign country	others	any time	before invention by applicant
Section 102(b)				
in public use or on sale	in this country	anyone	for more than one year	prior to the date of the application for patent in the U.S.
patented or described in a printed publication	in this or a foreign	anyone	for more than one year	prior to the date of the appli application for patent in the U.S.

§ 8. Doctrine of Late Claiming

A consequence implicit in, but not immediately apparent from a casual reading of, Section 102(b) is the so-called doctrine of late claiming. The following situation should bring this doctrine into focus: An inventor files a patent application disclosing and claiming an invention. After this filing, he puts into public use an invention embodying features which correspond to a hitherto unemphasized and unclaimed aspect of his disclosure. After more than one year of public use of the modified invention, he submits to the Patent Office claims reading on the modified invention. It has been held that where the amended or late claims are not fully supported by the disclosure as originally submitted to the Patent Office, the filing date does not insulate the applicant from public use of originally unclaimed features which occurred after that filing date.[35] It makes no difference whether it is the applicant or others who are responsible for the intervening public use. The doctrine of late claiming is, in effect, but a particular application of the rule that no new matter may be introduced.[36] Claims, whenever submitted, must be fully supported by the disclosure as this was originally filed. The doctrine of late claiming has no application where the late claims, though materially different from those originally submitted, are fully supported by the specification as originally filed. In fact, a court did not invoke the doctrine even where there was an amendment of the specification which went "no further than to make express what would have been regarded as an equivalent of the original; or to incorporate into one claim what was to be gathered from the perusal of all if read together."[37]

§ 9. Abandonment

Section 102(c) declares that a person is not entitled to a patent if he has abandoned his invention. No indication, however, is given in the statute of the nature of the acts which would constitute an abandonment of an invention. Before delving into what conduct the courts consider as constituting abandonment, it must be emphasized that there is a distinction between abandoning a patent application and abandoning the underlying invention disclosed in a patent application. By merely abandoning a patent application, the applicant does not abandon any invention disclosed therein. Consequently, he may file another patent application which discloses and claims the very same invention that was disclosed and claimed in an earlier filed, abandoned patent application. A patent application may be abandoned either by: (1) an express and formal declaration;[38] or (2) failure to take the required action upon the patent application within the applicable period set by law.[39] A patent application for which all rights of appeal have been exhausted, so that no further action by the applicant is possible, is also treated as an abandoned application. Section 102(c) relates not to the abandonment of patent applications, but rather to the abandonment of inventions!

A patent application will be regarded as abandoned if the issue (or final) fee is not timely paid.[40] An application abandoned by reason of failure to pay the issue fee was formerly referred to as a forfeited application.[41]

The abandonment of a patent application must be distinguished from the dedication of an issued patent or the disclaimer of one or more of its claims[42] and from the cancellation or amendment of the claims in an application pending before the Patent Office. The word "abandoned" is specifically applied by the Patent Act to inventions per se and to patent applications before they have matured into patents. Dedication to the public is, in effect, the abandonment of an issued patent. Dedication can be effected only in accordance with formalities spelled out in the Patent Act. A patentee may dedicate to the public the entire term of his patent or only a portion of it. The Patent Act also provides for what is, in essence, the formal abandonment of one or more claims of an issued patent. An abandonment of such is referred to as a disclaimer.

It should be noted that the Patent Act, in effect, draws a dichotomy on the subject of abandonment between rights in issued patents, on one hand, and rights in naked inventions or pending patent applications, on the other. Rights in issued patents may be relinquished or waived only expressly, that is, by some specified, formal act. Abandonment of rights in naked inventions or pending patent applications may be implied from conduct, even from failure to take certain action.

Another instance of loss of rights in pending applications occurs when an inventor amends his claims to overcome a rejection based on prior art made by the Patent Office. Where the allowed, amended claims are narrower than the rejected, earlier submitted claims, the patentee will be estopped to reassert in any subsequent infringement litigation any of the ground given up—in effect abandoned—in the Patent Office. This is the doctrine of file wrapper estoppel, which will be developed in detail in Chapter 15.

Before returning to the subject of abandoned inventions, a few words about unclaimed subject matter in issued patents seems to be in order. In drawing up his patent specification, the inventor may disclose more than he claims. Since the claims define the patent property, what is unclaimed will be deemed dedicated to the public, unless *timely* corrective action is taken. Mere failure to claim an invention in an issued patent does not of itself work an irretrievable abandonment or dedication to the public. There are three possible procedures by which such initially unclaimed subject matter may be recaptured by the patentee: (1) filing a reissue application; (2) filing a continuing patent application; (3) filing an independent application within the one year grace period, following issuance of the patent disclosing but not claiming the invention, before it becomes a statutory bar under Section 102(b).[43] The subjects of reissues and of continuing applications will be dealt with at length in Chapter 13. It should be noted here, however, that a reissue which contains broadened claims must be filed within two years from the date the original patent issues.[44]

Although the preceding discussion has taken us somewhat afield—from abandoned applications to abandoned patents—it should have brought out a rule of thumb: as the inchoate right of an inventor to a patent comes closer and closer to fruition, the conduct needed to work an abandonment of his rights becomes more and more explicit. Accordingly, before a patent application has been filed, the conduct that may be deemed by the law to constitute an abandonment of one's invention may be quite contrary to the inventor's intention. An inventor who designedly conceals his invention with a view of applying it indefinitely to his own profit, while obviously not intending to abandon such invention, has been deemed to have done so, where another has in the interim made the same invention and applied for a patent.[45] After reduction to practice, unreasonable delay in applying for a patent may be construed as an abandonment with the consequence that the public is entitled to rights in the invention.[46]

Section 102(d) precludes from patent protection in the United States an invention that was the subject of an earlier, foreign filed patent application, which foreign filing (1) occurred more than twelve months prior to the United States filing date, and (2) matured into a patent before an application therefor was filed in the United States. As will be discussed at length in Chapter 16, an invention which was the subject of a foreign filing that occurred *within* twelve months of the United States filing date is entitled to the benefit of the foreign filing date. If, however, the filing in the United States occurs *more than* twelve months after the earliest foreign filing date, the invention is not entitled to such favored treatment. In fact, the fate of such a late United States filing is dependent upon what has happened to any earlier filed foreign applications. If any foreign filed application issues as a patent at anytime before the date of actual filing in the United States, no United States patent may validly issue on that invention.

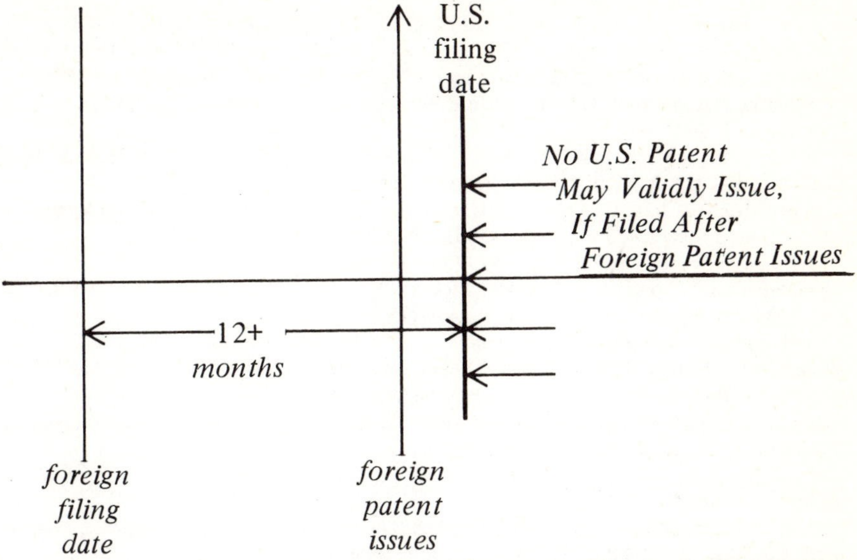

Section 102(e) is a codification of a Supreme Court case[47] which held that a United States patent is effective as a reference against a subsequently filed United States patent application of another as of its filing date, and not as of the date that it issued as a patent. Thus, the date as of which the specifications of United States patents become prior art relates back to their filing dates—a date on which their disclosures were not actually available to the public.

As will be discussed more fully in Chapter 16, the date as of which the specification of a United States patent becomes prior art is that on which application was *actually* made in the United States. It does not extend back to earlier foreign filings, even though the patent-reference may enjoy the benefit of an earlier foreign filing date.

Notes

[1] *In re* Huellmantel, 324 F.2d 998, 1000, 139 U.S.P.Q. 496, 498 (C.C.P.A. 1963).

[2] Scott Paper Co. v. Marcalus Mfg. Co., 326 U.S. 249, 256, 67 U.S.P.Q. 193, 196-197 (1945); Smith v. Dravo Corp., 203 F.2d 369, 373, 97 U.S.P.Q. 98, 101 (7th Cir. 1953).

[3] Traitel Marble Co. v. V.T. Hungerford Brass & Co., 18 F.2d 66 (2d Cir. 1927).

[4] See 35 U.S.C. 103.

[5] *In re* Tibbals, 316 F.2d 955, 958, 137 U.S.P.Q. 565, 567 (C.C.P.A. 1963); Ex parte Lawrence, 131 U.S.P.Q. 40, 41 (P.O. Bd. App. 1960).

[6] See Rubber Co. v. Goodyear, 76 U.S. (9 Wall.) 788, 795 (1869); Dominion Magnesium Ltd. v. United States, 320 F.2d 388, 138 U.S.P.Q. 306, 310 (Ct. Cl. 1963).

[7] Ex parte Smythe, 139 U.S.P.Q. 529 (P.O. Bd. App. 1963).

[8] Mast-Foos v. Stover, 177 U.S. 485, 494 (1900).

[9] Gaylor v. Wilder, 51 U.S. (10 How.) 477 (1850).

[10] Hamilton Laboratories, Inc. v. Massengill, lll F.2d 584, 45 U.S.P.Q. 594 (6th Cir.), cert. denied 311 U.S. 688 (1940); Ex parte Hershberger, 96 U.S.P.Q. 54 (P.O. Bd. App. 1952); Gulliksen v. Halberg, 75 U.S.P.Q. 252 (P.O. Bd. App. 1937).

[11] Ex Parte Garbo, 148 U.S.P.Q. 913 (P.O. Bd.App. 1964). Compare, *In re* Tenney, 254 F.2d 619, 117 U.S.P.Q. 348 (C.C.P.A. 1958).

[12] I.C.E. Corp. v. Armco Steel Corp., 250 F. Supp. 738, 743, 148 U.S.P.Q. 537, 540 (S.D.N.Y. 1966).

[13] *In re* Borst, 345 F.2d 851, 854, 145 U.S.P.Q. 554, 556 (C.C.P.A. 1965). Compare, Ex parte Kuzmitz, 113 U.S.P.Q. 255 (P.O. Bd. App. 1956).

[14] See Kirham v. Arden, 316 F.2d 242, 247, 137 U.S.P.Q. 370, 374 (C.C.P.A. 1963).

[15] *In re* Borst, N. 13, *supra.* See also, Bates v. Coe, 98 U.S. (8 Otto) 31, 46 (1878).

[16] Kendall v. Windsor, 62 U.S. (21 How.) 322, 327-328 (1858).

[17] Mason v. Hepburn, 13 App. D.C. 86 (1898).

[18] N. 12 *supra.*

[19] N. 16 *supra.*

[20] Electric Storage Battery Co. v. Shimadzu, 307 U.S. 5, 20, 41 U.S.P.Q. 155, 161 (1939); Brush v. Condit, 132 U.S. 39, 48-49 (1889).

[21] Brown v. Guild (Corn Planter Case), 90 U.S. (23 Wall.) 91 (1874).

[22] *In re* Blaisdell, 242 F.2d 779, 113 U.S.P.Q. 289 (C.C.P.A. 1957).

[23] Watson v. Allen, 254 F.2d 342, 117 U.S.P.Q. 68 (D.C.C. 1958).

[24] Elizabeth v. American Nicholson Pavement Co., 97 U.S. (7 Otto) 126 (1877).

[25] N. 23 *supra.*

[26] Egbert v. Lippmann, 104 U.S. (14 Otto) 333 (1881).

[27] Sperry Rand Corp. v. Bell Telephone Laboratories, 208 F. Supp. 598, 135 U.S.P.Q. 254 (S.D.N.Y. 1962).

[28] *Ibid.*

[29] Andrews v. Hovey, 123 U.S. 267 (1887).

[30] Shaw v. Cooper, 32 U.S. (7 Pet.) 292 (1833).

[31] National Tube Co. v. Steel Tubes, Inc., 90 F.2d 52, 33 U.S.P.Q. 406 (3d Cir. 1937).

[32] N. 22 *supra.*

[33] *Ibid.*

[34] Monroe Auto-Equipment Co. v. Heckethorn Mfg. & Supply Co., 332 F.2d 406, 141 U.S.P.Q. 549 (6th Cir. 1964).

[35] Muncie Gear Works, Inc. v. Outboard Marine & Mfg. Co., 315 U.S. 759, 53 U.S.P.Q. 1 (1942).

[36] 35 U.S.C. 132.

[37] Engineering Dev. Laboratories v. Radio Corp. of Am., 153 F.2d 523, 526, 68 U.S.P.Q. 238, 242 (2d Cir. 1946).

[38] Rule 138.
[39] 35 U.S.C. 133.
[40] Rule 316.
[41] M.P.E.P. 712.
[42] 35 U.S.C. 253.
[43] *In re* Gibbs, 437 F.2d 486, 168 U.S.P.Q. 578 (C.C.P.A. 1971).
[44] 35 U.S.C. 251.
[45] N. 17 *supra*.
[46] N. 23 *supra*.
[47] Alexander Milburn Co. v. Davis-Bournonville Co., 270 U.S. 390 (1926).

Chapter 7

UTILITY

> But a patent is not a hunting license. It is not a reward for the search, but compensation for its successful conclusion. "[A] patent system must be related to the world of commerce rather than to the realm of philosophy . . . ."
>
> A. Fortas, J.
> *Brenner v. Manson,*
> 383 U.S. 519, 536,
> 148 U.S.P.Q. 689, 696 (1966)

If novelty is the sine qua non of invention, then utility is its raison d'etre. Indeed, the Constitution speaks specifically not of novelty or invention, but rather of the *useful* arts, inventors, and their discoveries.

However, as will be presently demonstrated, the words "useful" and "utility" encompass a spectrum of concepts. And while, from the very first patent act, protection has been promised in regard to useful inventions, no statute has gone much beyond this word in defining the nature of the showing required. In fact, practically the only mention made of utility has been at the outset of each act, and there in general language, which essentially paraphrases the Constitutional provision.

In the present act, the word "useful" appears in Section 101:

> Whoever invents or discovers any new and *useful* process, machine, manufacture, or composition of matter, or any new and *useful* improvement thereof, may obtain a patent therefor, subject to the conditions and requirements of this title. [Emphasis added.]

The first paragraph of Section 112 further states:

> The specification shall contain a written description of the invention, and of the manner and process of making and *using* it, in such full, clear, concise, and exact terms as to enable any person skilled in the art to which it pertains, or with which it is most nearly connected, to make and *use* the same . . . . [Emphasis added.]

The foregoing two provisos are the only ones of the present act which make mention of utility. Nevertheless, courts have almost uniformly regarded an exhibition of utility—along with novelty and unobviousness (or invention)—to be the affirmative requisites of every valid patent. It is submitted, however, that the inclusion of the word "useful" in the patent statute is a direct carry over from the broad brush language employed by the framers of the Constitution, who associated usefulness with inventions more as a conviction than as a condition.

Thus, in a celebrated opinion, Justice Story couched the utility requirement in the form of a negative rule:[1]

> By useful invention, in the statute, is meant such a one as may be applied to some beneficial use in society, in contradistinction to an invention, which is injurious to the morals, the health, or the good order of society. It is not necessary to establish, that the invention is of such general utility, as to supercede all other inventions now in practice to accomplish the same purpose. It is sufficient, that it has no obnoxious or mischievous tendency, that it may be applied to practical uses, and that so far as it is applied, it is salutory. If its practical utility be very limited, it will follow that it will be of little profit to the inventor; and if it be trifling, it will sink into utter neglect. The law, however, does not look to the degree of utility; it simply requires, that it shall be capable of use, and that the use is such as sound morals and policy do not discountenance or prohibit.

Justice Story's discourse touches upon the shades of meaning implicit in the word "useful." At one extreme, useful means merely operative, that the invention is capable of some beneficial use. This is essentially the standard which Justice Story felt the statute imposed. It is the standard which has been consistently applied by the overwhelming majority of American courts.

To satisfy this standard, an inventor need not establish that his invention is better than, or that it is even as good as, existing means for accomplishing the same result. The degree of utility is immaterial, for the law does not ask *how* useful is the invention. An inventor need not carry his invention to the highest degree of perfection to be entitled to a patent therefor.[2] That is the role of improvement patents. The law, moreover, does not consider, as being material to the question of utility, the economic or commercial value of an invention. That is left to the marketplace.

Also held to have been wanting in utility were inventions that are injurious, or dangerous, or immoral.[3]

That the utility requirement has not been quantified is due, in large measure, to the practical impossibility of formulating a basis of comparison, a common denominator, that would reliably reflect the worth of each contribution. Should the standard by which utility is to be measured be in absolute terms or be tied to economics? A new approach may be faster (and in this sense be more useful than that known to the prior art) and yet be more hazardous and/or more expensive (thus, in a sense, being less useful than that known to the prior art). Moreover, what purpose or use should be selected as the criterion? Closely related structures may have different, multiple, or overlapping utilities. Where the contribution is closely related structurally to that known to the prior art invention may, indeed, reside in a utility wholly different from that possessed by cognate prior art structures.[4] And, of course, unobviousness may reside in the fact that a new structure is far more efficacious for the same purpose than its similarity with a prior art structure would suggest.

An inventor is free to choose any field which may suit his fancy. The only uses which the law proscribes are those which are immoral and/or illegal. Toys have long been a favorite and fruitful field for inventors.

The utility of most mechanical inventions is apparent from an examination of their structures. Consequently, their utility (or, more precisely, their operativeness) is presumed,[6] the exception, an obvious one, being perpetual motion machines. Nevertheless, it is customary to recite in patent specifications a number of objects which the invention can accomplish or advantages which it possesses.

It has been held that the inability of claimed structure to accomplish one or more of the disclosed objects set out in the specification does not vitiate the patent, so long as what is claimed is capable of accomplishing at least one of the recited objects.[7]

A patent will, of course, cover whatever structures read on its claims, including necessarily advantages neither apparent not appreciated nor disclosed by the inventor.[8]

The utility requirement with respect to inventions relating to compositions of matter and to processes of making the same is not quite so liberal. Some practical utility for the product of a chemical process must either be apparent to one skilled in the art or be disclosed in the specification for a patent application with claims directed to such process to satisfy the utility requirement.[9] This rule applies a fortiorari to product claims.[10] By "practical utility" is meant a specific, chemical utility. Mere usefulness in further chemical research will not suffice to satisfy the utility requirement. The Supreme Court held as failing to satisfy the utility requirement a patent application directed to a process of making a chemical compound for which there was no known specific utility. A chemical process must produce a useful product. The utility must be related to the composition's specific chemical structure; for all matter is useful, if only to the extent that it occupies space and possesses inertia. Moreover, the utility must be practical. This is in contradistinction to "usefulness" in the sense of being only an object of scientific research, and this is true whether that research be directed to (1) the production of other compositions which do possess demonstrated practical utilities; or (2) the finding of a practical utility for the composition which is claimed or is produced by the claimed process.

Not only must the requisite utility exist, but this must either be disclosed in the specification or be predictable. The Supreme Court found as insufficient the fact that another compound of the same class to which that under consideration belonged was known to possess tumor inhibiting properties.[11] Where an allegation of a specific utility is not mentioned in the specification and such is unknown to the prior art, the Patent Office may refuse to consider evidence thereof, on the ground that it would constitute new matter.[12]

Where, however, an allegation of a specific utility has been made in the specification, an applicant may submit evidence to prove such statements. In fact, where extravagent or incredible allegations of utility have been made in the specification, as that the invention is effective in treating baldness or cancer, the applicant may be required to submit proof thereof.[13]

It is interesting to note that while product claims are distinct from those directed to the use or method of using the product, a use for the product is an indispensible part of a product patent.

By virtue of the Federal Food, Drug and Cosmetic Act, the Federal Food and Drug Administration requires that it be demonstrated to its satisfaction that all new drugs, before the same can be marketed, are safe and effective for their intended uses.[14] The United States Court of Customs and Patent Appeals has rejected attempts by the

Patent Office to equate the utility requirement of the Patent Act with safety and effectiveness.[15] Accordingly, it is possible to patent a drug and yet be unable to market the same as such, for failing to meet the standards of the Federal Food and Drug Administration.

Notes

[1] Bedford v. Hunt, 3 Fed. Cas. 37 (No. 1217) (C.C.D. Mass. 1817). See also, Lowell v. Lewis, 15 Fed. Cas. 1018 (No. 8568) (C.C.D. Mass. 1817).

[2] The Telephone Cases, 126 U.S. 1 (1888). See also, *In re* Chilowsky, 229 F.2d 457, 108 U.S.P.Q. 321 (C.C.P.A. 1956); Hobbs v. Wisconsin Power & Light Co., 250 F.2d 100, 115 U.S.P.Q. 371 (7th Cir. 1957).

[3] Klein v. Russell, 86 U.S. (19 Wall.) 433 (1873) (injurious); Mitchell v. Tilghman, 86 U.S. (19 Wall.) 287 (1873) (dangerous); National Automatic Device Co. v. Lloyd, 40 Fed. 89 (N.D. Ill. 1889) (illegal); Brewer v. Lithtenstein, 278 Fed. 512 (7th Cir. 1922) (immoral).

[4] United States v. Adams, 383 U.S. 39, 148 U.S.P.Q. 479 (1966).

[5] See Parke-Davis & Co. v. H.K. Mulford Co., 189 Fed. 95, *aff'd* 196 Fed. 496 (2d Cir. 1911).

[6] See M.P.E.P. 608.01(p).

[7] Decker v. F.T.C., 176 F.2d 461, 81 U.S.P.Q. 519 (D.C.C.), cert. denied 338 U.S. 878 (1949). See also, Bennett v. Halahan, 285 F.2d 807, 128 U.S.P.Q. 398 (C.C.P.A. 1961).

[8] See Hall v. Wright, 240 F.2d 787, 112 U.S.P.Q. 210 (9th Cir. 1957).

[9] Brenner v. Manson, 383 U.S. 519, 148 U.S.P.Q. 689 (1966).

[10] *In re* Bremner, 182 F.2d 216, 86 U.S.P.Q. 74 (C.C.P.A. 1963).

[11] Brenner v. Manson, 383 U.S. 519, 532, 148 U.S.P.Q. 689, 694 (1966).

[12] See *In re* Cavallito, 282 F.2d 357, 127 U.S.P.Q. 202 (C.C.P.A. 1960). See generally, *In re* Honnig, 92 U.S.P.Q. 135 (C.C.P.A. 1951).

[13] *In re* Buting, 418 F.2d 540, 163 U.S.P.Q. 689 (C.C.P.A. 1969) (cancer); *In re* Oberweger, 115 F.2d 826, 47 U.S.P.Q. 455 (C.C.P.A. 1940) (baldness).

[14] 21 U.S.C. 1 *et seq.*

[15] *In re* Anthony, 414 F.2d 1383, 162 U.S.P.Q. 594 (C.C.P.A. 1969).

Chapter 8

NONOBVIOUSNESS

SYNOPSIS

There are every where a number of people who, being totally destitute of any inventive faculty themselves, do not readily conceive that others may possess it. They think of inventions as miracles; there might be such formerly, but they are ceased. With these, every one who offers a new invention is deem'd a pretender; he had it from some other country or from some book. A man of their own acquaintance, one who has no more sense than themselves, could not possibly, in their opinion, have been the inventor of any thing. They are confirmed, too, in these sentiments, by frequent instances of pretensions to invention, which vanity is daily producing. That vanity too, though an incitment to invention, is, at the same time, the pest of inventors. Jealousy and Envy deny the merit or the novelty of your invention; but Vanity, when the novelty and merit are established, claims it for its own . . . . One would not, therefore, of all faculties or qualities of the mind, wish, for a friend, or a child, that he should have that of invention. For his attempts to benefit mankind in that way, however well imagined, if they do not succeed, expose him, though unjustly, to general ridicule and contempt; and if they do succeed, to envy, robbery, and abuse.

B. Franklin,
Papers, Vol. V, pp. 526-527

The rationale for nonobviousness as a requisite of patentability has been sketched, in broad outline, in Chapter 4. The formulation of determinations of obviousness with prior art references is presented in Chapter 13. This chapter will endeavor to weld the myriad of decisions based on the notions of invention and nonobviousness into a consistent and coherent body of law. This will be accomplished by applying in tandem the following doctrines:

(1) Prima facie obviousness–
the "Negative Rules of Invention"

(2) Rebuttal of prima facie obviousness–
(a) Direct Evidence
criticality, unexpected result, etc.
(b) Circumstantial Evidence
"subtests" of unobviousness

Invention, by its very nature, defies positive definition;[1] for if invention could be precisely defined, there would be no such thing as invention! This paradox, no doubt, has lent a certain aura, if not mystery, to the subject. The reality of invention and its contributions to the amelioration of our civilization, however, are everywhere evident.

Once an invention has been disclosed, little mystery about it remains. There has not been an invention yet made which defies a law of nature. Even second rate scientists can formulate accurate theoretical explanations, in terms of known and accepted physical laws, of why an invention works, once its efficacy has been demonstrated. There is a distinction between making and doing something, on one hand, and offering an explanation therefor, on the other. The trick to making an invention is to so combine existing structures and/or operations as to yield a new and different effect or result.

Although it is not possible to define, in positive terms, all of the elements sufficient to constitute an invention, it is possible to specify some that are necessary and indispensible therefor. Prominent among these are novelty and utility. The law, however, has segregated novelty and utility from whatever else of substance it deems necessary to constitute a patentable invention and has elevated this something else to the status and dignity of a discrete and independent condition of patentability, to which the confusing title "invention" had been applied. The rationale for the imposition of this tertian quid is that all that is novel and useful may not be worthy of patent protection. The difference between what is old and what is merely technically or literally new may be so slight and trivial as to be readily, and perhaps even spontaneously, deducible upon demand from what is old and already known.

While novelty and utility are requirements of patentability separate and apart from invention, these three qualities so overlap, and are so interrelated, as to be incapable of being entirely segregated from one another. Indeed, some have suggested equating invention with the degree or quantum of novelty required for patentability.[2] While *how different from the prior art that which is novel must be to be patentable* is definitely a factor in determining whether invention is present, the degree of difference is not to be measured by structure alone. Caution should be used in applying such a yardstick, for experience has taught that many of the very greatest advances differed structurally only very slightly from the prior art. Edison's incandescent lamp,[3] and Bell's telephone,[4] are but a few of the many, many illustrations of this phenomenon. Laws, be they of physical or judicial origin, are but generalizations drawn from empirical observations and intuitive notions. To be acceptable, they must conform to these realities. Accordingly, the doctrine of small structural or physical change evolved. It was best articulated by Justice Learned Hand in the following words:[5]

> Very slight structural changes may be enough to support a patent, when they presuppose a use not discoverable without inventive imagination. We are to judge such devices, not by the mere innovation in their former material, but by the purpose which dictated them and discovered their function.

A perhaps dramatic illustration of this doctrine is the case in which the Supreme Court found invention merely in a change in the angle of inclination of a prior art structure.[6] Invention may reside in discovering the source of a problem as well as in solving it.[7]

Expressed in more direct, albeit homelier, terms: *It is not the difference, but the difference the difference makes that counts.* This formulation suggests an interrelation between the elements of novelty ("the difference") and utility ("the difference the difference makes"). It indicates, moreover, that "the difference" is to be placed in the perspective of the prior art. While suggesting that "the difference" must be significant, the foregoing illustrations and abstractions drawn therefrom offer no concrete clues as to the way or ways in which "the difference" must be significant. This is the point at which invention eludes more precise analysis in positive terms.

§ 1. The Negative Rules of Invention

There gradually emerged from the myriad of court decisions grappling with the requirement of invention, a number of recurring situations in which the baffling quality of invention was rather consistently found to be wanting. If a contribution could be characterized as corresponding to any of these situations it was prima facie deemed to lack invention. Thus, invention came to be defined in negative terms, that is, in terms of what it was not. The set of judicial pronouncements on the subject was often referred to as the "negative rules of invention." A list of the more significant of these negative rules follows:

(1) The exercise of ordinary mechanical skill does not amount to invention.[8]

(2) Mere perfection of workmanship does not amount to invention.[9]

(3) That which is logically deducible from the teachings of the prior art does not amount to invention.[10]

(4) The mere carrying forward of an old idea does not amount to invention.[11]

(5) That which would have been obvious to persons skilled in the art to which the subject matter relates does not amount to invention.[12]

(6) The substitution of a known equivalent for one of the elements of an old structure does not amount to invention.[13]

(7) Mere enlargement or change in size, degree, or form does not amount to invention.[14]

(8) Unification or multiplication of parts does not amount to invention.[15]

(9) Omission of an element and its attendant function, unless the omission produces a new result, does not amount to invention.[16]

(10) The application of an old process or machine to an analo-

gous subject, with no change in the manner of application, and no new result, does not amount to invention.[17]

The negative rules of invention were never invoked uniformly or consistently by the courts. There was no statute mandating their application. One difficulty in applying them to concrete situations lay in casting a contribution in terms of such indicia as "a change in degree," "a new result," etc. What constitutes ordinary skill in a given art? What might be obvious to one person, might be unobvious to another. Moreover, from time to time the courts invoked even more elusive and abstruse criteria. For example, on occasion, the Supreme Court decried the granting of patents for mere "gadgets"[18] What is a gadget? There was a time when many people regarded the telephone and phonograph as gadgets; perhaps some still do!

§ 2. The Nonobviousness Standard of Section 103

In an attempt to foster the establishment of at least a modicum of certainty and consistency, the following provision was incorporated into the 1952 Patent Act:

> *Section 103. Conditions for patentability; non-obviousness subject matter*
>
> A patent may not be obtained though the invention is not identically disclosed or described as set forth in section 102 of this title, if the difference between the subject matter sought to be patented and the prior art are such that the subject matter as a whole would have been obvious at the time the invention was made to a person having ordinary skill in the art to which said subject matter pertains. Patentability shall not be negatived by the manner in which the invention was made.

The second sentence of Section 103 was written into the statute to repudiate language in a Supreme Court opinion which could be interpreted as saying that the mental state of the invention was significant in determining whether a contribution satisfied the invention requirement. What the opinion actually said was:[19]

> [T]he new device, however, useful it may be, must reveal the

> flash of creative genius, not merely the skill of the calling.

If indeed the Court's position was that the mental state of the inventor is material, it was clearly at odds with reality and with the prior law which recognized that:[20]

> Invention is not always the offspring of genius; for frequently it is the product of plain hard work; not infrequently it arises from accident or carelessness; occasionally it is a happy thought of an ordinary mind; and there have been instances where it is the result of sheer stupidity. It is with the inventive concept, the thing achieved, not with the manner of its achievement or the quality of the mind which gave it birth that the patent law concerns itself.

The second sentence of Section 103 has dispelled any doubt that may have existed: A "flash of creative genius" is not a requisite of patentability.[21]

Section 103 makes patentability depend upon, in addition to novelty and utility, the nonobvious nature of the "subject matter sought to be patented." The first sentence of this section requires that the scope and content of the prior art be ascertained; and the level of ordinary skill in the pertinent art be resolved. Against this background, the obviousness or nonobviousness of the subject matter is to be determined.[22]

It will be observed that the test set out in the first sentence of Section 103 is couched as a negative rule, which focuses upon the obviousness or nonobviousness of the subject matter sought to be patented. While the word nonobvious is somewhat more descriptive and definitive than the word "invention," it is still quite general and, as was noted by Judge Learned Hand:[23]

> The test laid down is indeed misty enough. It directs us to surmise what was the range of ingenuity of a person "having ordinary skill" in an "art" with which we are totally unfamiliar; and we do not see how such a standard can be applied at all except by recourse to the earlier work in the art, and to the general history of the means available at the time. To judge on our own that this or that new assemblage of old factors was or was not, "obvious" is to substitute our ignorance for the acquaintance with the subject of those who were familiar with it.

In fact, the unobviousness test is so broad as to encompass most of the other negative rules of invention. Thus, to change arbitrarily merely the size or dimensions of a known machine or article of manufacture, or the amount or relative propositions of the constituents of a composition of matter, or the values of the operative parameters of a process can fairly said to be obvious. The omission of a component of a machine, or an ingredient of a composition of matter, or a step of a process, with only the corresponding loss of the omitted component's ingredient's, or step's function can fairly said to be obvious.

The Supreme Court regards Section 103 "merely as a codification of precedents embracing the Hotchkiss condition, with congressional directions that inquiries into the obviousness of the subject matter sought to be patented are a prerequisite of patentability."[24] The reader will recall that "the Hotchkiss condition," alluded to by the Supreme Court, refers to *Hotchkiss v. Greenwood,*[25] the earliest reported case to require that a patentable invention possess something more than novelty and utility.

While under Section 103, the test of invention or unobviousness (as the third requisite of patentability is now called) is ultimately subjective, the measurements comprising this test are to be made by those familiar with the pertinent art and not by a judiciary untutored in science and technology.[26] Section 103 makes it incumbent upon the judiciary to seek out and consider, in all but the simplest cases,[27] evidence in support of unobviousness. The outcome of the inquiry is not to be based wholly upon a judge's a priori and subjective notions, as it so often was under the law prior to the enactment of Section 103. The judiciary, nevertheless, is still free to interpret the test data and to decide what score passes muster under Section 103. Questions of patentability and unobviousness are still questions of law, not of fact, to be decided by judges and not by juries.[28]

Under Section 103, the frame of reference is the person having ordinary skill in the pertinent art. He has sometimes been characterized as a routineer.[29] In considering the testimony of those skilled in the pertinent art, care must be exercised lest the witness be too expert and base his conclusions not upon ordinary but upon extraordinary skill in the art.[30] Moreover, what might appear obvious to one unfamiliar with an art, may well be demonstrated to be nonobvious subject matter, as by a clear showing of obstacles which the art had theretofore found insurmountable.[31] While the person of ordinary skill is necessarily a hypothetical person, the difficulties to be encountered in ascertaining his capabilities should be comparable to those encountered in ascertaining the mental state of the man of ordinary care, known to the law of negligence.[32]

§ 3. Rebuttal of Prima Facie Obviousness

Section 103 requires that in ascertaining the obviousness of a contribution the subject matter as a whole be considered. This requires an examination of the entire picture, including such factors as, the relation between the advantage or utility attained and the means selected for effecting the same, the motivation for the change as well as the change itself, obstacles (real or apparent) existing in the art, and the source of the problem as well as its solution. What at first blush may appear obvious may be demonstrated to be, in fact, unobvious.

It would seem that the following approach carries out the mandate in Section 103 that the subject matter as a whole be considered:

(1) Determination of the change, or the modification, or actual point of (structural) novelty of the claimed contribution over the prior art. Standing by itself, if such modification appears to be arbitrary or obvious (as a change in the values of the parameters of a process or the dimensions of an apparatus), a case of prima facie obviousness has been made out.

(2) Possible rebuttal of the prima facie obviousness of the modification by considering the subject matter as a whole.

Just how much difference the difference must make to be unobvious is incapable of mechanical or general formulation. Each case must ultimately turn on its own peculiar facts. Where the claimed structure is simple and/or differs only slightly from the prior art, the inquiry may focus upon the utility or result effected.

Results which are truly unexpected, unusual, or surprising may render the invention as a whole unobvious, regardless of how little its structure differes from the prior art, so long as there is some actual difference.[33] With respect to patents directed to combinations of old elements, courts have, on occasion, said that "the whole must in some way exceed the sum of its parts."[34] This is merely a figurative expression of the need for an unexpected result.

A nice question is: How unexpected, unusual, or surprising must the result be? By how much must the whole exceed the sum of its parts? It has been held that the law does not recognize degrees of unobviousness.[35] It has also been held that the mere fact that the results attained are unexpectedly good is not controlling.[36] Where the prior art clearly indicates that a class of compounds will effect a certain general result, the fact that a specific member of that class is particularly efficacious does not render it or its application unobvious.[37] Obviousness does not require absolute predictability.[38] The act of selection should be beyond the capacity of commonplace imagination.[39] The argument that if one slavishly following the prior art, albeit with a little educated imagination, he will sometimes succeed and sometimes fail, then he is always entitled to a patent in case of success is untenable.[40] In other words, an invention can be said to be obvious if one ordinarily skilled in the art would consider that it was logical to anticipate with a high degree of probability that a trial would be successful.[41]

Not infrequently the prior art will teach that a certain general result can be attained by doing something in a certain general way. Someone then comes along asserting that by carrying out such prior art process employing the specific values of the operative parameters being claimed, results demonstrably superior to those indicated by the prior art will be attained. Such improved results standing alone are insufficient to establish unobviousness:[42]

> The prior art having taught generally the functional relationship described it does not rise to the dignity of invention to teach optimization of the function by making quantitative adjustments to achieve the most desirable result, there being involved in such process no discovery but only the exercise of prudence and skill.

However, the fact that the optimum conditions were arrived at by routine experimentation does not in and of itself negate unobviousness.[43]

Moreover, a claimed range within a range disclosed by the prior art may be patentable, if a substantial departure from the proportions claimed is accompanied by a result materially different from that being claimed. That is to say, where the prior art merely suggests a long list of possible combining chemical elements, the combination of them in proportions not specifically taught may be patentable, provided that the very proportions being claimed produce a composition having properties that are significantly different from these elements when they are combined in other than the claimed proportions.[44]

On the other hand, a refusal to consider superior results in no more warranted by Section 103 than a total preoccupation with them.[45] Merely because a certain approach might be obvious to try does not render it unpatentable, if upon trial, it is found that the approach yields a truly unexpected result. As the court noted:[46]

> [T]here is usually an element of "obviousness to try" in any research endeavor, that it is not undertaken with complete blindness but rather with some semblance of a chance of success, and that patentability determinations based on that as a test would not only be contrary to the statute but result in a marked deterioration of the entire patent system as an incentive to invest in those efforts and attempts which go by the name of "research."

The nature of unexpected results which may render apparently obvious structure patentable can be further characterized by the word "criticality." A demonstration, preferably quantitatively, that the very means or steps claimed produce a result or exhibit a property not produced or exhibited by means or steps which differ only slightly from those claimed would tend to establish the criticality of the very means or steps claimed. Comparative results are thus helpful in evaluating criticality. However, whether criticality amounts to unobviousness will also depend upon the nature of the result or property itself. As noted above, even if the precise structure being claimed is more efficacious than that known to the prior art, this may not suffice to establish unobviousness, if the prior art taught that the claimed structure or something analogous thereto exhibits that property, though not to the extent or degree demonstrated.

In the early days of the patent system inventors were preoccupied with the mechanical arts. Conseqeuntly, much of the law was cast in mechanical terminology, as "the mechanic of ordinary skill," alluded to in the *Hotchkiss* case. As the frontiers of science were pushed back, however, more and more attention became directed at the chemical arts. Many of the more recent cases, including some just discussed, relate specifically to chemistry. Because the precise consequences of chemical reactions are often not predictable from theoretical considerations, innovation in the chemical arts pose many interesting questions of unobviousness. Along these lines, the Supreme Court has noted:[47]

> Elements may, of course, especially in chemistry or electronics, take on some new quality or function from being brought into concert, but this is not a usual result of uniting elements old in mechanics.

Nevertheless, Section 103 applies equally to all inventions, whether chemical, mechanical, or electrical.[48] General precepts derived from consideration of chemical cases are applicable to analogous situations in the electrical and mechanical arts. It is just that the relative unpredictable nature of chemistry presents more opportunities for unobvious subject matter.

Unpredictability in chemistry has engendered a number of recurrent situations which raise particularly perplexing problems of obviousness. Prominent among these are: (1) structurally obvious compounds; (2) purity; and (3) synergism.

[1] Structurally Obvious Compounds

While there are probably an infinitely large number of different chemical compounds, these fall into a relatively limited number of classes. Class distinctions are based on the nature and arrangement of constituent atoms, members of a class possessing analogous structures and generally similar, albeit not identical, properties. In organic chemistry there are classes of compounds, known as homologous series, the members of which differ structurally from one another only in the number of units of atoms, according to a fixed formula. For example, the empirical formula for the alkane series of hydrocarbons is $(C_nH_{2n+2})_n$. All members of the alkane series possess generally similar chemcial and physical properties, and almost any two adjacent homologs possess nearly identical properties. It is thus often possible to extrapolate empirical observations, postulating the existence and predicting the properties of homologs not yet prepared.

Does the fact that the possible existence of a compound has been predicted by such extrapolation constitute an antiċipation? Does the fact that the possible existence of a compound could be predicted by extrapolation render it obvious? The answer depends upon whether the compound in fact possesses properties significantly different from those that have been or which are predictable. As the Court of Customs and Patent Appeals has noted:[49]

> From the standpoint of patent law, a compound and all of its properties are inseparable; they are one and the same thing. The graphic formulae, the chemical nomenclature, the systems of classification and study such as the concepts of homology, isomerism, etc., are mere symbols by which compounds can be identified, classified, and compared. But a formula is not a compound and while it may serve in a claim to identify what is being patented, as the metes and bounds of a deed identify a plot of land, the thing that is patented is not the formula but the compound identified by it. And the patentability of the thing does not depend on the similarity of its formula to that of another compound but of the similarity of the former compound to the latter. There is no basis in law for ignoring any property in making such a comparison. An assumed similarity based on a comparison of formula must give way to evidence that the assumption is erroneous.

The foregoing exposition of the law is but an application of the rule laid down in Section 103 that the subject matter as a whole must be considered. Close structural similarity between what is being claimed and the prior art raises a presumption of obviousness which may be rebutted by evidence of such an unexpected result as that the claimed compound possesses an unexpected or surprising property.

[2] Purity

A purer form of a known substance may be patentable where the purer form possesses properties significantly different from these exhibited by the impure form.[50]

[3] Synergism

The combined action of two or more agents that is greater than the sum of the action of each of the agents used alone is a phenomenon known as synergism. While the presence of synergism would seem to satisfy the requirement that the whole in some way exceed the sum of its parts, the existence of synergism is not in all cases determinative of unobviousness. The presence of a synergistic effect was held not to establish unobviousness where the prior art reasonably taught or suggested the expediency of the results achieved, albeit it did not teach that the effect would amount to synergism.[51] Where the compound claimed possessed a close structural relationship to one known to the prior art and the two possessed a specific, significant property in common, it was held that the fact that the one being claimed possessed an additional property efficacious for the use intended was not sufficient ground for a finding of unobviousness.[52]

§ 4. The Subtests of Invention

Of assistance in evaluating unobviousness are the so-called subtests of invention. These include evidence that the claimed innovation met with commercial success; or satisfied a longfelt demand; or met with commercial acquiescence. What they amount to are circumstantial evidence of unobviousness.

Unlike criticality, which focuses upon technical issues, the subtests look to economic and motivational facts as indicia of unobviousness. To the extent that the subtests view the impact made upon the marketplace or an industry as a whole, they are more objective than the direct approach, which in attempting to ascertain the level of ordinary skill, must rely heavily on the testimony of partisan witnesses.

Nevertheless, as the word "subtest" suggests, these considerations are clearly secondary. They are to be looked to only when unobviousness is in doubt, and in such case may tip the scales in favor of unobviousness.[53] Beyond this, courts have equivocated as to the amount of deference that is to be accorded to these secondary considerations. Thus the Supreme Court has said:[54]

> Such secondary considerations as commercial success, long felt but unsolved needs, failure of others, etc., might be utilized to give light to the circumstances surrounding the origin of the subject matter sought to be patented. As indicia of obviousness or nonobviousness, these inquiries may have relevancy.

And:[55]

> They may also serve to "guard against slipping into hindsight" . . . and to resist the temptation to read into the prior art teachings of the invention in issue.

More recently the Supreme Court noted:[56]

> It is, however, fervently argued that the combination filled a long felt want and enjoyed commercial success. But those matters "without invention will not make patentability."

[1] Commercial Success

Commercial success is perhaps the most frequently invoked of the subtests. The nexus between it and unobviousness is only indirect and inferential: (1) something of substantial commercial value, if obvious, would have appeared on the marketplace before; and (2) earlier attempts were made and failed.

It is important to bear in mind the distinction between commercial success, potential commercial worth, and unobviousness. Likelihood of commercial success is not a requisite of patentability and is not to be equated with unobviousness. An innovation may be truly unobvious and patentable and yet not be commercially feasible.

Commercial success is based upon the conduct of consumers. In evaluating evidence thereof, care must be exercised that the success is attributable to the claimed innovation and not to something else sold along with it. Moreover, the success must be due to the intrinsic merit of the innovation and not merely to such extrinsic factors as promotional activities on its behalf. As noted by the Supreme Court even before the advent of the mass media:[57]

> The argument drawn from the commercial success of a patented article is not always to be relied on. Other causes, such as the enterprise of the vendors, and the resort to lavish expenditures, may cooperate to promote a large marketable demand. Yet as was well said by Mr. Justice Brown, in the case of *Consolidated Brake-Shoe v. Detroit Co.*, 47 F. 894, "when the other factors in the case leave the question of invention in doubt, the fact that the device has gone into general use and has displaced other

devices which had previously been employed for analogous uses, is sufficient to turn the scale in favor of the existence of invention."

[2] Longfelt Demand

Longfelt demand and commercial success are complementary tests. A showing of longfelt demand coupled with a showing of commercial success are indirect but cogent evidence of unobviousness. The nexus between longfelt but unsatisfied demand and unobviousness is the same as that for commercial success, namely, that if the innovation were obvious, it would have appeared on the marketplace before in response to existing demand.[58] From the failure of others to solve the problem and meet a real, commercial demand, an inference of unobviousness can be drawn.

The amount and quality of the research expended, particularly by potential competitors, in unsuccessful attempts to solve an existing problem, are evidence of longfelt demand. Here again, however, there must be a correspondence between that for which the longfelt demand is demonstrated to have existed and that which was commercially successful.

[3] Commercial Acquiescence

Commercial acquiescence looks to the actions or inaction of competitors in regard to the patent in issue. The willingness of competitors to take a license or their efforts to design around or otherwise circumvent its claims may be a tacit recognition by them of the patent's validity and, hence, circumstantial evidence of the unobviousness of the innovation.[59] The more widespread the licensing, the stronger is the inference of unobviousness.

In evaluating evidence of commercial acquiescence, consideration must be given to the motivation therefor. Thus, the acquiescence may be attributable, not to the merit of the innovation, but rather to a conspiracy among competitors to restrain trade by agreeing not to challenge the validity of one another's patents.[60] Moreover, the royalties exacted may be so low as to have made it unwise, from a business standpoint, to challenge the patent's validity.

Questions of commercial success, longfelt demand, and commercial acquiescence may be raised in the Patent Office and in infringement litigation. However, issues involving commercial success and commercial acquiescence are far more frequently raised in litigation than in procurement, for the reason that they cannot really arise until the innovation has reached the marketplace. For commercial acquiescence, a showing before the Patent Office could possibly be based upon the willingness of competitors to take licenses under a patent application.

Notes

[1] McClain v. Ortmayer, 141 U.S. 419, 427 (1891).

[2] See Diamond Rubber Co. v. Consolidated Tire Co., 220 U.S. 428, 434-435 (1911).

[3] See The Incandescent Lamp Patent, 159 U.S. 465 (1895).

[4] See The Telephone Cases, 126 U.S. 1 (1888).

[5] Traitel Marble Co. v. V.T. Hungerford Brass & Co., 18 F.2d 66 (2d Cir. 1927); California Research Corp. v. Ladd, 356 F.2d 813, 148 U.S.P.Q. 404 (D.C.C. 1966).

[6] Eibel Process Co. v. Minnesota & Ontario Paper Co., 261 U.S. 45 (1923).

[7] *In re* Aufhauser, 399 F.2d 275, 159 U.S.P.Q. 351 (C.C.P.A. 1968).

[8] Hotchkiss v. Greenwood, 52 U.S. (11 How.) 248 (1850). See also, Pearce v. Mulford, 102 U.S. (12 Otto) 112, 117-118 (1880).

[9] Reckendorfer v. Faber, 92 U.S. (2 Otto) 347, 356 (1875).

[10] *In re* Urbanic, 319 F.2d 267, 272, 138 U.S.P.Q. 224, 228 (C.C.P.A. 1963); *In re* Adams, 284 F.2d 525, 527, 128 U.S.P.Q. 116, 117 (C.C.P.A. 1960).

[11] Smith v. Nichols, 88 U.S. (21 Wall.) 112, 119 (1875).

[12] Diamond Rubber Co. v. Consolidated Tire Co., 220 U.S. 428, 434-435 (1911); Pearce v. Mulford, 102 U.S. (12 Otto) 112, 117-118 (1880).

[13] Morley Mach. Co. v. Lancaster, 129 U.S. 263 (1889). Crouch v. Roemer, 103 U.S. (13 Otto) 797 (1880).

[14] Planing-Mach. Co. v. Keith, 101 U.S. (11 Otto) 479, 490 (1879).

[15] Howard v. Detroit Stove Works, 150 U.S. 164, 170 (1893).

[16] Hot Pouncing Mach. Co. v. Hedden, 148 U.S. 482, 489 (1892).

[17] Pennsylvania R.R. v. Locomotive Truck Co., 110 U.S. (10 Otto) 490, 498 (1883).

[18] Great Atlantic & Pacific Tea Co. v. Supermarket Equip. Corp., 340 U.S. 147, 156, 87 U.S.P.Q. 303, 307 (1950) (Douglas, J., concurring).

[19] Cuno Engineering Corp. v. Automatic Devices Corp., 314 U.S. 84, 91, 51 U.S.P.Q. 272, 275 (1941).

[20] Radiator Specialty Co. v. Buhot, 39 F.2d 373, 376, 4 U.S.P.Q. 205, 209 (3d Cir. 1930).

[21] Graham v. John Deere Co., 383 U.S. 1, 15, 148 U.S.P.Q. 459, 466 (1966).

[22] Graham v. John Deere Co., 383 U.S. 1, 17, 148 U.S.P.Q. 459, 467 (1966).

[23] Reiner v. I. Leon Co., 285 F.2d 501, 504-505, 128 U.S.P.Q. 25, 27 (2d Cir. 1960), *cert. denied* 266 U.S. 929 (1961).

[24] N. 21 *supra*.

[25] Hotchkiss v. Greenwood, 52 U.S. (11 How.) 248 (1850).

[26] Marconi Wireless Co. v. United States, 320 U.S. 1, 60-61, 57 U.S.P.Q. 471, 496-497 (1943) (Frankfurter, J., dissenting); Picard v. United Aircraft Corp., 128 F.2d 632-640, 53 U.S.P.Q. 563, 569 (2d Cir. 1943) (Frank, J., concurring).

[27] See generally, St. Regis Paper Co. v. Tee-Pak, Inc., 352 F. Supp. 309, 176 U.S.P.Q. 259 (N.D. Ohio 1973).

[28] N. 22 *supra.* See also, Allen v. Standard Crankshaft & Hydraulic Co., 323 F.2d 29, 34, 139 U.S.P.Q. 20, 24 (4th Cir. 1963).

[29] *In re* Laverne, 356 F.2d 1003, 1006, 148 U.S.P.Q. 674, 676 (C.C.P.A. 1966)

[30] See Kohn v. Eimer, 265 F. 900, 902 (2d Cir. 1920).

[31] See *In re* Harris, 324 F.2d 316, 320, 139 U.S.P.Q. 292, 295 (C.C.P.A. 1963).

[32] Graham v. John Deere Co., 383 U.S. 1, 18, 148 U.S.P.Q. 459, 467 (1966).

[33] United States v. Adams, 383 U.S. 39, 148 U.S.P.Q. 479 (1966).

[34] Great Atlantic & Pacific Tea Co. v. Supermarket Equip. Corp., 340 U.S. 147, 152, 87 U.S.P.Q. 303, 305 (1950).

[35] *In re* Petering, 301 F.2d 676, 683, 133 U.S.P.Q. 275, 280 (C.C.P.A. 1962).

[36] *In re* Szumski, 302 F.2d 753, 756, 133 U.S.P.Q. 551, 553 (C.C.P.A. 1962).

[37] *In re* Moreton, 288 F.2d 940, 129 U.S.P.Q. 288 (C.C.P.A. 1961).

[38] *In re* Farnham, 342 F.2d 455, 458, 144 U.S.P.Q. 746, 748 (C.C.P.A. 1965).

[39] B.G. Corp. v. Walter Kidde & Co., 79 F.2d 20, 26 U.S.P.Q. 288 (2d Cir. 1935).

[40] N. 37 *supra.*

[41] *In re* Pantzer, 341 F.2d 121, 126, 144 U.S.P.Q. 415, 418-419 (C.C.P.A. 1965).

[42] A.R. Inc. v. Electro-Voice, Inc., 311 F.2d 508, 512, 136 U.S.P.Q. 46, 50 (7th Cir. 1962).

[43] *In re* Fay, 347 F.2d 597, 602, 146 U.S.P.Q. 47, 51 (C.C.P.A. 1965).

[44] *In re* Russell, 439 F.2d 1228, 169 U.S.P.Q. 426 (C.C.P.A. 1971); Becket v. Coe, 98 F.2d 332, 38 U.S.P.Q. 26 (D.C.C. 1938).

[45] *In re* Lindell, 385 F.2d 453, 455, 155 U.S.P.Q. 521, 523 (C.C.P.A. 1967).

[46] *In re* Tomlinson, 363 F.2d 928, 931, 150 U.S.P.Q. 623, 626 (C.C.P.A. 1966).

[47] N. 34 *supra.*

[48] Hedman v. Comm'r, 253 F. Supp. 515, 520 148 U.S.P.Q. 582, 586 (D.D.C. 1966).

[49] *In re* Papesch, 315 F.2d 381, 391, 137 U.S.P.Q. 43, 51 (C.C.P.A. 1963). Compare, Carter-Wallace, Inc. v. Otte, as Trustee in Bankruptcy of Davis Edwards Pharmacal Corp., 474 F.2d 529, 176 U.S.P.Q. 2 and 452 (2d Cir. 1972, 1973), *cert. denied* 412 U.S. 929 (1973); Eli Lilly & Co. v. Generix Drug Sales, Inc., 460 F.2d 1096, 174 U.S.P.Q. 65 (5th Cir. 1972).

[50] See Parke-Davis & Co., v. Mulford, 196 Fed. 496 (2d Cir. 1912).

[51] N. 36 *supra.* Sterling Drug, Inc. v. Brenner, 256 F. Supp. 1000, 150 U.S.P.Q. 584 (D.D.C. 1966).

[52] *In re* Mod, 408 F.2d 1055, 1057, 161 U.S.P.Q. 281, 283 (C.C.P.A. 1969).

[53] Graham v. John Deere Co., 383 U.S. 1, 36, 148 U.S.P.Q. 459, 474 (1966).

[54] Graham v. John Deere Co. 383 U.S. 1, 17, 148 U.S.P.Q. 459, 467 (1966).

[55] N. 53 *supra.*

[56] Anderson's-Black Rock, Inc. v. Pavement Salvage Co., 396 U.S. 57, 61, 163 U.S.P.Q. 673, 674 (1969). For an interesting collateral review of the weight to be accorded to long felt need and commercial success, see Moran v. Tegtmeyer, 363 F. Supp. 377, 179 U.S.P.Q. 526 (D.D.C. 1973).

[57] Kremetz v. S. Cattle Co., 148 U.S. 556, 560-561 (1893). See also, *In re* Ernest, 305 F.2d 468, 472, 134 U.S.P.Q. 251, 254 (C.C.P.A. 1962); Stiegle v. J.M. Moore Import-Export Co., 312 F.2d 588, 136 U.S.P.Q. 230, 232 (2d Cir. 1963).

[58] Expanded Metal Co. v. Bradford, 214 U.S. 366, 381 (1908); Norman v. Lawrence, 285 F.2d 505, 505-506, 128 U.S.P.Q. 28, 29 (2d Cir. 1960).

[59] Wahl Clipper Corp. v. Andis Clipper Co., 66 F.2d 162, 165, 18 U.S.P.Q. 179, 182 (7th Cir. 1933). Compare, Deering Milliken & Co. v. Temp-Resisto Corp., 274 F.2d 626, 633, 124 U.S.P.Q. 147, 153 (2d Cir. 1960); Kleinman v. Kobler, 230 F.2d 913, 914, 108 U.S.P.Q. 301, 302 (2d Cir.), *cert. denied,* 352 U.S. 830 (1956).

[60] See generally, United States v. Singer Mfg. Co., 374 U.S. 174, 137 U.S.P.Q. 808 (1963); Chas. Pfizer & Co., F.T.C., 401 F.2d 574, 159 U.S.P.Q. 193 (6th Cir. 1968), *cert. denied* 394 U.S. 920 (1969).

–Part III–

COMPETING RIGHTS TO THE SAME PATENT

Inventors are a meritorious class. They are public benefactors. They add to the wealth and comfort of the community, and promote the progress of civilization.

Swayne, J.
Consolidated Fruit-Jar v. Wright,
94 U.S. (4 Otto) 92,96 (1876)

Whereas Part I and Part II are both concerned primarily with the rights of patent owners relative to the public at large, Part III focuses upon the allocation of patent rights among those asserting an interest in the same invention. Such interest may be based upon one's status as an inventor or as an investor.

Chapter 9

PRIORITY OF INVENTION

SYNOPSIS

> The prize of an exclusive patent falls to the one who had the fortune to be first. . . . The others gain nothing for all their toil and talents.
>
> B.N. Cardozo, J.
> *Radio Corporation of America v. Radio Engineering Laboratories, Inc.*, 293 U.S. 1, 3, 21 U.S.P.Q. 353, 354 (1934)

Inextricably tied to the problem of deciding what is new and what is old is the issue of priority of invention. Whereas the ordinary novelty determination focuses upon an invention in view of the prior art, the prime object of a priority contest is to determine which of two or more parties is entitled to a patent on the very same invention.

The issue of priority of invention, unlike nearly every other issue presented to the Patent Office, is a contest between adverse parties. The ordinary examination of patent applications is carried out ex parte. Priority contests, which are known as interferences, are inter partes proceedings. Most interferences begin within the Patent Office, but they may, under appropriate circumstances, be commenced in court.

The basis for the interference proceeding is the policy of the United States to award a patent only to the first inventor. This policy is declared in Section 102(g) of the Patent Act:

> A person shall be entitled to a patent unless: before the applicant's invention thereof the invention was made in this country by another who had not abandoned, suppressed, or concealed it. In determining priority of invention there shall be considered

> not only the respective dates of conception and reduction to practice of the invention, but also the reasonable diligence of one who was first to conceive and last to reduce to practice, from a time prior to conception by the other.

It should be noted that the approach which the United States takes to settling the issue or priority of invention differs from that taken by nearly every other country, wherein the conflict is resolved —and rather summarily too—on the sole basis of who was the first to file a patent application disclosing the invention. Thus, it has been said that the United States has a first-to-invent system, whereas the other countries have first-to-file systems. However, it will presently become apparent that even under United States law, priority does not necessarily go to the first to invent.

§ 1. Determination of Priority

To make possible rational determinations of priority, there must be a set of rules for determining what constitutes the making of an invention. For such purposes the inventive process has been broken down into two steps: (1) conception; and (2) reduction to practice. Conception is the mental part; reduction to practice, the physical part. These elements, to a limited extent, are analogous to those necessary to constitute a common-law crime: (1) mens rea—guilty mind; and (2) actus rea—guilty act.

An invention is not deemed to have been made until both conception and a reduction to practice have occurred.

[1] Conception

Conception, in the patent-law sense, involves the formulation, in the mind of the inventor, of the complete means for solving a problem. The mere recognition of a desirable result, or of a problem, or of a general approach to solving the same, without the formulation of the physical structure to accomplish that result or to solve the problem, will not suffice to constitute conception.[1]

[2] Reduction to Practice

A reduction to practice may be either actual or constructive. An actual reduction to practice involves the physical construction or carrying out of the invention. The actual reduction to practice of a process occurs when the constitutent steps have been performed.[2] The actual reduction to practice of a composition of matter occurs when the composition has been produced *and* its usefulness demonstrated by actual testing unless its utility is self-evident.[3] The actual reduction to practice of a design occurs when it has been incorporated in some structure other than a mere drawing.[4]

The word "constructive," when applied as a modifier to a legal relationship, signifies that which is deemed such in contemplation of law. The legal relationships involved in a constructive trust or a constructive contract are not consonant with those contemplated by a true trust or a contract, respectively. Nevertheless, for compelling reasons of policy, they are treated as such by the law. Accordingly, a constructive reduction to practice does *not* involve the building of the invention, but rather only the formal filing, in the Patent Office, of a patent application disclosing the invention.[5]

Construction or carrying out of the invention is not a condition precedent to patent validity. All that the law requires is that the invention, from the description in the patent specification, be capable of being constructed or carried out by one skilled in the art to which it relates.[6] An invention may be a purely mental product, or it may be the result of extensive experimentation.[7]

A drawing of even the simplest machine or device, perfect in every detail, and plainly demonstrating the principle, efficacy, and practical utility of the invention, will not constitute reduction to practice. Nor will the requirement of reduction to practice or use be satisfied by a construction clearly designed and intended as a model and nothing more. They are but evidence of conception. Some devices, however, are so simple, and their purpose and efficacy so obvious, that the complete construction of one of a size and form intended for and capable of practical use might well be regarded as a sufficient reduction to practice, without actual use or test in an effort to demonstrate their complete success or probable commercial value.[8]

The laws of nearly all foreign countries, by basing priority of invention solely upon filing dates, discourage prior construction and testing. The inevitable consequences of such first-to-file systems is a rush to the patent office and the filing of a plethora of paper applications on untried, speculative, and incomplete inventions. The United States attempts at least not to discourage construction and testing of inventions prior to filing, by giving credit for such conduct, treating earnest and sustained efforts to try out an invention as equivalent to the act of initiating the process of obtaining patent protection.

[3] Diligence

Diligence, as this word is used in Section 102(g), involves the continued application of the inventor or his representatives to the task of reducing the conceived invention to practice.[9] Efforts directed merely to the sale or other commercial exploitation of an invention do not contribute to its reduction to practice.[10] Diligence demands *activity* on the part of the inventor or his agents; a mere state of mind will not suffice.[11]

Diligence has the same significance whether there is reliance upon an actual or a constructive reduction to practice.[12] Where reliance is upon a constructive reduction to practice there must have been diligence in preparing and in filing the patent application.[13] An inventor is chargeable with his attorney's lack of diligence in filing the patent application.[14] An attorney's backlog of work may inure to the benefit of his client, as it has been held that an attorney who took up his client's application in chronological order acted diligently.[15]

The law does not require extraordinary diligence,[16] but rather only ordinary or reasonable diligence.[17] Diligence need not involve uninterrupted effort, nor the concentration of all of the applicant's energies upon the reduction of the invention in question to practice.[18] Reasonable vacation periods are not inconsistent with the exercise of diligence.[19]

The complexity of the invention may affect the degree of diligence which must be demonstrated: the simpler the invention, the more fixed and continuous must be the intent to reduce to practice.[20] The combination of lack of funds, preoccupation with other inventions having a more immediate cash value, and the belief of the inventor that he was a pioneer in the art without a rival in the offing has been cited by the Supreme Court as tending to excuse the absence of more concerted efforts to reduce to practice.[21] Even a total lack of activity may constitute diligence, where the inventor was physically or mentally incapable of exertion.[22] Some writers prefer to refer to such a situation as a valid excuse for a gap in diligence or as circumstances excusing diligence.[23] The role which the law accords to diligence may be likened to the manner in which equity views vigilance. To paraphrase an ancient maxim of equity jurisprudence: The law protects the diligent inventor; and not those who slumber on their conceptions.

Under our first-to-invent system, priority of invention belongs to the party who was the first to reduce to practice (whether actually or constructively), unless that invention was both (1) earlier conceived by another *and* (2) such other party exercised continued diligence from the time of his own conception until he reduced the invention to practice (whether actually or constructively).[24]

Once a party has (actually) reduced his invention to practice there is no requirement that he file an application to preserve his right to a patent.[25] It is this very feature which makes the system a first-to-invent system, rather than a first-to-file system. However, extended delay in filing a patent application may be taken as circumstantial evidence of abandonment, suppression, and concealment.[26] Diligence in the preparation and filing of a patent application is material only where the applicant relies upon a *constructive* reduction to practice.[27]

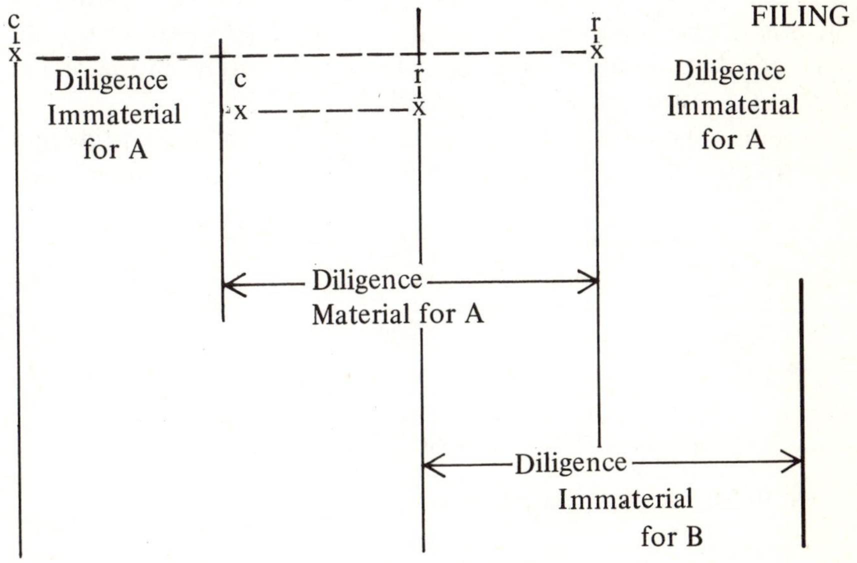

Diligence is only significant where one party was the first to conceive, but the last to reduce to practice, and then only during the interval beginning just prior to his rival's conception and ending with his own reduction to practice.[28] Throughout such interval, diligence must have been continuously maintained by the party who was the first to conceive, lest his rival prevail. There is no requirement that continued diligence in working to reduce to practice be commenced at the very time of one's own conception. It need only have started or been resumed at any time before a rival's conception.[29] The time interval during which continued diligence is significant is sometimes characterized as the critical period.[30]

Although a party was the first to conceive, he forfeits any claim to priority on the basis of such prior conception, if there is a gap in his diligence at any time after his rival's conception. Accordingly, one who was the first to conceive cannot recapture priority on the basis of his prior conception by spurting into renewed activity upon learning that another has entered the field. He thence can gain priority only by becoming the first to reduce to practice.

Where one of the parties did not himself conceive the invention, but rather derived it from his rival, prior reduction to practice by the party who derived the conception is unavailing to win him priority. The party who conceived the invention will prevail, even in the absence of diligence and even though he concealed his invention or was stirred into activity by his opponent.[31]

An understanding and appreciation of the foregoing principles should be facilitated by a consideration of the following illustrations:

I. The first to conceive is also the first to reduce to practice.

A prevails. Diligence is irrelevant.

II. Both conceive simultaneously.

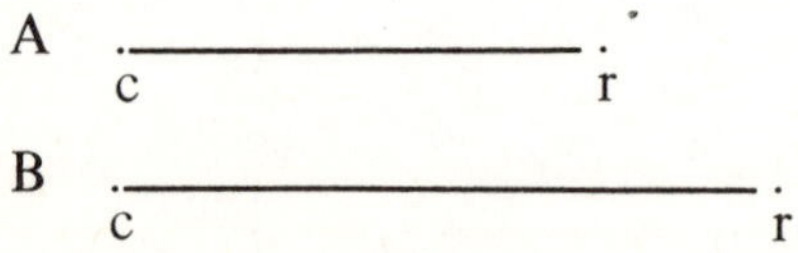

A prevails. Diligence is irrelevant.

III. The party first to conceive is the last to reduce to practice.

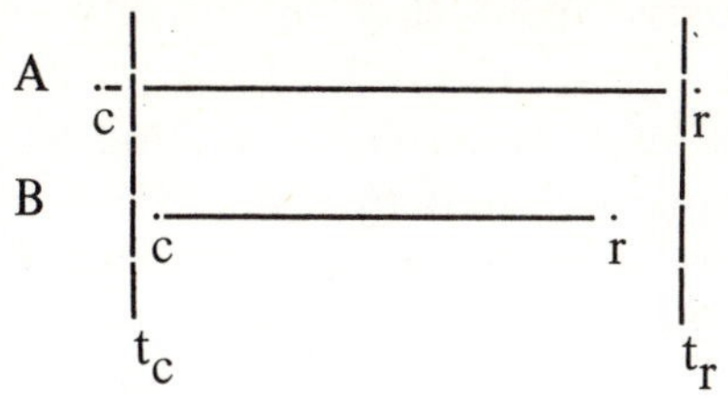

A will prevail only if diligent continuously throughout the time interval t_c to t_r.

It should be noted that in every instance, a constructive reduction to practice is treated as fully equivalent to an actual reduction to practice. Priority focuses upon which party was the first to make a reduction to practice.

The preceding discussion and illustrations all involved but two parties. The same principles are applicable to situations involving three or more parties, with the question of priority being readily resolved by breaking such a situation down into sets of situations, each of which involves but two of the parties.

Consider the following:

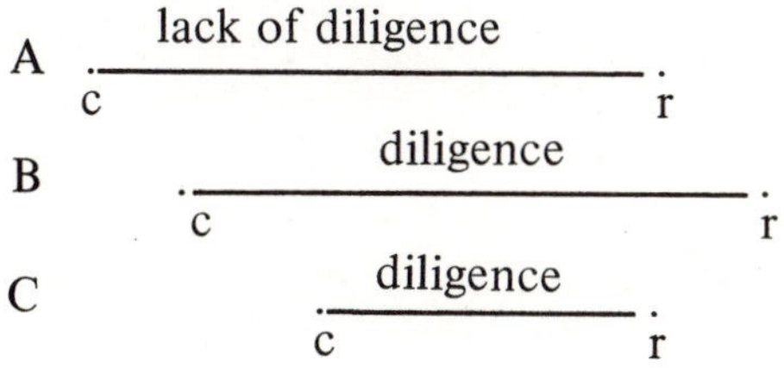

A prevails against B.
B prevails against C.
C prevails against A!

§ 2. Adjudication

While most patent matters are adjudicated by the Patent Office in proceedings ex parte, the question of priority of inventorship is resolved, both within and without the Patent Office, by inter partes proceedings. Accordingly, the mode of procedure in priority contests or interferences, as they are more often called, before the Patent Office differs quite markedly from that in other patent causes presented to the Office.

The difference having perhaps the most far reaching consequences is the nature of the evidence required to establish priority. In ex parte matters, the affidavit of an applicant will usually suffice as proof of facts alleged. On the contrary, the rule adhered to in interference practice is that the *testimony of an applicant–standing alone–will not suffice as proof of any critical facts,* that is, those tending to establish dates of conception and of (actual) reduction to practice and diligence.[32] This is not to say, however, that the testimony of an applicant on these issues is inadmissible. Such testimony is both relevant and competent, and it should never be totally ignored.[33]

To establish dates of conception and of (actual) reduction to practice and diligence, however, the testimony of an applicant on these points must always be supported or corroborated by at least one other witness.[34] The corroborating evidence must be in the form of testimony. Mere documentary evidence will not suffice. The corroborating witness must be able to testify that he personally observed acts tending to establish the critical facts as of the dates sought to be established. Of course, an applicant may have worked out an invention all alone. In such case, the earliest date that a corroborating witness could establish would be the date on which the applicant confided his invention to that witness. The rationale for requiring corroboration has been explained in the following terms.[35]

> A would-be inventor frequently has a nebulous and general idea of a result he wishes to accomplish and possibly a general idea of means to accomplish that result, but, being unable to give his ideas practical form, allows them to slumber. Upon learning that another has successfully worked out such ideas, the mists of uncertainty are immediately dissipated, vagueness takes definite form and the would-be inventor becomes, in his own mind, the actual inventor and acts accordingly. The danger and opportunity for fraud or mistake in such cases are so great that proof should be very clear and very convincing to warrant an award to the dilatory party.

Notebooks and other records are no substitute for testimonial evidence. Their chief value resides in the fact that information contained therein is available for refreshing the recollection of witnesses. Relegating records to a secondary role is not peculiar to interference practice, but applies wherever the rules of evidence prevail. Particular note should be taken of the fact that these rules also preclude, as corroborating evidence: (a) hearsay, i.e., evidence based upon what the witness heard someone else say; and (b) self-serving declarations.

The popular practice of mailing a disclosure to one's self or another person by registered mail is of questionable efficacy in establishing a date of conception. Recently, the Patent Office has made provision for the acceptance and preservation for a limited time of disclosure documents as evidence of the dates of conception of inventions.[36] Each such disclosure document will be retained by the Patent Office for two years and then be destroyed unless within that time it is referred to in a separate letter in a related patent application. A disclosure document is not a patent application, and the date of its receipt in the Patent Office will not become the effective filing date of any patent application subsequently filed. All disclosure documents will be held in confidence by the Patent Office.

Testimony to the effect that an applicant as of a certain date related knowledge of an invention to a witness, while literally evidence of what someone other than that witness said, is not deemed hearsay, if what is sought to be proved is not that such knowledge is valid (that is, that the invention is operable or that the knowledge originated with that applicant), but rather merely that, as of the date it was related, the applicant was in possession of the invention. Such testimony is thus competent evidence of conception.[37] Since conception is a purely mental act, proof thereof can be corroborated only by resort to evidence based upon what the putative inventor said or wrote. Testimonial evidence is necessary to establish the date relied upon.

While it is true that actual and constructive reductions to practice are equivalent, a party relying upon a constructive reduction to practice has an important procedural advantage in that his own case depends on no evidence other than that of his filing date, which, of course, is easily established.

The parties to an interference are styled the "interferants." The party possessing the earlier filing date is styled the "senior party." The senior party is prima facie the first inventor; the junior party has the burden of proving that he was the first inventor, and must resort, for proof thereof, to evidence of earlier actual reduction to practice and/or conception. It must not be forgotten that the senior party may go behind his own filing date too, to prove a still earlier (actual) reduction to practice and/or conception. The junior party has the burden of proving his case by a preponderance of the evidence.[38] For applications to which a right of foreign priority under the Paris Convention attaches, the earliest filing date abroad, known as the effective filing date, may be relied upon.[39] However, no evidence of activities abroad is admissible to establish a date of invention.[40] Thus, for inventions made abroad, it is not possible to establish a date of invention earlier than the effective date thereof.

An interference is possible between pending applications; between pending applications and issued patents; or between issued patents. The Patent Office has no jurisdiction over interferences entirely between issued patents. Such interferences must be commenced by one of the patentees in a United States district court.[41]

The Patent Office endeavors to screen pending applications for interfering subject matter. Its scrutiny, however, is confined to what applicants *have claimed* or, at most, to what there is an evident *intention* to claim, such intention being gleaned from such portions of an applicant's disclosure as the summary of his invention and/or abstract of his diclosure. Mere disclosure by an applicant of an invention, which he is not claiming, does not afford a ground for the Patent Office to extend an invitation to such applicant to claim subject matter which would create a conflict with what another is claiming.[42]

It is important for the reader to realize that the inventions of rival parties, as such are claimed, must be very close to warrant the declaration of an interference between them. While the claims need not be identical in language, and may vary in scope and in immaterial details, no express limitation may be ignored, nor may limitations be read into a claim.[43] The doctrine of equivalents, applicable to questions of patentability, is not applicable to interferences.[44]

It is Patent Office policy not to declare an interference between applications if there is a difference of more than three months in the effective filing dates of the oldest and next oldest applications, in the case of inventions of a simple character, or a difference of more than six months in the effective filing dates of the applications in other cases.[45]

Under present practice in the Patent Office, as a general rule, an interference will not be declared unless it appears that at least one of the conflicting cases contains patentable claims.[46] The object of this rule is to avoid premature interferences–to minimize the chance that the time and expense in resolving the issue of priority will have been in vain. For the same reason, an interference will normally not be instituted between applications having a common owner.[47] Elimination of conflicting claims therefrom may be required pursuant to Rule 78(b).

As the status and content of all pending patent applications is not a matter of public record, conflicts among applications can normally be detected only by the Patent Office. By contrast, the applicant or assignee of a pending application may become aware of a conflict between his application and an issued patent. Accordingly, interferences involving one or more issued patents may be instituted on the initiative of one or more of the parties.

The issue of priority is determined with respect to one or more claims, which are styled the counts of the interference. These may be analogized to the causes of action in general, civil litigation. One party may prevail with respect to some of the counts, while another may prevail with respect to other counts. However, in setting up an interference, one party must be senior as to all counts or junior as to all counts.

Where the interference involves only pending applications, it is the Primary Examiner who determines what the content of the counts is to be. Where the interference involves an issued patent, the counts nearly always correspond precisely to one or more of the claims of the patent.

So as to create sharply defined issues for adjudication, cases containing conflicting subject matter, before an interference will be formally declared between them, must have claims drawn to the common subject matter couched in substantially identical phraseology.

Where the conflict exists between applications, the Examiner may suggest such claims to one or more of the parties. Where one of the applications already contains claims which express the common invention, the Examiner may suggest these claims to the other party or parties. Where none of the applications contain an acceptable claim, the Examiner may formulate a claim or claims covering the common subject matter and suggest the same to all the parties. The parties to whom claims are suggested will be required to make those claims (that is, to present the suggested claims in their respective applications by amendment thereof) within a specified time, not less than thirty days, in order that an interference may be declared. The failure or refusal of any applicant to make any claim suggested within the time specified, is taken without further action as a disclaimer of the invention covered by that claim unless the time for response has been extended.[48]

The claims of a patent (barring a reissue) are fixed and unalterable. Therefore, an Examiner could not "suggest" claims to a patentee. An application with which a patent conflicts may, however, be amended. Therefore, an applicant may adopt or "copy" into his own application the claim or claims of a patent having conflicting subject matter, thereby provoking an interference with such patent. However, support must be present in his own application for every limitation recited in a copied claim. While an interference involving a patent is often proposed by an applicant, the Examiner may attempt to provoke an interference on his own initiative by requiring the applicant to amend his application by copying the claims of the patent which contain the common subject matter, giving the applicant thirty days to do so. Failure of the applicant to adopt such claims does not of itself constitute a disclaimer of such subject matter. However, that applicant would be precluded from later making such claims on the ground of double patenting–that only one patent (the one already issued) may be granted for one invention.

Where a patent has issued, the time within which a claim therein may be copied into a pending application is limited by Section 135(b) to one year from the patent's date of issue. This provison may be viewed as constituting a Section 102(b) bar against the applicant. The bar applies even where the pending application enjoys a filing date earlier than that of the already issued patent. In effect, the grant and issuance of the first patent has given the public an intervening right to have the monopoly on the subject matter disclosed therein expire seventeen years from the date that subject matter became publicly available through the issuance of the patent.

It should be noted that it may be possible for an applicant to overcome a patent whose disclosure has been cited as prior art against his claims by means of an affidavit made pursuant to Rule 131. Such affidavit must establish that the applicant completed the invention which he claims in the United States before the earliest effective filing date of the cited patent reference. If that patent has already been in existence for more than one year, an affidavit under

Rule 131 will be ineffective to overcome an art rejection based thereon. Of course, where a United States patent reference not only discloses but also claims the inventions being claimed by the applicant, a mere Rule 131 affidavit will not suffice to obviate the patent.

An interference can be declared only between cases claiming "substantially the same invention."[49] Where at all possible, that common invention should be expressed in identical phraseology. However, as every word recited in a claim must find support in its own specifications, it may not be possible for the parties to adopt counts which exactly coincide word for word. Therefore, where necessitated by circumstance, an interference may be declared: (1) between a set of counts which differ from one another by only immaterial limitations or variations; or (2) using a Modified Count, that is, one which is not completely supported by the specification of any of the parties.[50] The party who ultimately prevails in such interference will be entitled to claim only that for which there is complete support in his own specification.[51]

It must be emphasized that a variation in the counts of the parties to be permissible must be truly immaterial, as, for example, that one recites an inherent property, while the other does not; or that one contains a recitation of intended use, which the other does not.[52] However, limitations not expressly defined cannot be read into the counts.[53] An actual physical difference, albeit an obvious one, is not an immaterial variation. An example of a modified count which neither party can make would be a Markush group reciting ABCXY, where the specification of one party discloses the equivalence of A, B, C, and X and the specification of the other party discloses the equivalence of A, B, C, and Y.

Before an interference will be declared, not only must all the cases contain claims drawn to substantially the same invention, but it must also appear that there exists a reasonable possibility that the junior party would prevail. Thus, in the case of an apparent conflict between pending applications, the Patent Office will normally not institute an interference if there is a difference of more than three months in the effective filing dates of the oldest and next oldest applications, in the case of inventions of a simple character, or if there is a difference of more than six months in the effective filing dates of the applications in other cases. Moreover, an Examiner, pursuant to Rule 202, may require a junior applicant to state in writing under oath the date and the character of the earliest fact or act, susceptible of proof, which can be relied upon to establish conception of the invention under consideration, for the purpose of establishing priority of inventorship. In the event that the junior applicant makes no reply within the time specified (which may not be less than thirty days) or if the earliest date alleged is subsequent to the filing date of the senior party, the interference ordinarily will not be declared.

Where the conflict involves a patent and the applicant is the junior party (that is, the applicant's filing date is later than the filing date of the patent), that applicant must file an affidavit, pursuant to Rule 204, to the effect that he made the invention in controversy before the effective filing date of the patentee. And, where the applicant's filing date is more than three months subsequent to the effective date of the patentee, the applicant must, in addition: (1) set out in his affidavit pursuant to Rule 204 a factual description of acts and circumstances which would prima facie entitle him to an award of priority; and (2) submit an affidavit by at least one corroborating witness in support of his position. Where the applicant is the senior party, he is not required to make a showing under Rule 204.

When the cases containing conflicting subject matter have claims drawn thereto and the Primary Examiner has determined that the junior party may be able to establish priority of invention, he fills out a form known as the Initial Memorandum (which provides authorization for preparation of the Notices of Interference and the Declaration Sheet and which indicates the claims of each applicant or patentee that are to form the respective counts of the interference and whether any party is entitled to the benefit of the filing date of any prior application as to the subject matter in issue) and forwards this memorandum along with the file wrappers of the cases to the Board of Patent Interferences (Bd. Pat. Int.).[54]

Upon receipt thereof, a member of the Board of Patent Interferences will formally institute and declare the interference by forwarding a Notice of Interference to each of the parties to the proceeding. Each Notice of Interference identifies, by name, the other parties; the serial numbers and filing dates of their cases; and the counts of the interference.[55] Each notice also sets a schedule of times for filing the Preliminary Statement, required by Rule 215, and for filing motions, provided for under Rule 231.

Mailing to the parties of their Notices of Interference has the effect of transferring jurisdiction of any pending application from the Primary Examiner to the Board of Patent Interferences, further ex parte prosecution thereby being suspended.[56] While the Board of Patent Interferences thenceforth technically assumes jurisdiction and retains it until the issue of priority is resolved, all issues relating to the propriety of the counts are to be decided by the Primary Examiner and not by the Board of Patent Interferences, during what is known as the motion period. Since one party is free to oppose the motion of another party, motion practice before the Primary Examiner is in the nature of an inter partes proceeding.

The Preliminary Statement is, in essence, a concise summary or outline of the material facts constituting each party's case. If a party intends to establish a date of invention earlier than his earliest effective filing date, he must, under oath, set out in his Preliminary Statement certain critical events and their dates. These include:

(1) the date upon which the first drawing of the invention was made;

(2) the date upon which the first written description of the invention was made;

(3) the date upon which the invention was first disclosed to another person;

(4) the date of the first act susceptible of proof which would establish conception of the invention;

(5) the date of the actual reduction to practice of the invention;

(6) the date after conception of the invention when active exercise of reasonable diligence toward reducing the invention to practice began.

The nonexistence or nonoccurrence of any of the foregoing items or events must be affirmatively stated in the Preliminary Statement.

The information called for in the Preliminary Statement does not constitute evidence. Statements made therein are treated as mere conclusions or allegations of fact, analogous to those set forth in the pleadings of general, civil litigation. The purpose of the Preliminary Statement is to commit each party to a position from which it may not advance, thereby precluding one party from manufacturing proof of a still earlier date of invention upon learning of the date being relied upon by the opposition. Accordingly, a party will not be allowed to establish by evidence any date earlier than that alleged in his Preliminary Statement. Rule 223(b) provides:

> If a party proves any date earlier than that alleged in his preliminary statement, such proof will be held to establish the date so alleged and none earlier.

Moreover, amendment of a Preliminary Statement will be permitted only where error or omission can be clearly established, as where an incorrect filing date was recited.[57]

Each party will be allowed at least two months, from the date the interference was declared to prepare his Preliminary Statement.[58] Each Preliminary Statement must be filed in the Patent Office, within the allotted time, in a sealed envelope bearing the name of the party filing it and the number and title of the interference.[59] Upon filing his Preliminary Statement, each party is required to serve a Notice of Filing upon all his adversaries. Not less than fifteen days after the expiration of the time for filing Preliminary Statements, each party that has filed a Preliminary Statement is required to serve a copy thereof upon each of the other parties that has done so. Accordingly, no party has access to the Preliminary Statement of an adversary until all have committed themselves.[60]

After mailing of the Notices of Interference, each party thereto has the right of access to the applications identified in such notices except for any affidavits filed pursuant to Rules 131, 202, and 204.[61] The reason for this exception is that such affidavits would contain information bearing on an opponent's date of invention. Such affidavits will become open for inspection only after the date set for the serving of copies of the Preliminary Statements.

If a junior party to an interference fails to file a Preliminary Statement, or if his statement fails to overcome the prima facie case made by the filing date of the application of another party, judgment on the record will be entered against such junior party unless he has filed a motion within the time set therefor, for some action in the interference.

Not less than four months from the date of declaration of the interference, each party thereto has the right to make one or more Motions, pursuant to Rule 231, before the Primary Examiner. Also, the Primary Examiner upon his own motion, pursuant to Rule 237, may (1) dissolve the interference where he finds all or part of the counts unpatentable; (2) add a new party where he finds another case claiming substantially the same subject matter in issue. In general, motions pursuant to Rule 231 have as their object the alteration of the scope of the interference, either with respect to the counts, the parties, or the cases. For example, the moving party may attack, by way of a Rule 231 motion, the propriety of one or more of the counts on the basis that one or more of the cases cannot support the same. A motion made pursuant to Rule 231 may seek:

(1) to dissolve the interference as to one or more counts;

(2) to amend the issue by addition or substitution of new counts;

(3) to substitute any other application owned by him as to the existing issue, or to include any other application or patent owned by him as to any subject matter other than the existing issue but disclosed in his application or patent involved in the interference and in an opposing party's application or patent in the interference which should be made the basis of interference between himself and such other party;

(4) to shift the burden of proof, or be accorded the benefit of an earlier application which would not change the order of the parties;

(5) to amend an involved application by adding or removing the names of one or more inventors.

A motion to dissolve on the ground that a count is unpatentable over the prior art will not be entertained where one or more of the interferants is a patentee.[62]

Each motion made pursuant to Rule 231 must contain a full statement of the grounds therefor and reasoning in support thereof. Any opposition to a motion must be filed within twenty days of the expiration of the time set for filing motions and the moving party may, if he desires, file a reply to such motion within fifteen days of the date the opposition was filed. With respect to motions made pursuant to Rule 231, neither oral argument nor requests for reconsideration will be entertained. There is normally no appeal from decisions rendered on motion.

Motions relating to matters other than those specified in Rule 231 will be determined by a Patent Interference Examiner or by the Board of Patent Interferences, as may be deemed appropriate.

The Board of Patent Interferences is competent to determine the question of priority of invention, having the power to award priority to the party who, to its satisfaction, has established his case by a clear preponderance of the evidence.[63]

The Board of Patent Interferences must base its decision upon the evidence submitted.[64] Testimonial evidence must be presented in the form of depositions taken on oral examination as answers to interrogatories.[65]

There is a Final Hearing, but this is confined to the oral arguments of opposing counsel relating to: (1) the evaluation of the evidence to determine priority; (2) certain ancillary matters raised on motion.[66] Questions relating to the patentability of a claim over the prior art are not considered ancillary to the question of priority and, therefore, are not reviewable by the Board of Patent Interferences.[67]

An interference may be terminated either by dissolution or by judgment. A judgment will normally recite an award of priority to the prevailing party.

An applicant or a patentee involved in an interference may, at any time, file a written disclaimer or concession of priority, or abandonment of the invention. Such must be signed by the inventor with the written consent of any assignee, and a copy thereof must be filed in the Patent Office.[68] A concession of priority may not be made by an assignee.[69]

A party dissatisfied with the decision of the Board of Patent Interferences may appeal its decision to either the United States District Court for the District of Columbia or to the United States Court of Customs and Patent Appeals, at his election.[70]

The Patent Office has no jurisdiction over interferences involving only issued patents. The owner of an interfering patent may have relief against the owner of another by civil action, and the court may adjudge the question of the validity of any of the interfering patents in whole or in part.[71]

A final judgment adverse to a patentee from which no appeal or other review has been or can be taken or had constitutes cancellation of the claims involved from the patent, and notice thereof will be endorsed on copies of the patent thereafter distributed by the Patent Office. Where the prevailing party is an applicant, the Commissioner may grant a patent to such person, even though a patent for the same invention had been previously granted to another.[72]

Highlights of Patent Office Interference Proceedings

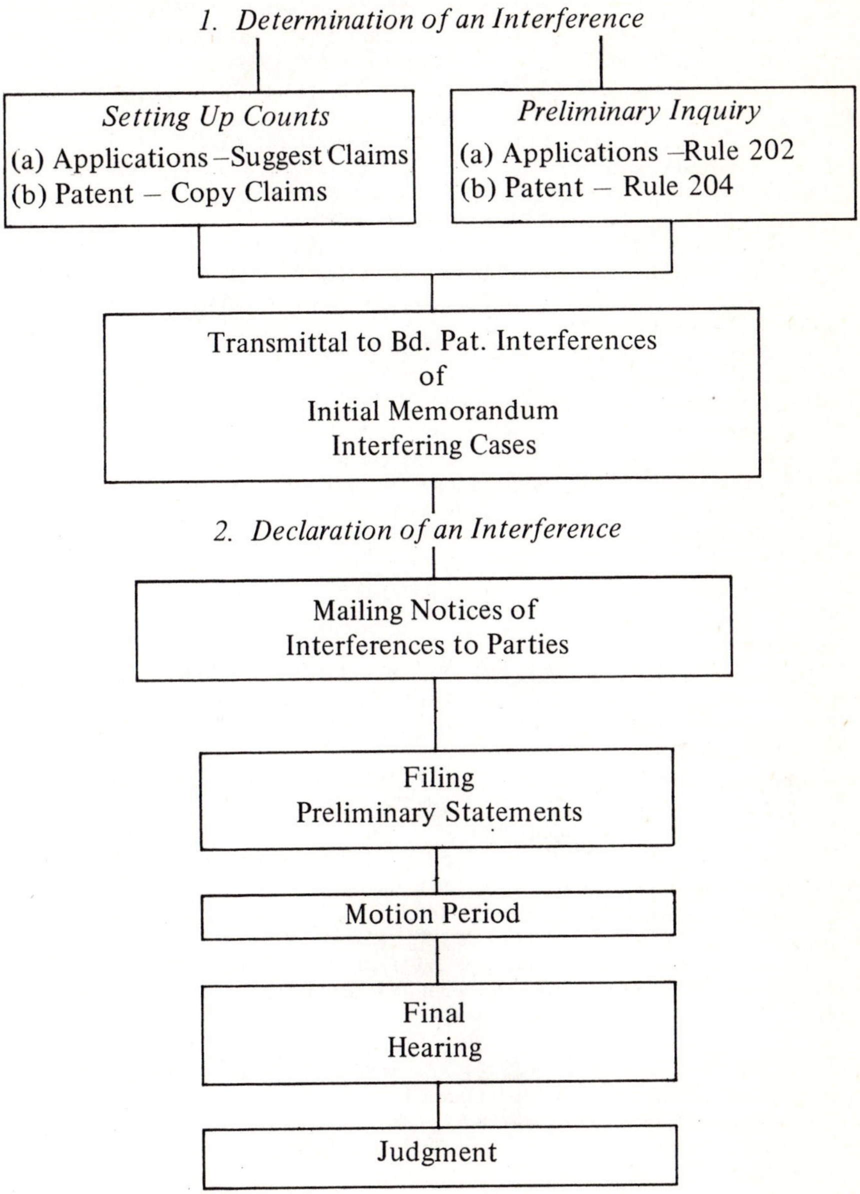

Notes

[1] Townsend v. Smith, 36 F.2d 292, 295, 4 U.S.P.Q. 269, 271 (C.C.P.A. 1929); Mergenthaler v. Scudder, 1897 C.D. 724, 731, 11 App. D.C. 264, 276 (D.C.C. 1897).

[2] Corona Cord Tire Co. v. Dover Chem. Corp., 276 U.S. 358, 383 (1928).

[3] Guinot v. Hull, 204 F.2d 281, 97 U.S.P.Q. 441 (C.C.P.A. 1953).

[4] Fitzgerald v. Arbib, 268 F.2d 763, 122 U.S.P.Q. 167 (C.C.P.A. 1959); Bomart v. Noymer, 141 U.S.P.Q. 252 (Bd. Pat. Int. 1963).

[5] General Elec. Co. v. DeForest Radio Co., 17 F.2d 90 (D. Del. 1927).

[6] See Farrington v. Mikeska, 155 F.2d 412, 414, 69 U.S.P.Q. 509, 511 (C.C.P.A. 1946).

[7] Kendall v. Searles, 173 F.2d 986, 81 U.S.P.Q. 363 (C.C.P.A. 1949).

[8] Mason v. Hepburn, 13 App. D.C. 86, 89 (D.C.C. 1898).

[9] Preston v. White, 97 F.2d 160, 37 U.S.P.Q. 802 (C.C.P.A. 1938).

[10] Teter v. Kearby, 169 F.2d 808, 79 U.S.P.Q. 65 (C.C.P.A. 1948).

[11] Rines v. Morgan, 250 F.2d 365, 116 U.S.P.Q. 145 (C.C.P.A. 1958); Powell v. Poupitch, 77 U.S.P.Q. 379 (C.C.P.A. 1948).

[12] Dickinson v. Swinehart, 263 F.474 (D.C.C. 1920).

[13] Mayhew v. Wardwell, 1869 C.D. 5 (Comm. Pat. 1869). See also, Christersen v. Ellis, 17 App. D.C. 498, 1901 C.D. 326 (D.C.C. 1901).

[14] Scharmann v. Kassel, 179 F.2d 365, 116 U.S.P.Q. 145 (C.C.P.A. 1958).

[15] Rines v. Morgan, 250 F.2d 365, 116 U.S.P.Q. 145 (C.C.P.A. 1958).

[16] Keizer v. Bradley, 270 F.2d 396, 123 U.S.P.Q. 215 (C.C.P.A. 1959).

[17] Radio Corp. of Am. v. Radio Engineering Laboratories, Inc., 293 U.S. 1, 13-14, 21 U.S.P.Q. 353, 358 (1934).

[18] N. 12 *supra*.

[19] Walker v. Bailey, 245 F.2d 486, 114 U.S.P.Q. 302 (C.C.P.A. 1959).

[20] N. 16 *supra*.

[21] N. 17 *supra*.

[22] Ballard v. City of Pittsburgh, 12 Fed. 783, 784 (C.C.W.D. Pa. 1882). See also, Smith v. Dental Vulcanite Co., 93 U.S. (3 Otto) 486, 491 (1877) (extreme poverty).

[23] Morway v. Bondi, 203 F.2d 742, 97 U.S.P.Q. 318 (C.C.P.A. 1953).

[24] 35 U.S.C. 102(g).

[25] Kirkham v. Arden, 316 F.2d 242, 247, 137 U.S.P.Q. 370, 374 (C.C.P.A. 1963).

[26] Watson v. Allen, 254 F.2d 342, 346, 117 U.S.P.Q. 68, 70 (D.C.C. 1958).

[27] See generally, Hull v. Davenport, 90 F.2d 103, 33 U.S.P.Q. 506 (C.C.P.A. 1937).

[28] Conner v. Joris, 241 F.2d 944, 113 U.S.P.Q. 56 (C.C.P.A. 1957); Tansel v. Higonnet, 215 F.2d 457, 103 U.S.P.Q. 58 (C.C.P.A. 1955).

[29] D'Amico v. Koike, 347 F.2d 867, 869, 146 U.S.P.Q. 132, 133 (C.C.P.A. 1965); Jepson v. Egly, 231 F.2d 947, 951, 109 U.S.P.Q. 354, 357 (C.C.P.A. 1956).

[30] See for example, Keizer v. Bradley, 270 F.2d 396, 398, 123 U.S.P.Q. 215, 216 (C.C.P.A. 1959); Fitzgerald v. Arbib, 268 F.2d 763, 766, 122 U.S.P.Q. 530, 532 (C.C.P.A. 1959).

[31] Chamberlain v. Kleist, 112 F.2d 846, 46 U.S.P.Q. 93 (C.C.P.A. 1940); Weston v. Beneke, 1908 C.D. 266, 137 O.G. 1709 (Comm. Pat. 1908).

[32] Kear v. Roder, 115 F.2d 810, 47 U.S.P.Q. 458 (C.C.P.A. 1940).

[33] Winslow v. Austin, 14 App. D.C. 137, 1899 C.D. 301 (D.C.C. 1899).

[34] N. 32 *supra*.

[35] Schmidt v. Clark, 32 App. D.C. 290, 294-295, 1909 C.D. 280, 283-284 (D.C.C. 1908).

[36] M.P.E.P. 1706.

[37] See generally, Fersing v. Fast, 121 F.2d 531, 50 U.S.P.Q. 112 (C.C.P.A. 1941).

[38] Rule 257. See also, Henning v. Hunt, 223 F.2d 926, 106 U.S.P.Q. 307 (C.C.P.A. 1955).

[39] 35 U.S.C. 104. Rule 217(2).

[40] 35 U.S.C. 104.
[41] 35 U.S.C. 291.
[42] M.P.E.P. 1101.01.
[43] M.P.E.P. 1101.
[44] Martin v. Snyder, 214 F.2d 177, 102 U.S.P.Q. 306 (C.C.P.A. 1955); Potts v. Kimball, 134 F.2d 327, 56 U.S.P.Q. 556 (C.C.P.A. 1943).
[45] M.P.E.P. 1101.
[46] M.P.E.P. 1101.01.
[47] M.P.E.P. 1101.
[48] Rule 203(b).
[49] Rule 201(b).
[50] See Ex parte Card & Card, 1904 C.D. 383, 112 O.G. 499 (Comm. Pat. 1904).
[51] Tolle v. Starkey, 255 F.2d 935, 936, 118 U.S.P.Q. 292, 294 (C.C.P.A. 1958).
[52] See for example, Natta v. Baxter, 179 U.S.P.Q. 692 (Bd. Pat. Int. 1973).
[53] Clauss v. Foulke, 379 F.2d 586, 154 U.S.P.Q. 85 (C.C.P.A. 1967); Ludwig v. Sohn, 324 F.2d 1004, 139 U.S.P.Q. 500 (C.C.P.A. 1963); McKee v. Noonan, 86 F.2d 986, 32 U.S.P.Q. 44 (C.C.P.A. 1936).
[54] M.P.E.P. 1102.01, 1102.01(a).
[55] Rule 207, M.P.E.P. 1102.02.
[56] Rule 211.
[57] Rule 222.
[58] Rules 218, 207(b), 245.
[59] Rule 219.
[60] Rule 227.
[61] Rule 226.
[62] Rules 231, 237.
[63] Rule 211.
[64] Rule 258.
[65] Rules 272, 277, 278.
[66] Rule 256.
[67] Rule 258. See generally, Moler v. Purdy, 131 U.S.P.Q. 276 (Bd. Pat. Int. 1960). See also Kreek, "Ancillary and Nonancillary Matters in Patent Interferences," 36 J. Pat. Off. Soc'y 7 (1954).
[68] 35 U.S.C. 135(c).
[69] Rule 262.
[70] 35 U.S.C. 141, 145.
[71] 35 U.S.C. 291.
[72] 35 U.S.C. 135.

Chapter 10

THE INVENTIVE ENTITY
AND
EMPLOYER-EMPLOYEE RIGHTS

SYNOPSIS

> Today the solitary inventor, tinkering in his shop, has been overshadowed by task forces of scientists, in laboratories and testing fields.
>
> D.D. Eisenhower,
> Farewell Address, 1961

In the popular mind, the inventor is a lone individual, almost heroic in stature, who has, all by himself, created his invention and who enjoys fruits fully commensurate with his contribution to civilization. Goodyear, Edison, Bell, and Westinghouse are but a few of the very many who fit this stereotype. In the eyes of the law, however, two unwarranted conclusions are present in this peculiarly American folk legend: (1) that an invention is necessarily the product of one mind; and (2) that the person who does the inventing owns the patent rights flowing from his invention.

This chapter will take a closer look at two related problems arising from the fact that more than a single individual may have an interest in the making or ownership of an invention. Stated simply, these problems are: (1) In securing a patent, who must be named as co-inventors? (2) How are patent rights to be allocated between employer and employee?

At the outset, it should be noted that there is a distinction between: (1) who gets nominal credit for an invention, that is, who must be named in a patent as joint or co-inventors; and (2) who has a proprietary interest in the patent. These two issues are treated differently, in that the solution to the first, under a given set of facts, is prescribed by law—and by federal law at that! Agreement between the parties cannot make one an inventor who in fact is not an inventor.[1] On the contrary, the allocation of proprietary rights in an invention is subject to agreement between the parties. Moreover, the construction of such agreements is governed by state common law, rather than by federal law.

§ 1. The Inventive Entity

Although it is convenient to speak of an invention as the product of *an* inventor, an invention may be the product of more than one mind. Indeed, the law mandates that application for a patent be made only in the name of no less than and no more than *all* its joint inventors. The statutory basis for this rule is found in Sections 102(f) and 116 of the Patent Act, which couch this requirement in the following language:

> *Section 102(f)*: A person shall be entitled to a patent unless he did not himself invent the subject matter sought to be patented . . . .
>
> *Section 116*: When an invention is made by two or more persons jointly, they shall apply for patent jointly and each sign the application and make the required oath, except as otherwise provided in this title.

Generic to "inventor" and "inventor*s*" is the term "inventive entity," which term will hereinafter be used to signify the person or persons, as the case may be, that were jointly responsible for the making of an invention.

A recent court opinion well sums up the law relating to the question of the nature of the contribution which entitles one to the status of a joint or co-inventor:[2]

> The exact parameters of what constitutes joint inventorship are quite difficult to define. It is one of the muddiest concepts in the muddy metaphysics of the patent law. On the one hand, it is reasonably clear that a person who has merely followed instructions of another in performing experiemnts is not a co-inventor of the object to which those experiments are directed.

> To claim inventorship is to claim at least some role in the final conception of that which is sought to be patented. Perhaps one need not be able to point to a specific component as one's sole idea, but one must be able to say that without his contribution to the final conception, it would have been less—less efficient, less simple, less economical, less something of benefit.

To the foregoing should be added the fact that, while merely supplying data or other information does not constitute one an inventor,[3] one is not precluded from making an inventive contribution because he is subject to the supervision of another. In the course of performing experiments or tests, an assistant may make a suggestion which raises him to the dignity of a joint or even the sole inventor.[4] The law draws the distinction between those who plan or design and those who merely build according to the preconceived plans of another.[5] In order to constitute two persons as joint inventors, it is not necessary that the inventive concept have come to both simultaneously; some features may be contributed by one and other features by the other.[6] However, all those parties named as joint inventors must have made some contribution to <u>all</u> the claims.[7]

One is not entitled to claim the rank of inventor merely because of his employer status.[8] That employees are under a contractual obligation to assign their inventions does not ipso facto make the employer a co-inventor.

An application for a patent made by two or more persons claiming to be joint inventors is prima facie evidence that they are such.[9] The Patent Office may rely upon such a representation, and the burden is on one attacking the relationship to show affirmatively by extrinsic proof that it is erroneous.

While perhaps self-evident to the reader, mention will nevertheless be made of the distinction between joint inventorship and priority of invention. Joint inventors all collaborate in and contribute to a common result. Priority of invention involves competing rights of strangers, each of whom separately and independently of the other contestants arrived at the same complete result. Joint inventors share credit for their efforts. In the absence of any agreement to the contrary, each joint inventor may make, use, or sell the patented invention without the consent of and without accounting to the other owners.[10] The question of priority of invention, on the contrary, is resolved in favor of the one party, at the expense of all the others. Of course, it is possible to have a priority contest between parties one or more of whom are joint inventors. Priority of invention is treated at length in Chapter 9.

It is most important to bear in mind that the law deems each different combination of inventors as an entirely separate and distinct entity. Thus, a patent granted to *X* and *Y*, as joint inventors, is effective as prior art against a subsequent invention made by *X, Y,* and *Z* jointly. Similarly, a joint application or patent and a sole application or patent by one of the joint inventors are different legal entities and, accordingly, upon issuance as a patent, the earlier filed application becomes a reference for everything it discloses. Different entities constitute, in effect, different inventors.[11]

§ 2. Nonjoinder and Misjoinder

The failure to name less than all who jointly contributed to the making of an invention is called nonjoinder; the naming of one or more persons who did not contribute to the making of an invention is called misjoinder.

Formerly, nonjoinder or misjoinder made a patent fatally and incurably defective.[12]

Section 116 of the present Patent Act provides a remedy for the nonjoinder or misjoinder of inventors in a pending application:

> Whenever a person is joined in an application for patent as joint inventor through error, or a joint inventor is not included in an application through error, and such error arose without any deceptive intention on his part, the Commissioner may permit the application to be amended accordingly, under such terms as he prescribes.

Section 256 of the present Patent Act provides a remedy for the nonjoinder or misjoinder of inventions in an issued *patent:*

> Whenever a patent is issued on the application of persons as joint inventors and it appears that one of such persons was not in fact a joint inventor, and that he was included as a joint inventor by error and without any deceptive intention, the Commissioner may, on application of all parties and assignees, with proof of the facts and such other requirements as may be

imposed, issue a certificate deleting the name of the erroneously joined person from the patent.

Whenever a patent is issued on the application of persons as joint inventor, but was omitted by error and without deceptive intention on his part, the Commissioner may, on application of all the parties and assignees, with proof of the facts and such other requirements as may be imposed, issue a certificate adding his name to the patent as a joint inventor.

The misjoinder or nonjoinder of joint inventors shall not invalidate a patent, if such error can be corrected as provided in this section. The court before which such matter is called in question may order correction of the patent on notice and hearing of all parties concerned and the Commissioner shall issue a certificate accordingly.

It is important to bear in mind that nonjoinder and misjoinder may be corrected only as provided for by the above statutes. Thus, it has been held that assignment to the first inventor was ineffective to cure a defect in that patent, where the defect was that the application had been made by one who was not the inventor.[13]

Not too long ago, the New Jersey state courts were called upon to resolve an interesting question relating to the right of an inventor to receive nominal credit for his (actually in this case, her) invention. The plaintiff alleged that she had, while in the course of the defendant's employment, made an invention covering a method of making and using a certain chemical compound. The defendant corporation had a patent application, in the name of another, prepared and filed, which application disclosed (1) that compound and (2) the method of making and using the compound alleged to have been invented by the plaintiff. The plaintiff conceded that she was not an inventor of the compound per se. The application, which eventually matured into a patent, made no mention of the plaintiff as a joint inventor. Although there subsisted a valid contract which assigned to the defendant corporation all proprietary rights in inventions to be made by the plaintiff during the course of her employment, the plaintiff sued on the theory that the failure to name her as a co-inventor constituted an actionable wrong. The court ultimately held for the defendant on the ground that the patent contained claims directed solely to the compound per se, no claims being directed to plaintiff's method of making and us.[14] It should be noted, however, that disclosure of a method of making and using the chemical composition is an essential part of every patent claiming a composition of matter![15]

§ 3. Rights of Employer and Employee Inter Se

While the abstract rules of law relating to the allocation of proprietary rights between an employee-inventor and his employer are simple, their application to concrete facts is often difficult. Though this law is largely state-created common law, and thus subject to vary from jurisdiction to jurisdiction, the decisions in this field have exhibited an almost uncanny uniformity, which fit into the following pattern:

(1) Where there subsists a contract between employer and employee covering the subject of employee-made inventions, the terms of such contract control the allocation of proprietary rights between the parties.

An employer may claim a proprietary interest in inventions made by his employee, if the contract of employment either:

(a) expressly calls for the assignment of employee made inventions to the employer; or

(b) is to the effect that the employee has been hired to make a particular invention or to give himself to the task of solving a particular problem.

(2) In the absence of a contract between employer and employee covering the subject of employee-made inventions, andy inventions made by the employee are his exclusive property with the qualification that the employer is entitled to a non-exclusive license to make and use the invention of his employee to which the employer has made some contribution, as that they were made during the hours of employment and/or using the employer's equipment and materials.[16] Such a nonexclusive license is known as an employer's "shop right."

Courts are reluctant to imply or infer an agreement by the employee to assign to his employer a proprietary interest in what he has invented.[17] Before the law will require of an employee that he turn over to his employer any invention made by him, it must be abundantly clear that the subject matter of the invention in question falls squarely withing the scope of his employment. Where the contract of employment falls short of calling for the assignment of employee inventions, the employer will be entitled to an assignment only where he can establish that the employee had been hired to make that invention, that is to say, the employer must demonstrate that the invention was the precise object of the inventor's employment. The fact that the invention falls within the field in which the employee has been hired to work does not make it the property of the employer. Moreover, employment merely to design, or to construct, or to devise methods of manufacture is deemed general employment, as distinguished from employment to invent.[18]

It was held by the United States Supreme Court that employees of the United States whose job it was to solve the problem of operating a relay for remote control of bombs, who during the hours of such employment and with the knowledge and cooperation of their supervisors, also devoted themselves, with the use of government-owned facilities, to the problem of applying alternating current to broadcast receiving sets, were personally entitled to the patents flowing from the latter activity. The government-employer gained for itself but a shop right—a royalty-free, nonexclusive license.[19]

It should be noted that a contract of employment may properly call for the assignment to the employer of even those inventions which may be made entirely on the employee's own time and/or entirely with his own funds and/or totally unrelated to the field in which he is employed. It may further call for the assignment of inventions made prior to the date employment commenced and/or for a reasonable time after employment is terminated. Moreover, rather than specifying inventions made by the employee, it may call for inventions "conceived and/or reduced to practice by" the employee. A recent case has held that a corporation had no proprietary interest in an invention that was admittedly *conceived* by one of its former employees while he was in its service, where the contract of employment only called for the assignment to the corporation of inventions *made* by that former employee.[20]

§ 4. An Employee's Obligations in Regard to His Employer's Trade Secrets

A significant problem engendered by the employer-employee relationship involves the rights and obligations of an employee, or former employee, in regard to trade secrets which the employee has not himself created or developed, but which were merely confided to him by the employer in the course of his employment.

A contract of employment may expressly prohibit an employee from divulging or making unauthorized use of his employer's trade secrets, and may further preclude the employee from employment with a competitor. Such restrictive covenants, if not unreasonable, and if ancillary to employment, are enforceable in most jurisdictions.[21] In measuring the reasonableness of a restrictive covenant, weight will be accorded to such factors as the duration and geographical extent of the restriction. The more it is limited in time and geography, the more likely it will be found to be reasonable and enforceable.

Even in the absence of an express covenant, an employee or former employee is, in most jurisdictions, precluded, at least theoretically, from divulging or making use of, for his personal benefit, confidential information that was acquired by him as a necessary consequence of his employment.[22]

However, in the absence of a restrictive covenant, most courts are extremely reluctant to enjoin an employee from employment of his choosing. An employee is entitled to use the skill and knowledge of his trade or profession which he has learned in the course of his employment, for the benefit of himself and the public, if he does not violate a contractual or fiduciary obligation in doing so.[23] As a practical matter, if his employment is not enjoined, it is nigh impossible to stop the employee from making use, in such employment, of all that he knows, including any trade secrets.

Where improper use has been made of trade secrets, there is a split of authority on whether an injunction against the wrongdoer is to continue after the information has become generally known. One line of cases, following the so-called "Conmar rule," holds that the sanctions survive.[24] A majority of American jurisdictions, however, follow the so-called "Shellmar rule," which is that an injunction issued to protect a trade secret terminates after its secrecy ends.[25]

Notes

[1] Lorenz v. Berkline Corp., 215 F. Supp. 869, 137 U.S.P.Q. 29 (N.D. Ill. 1963); Koehring Co. v. E.D. Etnyre & Co., 254 F. Supp. 334, 149 U.S.P.Q. 263 (N.D. Ill. 1966).

[2] Mueller Brass Co. v. Reading Indus., Inc., 352 F. Supp. 1357, 1372, 176 U.S.P.Q. 361, 372 (E.D. Pa. 1972).

[3] See O'Reilly v. Morse, 56 U.S. (15 How.) 61, lll (1853).

[4] De Laski & Thropp C.W.T. Co. v. Wm. R. Thropp & Sons Co., 218 Fed. 458, 464 (D.N.J. 1914), *aff'd* 226 Fed. 941 (3d Cir. 1915). Compare, Agawam Woolen Co. v. Jordan, 74 U.S. (9 Wall.) 583 (1869).

[5] Bull v. Logetronics, Inc., 323 F. Supp. 115, 129, 168 U.S.P.Q. 342, 352 (E.D. Va. 1971).

[6] Moler & Adams v. Purdy, 131 U.S.P.Q. 276 (Bd. Pat. Int. 1960); Cheshier v. Cox Multi-Mailer Co. v. Krause, 151 Fed. 1012 (6th Cir. 1907).

[7] De Laval Separator Co. v. Vermont Farm Mach. Co., 135 Fed. 772 (2d Cir. 1904).

[8] Koehring Co. v. E.D. Etnyre & Co., 254 F. Supp. 334, 149 U.S.P.Q. 263, 266 (N.D. Ill. 1966).

[9] Van Otteren v. Hafner, 278 F.2d 738, 126 U.S.P.Q. 151 (C.C.P.A. 1960). See also, Holstensson v. Webcor, 150 F. Supp. 441, 112 U.S.P.Q. 463 (N.D. Ill. 1957).

[10] Drake v. Hall, 220 Fed. 905 (7th Cir. 1914).

[11] Ex parte Utshig, 156 U.S.P.Q. 157 (P.O. Bd. App. 1967).

[12] City of Milwaukee v. Activated Sludge, Inc., 69 F.2d 577, 587, 21 U.S.P.Q. 69, 79 (7th Cir.), *cert. denied* 293 U.S. 576 (1934).

[13] Lorenz v. Berkline Corp., 215 F. Supp. 869, 137 U.S.P.Q. 29 (N.D. Ill. 1963).

[14] Misani v. Ortho Pharmaceutical Corp., 141 U.S.P.Q. 53 (N.J. Sup. Ct.), *cert. denied* 382 U.S. 203 (1965).

[15] 35 U.S.C. 112.

[16] Cahill v. Regan, 121 U.S.P.Q. 58 (N.Y. Ct. App. 1959).

[17] United States v. Dubilier Condenser Corp., 289 U.S. 178, 188, 17 U.S.P.Q. 154, 158 (1933).

[18] *Ibid.*

[19] United States v. Dubilier Condenser Corp., 289 U.S. 178, 192, 17 U.S.P.Q. 154, 160 (1933).

[20] Jamesbury Corp. v. Worcester Valve Co., 443 F.2d 205, 170 U.S.P.Q. 177 (1st Cir. 1971).

[21] See generally, United States v. Addyston Pipe & Steel Co., 175 U.S. 211 (1899).

[22] E.I. du Pont de Nemours & Co. v. American Potash & Chem. Corp., 200 A.2d 428, 141 U.S.P.Q. 447 (Ct. Chan. Del. 1964); B.F. Goodrich Co. v. Wohlgemuth, 192 N.E.2d 99, 137 U.S.P.Q. 804 (Ohio Ct. App. 1963).

[23] Space Aero Prod. Co. v. R.E. Darling Co., 145 U.S.P.Q. 356, 362 (Md. Ct. App. 1965); Koehring Co. v. E.D. Etnyre & Co., 254 F. Supp. 334, 362, 149 U.S.P.Q. 263, 286 (N.D. Ill. 1966).

[24] Conmar Prod. Corp. v. Universal Slide Fastener, 172 F.2d 150, 80 U.S.P.Q. 108 (2d Cir. 1949).

[25] Shellmar Prod. Co. v. Allen-Qualley Co., 87 F.2d 104, 32 U.S.P.Q. 24 (7th Cir.), *cert denied* 301 U.S. 695 (1936).

Chapter 11

GOVERNMENT INTERESTS IN PATENTS: PROCUREMENT & OWNERSHIP

SYNOPSIS

> When a government enters into a contract with an individual, it deposes, as to the matter of the contract, its constitutional authority, and exchanges the character of legislator for that of a moral agent, with the same rights and obligations as an individual. Its promises may be justly considered as excepted out of its power to legislate unless in aid of them. It is in theory impossible to reconcile the idea of a promise which obliges, with a power to make a law which can vary the effect of it.
>
> A. Hamilton,
> 3 *Hamilton's Works* 518-519

The United States acts in a dual capacity with respect to patents, in that it is both the grantor and a user of patent rights. The fact that the United States grants a patent, however, in and of itself gives the government no license to use the same. The ways in which it is possible for the United States or any of the states to gain access to patent rights include: (1) those by which a corporation may gain access to such rights (viz., by contract, as by purchase or as a result of the creative efforts of its employees); and (2) those special procedures reserved for a sovereign, that is, by taking under the power of eminent domain or pursuant to an exercise of the police power.

§ 1. Inventions Made with Federal Funds

The United States may have a proprietary interest in an invention because the research which generated the same was federally funded. Into this category fall inventions made not only by actual employees of the United States but also inventions made by private contractors and employees of private contractors in the course of carrying through projects funded by the United States. The extent of the government's proprietary interest in such inventions varies according to such factors as the extent to which government funds were used, the nature of the invention made, and the particular agency from which the funds were received.

[1] By Federal Employees

It has been held that, in the absence of agreement or controlling regulations, established common-law doctrines define the rights in inventions made by federal employees.[1] Since 1950, however, the rights of the United States in inventions made by its employees have been subject to Executive Order 10096, which sets a uniform, government-wide policy in regard to inventions made by any federal employee, civilian or military. Prior to that time each agency and department was largely free to formulate its own rules.

Executive Order 10096 (January 23, 1950) provides inter alia:

> (a) The United States shall obtain the entire right, title and interest in and to all inventions made by any Government employee made (1) during working hours; *or* (2) with a contribution by the Government of facilities, equipment, materials, funds or information, or of time or services of other Government employees on official duty; *or* (3) which bear a direct relation to or are made in consequence of the official duties of the inventor.
>
> (b) In any case where the contribution of the United States, as measured by any one or more of the criteria set forth in paragraph (a) above, to the invention is insufficient equitably to justify a requirement of assignment to the United States of the entire right, title and interest in such invention, or in any case where the United States has insufficient interest in an invention to obtain entire right, title and interest therein, the Government agency concerned, subject to the approval of the Chairman of

the Government Patent Board, shall leave title to such invention in the employee, subject, however, to the reservation to the Government of a nonexclusive, irrevocable, royalty-free license in the invention with power to grant licenses for all government purposes, such reservation to appear, where practicable, in any patent, domestic or foreign, which may issue on such invention.

(c) Inventions made by federal employees under any of the following circumstances are presumed to fall within the provisions of paragraph (a) above if: (i) The invention was made by an employee who was employed or assigned to invent or improve or perfect any art, machine, manufacture, or composition of matter; (ii) to conduct or perform research, development work, or both, (iii) to supervise, direct, coordinate, or review Government financed or conducted research, development work, or both; or (iv) to act in a liaison capacity among governmental or non-governmental agencies or individuals engaged in such work, or made by an employee included within any other category of employees specified by regulation. Inventions made by federal employees under any other circumstances are presumed to fall under paragraph (b) above. Either presumption may be rebutted by the facts or circumstances attendant upon the condition under which any particular invention is made and, notwithstanding the foregoing, shall not preclude a determination that the invention falls within the provisions of paragraph (d).

(d) In any case wherein the Government neither (1) pursuant to the provision of paragraph (a) above, obtains entire right, title and interest in and to an invention nor (2) pursuant to the provisions of paragraph (b) above, reserves a non-exclusive, irrevocable, royalty-free license in the invention with power to grant licenses for all governmental purposes, the Government shall leave the entire right, title and interest in and to the invention in the Government employee, subject to law.

In addition to the possibility of gaining proprietary rights in inventions in which the Government is either not interested or to which it has made minimal financial contribution, federal employees are entitled to cash awards for special contributions or services, including inventions. The amount of an award ranges from a token sum to thousands of dollars, depending on the inventor-employee's agency and the value of the invention to the Government.

Officers and employees of the Patent Office are precluded, by statute, during the period of their appointments and for one year thereafter, from applying for a patent and acquiring, directly or indirectly, except by inheritance or bequest, any patent or any right or interest in any patent, issued or to be issued by the Office. In patents applied for thereafter, former officers and employees of the Patent Office are not entitled to any priority date earlier than one year after the termination of their appointment.[2]

The Government Patent Board established by Executive Order 10096 was abolished by Executive Order 10930 (March 24, 1961), which Order also transferred all of the Government Patent Board's functions to the Secretary of Commerce, who in turn authorized the Commissioner of Patents to arrange for the performance of these duties.[3] Pursuant to this authority, the Commissioner of Patents now reviews cases arising from all agencies except the Atomic Energy Commission (which has its own Compensation Board) to determine the extent of a government employee's domestic rights.[4] The Commissioner of Patents may revise the terms set by the employee's own agency. An employee dissatisfied with the Commissioner's decision may take his case to the United States Court of Claims.

Government agencies are authorized by Executive Order 10096, with respect to inventions made under circumstances defined in paragraph 1(a) of this Order, either to prepare and file an application for patent therefor in the United States Patent Office or fully to disclose by publication such inventions, provided that the disclosure would not be detrimental to national security, or public health, safety, or welfare.

It should be noted that a protracted statute of limitations is provided for by 35 U.S.C. 267 for patent applications which are the property of the United States. It provides that notwithstanding the provisions of 35 U.S.C. 133 and 35 U.S.C. 151, the Commissioner may extend the time for taking any action to three years, when an application has become the property of the United States and the head of the appropriate department or agency of the Government has certified to the Commissioner that the invention disclosed therein is important to the armament or defense of the United States.

[2] By Nonfederal Employees

There is no uniform policy among the agencies and departments of the federal government, comparable to that set for federal employees by Executive Order 10096, with respect to inventions made in the course of or under contract with outside organizations with federal funds. Rather, each agency and department is left free to establish its own policy within the broad guidelines set out in President Kennedy's Memorandum and Statement of Government Patent Policy (October 10, 1963). This memorandum provides inter alia that:

> (a) Where (1) a principal purpose of the contract is to create, develope, or improve products, processes, or methods which are intended for commercial use (or which are otherwise intended to be made available for use) by the general public at home or abroad, or which will be required for such use by governmental regulations; or (2) a principal purpose of the contract is for exploration into fields which directly concern the public health or public welfare; or (3) the contract is in a field of science or technology in which there has been little significant experience outside of work funded by the government, or where the government has been the principal developer of the field, and the acquisition of exclusive rights at the time of contracting might confer on the contractor a preferred or dominant position; or (4) the services of the contractor are (i) for the operation of a government-owned research or production facility; or (ii) for coordinating and directing the work of others, the government shall normally acquire or reserve the right to acquire the principal or exclusive rights throughout the world in and to any invention made in the course of or under the contract. In exceptional circumstance the contractor may acquire greater rights than a non-exclusive license at the time of contracting, where the head of the department or agency certifies that such action will best serve the public interest. Greater rights may also be acquired by the contractor after the invention has been identified, where the invention when made in the course of or under the contract is not a primary object of the contract, provided the acquisition of such greater rights is consistent with the intent of this Section 1(a) and is a necessary incentive to call forth private risk capital and expense to bring the invention to the point of practical application.
>
> (b) In other situations, where the purpose of the contract is to

build upon existing knowledge or technology, to develop information, products, processes, or methods for use by the government, and the work called for by the contract is in a field of technology in which the contractor has acquired technical competence (demonstrated by factors such as know-how, experience, and patent position) directly related to an area in which the contractor has an established nongovernmental commercial position, the contractor shall normally acquire the principal or exclusive rights throughout the world in and to any resulting inventions, subject to the government acquiring at least an irrevocable nonexclusive royalty-free license throughout the world for governmental purposes.

(c) Where the commercial interests of the contractor are not sufficiently established to be covered by the criteria specified in Section 1(b), above, the determination of rights shall be made by the agency after the invention has been identified, in a manner deemed most likely to serve the public interest as expressed in this policy statement, taking particularly into account the intentions of the contractor to bring the invention to the point of commercial application and the guidelines of Section 1(a) hereof, provided that the agency may prescribe by regulation special situations where the public interest in the availability of the inventions would best be served by permitting the contractor to acquire at the time of contracting greater rights than a nonexclusive license. In any case the government shall acquire at least a nonexclusive license throughout the world for governmental purposes.

The manner in which each of the departments and agencies most concerned with research and development has implemented the foregoing policy will now be summarized.

[3] The Atomic Energy Commission

Unless it waives the rights, the Atomic Energy Commission (AEC) owns the inventions made by its contractors.[6]

Moreover, Section 151(a) of the Atomic Energy Act of 1954 specifically precludes from patent protection "any invention or discovery which is useful solely in the utilization of special nuclear material or atomic energy in an atomic weapon."[7] In lieu of patent protection, that Act establishes a Patent Compensation Board,[8] which has the power to grant just compensation to inventors of atomic weapons, as well as to inventors of other inventions in the atomic energy field which the Commission has declared are "affected with a public interest"[9] and to which a compulsory license has been acquired by the Commission or by other interested parties.[10] The Patent Compensation Board also passes upon the proprietary rights in inventions in the atomic energy field made pursuant to government contract.

Section 151(c) of the Atomic Energy Act of 1954[11] requires the Commissioner of Patents to notify the Atomic Energy Commission of all applications for patent which, in his opinion, disclose or which appear to disclose, or which purport to disclose, inventions or discoveries relating to atomic energy.[12]

[4] The National Aeronautics and Space Administration

The National Aeronautics and Space Administration Act not only provides that all inventions made by its contractors are the exclusive property of the United States, but further that all patents covering inventions which appear to the Commissioner of Patents to have significant utility in the conduct of aeronautical and space activities shall issue in the name of the Administrator of the National Aeronautics and Space Administration (NASA) on behalf of the United States, unless the applicant can establish that he made the invention independently of the performance of any work under any contract of the administration.[13] In order to prevent the patent from issuing in the name of the Administrator, the applicant must file with the Commissioner of Patents, either when he files his patent application or within thirty days after request therefor by the Commissioner, a written statement executed under oath setting forth the full facts concerning the circumstances under which such invention was made and stating the relationships (if any) of such invention to the performance of any work under any contract of the Administration.[14] If the Administrator contests the right of the applicant to a patent, the matter is referred to the Patent Office Board of Patent Interferences, whose decisions in such matters are subject to review by the Court of Customs and Patent Appeals.[15]

The Administrator is authorized to waive all or any part of the rights of the United States with respect to inventions made in the performance or any work required by any contract of the Administration, if the Administrator determines that the interests of the United States will be served thereby. Each such waiver shall be subject to the reservation by the Administrator of an irrevocable, nonexclusive, nontransferable, royalty-free license for the practice of such invention throughout the world by or on behalf of the United States or any foreign government pursuant to any treaty or agreement with the United States. To assist the Administrator in deciding whether and what rights should be waived, the National Aeronautics and Space Act provides for an Inventions and Contributions Board. Each proposal for a waiver is referred to the Inventions and Contributions Board, which holds hearings and makes findings of fact and recommendations which are transmitted to the Administrator.[16]

[5] The Tennessee Valley Authority

The statute creating the Tennessee Valley Authority (TVA) specifically provides that all inventions by employees of the Authority and of the United States made "by virtue of and incidental to" their employment are the sole and exclusive property of the Authority.[17] The board of directors of the Authority may pay to such inventors such sums from the income from the sale of licenses as it may deem proper.

This statute, moreover, grants the Authority access to any "process for the production of fixed nitrogen, or any essential ingredient of fertilizer, or any method of improving and cheapening the production of hydroelectric power."[18] The exclusive remedy of the patent owner whose rights are thereby infringed is a cause of action against the Authority in the appropriate district court of the United States, for the recovery of reasonable compensation for such infringement. The Authority does not have access to pending applications for patent.

[6] Other Government Agencies and Departments

Most other government agencies have no special laws governing their patent activities, being subject only to the aforementioned statements of executive policy and whatever regulations each agency has promulgated pursuant thereto. The policies of these agencies toward inventions made by their own employees and by outside contractors depends largely upon the extent to which the subject matter of the work being performed is intended to have commercial applications for public use. Accordingly, where the principal objective of the project is of a military nature, as in many of those sponsored by the Department of Defense, the government often takes merely a royalty-free, irrevocable, worldwide, nonexclusive license, for government use, leaving the employee or contractor with title to the invention and the commercial patent rights. On the other hand, where the principal objectives of the project are commercial and consumer oriented, as are many of those conducted by the Departments of Agriculture; Health, Education and Welfare; and the Interior, the government will take title to the invention and to any patents issuing thereon.

§ 2. Public Access to Government-Owned Inventions

It can be argued that inventions and patents generated with tax dollars should be freely available to all taxpayers.[19] It is a curious paradox of economic reality, however, that the public may enjoy an invention less when freely available than when the same is subject to an exclusive right to manufacture. Additional capital is needed to transform an idea into a reality. Private investors are reluctant to risk their capital on new and untried products, absent a sheltered market therefor.

Accordingly, it is the policy of the United States to grant, through the appropriate agency, nonexclusive, royalty-free licenses to all government-owned inventions upon request.[20] Such licenses are revocable either upon the failure of the licensee to market the invention within a reasonable period or to report on its utilization. If after the invention has been published as available for licensing on a nonexclusive, royalty-free basis for a period of at least six months, no such licenses have been granted and utilization is believed not to exist, the invention will then be offered to the general public on an exclusive license basis for a limited period, not to exceed five years, unless the head of the government agency involved determines on the basis of a written submission supported by a factual showing that a longer period is reasonably necessary to permit the licensee to enter the market and recoup his reasonable costs in so doing.[21] An exclusive license on a government invention may require the payment of royalties. The regulations under which exclusive licenses may be granted contain numerous safeguards to protect the public interest. Nevertheless, a United States district court, in a suit brought by a consumer advocate group, has voided the regulations relating to the granting of exclusive licenses on government owned patents, holding that the Constitution prohibits the granting of exclusive licenses on government-owned patents and inventions without congressional authorization.[22] This ruling has been appealed.

§ 3. Government Access to Privately Owned Patents

Government access to privately-owned inventions begins at the patent application stage. As was noted above, the Atomic Energy Act of 1954 and the National Aeronautics and Space Act of 1958 require the Commissioner of Patents to screen all applications for atomic energy and aeronautics and space subject matter.

Section 181 of the Patent Act further requires that the Commissioner of Patents make all applications for patent, the publication of which might, in his opinion, be detrimental to the national security, available for inspection by the Atomic Energy Commission, the Secretary of Defense, and the chief officer of any other department or agency of the Government designated by the President as a defense agency of the United States—even in regard to inventions in which the Government clearly has no proprietary interest.

If, in the opinion of any of the foregoing agencies, the publication or disclosure of any invention by the granting of a patent therefor would be detrimental to the national security, the chief officer of such agency must notify the Commissioner of Patents, and the Commissioner must order that the invention be kept secret and withhold the grant of a patent for such period as the national interest requires, and notify the applicant thereof. Upon proper showing by the head of the agency who caused the secrecy order to be issued that the examination of the application might jeopardize the national interest, the Commissioner shall thereupon maintain the application in a sealed condition and notify the applicant thereof.

In peacetime, an invention cannot be ordered kept secret and the grant of a patent withheld for a period of more than one year. The Commissioner may, however, renew the order at the end of the year, or at the end of any renewal period, for additional periods of one year upon notification by the head of the agency who caused the order to be issued that an affirmative determination has been made that the national interest continues so to require.

Section 183 of the Patent Act provides for compensation for the damage to the applicant caused by an order of secrecy. This section authorizes the head of the agency that was responsible for the imposition of the order of secrecy, upon the presentation of a claim, to determine the amount of compensation to which the applicant or patentee is entitled by reason of the order of secrecy. A claimant dissatisfied with the amount of the award offered by the agency may accept seventy-five percent of the sum proffered thereby and sue for the difference between that sum and the amount of compensation to which he feels entitled in the Court of Claims or in the District Court of the United States for the district in which the claimant is a resident. If the claimant does not apply to the agency that was responsible for the secrecy order, he may wait until the patent issues and then sue for the entire amount of just compensation in the Court of Claims.

Section 182 provides that the publication, disclosure, or foreign filing of an application for patent in violation of an order of secrecy may result in a holding of abandonment. A holding of abandonment constitutes forfeiture by the applicant or his successors of all claims against the United States based upon the invention.

Access to confidential information belonging to private citizens under the aforementioned circumstances represents a reasonable exercise of the police power to protect the national security and the proprietary rights of the government. In the interest of self-preservation, a government must assume power to protect itself against, as by the suppression of, the disclosure of potentially destructive weapons and other instruments of warfare. An applicant for patent suffers no damage by reason of the government's mere inspection of his invention. Indeed, some form of governmental inspection is a condition precedent to every grant of patent. Actual use thereof by the government or damage suffered by the inventor by reason of the government's suppression, however, constitutes a taking of private property for public use—an exercise of the power of eminent domain, entitling the property owner to just compensation, as provided for by the Fifth Amendment.

The provisions made in the Patent Act for the suppression of information affecting the national security that is contained in applications for patent are but a specific application of the power of eminent domain at the patent application stage. Both the federal and state governments are vested with a general power to make use of, and to authorize others to use, patented inventions for public purposes. At least insofar as the federal government is concerned, most instances in which privately owned patent rights are taken for public use involve national defense.

The urgency and complexity of its defense needs make it impractical for the federal government to negotiate a license with each patentee whose property may be involved in the fabrication of sophisticated weaponry. Moreover, most of the supplies used by the government are procured under contract from private sources. To prevent the obstruction of government activities by disputes or litigation between private parties respecting patent rights, there exists a statute which limits the patent owner's remedy for infringement of inventions that are used or manufactured by or for the United States, without license of the owner, to an action agianst the United States in the Court of Claims for the recovery of reasonable and entire compensation for such use and manufacture.[23] By virtue of this statute, a patent owner is precluded from enjoining the United States and its suppliers from making or using his invention for governmental purposes.

In awarding government contracts, in order to secure the maximum amount of competition from firms qualified and willing to undertake the production of articles for the United States, no preference is given to a patentee or his licensee by reason of the fact that manufacture by them would not involve patent infringement. A bidder who is willing to indemnify the United States against damage claims for patent infringement stands on the same footing as the patent owner and his licensees.[24]

The Fifth Amendment, impliedly sanctions the taking of private property for public use, by requiring only that just compensation be paid therefor. Of course, public use is not defined by the Constitution. Few, however, would dispute that articles intended for use directly by the government and/or its agents fall within the meaning of a public use. Moreover, public use includes not only what is necessary for national security but also what is needed for maintaining public health and safety. Accordingly, a court, in the interest of public health, has refused to enjoin the operation of a municipal sewage disposal plant, albeit it was infringing the plaintiff's patent.[25]

Instances of expropriation initiated by judicial fiat, however, have been extremely rare. Where actually imposed, it has usually been in retaliation for blatantly culpable, or at least unconscienable, conduct.[26] To such expropriation, the euphemistic label "compulsory licensing" is usually applied. Indeed, where authorized by statute in specific areas of technology the government's usurpation of patent rights generally has taken the form of a compulsory licensing, as in the Tennessee Valley Authority Act,[27] the Atomic Energy Act of 1954,[28] and most recently in the Clean Air Act of 1970.[29] These statutes generally provide for public access to private patent rights in narrowly and well-defined fields of technology that are affected with a substantial and overriding public interest.

A significant question posed by our federal system is the extent to which the states may interfere or otherwise regulate rights created by the federal government. Chief Justice Marshall in striking down the tax imposed by the state of Maryland upon notes issued by a federally chartered bank, analogized those rights with patent rights.[30] While the states may not tax patent rights directly, they may, and do, levy taxes upon income derived therefrom. In fact, it was subsequently held by the Supreme Court that patent rights are subject, to the same extent as any other species of property, to control by the states in the legitimate exercise of their power over their purely domestic affairs, whether of internal commerce or of police.[31]

Notes

[1] United States v. Dubilier Condenser Corp., 289 U.S. 178, 17 U.S.P.Q. 154 (1933).

[2] 35 U.S.C. 4.

[3] 26 Fed. Reg. 3118.

[4] 27 Fed. Reg. 3289.

[5] 28 Fed. Reg. 200.

[6] 42 U.S.C. 2182.

[7] 42 U.S.C. 2181(a).

[8] 42 U.S.C. 2187.

[9] 42 U.S.C. 2223.

[10] 42 U.S.C. 2186.

[11] 42 U.S.C. 2181(c).

[12] See Rule 14(c).

[13] 42 U.S.C. 2457(a).

[14] 42 U.S.C. 2457(c).

[15] 42 U.S.C. 2457(d).

[16] 42 U.S.C. 2457(f).

[17] 16 U.S.C. 831d.

[18] 16 U.S.C. 831r.

[19] See generally, Tektronix v. United States, 351 F.2d 630, 147 U.S.P.Q. 216 (Ct. Cl. 1965).

[20] 41 C.F.R. 101-4.103-2.

[21] 41 C.F.R. 101-4.103-3.

[22] 28 U.S.C. 1498.

[23] Public Citizen, Inc. v. Sampson, 180 U.S.P.Q. 497 (D.D.C. 1974).

[24] 38 Op. Comp. Gen. 276 (1958).

[25] City of Milwaukee v. Activated Sludge, Inc., 69 F.2d 577, 21 U.S.P.Q. 69 (7th Cir. 1934). See also, Aerovox Corp. v. Micamold Radio Corp., 83 F.2d 409, 29 U.S.P.Q. 456 (2d Cir. 1936).

[26] Chas. Pfizer & Co. v. F.T.C., 401 F.2d 574, 159 U.S.P.Q. 193 (6th Cir. 1968), *cert. denied* 394 U.S. 920 (1969); Besser Mfg. Co. v. United States, 343 U.S. 444, 93 U.S.P.Q. 321 (1952). Compare, United States v. National Gypsum Co., 352 U.S. 457, 112 U.S.P.Q. 340 (1957); United States v. National Lead Co., 332 U.S. 319, 73 U.S.P.Q. 498 (1947); Hartford-Empire Co. v. United States, 323 U.S. 386, 414-417, 64 U.S.P.Q. 18, 38-40 (1944). See also, Allied Research Prod. Inc. v. Heatbath Corp., 300 F. Supp. 656, 161 U.S.P.Q. 529 (N.D. Ill. 1969).

[27] 16 U.S.C. 831r.

[28] 42 U.S.C. 2183, 2184.

[29] 42 U.S.C. 1857h-6 (1970).

[30] M'Culloch v. Maryland, 17 U.S. (4 Wheat.) 316, 431 (1819).

[31] Patterson v. Kentucky, 97 U.S. (7 Otto) 501, 503 (1878).

– Part IV –

OBTAINING PATENT PROTECTION

The inventor of a new and useful improvement certainly has no exclusive right to it, until he obtains a patent. This right is created by the patent, and no suit can be maintained by the inventor against any one for using it before the patent is issued. But the discovery of a new and useful improvement is vested by law with an inchoate right to its exclusive use, which he may perfect and make absolute by proceeding in the manner which the law requires.

Taney, Ch. J.
Gayler v. Wilder,
51 U.S. (10 How.) 477, 493 (1850)

The Constitution empowers the United States to grant patents for inventions. By the wording of the Constitution, this power, however, is not self-executing, but requires Congressional legislation for its implementation. Moreover, the language of the Constitution concerning patents is couched with generality comparable to that of other Constitutional grants of Congressional power, Congress having wide discretion in prescribing the conditions under which patents will be granted.

Consequently, there is a distinction between a bald invention and a patented invention. One who makes an invention, however meritorious, does not, by that act alone, automatically acquire protection. Upon making an invention, the inventor has but an inchoate right to patent protection. Such inchoate right can be perfected into a patent only upon at least apparent compliance with a plethora of elaborate formalities prescribed by Congress and by the Patent Office acting on behalf of Congress. Patent protection must be sought or solicited from the government. The process of soliciting patents from the government is often spoken of as "procurement" or as prosecution."

Chapter 12

PREPARATION OF PATENT APPLICATIONS

SYNOPSIS

The specification and claims of a patent, particularly if the invention be at all complicated, constitute one of the most difficult legal instruments to draw with accuracy, and in view of the fact that valuable inventions are often placed in the hands of inexperienced persons to prepare such specification and claims, it is no matter of surprise that the latter frequently fail to describe with requisite certainty the exact invention of the patentee, and err either in claiming that which the patentee had not in fact invented, or in omitting some element which was a valuable or essential part of his actual invention.

Brown, J.
Topliff v. Topliff,
145 U.S. 156, 171 (1892)

A complete application comprises:[1]

(1) A petition or request for a patent, see Rule 61.
(2) A specification, including a claim or claims, see Rules 71 to 77.
(3) An oath or declaration, see Rule 65.
(4) Drawings, when necessary, see Rules 81 to 88.
(5) The prescribed filing fee. (See Rule 21.)

The petition, specification, and oath or declaration must be in the English language. All papers which are to become a part of the permanent records of the Patent Office must be legibly written or printed in permanent ink.[2]

The specification and claims, and also papers subsequently filed, must be plainly written on but one side of the paper. A wide margin must be reserved on the left-hand side and on the top of each page and the lines must not be crowded too closely together. Legal paper, eight to eight-and-one-half by twelve and one-half to thirteen inches, typewritten and double-spaced with margins of one and one-half inches on the left-hand side and top is deemed preferable. Typewritten or printed papers suitable for use by the Office may be required if the papers originally filed are not correctly, legibly, and clearly written.[3]

Any interlineation, erasure or cancellation, or other alteration, made before the application was signed and sworn to, or declaration made, should be clearly referred to in a marginal note or footnote on the same sheet of paper, and initialed or signed and dated by the applicant to indicate such fact.[4]

§ 1. The Petition

In substance, the petition simply requests or prays that letters patent be granted for the invention set out in the accompanying specification.[5] It must be addressed to the Commissioner of Patents and must state the residence and post office address of the petitioner, if the same do not appear elsewhere in the application. The petition may be combined with the oath or declaration and power of attorney.[6] The petition need not be separately signed when part of and attached to the specification and oath or declaration, otherwise it must be signed by the petitioner.

The following form has been approved by the Patent Office as a petition for patent by a sole inventor:

To the Commissioner of Patents

Your petitioner, ______ ,a citizen of the United States and a resident of ______ , State of ______ ,whose post-office address is ______ , prays that letters patent may be granted to him for the improvement in ______ , set forth in the following specification.

(The specification and oath follow the petition.)

§ 2. The Oath or Declaration

As part of his application, each applicant must state:

(1) that he verily believes himself to be the original and first inventor or discoverer of the process, machine, manufacture, composition of matter, or improvement thereof, for which he solicits a patent; that he does not know and does not believe that the same was ever known or used before his invention or discovery thereof, and of what country he is a citizen and where he resides and whether he is a sole or joint inventor of the invention claimed in his application;

(2) whether or not any application for patent on the same invention has been filed in any foreign country, either by himself, or by his legal representatives or assigns. If any such application has been filed, the country in which the earliest such application was filed must be named, as must the day, month and year of its filing; every such foreign filed application filed more than twelve months[8] before the filing of the application in this country must be identified by country and by day, month, and year of filing.

In every original application, the applicant must further state:

(3) that to the best of his knowledge and belief the invention has not been in public use or on sale in the United States more than one year prior to his application or patented or described in any printed publication in any country before his invention or more than one year prior to his application or patented in any foreign country.

An application for a plant patent must, in addition to the above statements, contain an averment that the applicant has asexually reproduced the plant, and where the plant is a newly found plant, it must also be stated that the plant was found in a cultivated area.[9]

The above statements (1) must be subscribed to by the applicant and (2) must either be sworn to (or affirmed) as provided in Rule 66, or include the personal declaration of the applicant as prescribed in Rule 68.

A declaration made pursuant to Rule 68 must contain *in addition* to the averments made in an oath the following statements:

(1) that all statements made of the declarant's own knowledge are true and that all statements made on information and belief are believed to be true;

(2) a warning that willful false statements and the like are punishable by fine or imprisonment, or both (18 U.S.C. 1001) and may jeopardize the validity of the application or any patent issuing thereon.

Strictly speaking, an oath involves a swearing of the person making the same, and is, in this respect, to be distinguished from an affirmation. As used in the *Rules of Practice*, however, the distinguishing characteristic of an oath is the attestation of an authorized official (e.g., a notary public), whether the statement is sworn to or affirmed. A declaration, while it involves an affirmation, is to be distinguished from an oath in that a declaration is executed entirely by the person making the same, there being no attestation by a notary public or other authorized official.

It should be noted that the applicant who elects to submit a declaration in lieu of an oath makes a commitment beyond that made by the applicant who submits an oath, to the effect that all statements made of his own knowledge are true and that all statements made on information and belief are believed to be true. Absent this commitment, an applicant does not vouch for the truth or validity of statements made in his specification. Absent the submission of a declaration, an applicant may make, in his specification, what he knows are spurious statements with impunity. By an oath, essentially all that an applicant commits himself to is that he believes himself to be the original and first inventor of what he claims.[10] Neither by oath nor declaration does an applicant vouch for the operability of what he claims.

The oath or declaration must be submitted within a reasonable time after its execution, lest it become stale. As a general rule, if more than five weeks have elapsed between the date of execution of the oath or declaration and the filing of the patent application a new oath or declaration will be required by the Patent Office. If no date of execution appears, the applicant is required to file either a new oath or declaration or a certificate from the notary giving the actual date when the oath was taken.[11]

The wording of an oath or declaration cannot be amended. If the wording is not correct or if all of the required averments have not been made or if it has not been properly subscribed to, a new oath or declaration must be submitted.[12]

Where the date of filing the application is not the date that determines the statutory twelve months' period, as in divisional and continuation cases, it is immaterial, so far as concerns the acceptability of the oath or declaration, how long a time intervenes between the execution of the oath or declaration and the filing of the application.[13] Moreover, in some cases, the oath or declaration of a divisional or continuation application may consist merely of a copy of the oath or declaration contained in the parent application.[14]

When an applicant presents a claim for matter originally shown or described but not substantially embraced in the statement of invention or claims originally presented, he must file a supplemental oath or declaration which in addition to the averments contained in the original oath or declaration further state that the subject matter of the proposed amendment was part of his invention.[15]

It is permissible to combine into a single instrument the petition, declaration, and power of attorney.

Declaration, Power of Attorney, and Petition

We, ____________ and ____________, declare that we are citizens of the United States, residing at ____________, County of ____________, State of ____________, and ____________, County of ____________, State of ____________, respectively; that we have read the foregoing specification and claims and we verily believe that we are the original, first, and joint inventors of the invention in

described and claimed therein; that we do not know and do not believe that this invention was ever known or used before our invention thereof, or patented or described in any printed publication in any country before our invention thereof, or more than one year prior to this application; or in public use or on sale in the United States more than one year prior to this application; that this invention has not been patented in any country foreign to the United States on an application filed by us or our legal representatives or assigns more than twelve months before this application; and that no application for patent on this invention has been filed by us or our representatives or assigns in any country foreign to the United States, except as follows:

And we hereby appoint __________, Registration No. __________, our attorney to prosecut this application and to transact all business in the Patent Office connected therewith.

WHEREFORE, we pray that Letters Patent be granted to us for the invention or discovery described and claimed in the foregoing specification and claims, and we hereby subscribe our names to the foregoing specification and claims, declaration, power of attorney, and this petition.

The undersigned petitioners declare further that all statements made herein of their own knowledge are true and that all statements made on information and belief are believed to be true; and further that these statements were made with the knowledge that willful false statements and the like so made are punishable by fine or imprisonment, or both, under Section 1001 of Title 18 of the United States Code and that such willful false statements may jeopardize the validity of the application or any patent issuing thereon.

DATED: __________.

X __________

Post Office Address: X __________

A patent must be applied for and the application papers must be signed and the necessary oath or declaration executed by the actual inventor(s) in all cases, except where an inventor is deceased, or is insane or legally incapacitated, or where another has a proprietary interest in the invention and the inventor either refuses to execute the application or cannot be found or reached after a diligent effort. However, the National Aeronautics & Space Act provides that no patent may be issued to any applicant other than the Administrator of the National Aeronautics & Space Agency for any invention in which the Administration has a proprietary interest.[16]

Rule 42. When the inventor is dead. In case of death of the inventor, the legal representative (executor, administrator, etc.) of the deceased inventor may sign the application papers and make the necessary oath or declaration and apply for and obtain the patent. Where the inventor dies during the time intervening between the filing of his application and the granting of a patent thereon, the letters patent may be issued to the legal representative upon proper intervention by him.

Rule 43. When the inventor is insane or legally incapacitated. In case an inventor is insane or otherwise legally incapacitated, the legal representative (guardian, conservator, etc.) of such inventor may sign the application papers and make the necessary oath or declaration, and apply for and obtain the patent.

Rule 47. Filing by other than inventor. This rule provides, inter alia: (a) If a joint inventor refuses to join in an application for patent or cannot be found or reached after diligent effort, the application may be made by the other inventor on behalf of himself and the omitted inventor. (b) Whenever an inventor refuses to execute an application for patent, or cannot be found or reached after diligent effort, a person to whom the inventor has assigned or agreed in writing to assign the invention or who otherwise shows sufficient proprietary interest in the matter justifying such action may make application for patent on behalf of and as agent for the inventor.

§ 3. The Drawing

A drawing of the invention forms a necessary part of an application for patent whenever the nature of the case admits of it.[17]

Illustrations facilitating an understanding of the invention (for example, flow sheets in cases of processes, and diagrammatic views) may also be furnished in the same manner as drawings and may be required by the Patent Office when considered necessary or desirable.[18]

It has long been the practice, however, to accept a case having only process or method claims which is filed without a drawing.[19] The same practice has been followed in composition cases and in the following other situations:

(1) Coated articles or products where the invention resides solely in coating or impregnating a conventional sheet;

(2) Articles made from a particular material or composition where the invention consists in making an article of a particular material or composition, unless significant details of structure or arrangement are involved in the article claims;

(3) Laminated structures where the claimed invention involves only laminations of sheets (and coatings) of specified material, unless significant details of structure or arrangement (other than the mere order of the layers) are involved in the article claims;

(4) Articles, apparatus, or systems where the invention resides in and the sole distinguishing feature is the presence of a particular material.

Any drawings submitted along with the specification are deemed part of the original disclosure.[20] Accordingly, it is impermissible to amend the drawing so as to introduce new matter therein.[21] However, a drawing may be amended to include matter for which there is sufficient verbal support in the specification. Similarly, the verbal description of the invention contained in the specification may be amended to describe features clearly shown in the drawing. Where the examiner requires a drawing, such is to be merely illustrative of what already is described in the specification, though, in such case, the written description of the invention must be suitably amended to contain reference to the new illustration.[22]

> *Rule 83.* Content of drawing. (a) The drawing must show every feature of the invention specified in the claims. However, conventional features disclosed in the description and claims, where their detailed illustration is not essential for a proper understanding of the invention, should be illustrated in the drawing in the form of a graphical symbol or a labeled representation (e.g. a labeled rectangular box). (b) When the invention consists of an improvement on an old machine the drawing must when possible exhibit, in one or more views, the improved portion itself, disconnected from the old structure, and also in another view, so much only of the old structure as will suffice to show the connection of the invention therewith.
>
> *Rule 84.* Standards for drawings. This rule prescribes the following regulations with respect to drawings:
>
> *(a) Paper and ink.* Drawings must be made upon pure white paper of a thickness corresponding to two-ply or three-ply bristol-board. The surface of the paper must be calendered and smooth and of a quality which will permit erasure and correction. India ink alone must be used for pen drawings to secure perfectly black solid lines. The use of white pigment to cover lines is not acceptable.
>
> *(b) Size of sheet and margins.* The size of a sheet on which a drawing is made must be exactly eight and one-half by fourteen inches. One of the shorter sides of the sheet is regarded as its top. The drawing must include a top margin of two inches and bottom and side margins of one-quarter inch from the edges, thereby leaving a sight precisely eight by eleven and three-quarters inches. Margin border lines are not permitted. All work

must be included within the sight. The sheets may be provided with two quarter-inch-diameter holes having their centerlines spaced eleven-sixteenths inches below the top edge and two and three-quarter inches apart, said holes being equally spaced from the respective side edges.

(c) Character of lines. All drawings must be made with drafting instruments or by photolithographic process which will give them satisfactory reproduction characteristics. Every line and letter (signatures included) must be absolutely black. This direction applies to all lines however fine, to shading, and to lines representing cut surfaces in sectional views. All lines must be clean, sharp, and solid, and fine or crowded lines should be avoided. Solid black should not be used for sectional or surface shading. Freehand work should be avoided wherever it is possible to do so.

(d) Hatching and shading. (1) Hatching should be made by oblique parallel lines, which may be not less than about one-twentieth inches apart. (2) Heavy lines on the shade side of objects should be used except where they tend to thicken the work and obscure reference characters. The light should come from the upper left hand corner at an angle of forty-five degrees. Surface delineations should be shown by proper shading, which should be open.

(e) Scale. The scale to which a drawing is made ought to be large enough to show the mechanism without crowding when the drawing is reduced in reproduction, and views of portions of the mechanism on a larger scale should be used when necessary to show details clearly; two or more sheets should be used if one does not give sufficient room to accomplish this end, but the number of sheets should not be more than is necessary.

(f) Reference characters. The different views should be consecutively numbered figures. Reference numerals (and letters, but numerals are preferred) must be plain, legible and carefully formed, and not be encircled. They should, if possible, measure at least one-eighth of an inch in height so that they may bear reduction to one twenty-fourth of an inch; and they may be slightly larger when there is sufficient room. They must not be so placed in the close and complex parts of the drawing as to interfere with a thorough comprehension of the same, and therefore should rarely cross or mingle with the lines. When

necessarily grouped around a certain part, they should be placed at a little distance, at the closest point where there is available space, and connected by lines with the parts to which they refer. They should not be placed upon hatched or shaded surfaces but when necessary, a blank space may be left in the hatching or shading where the character occurs so that it shall appear perfectly distinct and separate from the work. The same part of an invention appearing in more than one view of the drawing must always be designated by the same character, and the same character must never be used to designate different parts.

(g) Symbols, legends. Graphical drawing symbols and other labeled representations may be used for conventional elements when appropriate, subject to approval by the Office. The elements for which such symbols and labeled representations are used must be adequately identified in the specification. While descriptive matter on drawings is not permitted, suitable legends may be used, or may be required, in proper cases, as in diagrammatic views and flowsheets or to show materials or where labeled representations are employed to illustrate conventional elements. Arrows may be required, in proper cases, to show direction of movement. The lettering should be as large as, or larger than, the reference characters.

(h) Location of signature and names. The signature of the applicant or the name of the applicant and signature of the attorney or agent, may be placed in the lower right-hand corner of each sheet within the marginal line, or may be placed below the lower marginal line.

(i) Views. The drawing must contain as many figures as may be necessary to show the invention; the figures should be consecutively numbered if possible in the order in which they appear. The figures may be plane, elevation, section, or perspective views, and detail views of portions or elements, on a larger scale if necessary, may also be used. Exploded views, with the separated parts of the same figure embraced by a bracket, to show the relationship or order of assembly of various parts are permissible. When necessary, a view of a large machine or device in its entirety may be broken and extended over several sheets if there is no loss in facility of understanding the view (the different parts should be identified by the same figure number but

followed by the letters, a, b, c, etc., for each part). The plane upon which a sectional view is taken should be indicated on the general view by a broken line, the ends of which should be designated by numerals corresponding to the figure number of the sectional view and have arrows applied to indicate the direction in which the view is taken. A moved position may be shown by a broken line superimposed upon a suitable figure if this can be done without crowding, otherwise a separate figure must be used for this purpose. Modified forms of construction can only be shown in separate figures. Views should not be connected by projection lines nor should center lines be used.

(j) Arrangement of views. All views on the same sheet must stand in the same direction and should, if possible, stand so that they can be read with the sheet held in an upright position. If views longer than the width of the sheet are necessary for the clearest illustration of the invention, the sheet may be turned on its side. The space for a heading must then be reserved at the right and the signatures placed at the left, occupying the same space and position on the sheet as in the upright views and being horizontal when the sheet is held in an upright position. One figure must not be placed upon another or within the outline of another.

(k) Figure for Official Gazette. The drawing should, as far as possible, be so planned that one of the views will be suitable for publication in the Official Gazette as the illustration of the invention.

(l) Extraneous matter. An agent's or attorney's stamp, or address, or other extraneous matter, will not be permitted upon the face of a drawing, within or without the marginal line, except that the title of the invention and identifying indicia, to distinguish from other drawings filed at the same time, may be placed below the lower margin.

(m) Transmission of drawings. Drawing transmitted to the Office should be sent flat, protected by a sheet of heavy binder's board, or may be rolled for transmission in a suitable mailing tube; but must never be folded. If received creased or mutilated, new drawings will be required.[23]

Rule 82. Signature to drawing. Signatures are not required on the drawing if it accompanies and is referred to in the other papers of the application, otherwise the drawing must be signed.

> The drawing may be signed by the applicant in person or have the name of the applicant placed thereon followed by the signature of the attorney or agent as such.

Where a case admits a drawing, a filing date cannot be accorded the application until the drawing is supplied. A drawing not executed in conformity with Rule 84, may be admitted if suitable for reproduction, and a filing dated accorded the application, but in such case the drawing must be corrected or a new one furnished, as required. The necessary corrections will be made by the Office upon applicant's request and at his expense.[24] If photoprints are submitted, the applicant will be notified that formal drawings, in compliance with Rule 84, together with a comparison fee, are required within two months of the mailing of the notification, to avoid abandonment.[25] Photographs or photomicrographs, however, are acceptable in lieu of India ink drawings to illustrate inventions which are incapable of being accurately or adequately depicted by India ink drawings, restricted to the following categories: crystalline structures, metallurgical microstructures, textile fabrics, grain structures, and ornamental effects. Such photographs to be acceptable must be made on paper having the following characteristics: double weight paper with a surface described as smooth; tint, white.[26]

§ 4. Exhibits

The Patent Office has the power to require the submission of physical exhibits, such as a working model of an apparatus or a specimen of a composition of matter.[27] In fact, models were once required in all cases admitting a model, as a part of the application, and these models became a part of the record of the patent. Such models are no longer generally required (the description of the invention in the specification, and the drawings, must be sufficiently full and complete, and capable of being understood, to disclose the invention without the aid of a model). Today, moreover, a model will not be admitted unless specifically called for,[28] and they very rarely are!

§ 5. Specification

A specification contains a number of distinct items which should be arranged in the following order:[29]

(1) Title of the invention.

(2) Abstract of the disclosure.

(3) Cross-references to related applications, if any.

(4) Brief summary of the invention.

(5) Brief description of the several views of the drawing, if there are drawings.

(6) Detailed description.

(7) Claim or claims.

(8) Signature.

[1] Title and Abstract

Rule 72. Title and abstract. (a) The title of the invention, which should be as short and specific as possible, should appear as a heading on the first page of the specification, if it does not otherwise appear at the beginning of the application.

(b) A brief abstract of the technical disclosure in the specification must be set forth immediately following the title and preceding the disclosure in a separate paragraph under the heading "Abstract of the Disclosure." The purpose of the abstract is to enable the Patent Office and the public generally to determine quickly from a cursory inspection the nature and gist of the technical disclosure, and the abstract shall not be used for interpreting the scope of the claims.

[2] Cross-References to Other Applications

Rule 78. Cross-references to other applications. (a) When an applicant files an application claiming an invention disclosed in a prior filed copending application of the same applicant, the second application must contain or be amended to contain in the first sentence of the specification following the title and abstract a reference to the prior application, identifying it by serial number and filing date and indicating the relationship of the applications, if the benefit of the filing date of the prior application is to be claimed. Cross-references to other related applications may be made when appropriate.[30]

[3] Summary

Rule 73. Summary of the invention. A brief summary of the

invention indicating its nature and substance, which may include a statement of the object of the invention, should precede the detailed description. Such summary should, when set forth, be commensurate with the invention as claimed and any object recited should be that of the invention as claimed.

[4] Reference to Drawings

Rule 74. Reference to drawings. When there are drawings, there shall be a brief description of the several views of the drawings and the detailed description of the invention shall refer to the different views by specifying the number of the figures and to the different parts by use of reference letters or numerals (preferably the latter).

[5] Detailed Description

Rule 71. Detailed description and specification of the invention.
(a) The specification must include a written description of the invention or discovery and of the manner and process of making and using the same, and is required to be in such full, clear, concise, and exact terms as to enable any person skilled in the art or science to which the invention or discovery appertains, or with which it is most nearly connected, to make and use the same.
(b) The specification must set forth the precise invention for which a patent is solicited, in such manner as to distinguish it from other inventions and from what is old. It must describe completely a specific embodiment of the process, machine, manufacture, composition of matter or improvement invented, and must explain the mode of operation or principle whenever applicable. The best mode contemplated by the inventor of carrying out his invention must be set forth.
(c) In the case of an improvement, the specification must particularly point out the part or parts of the process, machine, manufacture, or composition of matter to which the improvement relates, and the description should be confined to the specific improvement and to such parts as necessarily cooperate with it or as may be necessary to a complete understanding or description of it.

Rule 71(b) is based upon Section 112(1) which reads as follows:

> The specification shall contain a written description of the invention, and of the manner and process of making and using it, in such full, clear, concise, and exact terms as to enable any person skilled in the art to which it pertains, or with which it is most nearly connected, to make and use the same, and shall set forth the best mode contemplated by the inventor of carrying out his invention.

It should be noted that Section 112, first paragraph, requires that the disclosure contained within the specification include all of the following:

(1) a description of the invention;
(2) the manner and process of making the invention;
(3) the manner and process of using the invention;
(4) the best mode contemplated by the inventor of carrying out his invention.

Apparently, the how-to-make requirement is separate and distinct from the description-of-the-invention requirement.[31]

Still unsettled is the degree of particularity with which (that is, how completely) the best mode must be set out in the specification. Although Rule 71(b) does declare that the specification must describe completely a specific embodiment of the invention, it has been held that no direct statutory basis exists for this requirement other than the best-mode requirement of Section 112.[32] Moreover, for a number of years, the Court of Customs and Patent Appeals has declined to equate the best mode with a specific embodiment, being of the opinion that all that was intended by the language mandating that the best mode be set out was to restrain inventors from applying for patents while at the same time concealing from the public preferred embodiments of their inventions which they have in fact conceived.[33] According to this interpretation, all that, in essence, the best-mode requirement mandates is nonconcealment of preferred embodiments.[34]

The inclusion of a specific embodiment, while it may not be necessitated by the best-mode requirement, may be necessary in order to enable one skilled in the art to practice the claimed invention.[35] The parameters values for which must be recited in the specification, to constitute an enabling disclosure, will depend upon the particular facts of the case, including the level of ordinary skill in the art to which the invention most nearly relates. Whatever details are required to render a disclosure enabling, the absence of a working example, denominated as such, does not compel a conclusion that the specification does not satisfy the requirements of Section 112. It will suffice if such information can be gleaned from the four corners of the specification.[36]

The test of whether a given disclosure is enabling is always whether, having the disclosure before him one possessing ordinary skill in the art could practice the claimed invention without the exercise of inventive faculties. If undue experimentation would be required to practice the claimed invention, the disclosure is insufficient.[37]

It should be noted that the statement in Rule 71(b) that the specification "must explain the mode of operation or principle of the invention" does not mean that the specification must offer a theoretical explanation of why the invention operates. All that is required is that the specification contain sufficient information to enable one of ordinary skill in the art to practice the invention. It is well settled that it is not necessary that the patentee understand the scientific principles underlying his invention.[38] There is a difference between a physical procedure for achieving a given result and a theoretical explanation of why a given physical procedure produces the result it does. The former belongs to the realm of invention; the latter to the realm of science.

In drafting a specification, it is advisable to make the disclosure as complete and thorough as possible. If there is any doubt as to whether information lies within or without the level of ordinary skill in the art, it is by far the wiser practice, in view of the strictures against new matter, to incorporate such information in the specification.

Rule 58 sets out standards for incorporating chemical and mathematical formulas and tables in the specification. In essence, this rule provides that chemical and mathematical formulas may be incorporated in the specification, including the claims, but drawings or flow diagrams may not. The description portion of the specification may contain tables; claims may contain tables only if necessary to conform to 35 U.S.C. 112.

In setting out an invention in the specification, reference must sometimes be made to the prior art. Where such prior art was not part of the specification as originally filed, it is, under certain, limited circumstances, permissible to amend the specification to incorporate by reference such prior art. Where the prior art is necessary for the support of the claims, reference may be made only to United States patents or to allowed United States patent applications. Where the prior art sought to be incorporated by reference is not necessary for the support of any of the claims, but rather is merely for such purposes as indicating the background of the invention or illustrating the state of the art, sources which may be cited include patents issued by the United States or foreign countries; prior filed, commonly owned United States patent applications; and nonpatent publications.[39]

The identification of a composition of matter by means of a trademark or proprietary name may be objectionable, as the relationship between the trademark and the product it identifies is sometimes indefinite, uncertain, and arbitrary. The formula or character of the product may change from time to time, at the pleasure of the manufacturer, and yet it may continue to be sold with the same trademark. Accordingly, the generic or common descriptive name of the product should be used in the specification. A trademark, however, may be recited in a specification where it is properly characterized as such (as by being capitalized) and the mark has a fixed and definite meaning.[40] The sufficiency of a disclosure containing a trademark will be decided on an individual, case-by-case basis.[41]

A mere written description of an invention involving the use of a microorganism which is unknown or not readily available to the public is by itself insufficient to enable the public to practice any invention described therein. In such a case, to comply with the disclosure requirements of Section 112, it is encumbent upon the applicant to make a deposit of a culture of the microorganism in a depository affording permanency of the deposit and ready accessibility thereto by the public if a patent is granted, no later than the effective United States filing date of the application.[42]

While there may be disclosures which are so defective as to be incapable of supporting any claim whatever, the sufficiency of most disclosures is relative to the breadth of the claims presented. That is to say, a given disclosure may be sufficient to support some claims, but insufficient to support others. In applications directed to inventions in arts where results are predictable, broad claims may properly be supported by the disclosure of a single species.[43] However, in applications directed to inventions in arts where results are unpredictable, the disclosure of a single species usually does not provide an adequate basis to support generic claims. This is because in arts such as chemistry it is not obvious from the disclosure of one species what other species will work.[44] Moreover, it would be unjust to allow an applicant to preempt a large field of chemistry by the simple expedient of making broad prophetic statements without having performed research to verify his speculations.[45]

It has been held improper, however, for an examiner to reject a claim drawn to a genus on the ground that it does not properly define his invention.[46] Section 112, second paragraph, allows an applicant to claim whatever he regards as his invention! It has also been held improper to reject a claim drawn to a genus where the sole basis therefor is merely that the examiner is of the opinion that there are an insufficient number of working examples disclosed to support a generic claim. Mention of representative compounds encompassed by generic claim language clearly is not required by Section 112 or any other portion of the statute.[47] That a claim is readable on inoperative embodiments, because values of operating conditions are not recited therein, is an insufficient basis for rejecting such claim, where the selection of values of conditions which would render the claim operable would be obvious to a person of ordinary skill in the art.[48]

[6] The Claims

The function of a patent specification is twofold: (1) to explain and describe the invention in such terms that any person skilled in the art to which it appertains may make and use it after the expiration of the term of the patent; and (2) to inform the public during the life of the patent of the limits of the monopoly asserted.[49] The part of the specification which informs the public of the limits of the monopoly asserted is known as the claim(s). As used in the Patent Act, the term "specification" is clearly inclusive of the claims.[50] In practice, however, the term "specification" is often used to connote the descriptive part of the specification which precedes the claims.

The statutory requirements for both the written description of the invention and the claims are contained in Section 112. Those relating to the claims form the subject matter of the second and third paragraphs of this section:

> The specification shall conclude with one or more claims particularly pointing out and distinctly claiming the subject matter which the applicant regards as his invention. A claim may be written in independent or dependent form, and if in dependent form, it shall be construed to include all the limitations of the claim incorporated by reference into the dependent claim.
> An element in a claim for a combination may be expressed as a means or step for performing a specified function without the recital of structure, material, or acts in support thereof, and such claim shall be construed to cover the corresponding structure, material, or acts described in the specification and equivalents thereof.

Rule 75 is essentially an elaboration of Section 112(2):

> *Rule 75*. Claim(s). (a) The specification must conclude with a claim particularly pointing out and distinctly claiming the subject matter which the applicant regards as his invention or discovery.
> (b) More than one claim may be presented provided they differ substantially from each other and are not unduly multiplied.
> (c) When more than one claim is presented, they may be placed in dependent form in which a claim may refer back to and further restrict a single preceding claim. Claims in dependent form shall be construed to include all the limitations of the claim incorporated by reference into the dependent claim.
> (d)(1) The claim or claims must conform to the invention as set forth in the remainder of the specification and the terms and phrases used in the claims must find clear support or antecedent basis in the description so that the meaning of the terms in the claims may be ascertainable by reference to the description.
> (2) See Rules 141 to 147 (which govern restriction practice) as to claiming different inventions in one application.
> (e) Where the nature of the case admits, as in the case of an improvement, any independent claim should contain in the following order, (1) a preamble comprising a general description of all the elements or steps of the claimed combination which are

conventional or known, (2) a phrase such as "wherein the improvement comprises," and (3) those elements, steps and/or relationships which constitute that portion of the claimed combination which the applicant considers as the new or improved portion.

Detailed consideration of claim structure and construction forms the subject matter of Chapter 3. To that will now be added just a few refinements. If the meaning of a claim is to be precise and crystal clear, each term must have a definite and unambiguous meaning. The following practices have as their object the elimination of likely sources of indefiniteness:

[a] Multiple dependency not permitted

As indicated in Rule 75(c), each claim may refer back to and further restrict but a single preceding claim. Confusion would result as to just what are the operative limitations of a claim if it were recited that the claim incorporated the limitiations of "claims 1 or 2" or "claims 2 and 3." However, it is altogether proper for a dependent claim to be dependent upon another dependent claim.

[b] Antecedent basis must be present

An ambiguity would exist if an element were preceded by the definite article (*the* filament) when first mentioned in the claim. The question which would naturally enter one's mind would be: "What filament?" Accordingly, a foundation or antecedent basis must be laid for each element recited. This can be done, usually in the preamble, by introducing each element with the indefinite article ("a" or "an"). Subsequent mention of the element is to be modified by the definite article or by "said" or by "the said," thereby making the latter mention of the element unequivocally referable to its earlier recitation.

Illustration:[51] A signalling system comprising *a* generator of microwaves, *a* hollow wave guide connected thereto, *a* resonant cavity interposed in *said* wave guide having therein *a* gas at pressures sufficiently low in the millimeter pressure range to provide sharp molecular resonance absorption, *a* source of energy for irradiating *said* gas to vary the absorption coefficient of *said* gas whereby the amplitude of *the* microwaves transmitted through *said* gas is varied, and means utilizing *the* microwaves transmitted through *said* gas.

[c] Double inclusion of elements not permitted

Another source of indefiniteness is the recitation of the same element under different names in different parts of the claim. The same term must be used for an element, each and every time it is recited.[52]

[d] Alternative expressions are normally not permitted

Alternative expressions may render a claim indefinite if the limitation covers two different elements. If two equivalent parts are referred to, such as "rods or bars," the alternative expression may be considered proper.[53] In chemical type cases, wherein the applicant asserts the equivalence of two or more different materials, these may be recited in a form known as a Markush group[54] (a material selected from the group consisting of A, B, C, . . . and X). A Markush group represents, in essence, a synthetic generic expression. Accordingly, a reference disclosing even only one member of the Markush group in the context claimed constitutes an anticipation of the entire Markush group.

[7] Signature

Rule 57. Signature. The application must be signed by the applicant in person. The signature to the oath or declaration will be accepted as the signature to the application provided the oath or declaration is attached to and refers to the specification and claims to which it applies. Otherwise the signature must appear at the end of the specification after the claims. Full names must be given, including at least one given name without abbreviation together with any other given name or initial.

Notes

[1] Rule 51.
[2] Rule 52(a).
[3] Rule 52(b).
[4] Rule 52(e).
[5] Rule 61(a).
[6] Rule 61(a).
[7] Rule 65.
[8] Rule 153.
[9] Rule 162.
[10] Ex parte Quattlebaum, 84 U.S.P.Q. 377 (P.O. Bd. App. 1948).
[11] M.P.E.P. 602.05. See Ex parte Heinze, 1919 C.D. 67, 265 O.G. 145 (1919).
[12] M.P.E.P. 602.01.
[13] M.P.E.P. 602.05(a).
[14] See Rule 60.
[15] Rule 67.
[16] 42 U.S.C. 2457(c).
[17] 35 U.S.C. 113.
[18] Rule 81.
[19] M.P.E.P. 608.02.
[20] *In re* Gay, 309 F.2d 769, 774, 135 U.S.P.Q. 311, 316 (C.C.P.A. 1962).
[21] See Rule 118, M.P.E.P. 608.04.
[22] M.P.E.P. 608.02.
[23] See also, Rule 152 for design patent drawings; Rule 165 for plant patent drawings; and Rule 174 for reissue patent drawings.
[24] Rule 85.
[25] M.P.E.P. 608.02(a).
[26] M.P.E.P. 608.02.
[27] 35 U.S.C. 114. See Rules 92, 93.
[28] Rule 91.
[29] *In re* Ahlbrecht, 435 F.2d 908, 168 U.S.P.Q. 293 (C.C.P.A. 1971).
[30] *In re* Gay, 309 F.2d 769, 774, 135 U.S.P.Q. 311, 316 (C.C.P.A. 1962); *In re* Locher, 455 F.2d 1396, 173 U.S.P.Q. 172 (C.C.P.A. 1972).
[31] Rule 77.
[32] Rule 78.
[33] *In re* Gay, 309 F.2d 769, 772, 135 U.S.P.Q. 311, 315 (C.C.P.A. 1972).
[34] But see dicta in, *In re* Boon, 439 F.2d 724, 729, 169 U.S.P.Q. 231, 235 (C.C.P.A. 1971).
[35] *In re* Long, 368 F.2d 892, 151 U.S.P.Q. 640 (C.C.P.A. 1966).
[36] *In re* Honn, 364 F.2d 454, 150 U.S.P.Q. 652 (C.C.P.A. 1966).
[37] *In re* Mayhew, 481 F.2d 1373, 179 U.S.P.Q. 42 (C.C.P.A. 1973); *In re* Long, N. 33 *supra*. See also, *In re* Halleck, 422 F.2d 911, 164 U.S.P.Q. 647 (C.C.P.A. 1970); *In re* Borkowski, 422 F.2d 904, 164 U.S.P.Q. 642 (C.C.P.A. 1970).
[38] *In re* Libby, 255 F.2d 412, 118 U.S.P.Q. 94 (C.C.P.A. 1958).
[39] M.P.E.P. 608.01(p).
[40] M.P.E.P. 608.01(v).
[41] *In re* Metcalfe, 410 F.2d 1383, 161 U.S.P.Q. 789 (C.C.P.A. 1969).
[42] *In re* Argoudelis, 434 F.2d 211, 168 U.S.P.Q. 99 (C.C.P.A. 1970).
[43] *In re* Cook, 439 F.2d 730, 169 U.S.P.Q. 298 (C.C.P.A. 1971).
[44] M.P.E.P. 706.03(z).
[45] Ex parte Diamond, 123 U.S.P.Q. 167, 169 (P.O. Bd. App. 1959); Ex parte Ulfstedt, 122 U.S.P.Q. 392, 394 (P.O. Bd. App. 1958).

[46] *In re* Borkowski, 422 F.2d 904, 164 U.S.P.Q. 642 (C.C.P.A. 1970); *In re* Wakefield, 422 F.2d 897, 164 U.S.P.Q. 636 (C.C.P.A. 1970).

[47] *In re* Robins, 429 F.2d 452, 166 U.S.P.Q. 552 (C.C.P.A. 1970).

[48] *In re* Skrivan, 427 F.2d 801, 166 U.S.P.Q. 85 (C.C.P.A. 1970).

[49] Schriber-Schroth Co. v. Trust Co., 305 U.S. 47, 57, 39 U.S.P.Q. 242, 245 (1938); Permutit Co. v. Graver Corp., 284 U.S. 52, 11 U.S.P.Q. 118 (1931).

[50] 35 U.S.C. 112, paragraph 2.

[51] Specification of U.S. Pat. No. 2,819,450, claim 3.

[52] See Palmer v. United States, 423 F.2d 316, 320, 163 U.S.P.Q. 250, 253 (Ct. Cl. 1969). Compare, Ex parte White, 115 U.S.P.Q. 369 (P.O. Bd. App. 1958).

[53] M.P.E.P. 706.03(a).

[54] Ex parte Markush, 1925 C.D. 126, 340 O.G. 839 (Comm. Pat. 1925).

Chapter 13

PROSECUTING PATENT APPLICATIONS

SYNOPSIS

> [B]ut the antlike persistency of solicitors has overcome, and I suppose will continue to overcome, the patience of examiners, and there is apparently always but one outcome . . . .
>
> [W]ith a degree of obduracy which is exceptional even in the Patent Office, the claim to such a buffer was put forward after rejection, disguised in one way or another, three or more times, either deliberately to hoodwink the Examiner, or because the solicitor had become enmeshed, like a silkworm, in his own emanations.
>
> L. Hand, J.
> *Lyon* v. *Boh*, 1 F.2d. 48, 50, 51 (S.D.N.Y. 1924), *rev'd* 10 F.2d 30 (2d Cir. 1926)

The granting of patents has been delegated by Congress to the Patent Office, which, since 1925, has been a unit of the Commerce Department. The Act of 1790 made the processing of patent applications a function of the State Department. Under that Act, the decision whether to grant a patent was placed in the hands of a board composed of the Secretary of State, the Secretary of War, and the Attorney General.[1] The Act of 1793 abolished the board and made the grant of patent a purely ministerial function.[2] Such a system, wherein the merit of a contribution is not scrutinized prior to the grant of patent, is often referred to as a registration system. The Act of 1836 reinstituted the examination of applications for patent, relegating the administration of this function to a newly created office to be known as the Patent Office.[3] In 1849 the Patent Office was transferred from the State Department to the Interior Department.[4]

§ 1. The Patent Bar

Inventors may prosecute their own applications pro se, that is, without the assistance of counsel. It is, however, advisable to employ the services of a registered patent agent or attorney, both to prepare and to prosecute a patent application. The distinction between a patent agent and a patent attorney is that between a nonlawyer and lawyer, respectively.[5]

The general rule that prevails in regard to practice before federal administrative agencies is that any attorney admitted to practice before any state or territorial bar is competent to represent clients before a federal agency without additional qualifications.[6] Practice before the Patent Office in patent causes is an exception to this general rule.[7] Such practice requires not only an intimate understanding of the language and principles of the physical sciences, but also familiarity with a panoply of elaborate, intricate, and highly specialized rules and procedures, an outline of which forms the bulk of the subject matter of the instant chapter. While the rules involved in the preparation and prosecution of patent applications are very much legal principles, because these are so highly technical and specialized, they form a separate and distinct body of law. Accordingly, one who has mastered these and who possesses a sufficient scientific background can carry on as a preparer and prosecutor of patent applications without the benefit of general legal training.

The Patent Office has set up a scheme for the licensing (or registering, as the Patent Office calls it) of persons qualified to represent others before the Office in patent matters. Nonlawyer registrants are styled patent agents, whereas registrants who are also members of any state or territorial bar are styled patent attorneys. The distinction was instituted in 1938 at the urging of the general bar. All persons registered prior to November 15, 1938, whether attorneys-at-law or not, were styled patent attorneys. Those nonlawyers registered as patent attorneys have been permitted, by the Patent Office, to retain the title of patent attorney.

Generally, a candidate for registration today must have both: (1) successfully completed sufficient college-level courses to constitute a major in one of the physical sciences or be able to demonstrate that he possesses the equivalent in training and experience; *and* (2) either have passed a written examination (known as the Patent Agent's Exam) or have served as a Patent Examiner for a period of at least four years.[8] The Patent Agent's Exam is given at least once a year, usually sometime in September, by the Patent Office, at testing centers on designated federal premises throughout the country. Detailed information on the requirements for registration and an application to take the Patent Agent's Exam may be obtained on request by writing: Clerk of the Committee on Enrollment, U.S. Patent Office, Washington, D.C. 20231.

Collectively, the registrants are sometimes unofficially referred to as the patent bar or as the Patent Office bar. Copies of the roster of registrants, including their addresses and telephone numbers, are sold by the Superintendent of Documents, U.S. Government Printing Office, Washington, D.C. 20402.

Section 33 of the Patent Act makes unauthorized practice subject to a fine of not more than $1000. It may also be punishable under state law.[9] A registrant may maintain an office and carry out the practice of preparing and prosecuting patent applications anywhere in the United States, even though he is not a member of the bar in the jurisdiction where located.

It should be borne in mind that an agent or attorney acts in a representative capacity on behalf of his principal or client. A course of action taken or a commitment made by a duly authorized agent or attorney irrevocably binds his client. An applicant cannot undo what his agent or attorney has done, even if clearly erroneous, merely because it was done by an attorney or agent and not by the applicant personally. Rule 35 provides:

> When an attorney or agent shall have filed his power of attorney, or authorization, duly executed, the correspondence will be held with him; notices, official letters, and other communications in the case intended for the applicant will be sent to the attorney or agent at the address of which notice shall have been given in the case, and replies to Office actions, or other actions in the case, will be received by him. Double correspondence with an applicant and his attorney or agent, or with two representatives, will not be undertaken. If more than one attorney or agent be appointed, correspondence will be held with the one last appointed unless otherwise requested.

A patent agent is deemed competent to handle all aspects of patent application preparation and prosecution. There is, however, a possible distinction in the status of their relationships with clients. It has been suggested by at least one court that no attorney-client privilege exists between a mere patent agent and his client, whereas such privilege would seem to exist between a patent attorney and his client.[11]

While there is eminent logic to the imposition of special requirements for those who would handle patent applications for others before the Patent Office, such requirements are inconsistent with the absence of a similar standard with respect to those who handle appeals from the Patent Office in the courts. Any duly admitted attorney-at-law may represent another in any patent cause in court, without satisfying any of the special requirements imposed by the Patent Office. On the other hand, a patent agent is not permitted to represent a client in court, even in an appeal from the Patent Office.[12] Moreover, members of the judiciary, even some of the judges on the specialized Court of Customs and Patent Appeals, have had no formal technical training, no less having satisfied the requirements of the Patent Office for registration.[13]

§ 2. Filing the Patent Application

The importance of obtaining the earliest possible filing date should be apparent. Rule 55(a) provides that the filing date of an application is the date on which the complete application, acceptable for placing on the files for examination, is received in the Patent Office; or the date on which the last part completing such application is received in the case of an incomplete or defective application completed within six months.

Rule 51 defines a complete application as one which comprises:

(1) A petition or request for a patent, see Rule 61.

(2) A specification, including a claim or claims, see Rules 71-77.

(3) An oath or declaration, see Rule 65.

(4) Drawings, when necessary, see Rules 81-88.

(5) The prescribed filing fee, see Rule 21.

Complete applications are numbered in the order in which they are received. The applicant is informed of the serial number and filing date of the application by a filing receipt. All communications concerning an application should bear the identifying serial number.

[1] Benefit of the Filing Date of an Earlier Filed Application

Under certain circumstances, a patent application may be accorded the benefit of the filing date of an earlier filed application. The circumstances in which this may occur fall into two broad classes:

(1) Foreign Priority Applications (35 U.S.C. 119)—the instant application being the parallel of an earlier filed, foreign application, there having been compliance with the terms and conditions of the Paris Convention. Foreign Priority is discusses at length in Chapter 16.

(2) Continuing Applications (35 U.S.C. 120)—the instant application corresponding, at least in part, to the content of an earlier filed, copending United States application.

It should be noted that in order to gain the benefit of the filing date of an earlier filed application, whether based on foreign priority or as a continuing application, an express claim for such treatment must be recited in the later filed application. Reference, identifying the earlier filed application, must be made in the later filed application.

[2] Fees

Fees are set by Congress and defray the cost of operating the

Patent Office. Currently, the Patent Office recoup's less than half of its annual operating budget from all its revenues, including those derived from fees and such other services as the sale of copies of patent specifications at $.50 per copy.

The filing fee is a material part of every patent application. No application is deemed to be complete until the requisite filing fee has been paid. The filing fee for a design or reissue patent application is $20. The minimum filing fee for any other type of patent application is $65, for which the applicant is entitled to one independent claim and up to nine claims dependent thereon. An additional $10 is charged for each independent claim in excess of one and an additional $2 is charged for each claim (whether independent or dependent) in excess of ten. No charge is made for merely amending claims or for substituting new claims for a like number of cancelled claims. By way of comparison, the filing fee set by the Patent Act of 1790 was fifty cents plus ten cents per hundred words of specification.

The issue or final fee is charged only for applications which have been found by the Patent Office to be allowable. For design applications the issue fee is dependent upon the term elected by the applicant: three years and six months = $10; seven years = $20; fourteen years = $30. For all other applications the issue fee is computed as follows: $100 plus $10 for each page (or portion thereof) of specification as printed, and $2 for each sheet of drawing. The issue fee is imposed to defray the cost of printing copies of the specification.

Fees are also imposed for the following:

On appeal to the Board of Appeals: $50 for filing the Notice of Appeal; an additional $50 on filing the brief in support of the appeal. Filing a brief is necessary to perfect an appeal.

On filing each petition to the Commissioner for the revival of an abandoned application for a patent or for the delayed payment of the fee for issuing each patent $15. No fee is imposed for the filing of any other form of petition to the Commissioner.

On filing each disclaimer: $15.

For a certificate under 35 U.S.C. 222 (certificate of correction applicant's mistake) or under 35 U.S.C. 256 (misjoinder): $15.

For recording every assignment, agreement, or other paper relating to the property in a patent or application: $20, where the document relates to more than one patent or application, $3 for each additional item.

The complete schedule of fees is set forth in 35 U.S.C. 41.

Rule 26 provides that money paid by actual mistake in excess, such as a payment not required by law, will be refunded, but a mere change of purpose after the payment of money, as when a party desires to withdraw his application or to withdraw an appeal, will not entitle a party to demand such a return.

[3] Continuing Applications and Res Judicata

It is not always feasible to carry through the very same application from filing to patent, for any one of a number of reasons. An application may disclose a patentable invention which has been finally rejected for a technical defect by the Patent Office; there may be errors or omissions in the disclosure itself; an application may disclose two or more inventions which may better be prosecuted in separate applications. Under such circumstances, it may be possible to refile, such that the later filed application will be accorded the benefit of the filing date of an earlier filed application. The later filed application is often referred to as a continuing application. The earlier filed application on which a continuing application may rely for its effective filing date is often referred to as the original or parent of the continuing application. Under present practice, there is no limit to the number of prior applications through which a chain of continuing applications may be traced to obtain the benefit of the filing date of the earliest of a chain of prior continuing applications.[14]

To enjoy the status of a continuing application, there must be a continuity between the later and earlier filed applications in compliance with the following conditions:

(1) Both the earlier and later filed applications must be by the same inventor. The term "same inventor" has been construed to include a continuing application of a sole inventor derived from an application of joint inventors where a showing was made that the joinder involved error without any deceptive intent.[15]

(2) Both the earlier and later filed applications must disclose the same invention.

(3) There must have been copendency between the earlier and later filed applications, that is, the later application must have been filed before (a) the patenting, or (b) the abandonment of, or (c) the termination of proceedings in the earlier application.

(4) The later filed application must contain a specific reference to the earlier filed application(s) in its specification.

There are three different types of continuing applications.

[a] Continuation

A continuation is a second application for the same invention claimed in a prior application and filed before the original becomes abandoned.[16] Except as provided in Rule 45, the applicant in the continuation must be the same as in the prior application. The disclosure presented in the continuation must be the same as that of the original application, that is, the continuation should not include anything which would constitute new matter if inserted in the orignial application. A continuation enables an applicant to keep alive an earlier filing date by establishing a right to further examination by the Primary Examiner of the same subject matter in the form of a new application. A new set of claims may be introduced into the continuation. A special form of continuation, known as a "Streamlined Continuation" is one whose specification and any drawings are identical to that of the original application and which has claims directed to the same invention as that prosecuted in the original application. The application papers of the original application, excepting the claims, may be used in a streamlined continuation. The streamlined continuation program is no longer in effect.[17]

[b] Continuation-in-part

The continuation-in-part is an application filed during the lifetime of an earlier application by the same applicant, repeating some substantial portion or all of the earlier application *and adding matter not disclosed* in the earlier case.[18] A continuation-in-part application filed by a sole applicant may also derive from an earlier joint application showing a portion only of the subject matter of the later application, subject to the conditions stated in the case of a sole divisiônal application stemming from a joint application. Subject to the same conditions, a joint continuation-in-part application may derive from an earlier sole application.[19]

A continuation-in-part application enjoys the benefit of the filing date of the original or parent application from which it is derived only with respect to subject matter adequately disclosed in the earlier, supporting application. The added or new matter is accorded only the actual filing date of the continuation-in-part application.

Moreover, where a first application is found to be fatally defective because of insufficient disclosure to support allowable claims, a second application filed as a continuation-in-part of the first application to supply the deficiency is not entitled to the benefit of the filing date of the first application.[20]

[c] Division

A division or divisional application is a later application for a distinct or independent invention, carved out of a pending application and disclosing and claiming only subject matter disclosed in the earlier or parent application. Except as provided in Rule 45, both must be by the same applicant. The divisional application should set forth only that portion of the earliest disclosure which is germane to the invention as claimed in the divisional application.[21] While a divisional application may depart from the phraseology used in the parent case, there may be no departure therefrom in substance or variation in the drawing that would amount to new matter if introduced by amendment into the parent case. A design patent application is not to be considered to be a division of a utility patent application, and is not entitled to the filing date thereof, even though the drawings of the earlier filed utility application show the same article as that in the design application.[22]

While a divisional application is usually filed as a consequence of a requirement for restriction made by the Primary Examiner in an earlier application, an applicant may file a division on his own initiative. Where no requirement for restriction was made, however, there looms the possibility that the divisional application will be rejected on the ground of "double patenting." This problem will be discussed at greater length below.

[d] Res Judicata

To facilitate the visualization of the relations among the content of the three different types of continuing applications, the reader is urged to consider the following diagram:

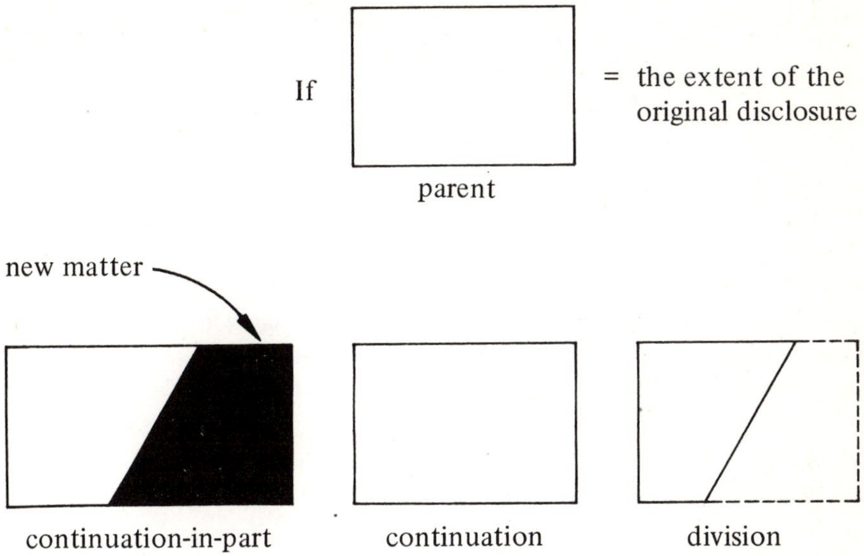

Whether any given application is, in fact, a continuation, a continuation-in-part, or a division will depend upon the operative facts. A mere designation by the applicant, albeit recited in his specification and approved by of the primary examiner, is not controlling.[23] An application which is in essence the duplicate of an application by the same applicant abandoned before the filing of the later application, which for any reason does not qualify as a continuation is designated a substitute application.[24] Current practice does not require the applicant of a substitute application to insert in such application any reference to the earlier case.[25]

A patent application having a disclosure and claims that are commensurate with the disclosure and claims of some earlier application made by the same applicant, whether or not the later application enjoys the status of a continuation, would seem to raise the question of whether the later filed application could be barred under the doctrine of res judicata. The doctrine of res judicata had its origin in judicial proceedings, wherein it is invoked to preclude the relitigation of a controversy between the same parties involving the same cause of action as was finally determined on the merits in the earlier proceeding.[26] Patent Office proceedings are not deemed to be of a judicial character, but rather administrative or quasi-judicial. Courts have recognized, however, that while the rules that govern the finality and conclusiveness of adjudications at common law do not apply, in the strict sense, to administrative or quasi-judicial action in the executive departments of government, yet in administrative action, as well as in judicial proceedings, it is both expedient and necessary that there should be an end to controversy.[27] Accordingly, the courts have apparently sanctioned the application of res judicata to patent prosecution, but only where: (1) in the earlier proceeding the refusal to grant a patent was adjudicated by a tribunal above the primary examiner level, such as the Patent Office Board of Appeals; and (2) no new issues are raised in the later case.[28] However, as almost any change in the specification or claims would involve a new issue, the applicability of the doctrine of res judicata in Patent Office proceedings is sorely limited.[29] The Patent Office admonishes its examiners, in rejecting on the ground of res judicata, also to reject on the basis of prior art.

§ 3. Outline of Ex Parte Prosecution

Within the Patent Office, with the exception of the seldom invoked Public Use Proceedings,[31] the examination of applications for patent, as to all issues except that of priority of invention,[32] is conducted ex parte. The public is not notified of the content of patent applications while they are pending before the Patent Office, Section 122 of the Patent Act requiring that all applications for patents be kept in confidence by the Patent Office and that no information concerning the same be ordinarily given without authority of the applicant or owner. The reason for this secrecy is to encourage inventors to avail themselves of the patent system, which grants a seventeen year monopoly in exchange for public disclosure. However, public disclosure occurs only after patent rights are granted. Were public disclosure made by the government before giving a promise of patent, inventors would be reluctant even to attempt to use the patent system, for public disclosure destroys secrecy, to which valuable rights attach at common law. Rather than a risk a total loss of rights by a combination of public disclosure and refusal to grant a patent by the government, most inventors would prefer to keep their inventions secret.[33]

While the Patent Act vests the Commissioner of Patents with the power to issue patents, the actual examination of applications therefor is conducted by a corps of professional employees of the Patent Office, having Civil Service status, who are styled patent examiners. To some of the more senior examiners, the Commissioner has formally delegated full signatory authority, which gives the incumbents the authority to allow patent applications on behalf of the Commissioner. An allowed application is one adjudged by the Patent Office, after due examination, to be entitled to a patent. Examiners having full signatory authority are styled Primary Examiners. Each, in effect acts as a court of original jurisdiction, making the initial decision whether or not a patent is to be granted upon an application. The proceeding to obtain a patent is quasi judicial in its character.[34] Each primary examiner examines in a particular art, that is, in a narrow area of technology. The cases in an examiner's docket will normally fall into that specialty. The actual examination of a large proportion of the applications is performed by junior or assistant examiners, whose work is supervised, in varying degrees, by a supervisory primary examiner. Only primary and supervisory primary examiners, however, have the authority to allow an application.

The papers comprising an application, before they reach the examiner, are placed in a folder known as the file wrapper. Papers introduced into the file wrapper during the course of prosecution, including all formal actions taken by the examiner, are numbered in chronological order. The file wrapper thus contains a complete record of the patent's prosecution history, including much pertinent information not found in the printed specification. The file wrapper and the contents thereof corresponding to every patent are available for public inspection in the Patent Office, as are the file wrappers of abandoned applications to which reference has been made in a patent.

Applications are taken up for examination by the examiners to whom they have been assigned in the order in which they have been filed, unless an application has been accorded special status. The applicant may petition the Commissioner to make special an application for one of a number of reasons set out in the *Manual of Patent Examining Procedure* § 708.02, as, for example, that the applicant is sixty-five or more years of age, or that the application is directed to an invention which will materially enhance the quality of the environment.

[1] Action Taken by the Examiner

The examiner to whom an application has been committed for

examination will study the contents of the file wrapper, make a search of what he deems to be the relevant prior art, and then act on the application accordingly. The primary object of the examination of an application is to determine whether or not the claims define a patentable advance over the prior art.[35]

Favorable action taken upon a claim is indicated by the examiner's allowance thereof. Adverse action is indicated by rejection. Defects purely in form, such as that an otherwise allowable claim is dependent upon a rejected claim, are indicated by objection. The examiner will also object to defects in the specification apparent to him. In appropriate instances, the examiner may make a requirement. Unlike either a rejection or an objection, a requirement spells out to the applicant the course of action that he is to take. Perhaps the most common type of requirement is a requirement for restriction between independent and distinct inventions, which topic will be discussed at length later in this chapter. An objection may be coupled with a requirement, such that compliance with the requirement will obviate the objection.

The distinction between a rejection, on one hand, and an objection or requirement, on the other, has a significant consequence. Rejections touch the merits of the claims, and, hence, are reviewable by appeal to the Patent Office Board of Appeals and thence, at the election of the applicant, by either the United States Court of Customs and Patent Appeals or by the United States District Court for the District of Columbia. An objection or requirement is reviewable by petition to the Commissioner. His refusal is reviewable by any United States District Court.

The status of the application, after the initial search and examination have been made, is communicated to the applicant (or his attorney) by means of an official letter. If all the claims are allowable and the application is in condition for allowance, a Notice of Allowance will be sent. First action allowances are still relatively rare. More often some objection, requirement, and/or rejection will be raised. This, including a concise explanation of the reasons therefor and indication of allowable claims (if any) are embodied in a written communication, known as an Office Action or letter.

Examiners normally do not state any reason for allowing a claim. This must be gleaned from the record as a whole. Giving the reason(s) for rejecting a claim, however, including the statutory basis therefore, would seem to be an element of due process of law. Such practice is specifically mandated by Section 132 of the Patent Act. The rationale for the rejection is supposed to give the applicant notice sufficient to enable him to judge the propriety of continuing the prosecution of his application and to frame an intelligent response. It also gives a reviewing tribunal a record upon which to base its decision. Where the Office action contains a rejection based upon prior art, a copy of each reference relied upon by the examiner is supplied by the Patent Office.

It should be noted that though an application contains allowed claims, it will not be passed to issue unless and until all the claims are allowable and any objections overcome and requirements met.

When an application is in condition for allowance except as to matters of form, a so-called Quayle Action will be sent to the applicant, giving him two months within which to comply with the outstanding requirement and apprising him that prosecution on the merits is closed.[36]

[2] Response by the Applicant

Section 132 of the Patent Act provides for the examination and reexamination of applications for patent. Accordingly, after being once formally refused a patent, an applicant has the right to reconsideration, upon filing a response to the examiner's refusal with a request for reconsideration. The paper (letter) submitted by the applicant in response to the examiner's refusal is often referred to as an amendment, although it may be a mere argument, pointing out wherein the applicant believes the examiner to be in error. The applicant, in his amendment, may amend or cancel one or more existing claims and/or introduce one or more new claims into the case.

Although Rule 2 provides that all business with the Patent Office should be transacted in writing and that the personal attendance of applicants or their attorneys or agents at the Patent Office is unnecessary, the personal appearance of an applicant and/or his attorney or agent before the examiner frequently facilitates the disposition of his case. It gives the applicant an opportunity to explain his invention and receive from the examiner an elaboration upon and/or a clarification of his position, so that a more intelligent response to an outstanding refusal may be drafted. Accordingly, Rule 133(a) provides for the conduct of interviews in the examiners' rooms at such times, within office hours, as the respective examiners may designate.

Rule 133(b) further provides that in every instance where reconsideration is requested in view of an interview with an examiner, a complete written statement of the reasons presented at the interview as warranting favorable action must be filed by the applicant. An interview does not remove the necessity for response to Office actions. Rule 2 also contains the following caveat:

> The action of the Patent Office will be based exclusively on the written record in the Office. No attention will be paid to any alleged oral promise, stipulation, or understanding in relation to which there is disagreement or doubt.

To secure an allowance, an applicant must file a written response to any and all outstanding grounds of refusal, however untenable may be the examiner's position. Moreover, such response must be submitted within the specified time, lest the application go abandoned. Section 133 of the Patent Act provides:

> Upon failure of the applicant to prosecute the application within six months after any action therein, of which notice has been given or mailed to the applicant, or within such shorter time, not less than thirty days, as fixed by the commissioner in such action, the application shall be regarded as abandoned by the parties, unless it be shown to the satisfaction of the Commissioner that such delay was unavoidable.

Shortened Statutory Periods have been set for response to all Office actions as follows:[37]

Requirement for restriction only	30 days
Quayle Action	2 months
Multiplicity rejection only	2 months
Winning party in terminated interference to reply to unanswered Office action	2 months
New ground of rejection in an Examiner's Answer on appeal	2 months
Any Office action on the merits	3 months

Any petition not filed within two months from the action complained of may be dismissed as untimely.[38]

The Commissioner may, upon written request and for good and sufficient cause, extend the time for reply up to six months from the date of an action, that is, up to a full statutory period.[39] The Commissioner is without statutory authority to extend a period of response beyond six months from the date of the action. Any request for an extension of time must be filed on or before the day on which action by the applicant is due. The mere filing of a request does not effect any extension.[40]

The date of an Office Action is the date of its mailing.[41] The date of a paper or letter submitted by or on behalf of an applicant is the date it is received in the Office.[42]

An application abandoned for failure timely to prosecute may be revived as a pending application if it is shown to the satisfaction of the Commissioner that the delay was unavoidable. A petition to revive an abandoned application must be accompanied by: (1) a verified showing of the causes of the delay; (2) the proposed response, unless it has been previously filed; and (3) the petition fee.[43]

[3] Reconsideration by the Examiner

If the applicant's response does not place the application in condition for allowance, the examiner will execute a second Office action, which will contain one or more grounds of rejection, objection, and/or requirement.

If the applicant has not amended his claims and the examiner persists in his rejection thereof on the same basis as the first action, an issue between the examiner and the applicant has been reached, and the examiner will make the rejection final. If the applicant has not amended his claims and the examiner introduces any new ground of rejection, the examiner may *not* properly make the second action final. If the applicant has amended his claims, the examiner may make the second action final notwithstanding the examiner's introduction of a new ground of rejection with respect to the claims amended by the applicant, where the new ground(s) of rejection was necessitated by amendment of the application by applicant.[44] It is the practice of the Office to expedite the processing of applications by, wherever possible, making the second action on the merits final.[45] A first action which is merely a requirement for restriction is not an action on the merits. A second action on the merits will not be made final if it includes a rejection, on newly cited art, of *any* claim not amended by applicant even though other claims may have been amended to require newly cited art. A requirement, which has been traversed by the applicant in his written response, will be made final by the examiner in his next Office action even though such action is not made final with respect to the rejection of the claims.[46]

The claims of a new application may be finally rejected in the first Office Action in those situations where: (l) the new application is a continuing application of, or a substitute for, an earlier application; and (2) all claims of the new application (a) are drawn to the same invention claimed in the earlier application and (b) would have been properly finally rejected on the art of record in the next Office Action if they had been entered in the earlier application.[47]

The examiner will clearly indicate the finality of any action or requirement by such a concluding statement as: "This is a FINAL rejection." "This requirement is made FINAL."[48] Similar language of like import may be used instead. The refusal of the primary examiner to withdraw a final rejection as being premature is petitionable and not appealable.[49]

It should be noted that formerly, applicants were given at least two actions on the merits before the final action. To expedite the processing of applications and thus reduce the huge backlog of pending applications, the Office, some years back, instituted a program known as "compact prosecution," prominent features of which are a thorough search and complete first action on the merits to be followed by a second, final action and the setting of the shortened statutory periods for response now applied.[50]

In large measure, a final rejection signifies (1) the final refusal of the primary examiner to allow one or more claims in an application pending before him and (2) the reaching of clear issues between the examiner and applicant. An application will be placed under final rejection even though it contains one or more allowed claims.[51] Requests for reconsideration proffered after an application has been properly placed under final rejection will be considered by the primary examiner, but only cursorily. Prosecution after final rejection is greatly curtailed. Before final rejection, an applicant has an almost unrestricted right to amend or introduce new claims. Amendments submitted before final are entered as a matter of course. After final rejection, an applicant only has the *right* to introduce amendments which adopt suggestions made by the examiner and/or remove issues from appeal, as by cancelling one or more claims; and/or which otherwise place the application in better condition for appeal.[52] Amendments after final rejection are governed by Rule 116. They will not be made part of the record of the application as a matter of course, but must first be approved by the examiner. Amendments which touch the merits of the application, may be admitted in the examiner's discretion, upon a showing of good and sufficient reasons why they are necessary and were not earlier presented. It would seem that amendment of claims made in response to a ground of rejection first presented in the final rejection satisfies this requirement. An amendment after final rejection may be denied entry on the ground that it raises one or more new issues that would require further search and/or consideration. The presentation of additional claims without the cancellation of a corresponding number of finally rejected claims is not considered as placing the application in better condition for appeal, and consequently such amendment may be summarily denied entry for this reason alone.[53]

The limitations imposed by a final rejection upon time are as significant as the constraints placed by an outstanding final rejection upon amendment. Upon the filing of a letter responsive to a nonfinal action, the statutory period ceases to run. Accordingly, an applicant is not prejudiced by the length of time that it takes the Office to reply to an applicant's letter responsive to a nonfinal action. No comparable tolling of the statutory period occurs by response to a final rejection.[54] Moreover, the filing of a petition does not stay the period for reply to an examiner's action which may be running against the application.[55] The harshness of this policy is mitigated somewhat by the fact that upon filing a first response to a final rejection, the shortened statutory period is automatically extended from three to four months, a timely first response to a final rejection being construed as including a request for a one month's extension of time.[56] Second and subsequent responses to a final rejection do not further extend the shortened statutory period, and, if submitted on the initiative of the applicant, will normally not be entered unless they merely cancel additional claims and/or place the case in condition for allowance. After final rejection, one personal interview by the applicant may be entertained, if circumstances warrant. In exceptional circumstances, a second personal interview may be initiated by the examiner if in his judgment this would materially assist in placing the application in condition for allowance.[57]

It will be noted here that amendments in the course of ex parte prosecution may also be made: (1) before first action (known as a preliminary amendment), such amendment must not introduce new matter; (2) after decision by the Board of Appeals in response to a new ground of rejection made thereby (Rule 196b); and (3) after allowance, such generally being limited to formal matters which do not change the scope of any claim (Rule 312).

Regardless of the point in prosecution at which an amendment is proffered, its form must conform to the following rules:

> *Rule 121.* Manner of making amendments. (a) Erasures, insertions, or alterations of the Office file papers and records must not be physically entered by the applicant. Amendments to the application (excluding the claims) are made by filing a paper (which should conform to rule 52), directing or requesting that specified amendments be made. The exact word or words to be stricken out or inserted by said amendment must be specified and the precise point indicated where the deletion or insertion is to be made.
>
> (b) Except as otherwise provided herein, a particular claim may be amended only by directions to cancel or by rewriting such claim with underlining below the word or words added and brackets around the word or words deleted. The rewriting of a claim in this form will be construed as directing the cancellation of the original claim; however, the original claim number followed by the parenthetical word "amended" must be used for the rewritten claim. If a previously written claim is rewritten, underlining and bracketing will be applied in reference to the previously rewritten claim with the parenthetical expression "twice amended," "three times amended," etc., following the original claim number.
>
> (c) A particular claim may be amended in the manner indicated for the application in paragraph (a) of this section to the extent of corrections in spelling, punctuation, and typographical errors. Additional amendments in this manner will be admitted provided the changes are limited to (1) deletions and/or (2) the addition of no more than five words in any one claim. Any amendment submitted with instructions to amend particular

claims but failing to conform to the provisions of paragraphs (b) and (c) of this section may be considered nonresponsive and treated accordingly.

(d) Where underlining or brackets are intended to appear in the printed patent or are properly part of the claimed material and not intended as symbolic of changes in the particular cliam, amendment by rewriting in accordance with paragraph (b) of this section shall be prohibited.

(e) In reissue applications, both the descriptive portion and the claims are to be amended as specified in paragraph (a) of this section.

Rule 126. Numbering of claims. The original numbering of the claims must be preserved throughout the prosecution. When claims are cancelled, the remaining claims must not be renumbered. When claims are added, except when presented in accordance with rule 121(b), they must be numbered by the applicant consecutively beginning with the number next following the highest numbered claim previously presented (whether entered or not). When the application is ready for allowance, the examiner, if necessary, will renumber the claims consecutively in the order in which they appear or in such order as may have been requested by applicant.

[4] Incomplete Actions and Incomplete Responses

Where an Office Action has been dispatched which is defective in some matter necessary for a proper response, the error or omission should be called to the attention of the Office before the expiration of the period for response. The examiner will then prepare a Supplementary Action, the mailing of which will restart the period for response, regardless of the time remaining in the original period.[58]

Where an applicant's communication is not fully responsive to an Office Action, the examiner may give the applicant one month or the remainder of the period for response, whichever is longer, to complete his response.[59] The period thus given is known as a "time limit" in contradistinction to a shortened statutory period.[60] Failure to respond within a time limit may be excused by the examiner, if the delay is satisfactorily explained. Failure to respond within a period for response (even a shortened statutory period) cannot be excused by the examiner, the only recourse being by petition to the Commissioner.[61]

§ 4. Appellate Review

[1] By the Patent Office Board of Appeals

An applicant for a patent, any of whose claims has been twice rejected, or who has been given a final rejection, may appeal from the decision of the primary examiner to the Board of Appeals (P.O. Bd. App.)[62]

The appeal must be initiated within the period of response to the outstanding Office Action from which the appeal is being taken.[63] This is accomplished by the filing of a Notice of Appeal, which recites the Office Action of the primary examiner (identified by its mailing date) and the rejected claims (identified by their numbers) being appealed.

Within the time allowed for response to the action appealed from or within sixty days from the filing of the Notice of Appeal, whichever is later, the applicant (who is now styled the "appellant") *must* file a brief setting forth his position and indicating whether he desires an oral hearing.[64] The Board of Appeals may, for sufficient cause shown, extend the time for filing the brief to a date not later than sixty days after the original expiration date. Any longer or further extension must be sought from the Commissioner. All requests for extensions must be filed prior to the expiration of the period sought to be extended. The appeal will be dismissed, if a brief is not filed within the time allowed.[65]

Following the submission of the appellant's brief, the examiner prepares a reply thereto, known as the Examiner's Answer, a copy of which is mailed to the appellant. The Examiner's Answer may contain a new ground of rejection, in which case the appellant is given sixty days from its mailing to file a reply brief.[66] Such reply may include any amendment or material appropriate to the new ground and may request remand to the examiner to consider such amendment or material. Appellant's brief *must* be responsive to every ground of rejection stated by the examiner, including new grounds stated in his answer. If an examiner's answer contains new points of argument, not amounting to a new ground of rejection, the appellant is given twenty days from the mailing of the answer within which he *may* file a reply thereto.

An oral hearing will be held only if requested by the appellant, and will normally be limited to one-half hour. The hearing is confined to arguments in support of the appellant's position, based on the record made before the primary examiner. The hearing is in no sense a trial. No new evidence can be introduced into the record, either by an appellant's brief or oral presentation, except in response to a new ground of rejection made in the examiner's answer.

The Board of Appeals, in its decision, may affirm or reverse the decision of the primary examiner in whole or in part on the grounds and on the claims specified by the primary examiner. The Board of Appeals may also make a new ground of rejection with its own reasons for so holding. The appellant may submit an appropriate amendment (known as a Rule 196b Amendment) of the claims so rejected or a showing of facts, or both, and have the matter reconsidered by the primary examiner or, waive such reconsideration before the primary examiner, and have the case reconsidered by the Board of Appeals.[67]

It should be noted that it is the Primary Examiner who has the power to allow a case. The function of the Board of Appeals is merely to review the propriety of decisions of the primary examiner that are adverse to an applicant. Accordingly, where the Board of Appeals reverses a decision of a primary examiner, the case will be remanded to the primary examiner to take further action in conformity with the decision rendered by the Board.[68] Technically, the Board of Appeals acquires jurisdiction over a case only after the examiner's answer has been written (or after he has considered appellant's reply thereto, where such is filed) and retains jurisdiction until it renders a decision.[69]

An appeal is generally heard and decided by a panel of three members of the Board of Appeals, who are styled "examiners-in-chief." There are two types of examiners-in-chief: (1) permanent members, who are appointed by, and serve at the pleasure of, the President; and (2) acting or temporary members, who are examiners of the primary grade designated by the Commissioner to serve on the Board of Appeals for periods of six months. Not more than one member of a panel may be an acting member of the Board.[70] The Commissioner of Patents and the assistant commissioners are ex officio members of the Board. On infrequent occasions the Board may be convened en banc, usually on rehearing, to consider important issues having implications beyond the instant case.

[2] Court Review

The decision of the Board of Appeals represents the decision of the Patent Office. Further proceedings are adversary in nature, in effect, pitting the Commissioner of Patents, represented by his solicitor, against the applicant. A primary examiner cannot take his case beyond the Patent Office. However, an applicant who is dissatisfied with the decision of the Board of Appeals may seek judicial review of the decision of the Board of Appeals, at his election, either before the United States Court of Customs and Patent Appeals (C.C.P.A.) or before the United States District Court for the District of Columbia (D.D.C.).

It should be noted that before an applicant is given his day in court, he must have "exhausted his administrative remedies," by first having submitted his case to the Patent Office Board of Appeals.[71] By going into court, moreover, an applicant loses his common-law right of secrecy, since all court proceedings are a matter of public record,[71] unless the court allows the proceedings to be conducted in camera.[72] All proceedings before the Patent Office, the reader will recall, are subject to the strictures of confidentiality imposed by 35 U.S.C. 122. The courts are not so bound.[73]

Court review of Board decisions must be initiated by the appellant within sixty days from the date of the decision of the Board, unless a petition for rehearing or reconsideration had been filed within thirty days after the date of the decision of the Board, in which case the time is extended to thirty days after the action on such petition.

Review by the Court of Customs and Patent Appeals is initiated by filing in the Patent Office a Notice of Appeal and reasons therefor.[74]

Review by the District Court for the District of Columbia is initiated by commencing a civil action against the Commissioner there.[75]

The nature and extent of the review differs drastically in the two forums. Proceedings before the Court of Customs and Patent Appeals are appeals in the true sense of the word. They are based strictly on the record made in the Patent Office.[76] Neither side may introduce new evidence or issues into the record. On the other hand, proceedings in the District Court for the District of Columbia are a trial de novo.[77] The Commissioner may introduce prior art and/or advance grounds of rejection other than that contained in the record made in the Patent Office. Moreover, the policy of the District Court is to accept the Commissioner's position unless the Court finds this to be "clearly erroneous."[78] The Court of Customs and Patent Appeals has been somewhat less inclined to accept the Patent Office's findings.[79]

It is interesting to note that until relatively recently the Court of Customs and Patent Appeals was deemed, by the Supreme Court, to be a mere "legislative" or Article I court, rather than a "constitutional" or Article III court.[80] What prompted the Supreme Court to change its mind was an appeal from a criminal conviction in which the defendant, who had been tried by a judge of the Court of Customs and Patent Appeals sitting by designation, argued that trial by a judge of an Article I court was a denial of due process, it being possible for Congress to reduce the compensation paid judges of such a court. Rather than set the defendant free, the Supreme Court changed its mind, holding that the Court of Customs and Patent Appeals was indeed an Article III court,[81] even though, at least in certain customs causes, the decisions of the court are reviewable by the President.[82]

An applicant or the Commissioner, if dissatisfied with the decision of the Court of Customs and Patent Appeals may seek review of its decision by the United States Supreme Court,[83] by petitioning the Supreme Court for a writ of certiorari. An applicant or the Commissioner, if dissatisfied with a decision of the District Court for the District of Columbia must first appeal to the United States Court of Appeals for the District of Columbia Circuit before petitioning the Supreme Court for a writ of certiorari.[84]

Proceedings before the Board of Appeals, the Court of Customs and Patent Appeals, and the District Court can be identified and distinguished by their distinctive captions: *Ex parte* signifies a case before the Board; *In re* (In the matter of the application of) signifies a case before the Court of Customs and Patent Appeals; and *Commissioner* v. ______ signifies a case before the District Court.

In considering the propriety of any review from the decision of the primary examiner, it is important to bear in mind, that, unlike other civil litigation, the applicant bears all the costs even if ultimately successful. This is particularly onerous with respect to appeals to the Court of Customs and Patent Appeals, the Court of Appeals for the District of Columbia Circuit, and the Supreme Court, where the appellant must pay for the printing of the record made before the Patent Office.[85]

§ 5. Restriction and Double Patenting

Section 121 of the Patent Act provides:

> If two or more independent and distinct inventions are claimed in one application, the Commissioner may require the application to be restricted to one of the inventions. If the other invention is made the subject of a divisional application which complies with the requirements of section 120 of this title it shall be entitled to the benefit of the filing date of the original application. A patent issuing on an application with respect to which a requirement for restriction under this section has been made, or on an application filed as a result of such a requirement, shall not be used as a reference either in the Patent Office or in the courts against a divisional application or against the original application or any patent issued or either of them, if the divisional application is filed before issuance of the patent or the other application. If a divisional application is directed solely to subject matter described and claimed in the original application as filed, the Commissioner may dispense with signing and execution by the inventor. The validity of a patent shall not be questioned for failure of the Commissioner to require the application to be restricted to one invention.

The phrase "independent and distinct inventions" is contrued as meaning "independent *or* distinct inventions," that is, as meaning distinct (or related) though dependent.[86] The concept of "independent inventions" embraces that of "distinct inventions."

The term "independent" means that there is no disclosed relationship between the two or more subjects disclosed, that is, they are unconnected in design, operation, or effect, as, for example: (1) species under a genus which species are not usable together as disclosed; and (2) process and apparatus incapable of being used in practicing the process.[87]

The term "distinct" means that two or more subject as disclosed are related, as, for example: (1) a combination and part (subcombination) thereof; (2) a process and apparatus for its practice; (3) a process and product made, which are each capable of separate manufacture, use or sale as claimed, and are patentable over each other.[88]

Restriction includes that practice of requiring the applicant to elect between dependent though distinct (related) inventions.

Two or more truly independent, and not merely distinct, inventions may not be claimed in one application except that more than one species of an invention, not to exceed five, may be specifically claimed in different claims in one application, provided the applicant also includes an allowable claim generic to all the claimed species and all the claims to each species in excess of one are written in dependent form or otherwise include all the limitations of the generic claim.[89] Claims to be restricted to species, must recite the mutually exclusive characteristics of such species.[90] The examiner will not require restriction to five species unless he is satisfied that he would be prepared to allow claims to each of the claimed species over the parent case, if presented in a divisional application filed according to the requirement.[91]

Restriction between two or more merely distinct inventions *may* be required by the primary examiner.

Where there is a combination-subcombination relationship between the claimed inventions, distinctiveness is established merely by demonstrating one of the following:[92]

(1) Separate classification thereof: This shows that each distinct subject has attained a recognition in the art as a separate subject for inventive effort, and also a separate field of search;

(2) A separate status in the art when they are classifiable together: Even though they are classified together, as shown by appropriate explanation, each subject can be shown to have formed a separate subject for inventive effort when an explanation indicates a recognition of separate effort by inventors;

(3) A different field of search: Where it is necessary to search for one of the distinct subjects in places where no pertinent art to the other subject exists, a different field of search is shown, even though the two are classified together. The indicated different field of search must in fact be pertinent to the type of subject matter covered by the claims.

To establish distinctiveness of a process and a product made thereby; or of apparatus and product made thereby; or of a process and apparatus for its practice, it must be demonstrated that *in addition* to satisfying one of the criterion for distinctiveness of combination-subcombination inventions, set out above, that:[93]

(1) For apparatus and product made thereby—

(a) that the process as claimed is not an obvious process of making the product and that the process as claimed can be used to made other and different products, or

(b) that the product as claimed can be made by another and materially different process.[94]

(2) For apparatus and product made thereby—

(a) that the apparatus as claimed is not the obvious apparatus for making the product and that the apparatus as claimed can be used to make other and different products, or

(b) that the product as claimed can be made by other and materially different apparatus.[95]

(3) For process and apparatus for its practice—

(a) that the process as claimed can be practiced by another and materially different apparatus or by hand, or

(b) that the apparatus as claimed can be used to practice another and materially different process.[96]

It should be noted that claims involving different statutory classes of invention, as those drawn to a process and apparatus for its practice, may raise different legal issues. However, the fact that the claims of an application are drawn to different statutory classes of invention is in and of itself an insufficient basis for requiring restriction between them.

In a sense, a claim drawn to a genus links together claims drawn to species subsumable thereunder. As has been noted above, the examiner must examine the generic claim along with up to five species claims.[97] The phenomenon of linking occurs also in regard to distinct inventions.[98] For example, a claim to "means" for practicing a process links proper apparatus and process claims.[99] A claim drawn to a combination is not, however, deemed to "link" claims drawn to subcombinations thereof.[100] Where true linking claims between distinct inventions are present in an application, the linking claims must be examined along with the claims drawn to the invention elected, and should any linking claims be allowed, rejoinder of the divided invention must be permitted.[101] Where linking claims are present, whether they link independent or distinct inventions, the examiner will either execute a letter including a restriction requirement only or telephone the applicant and request that he make an oral election.[102] The examiner will specify in his restriction requirement the linking or generic claims.[103]

A requirement for restriction between independent or distinct inventions may be made at any time before final action in the case, at the discretion of the examiner, although it is usually made either before or simultaneously with a first action on the merits.[104] The examiner may telephone the applicant and make an oral requirement, to be followed up in writing along with the next Office Action. If the applicant refuses to make an oral election, a written requirement will be executed. Where the examiner makes a requirement for restriction, the applicant must make a provisional election between the independent or distinct inventions as the claims drawn to each have been grouped by the examiner, *even though the applicant traverses the requirement.*[105] If the applicant traverses the requirement, its propriety will be reconsidered by the examiner and either be withdrawn or be made final in the next Office Action.[106] From the finality of the requirement, the applicant may petition the Commissioner for review.

Nonelected claims, even though withdrawn by the examiner from further consideration, are technically retained in the case until they are cancelled. An applicant who does not traverse a requirement for restriction, however, thereby looses the right to petition the Commissioner and the examiner, if the case is otherwise in condition for allowance, may himself cancel the nonelected claims by examiner's amendment, without even first consulting the applicant.[107] Where a requirement for restriction has been traversed and made final, the applicant may petition the Commissioner to review the requirement. Such petition may be filed at any time before appeal.[108] If the case is otherwise in condition for allowance, the examiner may give the applicant one month in which to cancel the nonelected claims or to petition the Commissioner pursuant to Rule 144. Failure to take action during such period will be treated as authorization to cancel the nonelected claims by examiner's amendment and to pass the case to issue.[109]

Before leaving the subject of restriction, it should be borne in mind that the motivation for requiring restriction between independent or distinct inventions is to obviate the burden that examining two or more different inventions in one application would place upon the Patent Office and its staff.

The issuance of two or more patents to the same inventive entity for the same invention is know as "double patenting."[110] Where plural, noncontinuing applications filed by the same inventive entity disclose the same invention, one cannot be used as a reference against another unless the earlier one becomes a statutory bar to a patent.[111] The wording of 35 U.S.C. 101, which states in the singular that an invention "may obtain *a* patent . . . ." is used, however, as the basis for denying a second patent on the very same invention to the same inventive entity.[112] Courts have also found double patenting where there is a merely obvious but real difference between the claims of two patents to the same inventive entity.[113] Thus, there are two types of double patenting: (1) the "same invention" type, which is based on 35 U.S.C. 101; and (2) the "obviousness" type, which is judicially created doctrine based on public policy rather than statute and which is primarily intended to prevent prolongation of monopoly by prohibiting claims in a second patent not patentably distinguishing from claims in a first patent.[114]

The language of 35 U.S.C. 121, third sentence, would appear to preclude a holding of double patenting in regard to a parent or any divisional applications thereof conforming to a requirement for restriction made by the Patent Office.[115] Some courts, however, have hinted that they would not feel precluded from holding double patenting where a requirement for restriction was improperly made.[116]

Double patenting is deemed offensive because: (1) if the patents are not to expire at the same time there is a prolongation of monopoly; and (2) if the patents become the property of different parties, there is a possibility of vexatious litigation. Accordingly, even where no requirement was made, a rejection based merely on the obviousness type of double patenting may be obviated by the filing of terminal disclaimers which include a provision that the patent shall expire immediately if it ceases to be commonly owned with the other application or patent.[117] The terminal disclaimer disclaims the terminal part of the patent that would extend beyond the expiration date of the other patent or application between whose claims there are merely obvious differences. A rejection based on the same invention type of double patenting, being predicated upon statute, cannot be obviated by the filing of a terminal disclaimer.[118]

§ 6. Rejections

An applicant in the United States has a *right* to a patent for his invention, unlike an applicant in the United Kingdom, where the granting of patents, at least in theory, is still at the *discretion* of the

Sovereign.[119] Before any United States patent issues, however, there must be at least apparent compliance with the requisites prescribed by law, as determined in first instance by the Patent Office. Upon presentation to the Patent Office of an application in the prescribed form, the applicant is prima facie entitled to a patent upon what he claims. However, upon the issuance of a rejection, it is incumbent upon the applicant to come forward and rebut or otherwise overcome the examiner's position. Much dispute and uncertainty has surrounded the extent to which the examiner's rejection must be overcome. Some years back, the Court of Customs and Patent Appeals took the position (known as the "Rule of Doubt") that in cases of doubt, the applicant is entitled to a patent. While the court has since retreated from this position, it should be apparent that as an abstract proposition, the rule or its repudiation is largely meaningless, as there is some degree of doubt in nearly every determination of patentability or unpatentability![120] It is utterly impossible to come up with anything even approaching a quantitative measure of doubt present in any case.

Broadly, the rejections that may be made against a claim fall into two categories: (1) those based on prior art; and (2) those not based on prior art. Even here there is overlap, because a claim may be so indefinite as to read on the prior art.

Prior art rejections are based on either 35 U.S.C. 102 or 35 U.S.C. 103. Rejections not based on prior art may fall under 35 U.S.C. 101, 35 U.S.C. 112, or 35 U.S.C. 132. In a few instances, rejections will be made without the invocation of a section of the Patent Act, recourse being had to some more general proposition of law, as, for example, rejections based upon res judicata or upon obviousness double patenting.

In making rejections based on prior art, it is the practice to cite one or more patent or literature references as evidence of the state of the prior art alleged by the examiner. However, there may be instances in which a feature is so well known that the citation of a specific reference showing the same is deemed unnecessary.[121] In such a case, it is said that "official" or judicial notice is taken of the fact alleged to be notoriously well known.[122]

[1] Under 35 U.S.C. 102

In making a rejection under 35 U.S.C. 102, the examiner will state that one or more specified claims "are rejected under 35 U.S.C. 102 as *anticipated* by" (emphasis added), a single reference. To constitute an anticipation, all material claimed features must be contained within the four corners of a single prior art reference.[123] There are, however, instances in which it is not improper, and indeed advantageous, to cite more than a single reference in applying 35 U.S.C. 102, as, for example, where the reference relied upon as an anticipation does not *expressly* disclose all the features or properties recited in the claim being rejected.[124] In such a situation, additional references may be cited as evidence of the inherency of features or properties not expressly mentioned in the alleged anticipating reference. Moreover, the date of a reference cited merely as evidence of the inherency of a feature of property alleged to be present in some other reference would seem to be irrelevant. It may well be subsequent to the effective filing date of the application whose claim is being rejected. In setting out a rejection under 35 U.S.C. 102, an examiner may merely cite the alleged anticipating reference without further elaboration, believing that its application to the claim is self-explanatory. Where the correspondence of a claimed feature to that disclosed in the reference is obscure or inherent, the examiner may indicate in his rejection, the portion of the reference on which he is relying.[125] In rejections under 35 U.S.C. 102, it is permissible to employ a reference the disclosure of which literally reads on what is claimed, though the reference is from a wholly unrelated art.[126] In making such a rejection, the examiner is, in effect, telling the applicant that his claim is so broad as literally to read on the cited unrelated art.

[2] Under 35 U.S.C. 103

In making a rejection under 35 U.S.C. 103, the examiner will state that one or more specified claims "are rejected under 35 U.S.C. 103 as *unpatentable over*" (emphasis added) one or more references. Where more than one reference is applied, it will be stated that the claim is unpatentable over one reference (known as the primary reference) "in view of" or "in light of" one or more other (secondary, tertiary, etc.) references. There is no limit to the number of references that may be combined in a rejection under 35 U.S.C. 103.[127] However, where the invention is relatively uncomplicated, the citation of a large number of prior art references, none of which hit upon the crux of applicant's invention, has been taken by some courts as evidence of unobviousness.[128] As a general rule, the vintage of a reference is immaterial, absent some showing that the art tried and failed to solve some problem notwithstanding its presumed knowledge of the reference.[129] Nevertheless, the lapse of about a half century between the vintage of the references and the making of the claimed invention by the patentee has been taken as evidence of the fact that it would not have been obvious to combine the references to arrive at the claimed invention.[130]

There is no universal, mechanical formula for permissible combining and/or modifying of prior art references to guide the examiner in formulating rejection based on obviousness. Each case, must ultimately turn on its own peculiar facts.[131] It is generally accepted, however, that it is improper to change the basic principle under which the primary reference was intended to operate.[132] A combination of references is improper if it renders the primary reference inoperative for its intended purpose.[133] It is not improper, however, to take a feature out of context and employ it in a different, though analogous, context.[134] A combination of references may be proper even though the secondary reference cannot be bodily incorporated, as by substitution, into the primary reference.[135] It is insufficient to show merely that each separate element of a claimed combination can be found in one or various prior art references.[136] There should be some teaching, or at least suggestion, in the prior art that the individual elements can, or should, be combined as claimed.[137] The question always is whether one skilled in the art, with the references before him, could make the combination of elements claimed without the exercise of inventive faculty.[138] Thus, it would seem not improper to rely upon a reference, though from a non-analogous art, where the feature therein relied upon is generally well known. The fact that a reference is technically classifiable in an art different from that to which the claimed invention relates would seem to be immaterial, if the feature therein relied upon is so well known that it either: (1) would be part of one's general knowledge, or (2) would at least be reasonable for one to look to such art for a solution to the problem at hand.

Still unsettled is the question of whether a rejection under 35 U.S.C. 103 on a combination of references is tenable where there is a good and obvious reason to combine them, but not the reason taught by the applicant.[139] The Supreme Court has sustained the validity of a patent the claims of which were drawn to an electrochemical battery, the electrodes of which were made of materials that the prior art showed were known to be suitable for such purpose, although no single prior art reference showed the claimed combination.[140] The specification taught that the claimed combination of electrodes possessed advantages which could not be discerned from a study of the relevant prior art.

Before turning to rejections not based on prior art, a significant point involving the interplay of 35 U.S.C. 102 and 35 U.S.C. 103 will be presented. Section 102(b) bars from patent protection an invention which was patented or described in a printed publication more than one year prior to the date of the application for patent in the United Staes. Section 102 has been construed as applying to anticipations. To be barred by Section 102, there must be a complete correspondence between the reference and what is claimed. Suppose, however, that after *A* makes an invention, a reference *X* is published which, while it does not anticipate *A's* invention, does render it obvious. *A* does not file an application for a patent on his invention until more than a year after reference *X* has been published.

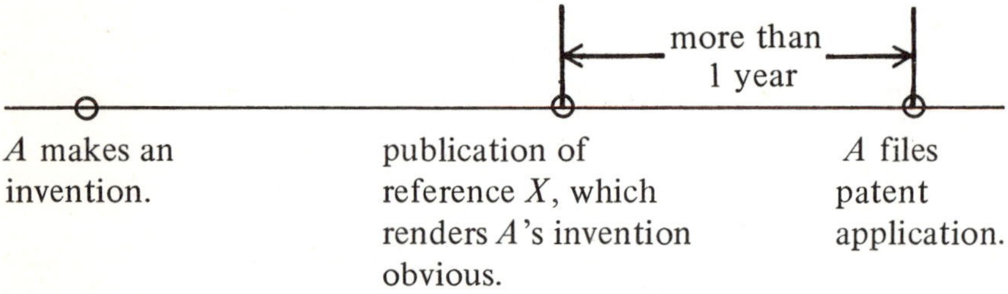
more than 1 year
A makes an invention.
publication of reference X, which renders A's invention obvious.
A files patent application.

Query: Is *X* a good reference against *A's* invention under 35 U.S.C. 103?

Answer: Yes.[141] Despite the fact that obviousness is to be gauged (according to the very language of 35 U.S.C. 103) "at the time the invention was made." At the time *A* made his invention, *X* was not in the public domain!

[3] Under 35 U.S.C. 101

The Patent Office and courts have found in this provision a basis for rejecting on the grounds of:

(1) lack of statutory subject matter (See Chapter 5).

(2) lack of utility. (See Chapter 7).

(3) "same invention" type of double patenting. (See this chapter infra).

[4] Under 35 U.S.C. 112

Most rejections not based on prior art are founded upon some language in 35 U.S.C. 112. There are three paragraphs to 35 U.S.C. 112, the first two of which relate to the required content of the disclosure and form of the claims, respectively. Failure of the specification to comply with the requisites of 35 U.S.C. 112, first paragraph, is grounds for objecting to the specification and for rejecting claims based thereon. Failure of the claims to satisfy the requisites of 35 U.S.C. 112, second paragraph, is grounds for rejecting the claims. Rejections made pursuant to 35 U.S.C. 112 may be broken down as follows:

[a] First Paragraph

Insufficient disclosure
Undue breadth

Rejections based upon 35 U.S.C. 112, first paragraph, are addressed to the adequacy of the disclosure. A disclosure may be so defective as to be incapable of supporting any claims whatever. Such a disclosure will vitiate not only the instant application, but also any purported continuation-in-part application which attempts to rely on the filing date of the fatally defective disclosure.[142] A disclosure may be sufficient to support certain claims, but too limited to support others. The claims lacking sufficient support may be rejected under 35 U.S.C. 112, first paragraph, on the ground of undue breadth.[143] The requisites of an adequate disclosure are outlined in Chapter 12.

[b] Second Paragraph

Vague and indefiniteness
Undue multiplicity
Prolixity
Omnibus claim
Old combination

Rejections based upon 35 U.S.C. 112, second paragraph, are addressed to the form of the claims and, hence, may be overcome by amendment. All rejections under this paragraph are, in essence, that the claims, as worded, fail particularly to point out and distinctly claim the subject matter which the applicant regards as his invention, and, hence, are vague and indefinite. There indeed is an element of vagueness and indefiniteness in unduly multiplied[144] and prolix claims.[145] Both practices tend to obscure the invention by raising numerous insignificant issues: a prolix claim by long recitations of unimportant details; unduly multiplied claims, by presenting a large number of claims which differ from one another by minor details. It should be borne in mind, however, that both the *Rules of Practice*[146] and the case law[147] confirm an applicant's right to restate, by plural claims, his invention in a reasonable number of ways.

The antithesis of a claim which particularly points out and distinctly claims what the applicant regards as his invention is a so-called omnibus or nonstatutory claim, which typically reads as: "A device substantially as shown and described." Such a claim is not permitted.

A claim is said to be drawn to an old combination where the recited combination is old, novelty residing merely in one of its constituent elements.[148] The fact that an applicant has improved one element of a combination which may be per se patentable does not entitle him to a claim to the improved element in combination with old elements where the elements perform no new function in the claimed combination.[149]

What constitutes vagueness and indefiniteness in claiming can best be gleaned from studying the rules of claim drafting set out in Chapter 3.

There are a few grounds of rejection which are, in a sense, akin to those based upon indefiniteness, and yet which find no clear support in literal wording of 35 U.S.C. 112, second paragraph. These include rejection based upon duplicity of claims and upon aggregation.

[i] Duplicate Claims—When two claims in an application are duplicates, or else are so close in content that they both cover the same thing, despite a slight difference in wording, it is proper after allowing one claim to reject the other as being a substantial duplicate of the allowed claim.[150]

[ii] Aggregation—A claim is said to be aggregative where it merely recites an assemblage of elements without pointing out any cooperation between them.[151]

[5] Under 35 U.S.C. 132

This section relates to the reexamination and amendment of claims. The final sentence declares: "No amendment shall introduce new matter into the disclosure of the invention."

Accordingly, a claim which is based on new matter will be "rejected under 35 U.S.C. 132 as drawn to new matter."

The rationale for precluding the introduction of new matter is to preserve the integrity of filing dates. All material aspects of a disclosure must correspond to what was contained in the specification when it was originally filed, with the exception of continuation-in-part applications, wherein there may be a departure in content from that of the parent application. The new matter will be entitled only to the benefit of the actual filing date of the continuation-in-part application.

"New matter" is a term of art, and may include the cancellation of material as well as the addition of material to the specification and/or drawing.[152] On the other hand, merely making explicit that which is clearly inherent in the specification may be deemed not to constitute new matter.[153]

It should be noted that the claims, as originally filed, are part of the original disclosure.[154] Where material contained in the claims, as originally presented, is not also part of the description of the invention, such description may be suitably amended to form an antecedent basis for what is claimed.[155]

§ 7. Affidavit Practice

Under certain circumstances, a rejection may be overcome by the submission of evidence in the form of an affidavit or a declaration.

An affidavit is a statement confirmed by oath or affirmation before an officer authorized to administer the same. A declaration contains: (1) an affirmation that all statements made of the declarant's own knowledge are true and that all statements made on information and belief are believed to be true; and (2) a warning that willful false statements are subject to the penalties of perjury.[156] Unlike an affidavit, a declaration is executed entirely by the declarant, there being no attestation by a notary public or other authorized official. An affidavit and declaration have precisely the same legal effect. That is to say, either is competent legal evidence of facts averred therein.

There are two ways in which an affidavit or declaration may overcome a rejection: (1) it may establish that the claimed invention was made before a disclosure which appears to be prior art became effective as a reference (Rule 131); (2) it may traverse a ground of rejection, as by demonstrating the inoperativeness of applied prior art or by distinguishing applied prior art from the claimed subject matter (Rule 132).

[1] Rule 131

The purpose of an affidavit or declaration made pursuant to Rule 131 is to antedate, and thereby eliminate, a reference applied by the examiner against an applicant's claims. By means of an affidavit or declaration, an applicant may establish that he made the invention which he claims prior to the date the cited material became effective as a reference and, hence, that such material is, with respect to his invention, not prior art. Thus, the effect of a Rule 131 affidavit or declaration is sometimes described as the "swearing back" of a reference or as the "carrying back" the date of invention.

An affidavit or declaration made pursuant to Rule 131 can overcome a reference which is a United States patent only if such patent merely discloses, and does not claim, what affiant or declarant claims. If a United States patent does claim the same invention claimed by the applicant, the only possible way of overcoming such patent is by an interference. The rationale of Rule 131 is consistent with the policy of United States law which accords priority to the first party to have reduced the invention to practice in the United States. Accordingly, an affidavit or declaration can be effective under Rule 131, only if it shows that the claimed invention was completed in the United States before the nominal publication date of a literature reference or foreign patent or before the filing date of a United States patent. A rule 131 affidavit is not competent to establish acts committed abroad.

In accordance with 35 U.S.C. 102(b), a Rule 131 affidavit or declaration is incapable of overcoming any reference which has been published, anywhere in the world, more than one year prior to the applicant's earliest effective filing date.

Rule 131 effective to overcome publication X, where:

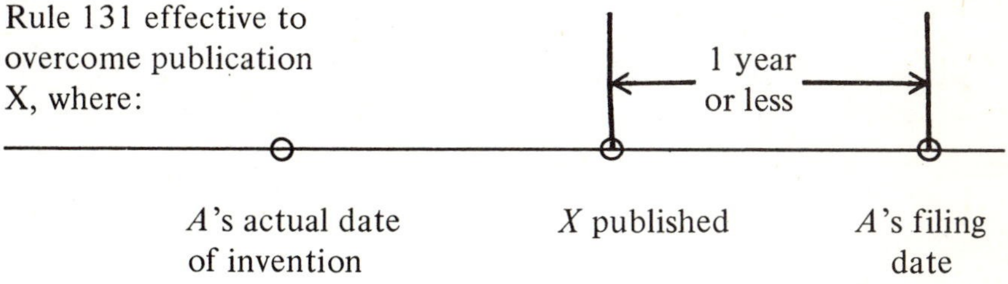

Unless it is a statutory bar, a rejection on a publication may be overcome by a showing that it was published either by the applicant himself or in his behalf.[157] When the unclaimed subject matter of a patent is the applicant's own invention, a rejection on that patent may be removed by:(1) an affidavit or declaration from the patentee establishing the fact that he derived his knowledge of the relevant subject matter from the applicant; and (2) a showing by the applicant that he himself made the invention upon which the relevant disclosure in the patent is based.[158]

To be effective, an affidavit or declaration must state facts, and not merely conclusions. An affidavit or declaration made pursuant to Rule 131 must be supported by exhibits evidencing the statements of fact made therein.[159] These may include copies of sketches, notebook entries, an accompanying model, and/or attached statements by witnesses. As in interference practice, where conception occurred prior to the date of the reference, but reduction to practice occurred after the date of the reference, diligence between the time of conception and reduction to practice must be shown. Moreover, completion of applicant's invention, as he claims it, must be shown. Completion of merely as much of the invention as the applied reference shows will not suffice.[160] Thus, even though a reference is applied under 35 U.S.C. 103, and discloses only part of what applicant claims (the difference alleged by the examiner to be obvious), the applicant must demonstrate that he was in possession of all that he claims prior to the date the disclosure being relied upon became a reference.

Affidavits or declarations made pursuant to Rule 131 are normally made by the inventor.[161] However, as already noted, where the applicant is relying upon witnesses for support, their affidavits or declarations may be included as exhibits.

[2] Rule 132

All affidavits or declarations presented which do not fall within or under other specific rules are treated or considered as falling under Rule 132.

Rule 132 affidavits or declarations, however, generally fall into five groups:

(1) Comparative tests or results;
(2) Operability of applicant's disclosure;
(3) Inoperability of references;
(4) Commercial success; and
(5) Sufficiency of disclosure.

An affidavit or declaration under Rule 132 is incapable of overcoming a rejection based upon a United States patent which claims the same invention being claimed by the applicant. The only possible way of overcoming such patent is by an interference.

An affidavit or declaration under Rule 132 must be timely presented. That is, it must be presented before final rejection, unless the affidavit or declaration is submitted in response to a new ground of rejection made in the final rejection or by the Board of Appeals.[162]

An affidavit or declaration under Rule 132 must state facts, not mere conclusions.

[a] Comparative Tests or Results

Affidavits or declarations comparing applicant's results with those of the prior art are generally submitted for the purpose of establishing an applicant's allegations of criticality or of an unexpected result. However, there should be some basis in applicant's specification for the criticality or unexpected result alleged. Statements in affidavits or declarations cannot be a substitute for proper disclosure in the application.[163]

[b] Operability of Applicant's Disclosure

Where the invention involved is of such a nature that it cannot be tested by known scientific principles, theoretical arguments in affidavit or declaration form are unacceptable, and the only satisfactory manner of overcoming the rejection is to demonstrate the operability by construction and operation of the invention.[164]

[c] Inoperability of References

Courts are wary of affidavits or declarations offered to show what a patentee states has been done cannot be done. The burden of proving inoperativeness of a patented invention is heavy.[165] Opinion affidavits or declarations carry little, if any, weight.[166]

[d] Commercial Success

Evidence of commercial success may serve as circumstantial evidence of unobviousness, but only where unobviousness over the prior art is in doubt. The affidavit or declaration must relate to the invention as claimed, and not merely as described and claimed.[167]

[e] Sufficiency of Disclosure

Affidavits or declarations may be presented to show that the disclosure of an application is sufficient to enable one skilled in the art to which it relates to practice the claimed invention. Such an affidavit or declaration may be made by anyone skilled in the art, though usually not by the applicant, as that would be self-serving. An affidavit or declaration which attempts to establish the sufficiency of a disclosure is obviously based largely upon the affiant's or declarant's opinion. Such document may not be used to supply deficiencies in the specification.[168]

§ 8. Fraud on the Patent Office

Misconduct in the course of procuring a patent may not only result in punishment of the culpable parties, but may vitiate the tainted patent or patent application as well. There also looms the possibility of liability under the antitrust laws for unlawful monopolization.

It is usual to speak of the misconduct as "fraud," whether or not the misconduct involves the commission of criminal acts (e.g., forgery, perjury, bribery). One of the earliest cases of fraud on the Patent Office, and the only one to implicate an employee of the Patent Office, involved the alteration, by the examiner, of Office records of a pending application.[169] The tainted application was stricken from the records of the Patent Office, and both the examiner and the attorney who had acted in collusion with him served prison sentences. More recently, it has been held that the participation of a retired examiner in the procurement of a reissue patent, the original of which he had examined, constituted a conflict of interest which voided the reissue, even though there was no evidence that the conflict of interest was the cause for the issuance of the reissue patent.[170]

Fraud in the procurement of a patent may be asserted in the following ways:

(1) A suit to cancel for fraud in the procurement. Such a suit, however, can be brought and maintained only by the United States.[171] It has been held, moreover, that a declaratory judgment action seeking the invalidity of a patent cannot be maintained where the sole basis therefor is an allegation of fraud in its procurement.[172]

(2) A proceeding brought before the Federal Trade Commission for violation of Section 5 of the Federal Trade Commission Act, which violation is in part based upon fraud in the procurement of a patent.[173]

(3) A defense[174] or counterclaim under the antitrust laws[175] to a suit for patent infringement.

Only as a defense or counterclaim to a suit for patent infringement is fraud in the procurement of such patent assertable by a private party. The theory underlying allowing a defendant to interpose fraud as a defense is the equitable doctrine of unclean hands, which holds that a court of equity will withhold enforcement of rights in property where the party seeking such enforcement, or those in privy with him, has indulged in inequitable conduct, which soils or dirties the hands of the plaintiff-patentee.

The elements constituting fraud which will render unclean the hands of a plaintiff-patentee generally correspond to those needed to establish a common-law cause of action for deceit, the party being deceived here being the United States acting through the Patent Office:

(1) a *Representation* of

(2) a *Material Fact*;

(3) the *Falsity* of such representation;

(4) *Scienter* or *Intent to Deceive* coupled with his knowledge of the falsity of the representation;

(5) *Reasonable Reliance* by the party to whom the misrepresentation is made;

(6) *Deception* of the party to whom the misrepresentation is made by reason of his reliance thereon;

(7) *Injury* to the party to whom the misrepresentation is made resulting from his reliance thereon.

Where the party accused of infringing a patent procured by fraud seeks to recover treble damages by means of a counterclaim under antitrust laws, he must very clearly establish that the patent would not have issued "but for" the misrepresentation.[176]

Perhaps the greatest difficulty in applying the common-law elements of deceit to patent procurement situations is in the determination of what conduct constitutes a misrepresentation. When is silence or the nondisclosure of information a misrepresentation? When is there a duty to speak? An applicant in his oath swears that he believes himself to be the first and original inventor of what he claims. Thus, if he knows of anticipatory art at the time he makes such an oath, he is committing perjury. Suppose, however, an applicant knows of art which, while not an anticipation, might, in the eyes of the examiner, render his invention obvious and therefore unpatentable. Is the applicant under a duty to call such art to the attention of the Patent Office? It would seem that such a duty does exist.[177] If an applicant becomes aware of anticipatory and only after he makes the oath is he under a duty to call it to the attention of the Patent Office? Another context in which the nondisclosure or suppression of information comes into play is in connection with the submission of affidavits or declarations pursuant to Rule 132. Where comparative results were submitted to the Patent Office to establish an unexpected result, the editing out of data unfavorable to the applicant's position was found to be culpable.[178] That a prior art patent may have been procured by fraud does not preclude its specification from being applied as a reference in *ex parte* prosecution.[179]

§ 9. Correction of Defective Patents

Three possible mechanisms exist for the correction of defective patents: a certificate of correction, a reissue patent and a disclaimer.

[1] Certificates of Correction

Certificates of Correction are available to obviate mistakes of a relatively minor character and for the correction of error in joining inventors.[180] The Patent Act and the *Rules of Practice* distinguish between certificates correcting Patent Office mistakes and those correcting an applicant's mistakes.

[a] Patent Office Mistake

Whenever a mistake in a patent, incurred through the fault of the Patent Office is clearly disclosed by the records of the Office, the Commissioner may issue a certificate of correction stating the fact and nature of such mistake, under seal, without charge, to be recoded in the records of patents. A printed copy thereof shall be attached to each printed copy of the patent, and such certificate shall be considered as part of the original patent. Every such patent together with such certificate, has the same effect and operation in law on the trial of actions for causes thereafter arising as if the same had been originally issued in such corrected form. The Commissioner may issue a corrected patent without charge in lieu of and with like effect as a certificate of correction.[181]

A certificate correcting an Office mistake may be issued at the request of the patentee or his assignee. Such certificate will not be issued at the request or suggestion of anyone not owning an interest in the patent, nor on motion of the Office, without first notifying the patentee (including any assignee of record) and affording him an opportunity to be heard.[182] If such mistakes are of such a nature that the meaning intended is obvious from the context, the Office may decline to issue a certificate and merely place the correspondence in the patented file.

[b] Applicant's Mistake

Whenever a mistake of a clerical or typographical nature, or of minor character, which was not the fault of the Patent Office, appears in a patent and a showing has been made that such mistake occurred in good faith, the Commissioner may, upon payment of the required fee, issue a certificate of correction, if the correction does not involve such changes in the patent as would constitute new matter or would require re-examination. Such patent, together with the certificate, has the same effect and operation in law on the trial of actions for causes thereafter arising as if the same had been originally issued in such corrected form.[183] A mistake is not of a minor character if the requested change would materially affect the scope or meaning of the patent.

[2] Reissue Patents

Reissue patents are available to correct errors made without any deceptive intention by the applicant, which errors are sufficiently material to render the original patent wholly or partly inoperative or invalid, by reason of a defective specification or drawing, or by reason of the patentee claiming more or less than he had a right to claim in the patent.[184]

No new matter may be introduced into the specification of a reissue patent.[185] A reissue application which seeks to broaden any claim, in any way, must be filed within two years of the issue date of the original patent.[186] Broadened claims, moreover, will be subject to the intervening rights of third parties.[187]

The term of a reissue is co-extensive with the unexpired part of the term of the original patent. That is to say, a reissue works no extension of the term of the patent which it replaces. Successive reissues may be obtained to correct errors in either the original or a subsisting reissue. Upon the demand of the applicant, separate reissues may be granted for each distinct invention contained in the original patent. The Patent Office, however, may not *require* restriction and election of distinct inventions present in an original patent.[188] The patent which a reissue corrects must be surrendered upon the grant of the reissue sought.[189]

It has been held that a reissue patent is available to correct misjoinder of inventions;[190] to correct the failure to claim the benefit of an earlier filing date, either based on the right of foreign priority[191] or as a continuing application;[192] and to obviate file wrapper estoppel, where it was found that a limitation added to a claim to obtain allowance was more restrictive than the prior art required.[193]

[3] Disclaimer

A patentee, whether of the whole or any sectional interest therein, may, on payment of the fee required by law, make disclaimer of any complete claim, stating therein the extent of his interest in such patent. Such disclaimer shall be in writing and recorded in the Patent Office; and it shall thereafter be considered as part of the original patent to the extent of the interest possessed by the disclaimant and by those claiming under him.[194]

[1] 1 Stat. 109 (1790).

[2] 1 Stat. 318 (1793).

[3] 5 Stat. 117 (1836).

[4] 9 Stat. 395 (1849). When established in 1849, the Department of the Interior was referred to as the *Home Department.*

[5] Rule 341(a), (b).

[6] P.L. 90-83, §500(b).

[7] P.L. 90-83, §500(e).

[8] Rule 341(c).

[9] People v. O'Brien, 142 U.S.P.Q. 239 (N.Y. Sup. Ct. 1964).

[10] Sperry v. Ex rel. Florida Bar, 373 U.S. 379, 137 U.S.P.Q. 578 (1963). See also, People v. Miller, 145 U.S.P.Q. 663 (N.Y. Sup. Ct. App. Div. 1st Dept't 1965).

[11] United States v. United Shoe Machinery, 89 F. Supp. 357, 358, 85 U.S.P.Q. 5, 6 (D. Mass. 1950).

[12] See Rules of the United States Court of Customs & Patent Appeals, Rule 2.

[13] See generally, Rifkind, "A Special Court for Patent Litigation? The Danger of a Specialized Judiciary," 37 *A.B.A.J.* 425 (1951). Compare, Posnack, "Special Judges for Patent Cases," 50 *A.B.A.J.* 475 (1964).

[14] *In re* Henriksen, 399 F.2d 253, 158 U.S.P.Q. 224 (C.C.P.A. 1968).

[15] *In re* Schmidt, 293 F.2d 274, 130 U.S.P.Q. 404 (C.C.P.A. 1961).

[16] M.P.E.P. 201.07.

[17] M.P.E.P. 201.07 (Rev. 36, Apr. 1973). See Rule 60.

[18] M.P.E.P. 201.08.

[19] M.P.E.P. 201.08.

[20] Hunt v. Mallinckrodt Chem. Works, 177 F.2d 583, 83 U.S.P.Q. 277 (2d Cir. 1949).

[21] M.P.E.P. 201.6.

[22] *In re* Campbell, 212 F.2d 606, 101 U.S.P.Q. 406 (C.C.P.A.) *cert. denied* 348 U.S. 858 (1954).

[23] N. 20 *supra*.

[24] Ex parte Komenak, 45 U.S.P.Q. 186 (Comm. Pat. 1940).

[25] M.P.E.P. 201.09.

[26] See generally, Comm'r v. Sunnen, 333 U.S. 591, 598, 77 U.S.P.Q. 29, 32 (1948).

[27] *In re* Barratt's Appeal, 14 App. D.C. 255, 257 (D.C.C. 1899).

[28] *In re* Fried, 312 F.2d 930, 136 U.S.P.Q. 429 (C.C.P.A. 1963).

[29] See *In re* Herr, 377 F.2d 610, 153 U.S.P.Q. 548 (C.C.P.A. 1967).

[30] M.P.E.P. 706.03(w).

[31] Rule 292.

[32] Rule 201.

[33] United States v. Bell Telephone Co., 128 U.S. 315, 363 (1888).

[34] See Universal Oil Prod. Co. v. Globe Oil & Refining Co., 322 U.S. 471, 484, 61 U.S.P.Q. 382, 388 (1944).

[35] M.P.E.P. 706.03.

[36] M.P.E.P. 714.14.

[37] M.P.E.P. 710.02(b).

[38] Rule 181(f).

[39] M.P.E.P. 710.02(e).

[40] Rule 136(b).

[41] M.P.E.P. 710.01(a).

[42] M.P.E.P. 710.01(a).

[43] Rule 137.

[44] M.P.E.P. 706.07(a).

[45] M.P.E.P. 706.07(a).

[46] M.P.E.P. 706.07(a).
[47] M.P.E.P. 706.07(b).
[48] M.P.E.P. 706.07.
[49] M.P.E.P. 706.07(c).
[50] See Whitmore, "The Significance of Compact Prosecution," 44 *J. Pat. Off. Soc'y* 719 (1962).
[51] Rule 113.
[52] M.P.E.P. 714.12.
[53] Rule 116(a).
[54] See generally, Lorenz v. Finkl, 333 F.2d 885, 889, 142 U.S.P.Q. 26, 29 (C.C.P.A. 1964).
[55] Rule 181(f).
[56] M.P.E.P. 714.12.
[57] M.P.E.P. 714.12. See also, M.P.E.P. 713.09.
[58] M.P.E.P. 710.06.
[59] M.P.E.P. 714.03.
[60] M.P.E.P. 710.02(d).
[61] 35 U.S.C. 133.
[62] 35 U.S.C. 134.
[63] Rule 191.
[64] Rule 192(a).
[65] Rule 192(b).
[66] M.P.E.P. 1208.01.
[67] Rule 196(b).
[68] Rule 197.
[69] M.P.E.P. 1210.
[70] 35 U.S.C. 7. But see, *In re* Denny, 397 F.2d 1020, 1022, 158 U.S.P.Q. 292, 294 (C.C.P.A. 1968) (Smith, J., dissenting); *In re* Wiechert, 370 F.2d 927, 152 U.S.P.Q. 247 (C.C.P.A. 1967).
[71] See Britt Technical Corp. v. L. & A. Prod. Inc., 223 F. Supp. 126, 139 U.S.P.Q. 334 (D. Minn. 1963).
[72] C.C.P.A. Rules of Practice, Rule 5.13(g).
[73] Hartley Pen Co. v. The United States District Court, 287 F.2d 324, 328, 129 U.S.P.Q. 152, 157-158 (9th Cir. 1961).
[74] 35 U.S.C. 141, 142.
[75] 35 U.S.C. 145.
[76] See Coakwell v. United States, 292 F.2d 918, 920, 130 U.S.P.Q. 231, 234 (Ct. Cl. 1961).
[77] Tietig v. Ladd, 228 F. Supp. 637, 141 U.S.P.Q. 372, 374 (D.D.C. 1964).
[78] Goodyear Tire & Rubber Co. v. Ladd, 349 F.2d 710, 711, 146 U.S.P.Q. 93, 95 (D.C.C. 1965).
[79] See Railex Corp. v. Joseph Guss & Sons, Inc., 256 F. Supp. 994, 995-996, 150 U.S.P.Q. 491, 492 (D.D.C. 1966).
[80] Ex parte Bakelite, 279 U.S. 438 (1929).
[81] Glidden v. Zdanak, 370 U.S. 530 (1962). See also, Brenner v. Manson, 383 U.S. 519, 526, 148 U.S.P.Q. 689, 692 (1966).
[82] 19 U.S.C. 1337 (1964). See generally, Metzger & Musrey, "Judicial Review of Tariff Commission Actions and Proceedings," 56 *Cornell L.R.* 285 (1971).
[83] 15 U.S.C. 2101.
[84] 28 U.S.C. 1252-1254.
[85] 35 U.S.C. 145.
[86] M.P.E.P. 802.01.

[87] M.P.E.P. 806.04.
[88] M.P.E.P. 808.02.
[89] Rule 141.
[90] M.P.E.P. 806.04(f).
[91] M.P.E.P. 806.04(h).
[92] M.P.E.P. 806.05(c).
[93] M.P.E.P. 808.02.
[94] M.P.E.P. 806.05(g).
[95] M.P.E.P. 806.05(f).
[96] M.P.E.P. 806.05(e).
[97] M.P.E.P. 809.02.
[98] M.P.E.P. 809.
[99] M.P.E.P. 809.03.
[100] M.P.E.P. 809.03.
[101] M.P.E.P. 809.
[102] M.P.E.P. 809.
[103] M.P.E.P. 809, 809.03.
[104] M.P.E.P. 811.
[105] M.P.E.P. 818.03(b).
[106] Rule 143, M.P.E.P. 818.03.
[107] M.P.E.P. 821.02.
[108] Rule 144.
[109] M.P.E.P. 821.01.
[110] M.P.E.P. 804.
[111] *In re* Facius, 408 F.2d 1396, 161 U.S.P.Q. 294 (C.C.P.A. 1969).
[112] M.P.E.P. 804.
[113] *In re* Thorington, 418 F.2d 528, 163 U.S.P.Q. 644 (C.C.P.A. 1969); *In re* White, 405 F.2d 904, 160 U.S.P.Q. 417 (C.C.P.A. 1969).
[114] See *In re* Carlson, 412 F.2d 255, 162 U.S.P.Q. 233 (C.C.P.A. 1969).
[115] M.P.E.P. 804.01.
[116] Eversharp, Inc. v. Phillip Morris, Inc., 256 F. Supp. 778, 150 U.S.P.Q. 98 (E.D. Va. 1966), *aff'd* 374 F.2d 511, 153 U.S.P.Q. 91 (4th Cir. 1967).
[117] M.P.E.P. 804.02.
[118] M.P.E.P. 804.
[119] See United States v. Bell Telephone Co., 128 U.S. 315, 363 (1888).
[120] *In re* Hofstetter, 362 F.2d 293, 298, 150 U.S.P.Q. 105, 109 (C.C.P.A. 1966), *cert.* granted 386 U.S. 990 (1967), *app. dism'd* 155 U.S.P.Q. 515 (1967). See also, *In re* Mixon, 470 F.2d 1374, 1378, 176 U.S.P.Q. 296, 299 (C.C.P.A. 1973).
[121] *In re* Fox 471 F.2d 1405, 1407, 176 U.S.P.Q. 340, 341 (C.C.P.A. 1973).
[122] M.P.E.P. 706.02(a).
[123] Soundscriber Corp. v. United States, 360 F.2d 954, 960, 148 U.S.P.Q. 298, 301 (Ct. Cl. 1966); Mueller Brass Co. v. Reading Indus., Inc., 352 F. Supp. 1357, 176 U.S.P.Q. 361, 368 (E.D. Pa. 1973).
[124] Package Devices, Inc. v. Sun Ray Drug Co., 432 F.2d 272, 167 U.S.P.Q. 193 (3d Cir. 1970).
[125] M.P.E.P.706.02.
[126] See *In re* Tibbals, 316 F.2d 955, 958, 137 U.S.P.Q. 565, 567 (C.C.P.A. 1963); Ex parte Lawrence, 131 U.S.P.Q. 40, 41 (P.O. Bd. App. 1960).
[127] Ex parte Fine, 1927 C.D. 84, 86, 364 O.G. 511, 512 (Comm. Pat. 1926).
[128] See Reynolds v. Whitin Mach. Works, 167 F.2d 78, 76 U.S.P.Q. 551 (4th Cir.), *cert. denied* 334 U.S. 844 (1948).
[129] *In re* McGuire, 416 F.2d 1322, 163 U.S.P.Q. 417 (C.C.P.A. 1969).

[130] Eastern Rotorcraft Corp. v. United States, 385 F.2d 465, 150 U.S.P.Q. 124 (Ct. Cl. 1966).
[131] *In re* Fotsch, 337 F.2d 1016, 1023, 143 U.S.P.Q. 291, 296 (C.C.P.A. 1964); Ex parte France, 132 U.S.P.Q. 211, 212 (P.O. Bd. App. 1961).
[132] *In re* Ratti, 270 F.2d 810, 123 U.S.P.Q. 349 (C.C.P.A. 1959).
[133] *In re* Flick, 210 F.2d 832, 101 U.S.P.Q. 70 (C.C.P.A. 1954).
[134] *In re* Bent, 339 F.2d 255, 144 U.S.P.Q. 28 (C.C.P.A. 1964).
[135] Canadian Ingersoll-Rand Co. v. Peterson Prod., Inc., 223 F. Supp. 803, 139 U.S.P.Q. 61 (N.D. Cal. 1963).
[136] *In re* Markham, 330 F.2d 358, 141 U.S.P.Q. 291 (C.C.P.A. 1964); *In re* Pennington, 241 F.2d 750, 113 U.S.P.Q. 81 (C.C.P.A. 1957); *In re* Hummer, 241 F.2d 742, 113 U.S.P.Q. 66 (C.C.P.A. 1957).
[137] *In re* Demarche, 210 F.2d 952, 105 U.S.P.Q. 65 (C.C.P.A. 1955).
[138] *In re* Shaffer, 229 F.2d 476, 108 U.S.P.Q. 326 (C.C.P.A. 1956); *In re* Carter, 212 F.2d 189, 101 U.S.P.Q. 290 (C.C.P.A. 1954).
[139] *In re* Mod, 408 F.2d 1055, 161 U.S.P.Q. 281 (C.C.P.A. 1969).
[140] See United States v. Adams, 383 U.S. 39, 148 U.S.P.Q. 479 (1966).
[141] *In re* Foster, 343 F.2d 980, 145 U.S.P.Q. 166 (C.C.P.A. 1965).
[142] Hunt v. Mallinckrodt Chem. Works, 177 F.2d 583, 83 U.S.P.Q. 277 (2d Cir. 1949).
[143] M.P.E.P. 706.03(z).
[144] M.P.E.P. 706.03(1).
[145] M.P.E.P. 706.03(g).
[146] Rule 75.
[147] *In re* Wakefield, 422 F.2d 897, 164 U.S.P.Q. 636 (C.C.P.A. 1970); *In re* Flint, 411 F.2d 353, 162 U.S.P.Q. 228 (C.C.P.A. 1969); Parke-Davis & Co. v. H.K. Mulford Co., 189 Fed. 95, 103 (C.C.S.D.N.Y. 1911).
[148] M.P.E.P. 706.03(j).
[149] *In re* Hall, 208 F.2d 370, 100 U.S.P.Q. 46 (C.C.P.A. 1953); Ex parte Silverstein, 125 U.S.P.Q. 238 (P.O. Bd. App. 1959).
[150] M.P.E.P. 706.03(k).
[151] M.P.E.P. 706.03(i).
[152] Rule 118. See Railway Co. v. Sayles, 97 U.S. (7 Otto) 554, 563-564 (1878).
[153] See generally, *In re* Oda, 443 F.2d 1200, 1203, 170 U.S.P.Q. 268, 270 (C.C.P.A. 1971).
[154] M.P.E.P. 608.01(1), 608.04(a), 706.03(n).
[155] Rule 117.
[156] Rule 68.
[157] M.P.E.P. 715.01(c).
[158] *In re* Facius, 408 F.2d 1396, 161 U.S.P.Q. 294 (C.C.P.A. 1969).
[159] Rule 131(b).
[160] *In re* Tanczyn, 347 F.2d 830, 146 U.S.P.Q. 298 (C.C.P.A. 1965).
[161] Rule 131(a).
[162] M.P.E.P. 715.09 (Rule 131); 715 (Rule 132).
[163] *In re* Oppenauer, 143 F.2d 974, 62 U.S.P.Q. 297 (C.C.P.A. 1944). See also, *In re* Honnig, 193 F.2d 191, 92 U.S.P.Q. 134 (C.C.P.A. 1951); Morton v. Ladd, 218 F. Supp. 824, 138 U.S.P.Q. 285 (D.D.C. 1963). Compare, Jennings v. Brenner, 255 F. Supp. 410, 150 U.S.P.Q. 167 (D.D.C. 1966).
[164] *In re* Chilowsky, 229 F.2d 457, 108 U.S.P.Q. 321 (C.C.P.A. 1956); Buck v. Ooms, 159 F.2d 462, 72 U.S.P.Q. 211 (D.C.C. 1947).
[165] *In re* Berry, 315 F.2d 916, 137 U.S.P.Q. 353 (C.C.P.A. 1963).
[166] See for example, *In re* Henrich, 268 F.2d 753, 122 U.S.P.Q. 388 (C.C.P.A. 1959).
[167] *In re* Hollingsworth, 278 F.2d 753, 126 U.S.P.Q. 56 (C.C.P.A. 1960).

[168] *In re* Smyth, 189 F.2d 982, 90 U.S.P.Q. 106 (C.C.P.A. 1951).
[169] *In re* Heany, 1911 C.D. 138, 171 O.G. 933 (Comm. Pat. 1911).
[170] Kearney & Trecker v. Giddings & Lewis, Inc., 452 F.2d 579, 171 U.S.P.Q. 650 (7th Cir.) *cert. denied* 405 U.S. 1066 (1971).
[171] United States v. Bell Telephone Co., 128 U.S. 315 (1888).
[172] E.W. Bliss Co. v. Cold Metal Process Co., 102 F.2d 105, 41 U.S.P.Q. 342 (6th Cir. 1939).
[173] Chas. Pfizer & Co. v. F.T.C., 401 F.2d 574, 159 U.S.P.Q. 193 (6th Cir. 1968), *cert. denied* 394 U.S. 920 (1969).
[174] Precision Instrument Mfg. Co. v. Automotive Maintenance Mach. Co., 324 U.S. 806, 65 U.S.P.Q. 133 (1945).
[175] Walker Process Equip., Inc. v. Food Mach. & Chem. Corp., 382 U.S. 172, 147 U.S.P.Q. 404 (1965).
[176] See Corning Glass Works, Inc. v. Anchor Hocking Glass Corp., 253 F. Supp. 461, 149 U.S.P.Q. 99 (D. Del. 1966), *rev'd on other grounds* 274 F.2d 473, 153 U.S.P.Q. 1 (3d Cir. 1967); Sticker Indus. Supply Corp. v. Blaw-Knox Co., 367 F.2d 744, 151 U.S.P.Q. 443 (7th Cir. 1966).
[177] See Union Carbide Corp. v. Filtrol Corp., 170 U.S.P.Q. 482, 521 (C.D. Cal. 1971); Elmwood Liquor Prod. Inc. v. Singleton Packing Corp., 328 F. Supp. 974, 170 U.S.P.Q. 398 (M.D. Fla. 1971).
[178] Monsanto Co. v. Rohm & Haas Co., 312 F.Supp. 778, 164 U.S.P.Q. 556 (E.D. Pa. 1970), *aff'd* 456 F.2d 592, 172 U.S.P.Q. 323 (3d Cir.), *cert. denied* 407 U.S. 934 (1972).
[179] *In re* Ludovici, 482 F.2d 958, 179 U.S.P.Q. 84 (C.C.P.A. 1973).
[180] 35 U.S.C. 256.
[181] Rule 322(b).
[182] Rule 322(a).
[183] 35 U.S.C. 254, 255.
[184] 35 U.S.C. 251.
[185] 35 U.S.C. 251.
[186] 35 U.S.C. 251.
[187] 35 U.S.C. 252.
[188] Rule 176.
[189] 35 U.S.C. 252.
[190] Ex parte Scudder, 169 U.S.P.Q. 814 (P.O. Bd. App. 1971).
[191] Brenner v. State of Israel, 400 F.2d 789, 158 U.S.P.Q. 584 (D.C.C. 1968).
[192] Sticker Indus. Supply Corp. v. Blaw-Knox Co., 321 F. Supp. 876, 167 U.S.P.Q. 442 (N.D. Ill. 1970).
[193] *In re* Richman, 409 F.2d 269, 161 U.S.P.Q. 359 (C.C.P.A. 1969).
[194] 35 U.S.C. 253.

–Part V–

EXPLOITING PATENT RIGHTS

> [T] he invention of fire-arms equalized the villein and the noble on the field of battle . . . .
>
> A. de Tocqueville
> *Democracy in America*, (1835)

All that a patent gives its recipient is the negative right to exclude others from the domain circumscribed by its claims.

The government leaves it to the patentee to translate this right into a financial return. A patent carries with it no assurance of government funds or other assistance. To enforce his rights, a patentee may resort to the courts, but he must hire, at his own expense, counsel to do so. Moreover, it is more than likely that he will find there a less than hospitable forum. Obviously, successful exploitation of a patent will depend upon much besides legal and inventive talents.

The exploitation of patents does, however, have its own peculiar legal problems. These arise: (1) when persons not authorized by the patentee attempt to compete with the patentee in the exploitation of his patented invention; (2) when the patentee attempts to transfer to or share with others his monopoly. Part V outlines each of these areas in a separate chapter.

Chapter 14

LICENSING AND ASSIGNMENT: THE SHARING & TRANSFER OF PATENT RIGHTS

SYNOPSIS

The fact that a patentee has the power to refuse a license does not mean that he has the power to grant a license on such conditions as he may choose.

Douglas, J.
Transparent-Wrap Mach. Co. v. *Stokes & Smith Co.*, 329 U.S. 637, 643, 72 U.S.P.Q. 148, 152 (1947)

> Within his domain, the patentee is czar. The people must take the invention on the terms he dictates or let it alone for 17 years. This is a necessity from the nature of the grant. Cries of restraint of trade and impairment of the freedom of sales are unavailing, because for the promotion of useful arts the constitution and statutes authorize this very monopoly.
>
> Baker, J.
> *Victor Talking Mach. Co.* v. *The Fair,*
> 123 Fed. 424, 426 (7th Cir. 1903)

An essential attribute of property is the ability to alienate or dispose of it. This is certainly no less true of patents than of other forms of property.

The reward derived from any patent will indeed be a function of the number of items embodying the patented invention from which the patentee can claim tribute. A patent to one having otherwise limited economic resources will not be nearly so valuable as it would be to one having virtually unlimited productive capacity. Since those who make inventions are not always in the position to derive the maximum economic return therefrom, a need exists for the ability to transfer or share patent rights.

The exclusivity that is the patent property may be split up and parcelled out in a myriad of different ways and along many different lines. While there are virtually an infinite number of ways in which the rights incident to a single patent may be divided up, there are but a relatively few which have significantly different legal consequences.

Perhaps the single most important distinction in farming out patent rights is that between an assignment and a license. The law allows a patentee to transfer to others his entire interest in a patent. The law also recognizes the transfer of less than an entire interest in a patent. The transfer of any *interest* in a patent is called an assignment. Federal law controls the assignment of patents. Section 261 of the Patent Act provides:

> Applications for patent, patents, or any interest therein, shall be assignable in law by an instrument in writing. The applicant, patentee, or his assigns or legal representatives may in like manner grant and convey an exclusive right under his application,

> patent, or patents, to the whole or any specified part of the United States. . . .
>
> An assignment, grant or conveyance shall be void as against any subsequent purchaser or mortgagee for a valuable consideration, without notice, unless it is recorded in the Patent Office within three months from its date or prior to the date of such subsequent purchase or mortgage.

A mere license is not deemed to constitute any *interest* in the patent. A license is but a promise by one having an interest in a patent to forbear from suing one who would commit what would be, but for the license, an infringement of that interest.[1] It is but permission to do that which otherwise would be unlawful.

A patent is, in effect, a bundle of rights which may be divided up and parcelled out along one or more different lines, as for example, by time, territory, field of use. One who acquires patent rights so limited acquires a divided interest in the patent. Such an interest is to be distinguished from an undivided interest, which includes a share in each and every right in the whole bundle of rights that is the patent. Holders of an undivided interest in a patent, as, for example, joint inventors, have the status of tenants in common.[2]

Section 261 provides, inter alia, for the recordation, in the Patent Office, of assignments, grants, and conveyances of interests in patents and patent applications. Accordingly, assignments, but not licenses, may be recorded there. Failure to record within the three-month period specified in the statute does *not* render the transfer absolutely void. An unrecorded, written assignment is good unless the rights that were purportedly transferred by such unrecorded assignment were later transferred to another. The transfer to the subsequent transferee would be good against an earlier, unrecorded transfer unless the earlier assignment were recorded within three months after the date of that earlier assignment or unless the subsequent transferee took with actual notice of the earlier transfer. Recordation is constructive notice of transfer.

Saying that one has an interest in a patent is shorthand for saying that he owns such interest. The evidence of ownership is sometimes referred to as title. The inter vivos transfer or conveyance of ownership from one individual to another of incorporeal or intangible rights, such as patent rights, is referred to as an assignment. The motivation for an assignment may be a sale, an exchange, or a gift.

Patents may also be acquired by bequest or by operation of law.

What, in essence, distinguishes ownership of an *interest* in a patent from a mere license is the right to sue infringers.[3] Such right is tantamount to the right to exclude others, and is an incident of ownership. In the absence of a provision to the contrary, moreover, a license is deemed a purely personal right, which may not be transferred to others, either in toto or in the form of sublicenses.[4] Indeed, the granting of a licnese is not deemed to involve a transfer of any rights. Licensing arrangements would be more accurately characterized as a sharing, rather than a transfer of patent rights, except that a patent owner may grant an exclusive license, going so far as to promise his licensee not even to make, use, or sell his own invention! Where the license does not expressly preclude the licensor from licensing others, it is referred to as a nonexclusive license.[5] The line of distinction between an assignment and an exclusive license is, in many instances, a hazy one, since by an exclusive license the licensee acquires exclusivity, with the licensor retaining only the right to enforce that exclusivity by resort to the courts, albeit largely for his licensee's benefit.

Patent licenses are not governed by the Patent Act, Section 261 being inapplicable to licensees. Accordingly, a license though oral may be wholly effective, provided it does not fall within the applicable statute of frauds.[6] The provision of the statute of frauds most likely to bring a patent license within its purview is that relating to contracts which cannot be performed within a year of their making.

It should be borne in mind that a patent license and any agreement embodied therein will be construed according to state-based common law of contract, which generally gives the parties wide latitude in setting up the terms and conditions under which they will do business. Parties are left free to make their own bargain, so long as it does not contravene the antitrust laws or any other positive statutory prohibitions. Much of the common law of patent licensing is composed of rules for the disposition of contingencies over which there is conflict, but for which the parties made no express provision. For example, in the absence of an express provision to the contrary, a license is not assignable. Freedom of contract allows the parties to agree otherwise, but the alternative will be sanctioned only where there has in fact been an agreement to that effect. It is significant to note that, in construing an agreement, a court will look to its substance, rather than to its label, as controlling. What purports by its caption to be a license, may in fact, by its operative terms, constitute an assignment, and vice versa. If the licensee is given exclusivity, the right to transfer his license, and the right to sue infringers, such license is really an assignment. Exclusivity; the right to transfer; and the right to sue infringers are the hallmarks which distinguish an assignment from a license, the right to sue infringers being indispensible to an assignment. That an agreement involves less than the entire remaining term of the patent, or that it is restricted to less than the whole of the United States, or that it is limited only to use and sale is not determinative of its status as a license or an assignment. Similarly, both a license and an assignment may impose any of a number of ancillary restraints, as, for example, that all products made be of a certain prescribed quality. Such provisions contained in an assignment are analogous to restrictive covenants in a deed to real property.

Before delving into the significant parameters of patent licenses and assignments, a most important consequence attached to joint patent ownership must be discussed. Where a patent is jointly owned, any joint-owner, regardless of the size of his share in the patent, may grant anyone and everyone a license to practice the patented invention without obtaining the consent of any of his co-owners.[7] Moreover, each joint owner is free, in the absence of a partnership agreement to the contrary, to retain all of the royalties that he receives from his licensees. Thus, the owner of a one one-thousandth interest in a patent may keep a hundred per cent of the royalties paid by his licensees. The status of joint patent owners is that of tenants in common.[8] The only significance attached to the proportion which each joint patentee owns is where there is a recovery of damages for infringement. In such case, each owner's share of the proceeds will be proportional to his share of ownership in the patent.[9]

Where a patent application lists a number of co-inventors, each will be deemed to have an interest equal to that of the others. Thus, where three inventors are named, each will have a one-third interest. Of course, they may among themselves settle upon a different allocation.

The possible provisions of a patent license or assignment may, from a contractual standpoint, be divided into the following two broad classes: (1) the parameters which define the extent of the property being licensed or conveyed; (2) ancillary conditions and covenants. Each will now be presented individually, with, where applicable, a concise summary of potential antitrust implications. Some, of course, such as royalties and duration, so overlap and are so interrelated that treatment under more than one heading will be necessary. This presentation will be followed by a more rigorous and generalized antitrust analysis. However, throughout this chapter the emphasis and arrangement is such as to make the reader mindful of potential antitrust consequences.

§ 1. Provisions Relating to the Extent of Patent Rights Conveyed or Licensed

[1] Duration

A patent owner may license or assign his patent for any period of time not to exceed the unexpired term of his patent. The practice of collecting royalties on a patent after it has expired, known as "post-expiration royalties," has been declared to be a patent misuse by the Supreme Court.[10] The significance of patent misuse will be explained presently.

[2] Manufacture, Use, or Sale

The patent grant is divisible into the rights to make, to use, and to sell.[11] A patent owner may split these three rights, granting another any one, any two, or all three.

[3] Field of Use

The field of operation may also be split up. An invention may have applications in more than one field or industry. A patent owner may limit an assignment or license on lines drawn according to field of use.[12] The patent rights to a drug which has both human and veterinary applications, for example, may be divided between these uses.[13] Similarly, rights in patents relating to vacuum tubes, which were suitable for use in both the home broadcasting and commercial fields were split along these lines, such allocation being sanctioned by the Supreme Court.[14] The patent owner may grant rights only in a defined field of use or he may except one or more fields of use from his assignment or license.

[4] Geographic

A United States patent is effective throughout the United States, its territories and possessions. A patent owner may split up his patent according to territory, giving one person rights in only one part of the United States and another person rights in another part of the country.[15] Section 261 of the Patent Act expressly sanctions the practice of granting an exclusive right under a patent "to the whole or any specified part of the United States."

[5] Quantity

Every patent potentially controls an indefinitely large number of physical objects, the class of such objects being coextensive with that which embodies the invention called for by the claims of the patent. As a general rule, the number of objects which may lawfully come into being during the term of the patent is dependent upon the pleasure of the patentee. It is well settled that a patentee need not work his invention and that others may not do so (except pursuant to an exercise of the power of eminent domain) without the patentee's consent.[16] From the foregoing precepts, it follows that a patentee may limit the quantity of physical objects embodying his invention that a licensee may produce.

§ 2. Ancillary Provisions

[1] Considerations

The primary consideration or tribute for access to a patented invention takes two forms: (1) money payments; (2) the exchange of patent rights.

[a] Money Payments

Money payments may be in the form of a royalty or rent. A royalty is payment for the mere right to exploit a patented invention, the patentee parting with nothing tangible. Rent is payment for the lease of a specified physical object. Where such object embodies one or more patented inventions, lease thereof by the patentee may include a license to use the same.[17]

It is well settled that, absent an exercise of the power of eminent domain, a patentee is free to exact royalties as high as he can negotiate with the leverage of the patent monoply.[18]

Various bases have been used to compute rents and royalties. While it seems eminently fair and reasonable to calculate rents and royalties on the basis of the money which the invention saves the user, it has been held a violation of Section 5 of the Federal Trade Commission Act to discriminate among lessees in the amount of rent charged, even where the differential was proportional to the amount each lessee would save by the use of the patented machines.[19] The Supreme Court has held it a violation of Section 4 of the Clayton Act to base royalty payments under a license on a patent drawn to a combination of elements only upon sales of an unpatented element of the combination, even where the license limited the payment of royalties to sales of that element to be used in the patented combination.[20] In a more recent case, the Supreme Court retreated somewhat from the position that the royalty base must fall wholly within the four corners of the patent claims, holding that a patent license provision which measures royalties by a percentage of the licensee's total sales is lawful if included for the "convenience of both parties," but unlawful if "insisted upon" by the patentee.[21]

[b] Exchange of Patent Rights

There exist a number of situations in which the barter of patent rights is more advantageous to patentees than would be mutual royalty patents. Accordingly, one patentee may agree to license another under one or more of his own patents in exchange for a license to use one or more patents owned by the other patentee. Such an arrangement is often referred to as cross-licensing. This type of bargain is most commonly struck where one party owns a patent whose claims dominate the claims of one or more patents held by the other. In such a situation, absent a license by each to the other, neither could the owner of the dominant patent make use of inventions covered by the claims of a subservient patent, nor could the owner of a subservient patent make use of the inventions covered by the claims of his own patents![22] An agreement may provide for the payment of royalties in addition to providing for the cross-licensing.

In industries generating a large number of important patents of diverse ownership, it has been found mutually advantageous for the interests owning these rights to pool their patents. This is generally effected by a multilateral agreement which provides for the creation and maintenance of a trust or holding company to control and manage their patents. Such was the origin of the Radio Corporation of America.[23] Generally, each party agrees to transfer to the holding company whatever patents it has or may thereafter acquire in that industry. The agreement assures each of the participating parties of access to all of the patents in the pool, either on a royalty-free basis or at a rate set forth in the agreement. Any royalties collected may either be plowed back into further research or distributed to the participants according to some agreed upon formula.

While cross-licensing and patent pools have been criticized by the Antitrust Division of the United States Department of Justice, these practices are not per se illegal under present law.[24] There are, however, a number of concessions exacted by patentees, as at least part of the consideration for access to their patented inventions, which have been declared unenforceable by the courts, on the theory that their implementation would constitute a patent misuse. Some of these practices may also form the basis of an antitrust violation.

The doctrine of patent misuse had its inception in a dispute involving the propriety of inserting what amounted to a requirements contract in licenses for the use of a patented salt tablet dispenser, whereby licensees agreed to purchase all salt tablets used in the dispensers from the licensor's wholly owned subsidiary. Rather than submit to such terms, the defendant infringed the patent, arguing, when sued for infringement, that by predicating the granting of a license upon acceptance by licensees of a condition whereby the licensees agreed to fill their requirements for unpatented tablets used in the patented dispensers only with tablets sold by the licensor's wholly owned subsidiary, plaintiff was violating Section 3 of the Clayton Act, in that plaintiff's scheme substantially lessened competition or tended to create a monopoly in unpatented salt tablets. The Supreme Court, without deciding whether plaintiff had violated the Clayton Act, declined to enjoin infringement of the plaintiff's patent while the requirements provision subsisted, the Court invoking the equitable doctrine of unclean hands in support of its position. The Court reasoned that the licensor's practice of conditioning access to a patented invention (the dispenser) upon exclusive purchase from it of unpatented goods (tablets) was an unlawful extension of the patent monopoly on the dispenser—a patent misuse—which amounted to inequitable conduct or unclean hands sufficient to justify a denial of equitable relief.[25] A legal monopoly may not be used as leverage to beget an illegal one. The Court implied that a suit for an injunction would be entertained if and when the improper practice was abandoned and all consequences of the patent misuse had been dissipated. An analogous result was reached by the Court in another suit wherein the licensor had conditioned access to its patented business machines upon purchase from it of the unpatented cards to be used in these machines.[26]

Patent misuse has been found in several contexts, the common thread among which is the existence of a tie-in, that is, the tying or conditioning of a patent license upon something deemed to lie outside the bounds of the patent monopoly. Provisions for the payment of post-expiration royalties may be viewed as a tying of a license to exploit a patent during its lawful term to an unlawful extension of that term.[27]

It should be noted that, in contradistinction to a tying arrangement, field-of-use and territorial restrictions by themselves lact the potential for creating monopolies in things not covered by the underlying patent grant. Rather, they split up the monopoly that is the patent into fields of use and territories, respectively.

So-called package licensing, in a sense, possesses an element of tying. Instead of licensing patents on an individual basis, a blanket or package license may be granted covering all the patents the licensor owns in a given field of technology. While there is an element of tying in such an arrangement, in that access to one patent is conditioned on taking a license for others, no extension of monopoly beyond the grant of patent is involved and no monopoly in that which is unpatented is created. Package licensing has the virtue of avoiding determination of whether each type of licensee's product embodies what may be any of the licensor's numerous patents. Accordingly, courts have acquiesced to package licensing where it has appeared that the arrangement was for the mutual convenience of the parties and was not exacted by the licensor as a condition for access by the licensee to part of the package really desired.[28]

Yet another arrangement possessing an element of tying is the grant back. An innovation in a field of technology may, at any time, make what is new today obsolete tommorrow. Progress is expensive both in terms of research and new equipment costs. It may be ruinous to those who fail to gain access to new developments. He who is in the forefront today may trail tomorrow; there is no finality in science and technology. To insure access to any improvements that may be made by a licensee on the licensor's patented invention, a grant-back clause may be inserted in the license. As the term suggests, a grant-back clause generally provides for the granting back or returning to the licensor of rights in whatever improvements the licensee may thereafter make or otherwise acquire upon the licensor's patents. Grant backs possess an element of tying in that license of existing inventions is conditioned upon or tied to access by the licensor of inventions not yet in being. The propriety of such arrangements is affected by the extent of the rights in the prospective patents to be granted back to the licensor. Where the licensee is only obliged to grant back to his licensor a non-exclusive license, the net potential effect of the agreement is to increase competition, for such grant-back provision only gives the licensor assured access to his licensee's prospective patents.[29] Where, however, a licensee agrees to grant back to his licensor an exclusive license or to assign to the licensor the licensee's future patents, the net effect of the arrangement may be to perpetuate a licensor's dominant market position, while relegating the licensee to a position of perpetual subservience. Moreover, a grant-back provision which would deprive the licensee of free access to patents which it acquires might very well tend to discourage it from carrying on research to generate new patents. The legality, under the antitrust laws, of restrictive grant-back provisions is open to question.[30]

It should be noted that an antitrust violation may co-exist with a patent misuse. Whether an antitrust violation will be found will depend upon whether all the elements of such violation are present in the patentee's conduct.[31]

[c] Cessation of Royalty Payments

In its decision striking down the doctrine of licensee estoppel, the Supreme Court indicated that a licensor could not collect royalties on a patent after it had been declared invalid.[32] Prior to this decision, without a stipulation to the effect that the licensee would be relieved of paying royalties should the patent be declared invalid, a licensee was obliged to continue paying royalties even if the licensed patent were declared invalid unless the license were an exclusive one. An exclusive licensee was able to resist paying further royalties on a patent which had been declared invalid on the theory of "eviction" from the license.[33] The rationale of the eviction defense was that the declaration of invalidity opened up the patented invention to the licensee's competitors and, therefore, he would no longer be getting that for which he had bargained—the exclusive right to exploit the patented invention. A license agreement may endeavor to safeguard a licensee's freedom from unauthorized competition by providing for the suspension of royalty payments so long as infringement continues. Such must be expressly provided for, as there is no implied covenant of quiet enjoyment in the license of patent rights.[34]

[d] Warranties by Patentee

In the absence of an express provision to the contrary, the patentee, in merely giving a license or making an assignment, does *not* warrant that the patent or patents being licensed or assigned are valid or even that the inventions claimed therein are operable.[35] Moreover, there is no implied warranty that the licensee or assignee will be able to exploit the invention covered by the claims of the licensed or assigned patent without infringing the claims of some other patent having claims which dominate those of the patents which are the subject of the license or assignment. If only because of the frequency with which courts hold patents invalid, patent owners are reluctant to warrant the validity of patents they license. However, patent owners are somewhat more willing to warrant the operability of their patents and of the non-existence of dominant patents belonging to third parties. Protection against the existence of a dominant patent belonging to a third person may take the form of an indemnity clause, whereby the licensor or assignor agrees to hold harmless the licensee or assignee for infringement of patent rights of others.[36]

[e] Police, Security, Access, and Quality Provisions

Patent owners have a legitimate interest in retaining a modicum of control over the exploitation of their patented inventions in the hands of licensees. Valuable rights may be lost if due caution is not constantly exercised. For example, the Patent Act disallows damages if there has been a failure to mark appropriately patented articles.[37] Accordingly, a patent license agreement may require the licensee to take appropriate precautions, including the marking of all articles manufactured by him. The patent owner may also want to have access to his licensee's facilities to discover unauthorized use by the licensee and to insure that royalties are being paid on the full extent of the patent's use. A patent owner who himself exploits his patents, in addition to licensing others to do so, particularly where the products are marketed under a common trademark, has a reputation to protect and, accordingly, may wish to provide in the license agreement that the products to be manufactured by the licensee be of specified grade and quality. It is also quite common to require licensees to undertake to use their best efforts to discover unauthorized uses and infringements and to report the same to the licensor.

[f] Most-Favored Licensee

In trade agreements between nations, it is common to insert what has become known as a most-favored nation clause. In essence, what such a clause provides is that in the event any subsequent agreement with more favorable terms is concluded with some third nation, the parties to the instant agreement will automatically enjoy the benefits of the more favorable terms of the later agreement. For example, suppose a trade agreement between countries *X* and *Y* provides for mutual import duties on widgets of 20 percent, but also provides for most-favored nation treatment. Subsequently, country *X* concludes a trade agreement with country *Z*, which agreement provides that the duties to be levied on widgets imported into country *X* from country *Z* will be at the rate of 15 percent. By virtue of the most-favored nation clause contained in the agreement between countries *X* and *Y*, widgets imported into country *X* from country *Y* will, from the date the agreement between countries X and Z goes into effect, be dutable at the rate of 15 percent. Applied to patent license agreements, this principle encourages the taking of licenses, for it insures against a hold out competitor gaining more favorable terms.[38]

[g] Miscellaneous Provisions

There are a number of standard clauses which may be inserted in contracts of a commercial nature to further define the rights and obligations of the parties, regardless of whether the contract involves patent or other property rights. These include a choice-of-law clause, which provides that any controversy arising from the contract be adjudicated in accordance with the laws of the jurisdiction specified, and an arbitration clause.

§ 3. Viability of Restrictions on the Physical Object

The viability of restrictions upon the exploitation of patented articles brings into focus the distinction between a patent and the invention it protects, on one hand, and physical objects embodying the invention, on the other hand. The problems implicit in this distinction can be better appreciated by considering the following situation. Suppose a license only permits the licensee to make, use, and sell the patented invention west of the Appalachian Mountains. Pursuant to this restriciton, the licensee makes and sells to a third person articles embodying the licensed invention within the permissible geographical area. Is the restriction appurtenant to the article, moving with it in the channels of commerce, such that third persons are bound thereby? May a subsequent vendee lawfully use or sell the patented article east of the Appalachian Mountains? Does the result turn upon whether a subsequent vendee had notice of the restriction? Territorial restrictions are binding only upon the licensee and not upon the licensee's vendee or upon subsequent vendees.[39] However, it has been held that a territorial use restriction was effective against a vendee from a licensee who took with actual notice of the restriction.[40] Of course, a mere lease may restrict the transport of the article being leased. A similar rule has prevailed with respect to price setting, maintenance of the price set by the licensor being enforceable only so far as the licensee's immediate vendee. Stated in other words, the set price extends no further than the first sale.[41] With respect to field-of-use restrictions, however, the Supreme Court has upheld the same against the licensee's vendee, where they took with notice of the restriction.[42]

§ 4. Antitrust Analysis and Critique

There is, if only in terminology, an apparent conflict between the patent and antitrust laws. The patent laws proffer a monopoly on and promise freedom from competition in the practice of patented inventions; the objectives of the antitrust laws are the suppression of monopolization and the fostering of competition.

The subject matter of a patent monopoly must be new and unobvious. Consequently, the public is not, because of patents, deprived of anything it enjoyed before. In fact, an object of the patent laws is to stimulate public disclosure of inventions. What is offensive about monopolies is not the mere element of exclusivity, but exclusivity in that which belongs to the public. Since the subject matter of every patent must be new and unobvious, patents remove nothing from the public domain. This distinction was recognized as long ago as the enactment of the English Statute of Monopolies of 1623, which forbade the Crown from creating monopolies save those for any manner of new manufacture introduced into the realm.[43] Furthermore, the extent of every patent monopoly is extremely limited. It is for but a limited time, no longer than seventeen years.[44] Because of the precision with which the invention must be defined in the claims, a patent can cover no more than a scintilla of technology!

Patents, moreover, may actually promote competition. A patent belonging to a struggling small- or medium-size firm in an industry dominated by a few well entrenched giants may give its owner a crucial tool with which to compete with its more powerful rivals. A patented innovation may be so revolutionary as to render hitherto existing practice obsolete. If the patentee of such an invention is unwilling to license his rivals, they may be compelled to attempt to design around his patent. Because a patent covers such a small and well-defined area of technology and because a patentee is compelled to educate his competition by disclosure, it is often possible to come up with an alternative which does not infringe—given enough time and research funds. The quest for alternatives sometimes also yields improvements. There is no final or ultimate invention; there is always room for improvements!

Every antitrust violation must be predicated upon the contravention of a statutory prohibition. However, whether specific conduct does in fact constitute a contravention of one of these statutes often requires involved analysis. The antitrust statutes relevant to the acquisition and exploitation of patents are few in number. The Sherman Act, Section 1; the Sherman Act, Section 2; and the Clayton Act, Section 3 embrace nearly all of the relevant substantive prohibitions. Each will be outlined separately in the paragraphs which follow. Section 4 of the Clayton Act provides for a private right of action by any person injured in his business or property by reason of anything forbidden in "the antitrust laws." This section provides for the recovery of treble damages and a reasonable attorney's fee for injuries sustained by reason of the violation. Section 5 of the Federal Trade Commission Act has been held to empower that Commission to take action against antitrust violations.[45]

[1] Sherman Act, Section 1

Patent licenses are almost invariably embodied in and are a part of a contract. Section 1 of the Sherman Act declares illegal "Every contract, combination . . . or conspiracy, in restraint of trade . . . ." Every patent license agreement is literally a contract and combination. However, not every contract or combination relating to trade is violative of the Sherman Act.[46] Every patent sharing arrangement necessarily has a positive competitive effect, in that someone in addition to the patentee thereby gains access to what was theretofore the exclusive domain of the patentee.

To what antitrust advocates object are certain terms and conditions (such as a price setting clause) which they claim have anticompetitive effects. Even such restrictive clauses, however, under certain circumstances, have positive competitive effects. Consider, for example, the small or medium-sized firm which, as a consequence of its stress on innovation, has come up with an invention for which there is an extensive market. Because of the patentee's limited productive capacity, the patentee is itself incapable of satiating market demand. It would be willing to license its larger and more entrenched rivals to help satisfy the demand, but because of economies of scale inherent in their operations, they might be able to so undersell the patentee, even after payment of a generous royalty, as possibly to drive the patentee out of business. The insertion of a price-setting clause in the license would obviate this possibility. It should be noted that in any non-patent context, any price setting arrangement, which in such other contexts would be branded as price-fixing, would be a per se violation of the Sherman Act.[47] That is to say, the mere existence of a price-fixing agreement is conclusively presumed to restrain trade. The parties thereto not being allowed to prove otherwise.[48]

Although certain licensing practices may have possible anticompetitive effects, it should be borne in mind that it is licensing which makes it feasible for smaller economic entities to derive from patents rewards that are commensurate with those enjoyed by larger economic entities without licensing. A motivation to license arises where the patentee lacks the resources to exploit by himself the full potential of his patent. A patentee with virtually unlimited capital would have no need to license. The patentee with limited resources must rely on licensing to reap a measure of reward equivalent to that enjoyed by larger economic entities!

[2] Clayton Act, Section 3

This section proscribes any arrangement whereby one party agrees not to use or deal in the goods of a competitor and the effect of such arrangement may be to substantially lessen competition or tend to create a monopoly in any line of commerce. Section 3 of the Clayton Act is more specific than is Section 1 of the Sherman Act. In effect, it defines one species of conduct, namely, a concerted refusal to deal, which constitutes a restraint of trade.[49] Most conduct that would be violative of Section 3 of the Clayton Act would also violate Section 1 of the Sherman Act. Section 3 of the Clayton Act is of interest in patent licensing because a contract tying a patent license to all purchases of an unpatented article used in connection with the patented invnetion is, in effect, an agreement not to use or deal in the goods of a competitor. Even where it cannot be established that the effect of a tying arrangement may be substantially to lessen competition or tend to create a monopoly in the unpatented goods which have been tied to the patented invention, a court may decline to grant an injunction to restrain infringement, on the ground that the tying arrangement of itself constitutes a patent misuse. The patentee will be penalized even where the patent has created a truly new use, and consequently a new market, for the old product!

[3] Sherman Act, Section 2

Section 2 of the Sherman Act declares illegal the monopolization of any part of the trade or commerce of the United States. While courts have drawn a distinction between monopoly and "monopolization," implicit in the sweeping language of Section 2 is the potential conflict between the antitrust and patent laws.[50] The Supreme Court has said "the mere accumulation of patentee, no matter how many, is not in and of itself illegal."[51] Suppose, however, a corporation embarks upon a deliberate plan to attain by purchase and otherwise, a dominant patent position in an industry. Would such a scheme constitute an attempt to monopolze in violation of Section 2 of the Sherman? Suppose one corporation having a strong patent position agreed to sell its patents to another corporation having an equally strong patent position. Would that agreement constitute a contract and combination in restraint of trade in violation of Section 1 of the Sherman Act?

It has been held that a scheme among defendant corporations to monopolize an industry, which scheme included a concerted policy of acquiring relevant dominant patents, violated the antitrust laws.[52] It has also been found that the bringing of an infringement suit constituted an element in a plan to eliminate competition and monopolize an industry.[53] In these instances, however, the defendants also committed some culpable act apart from the mere acquisition and assertion of patent rights.

It has been held by the Supreme Court that the enforcement of a patent procured by an intentional fraud on the Patent Office may be violative of Section 2 of the Sherman Act provided the other elements necessary to a Section 2 case are present.[54] To establish monopolization or attempt to monopolize a part of trade or commerce under Section 2 of the Sherman Act, it would be necessary to appraise the exclusionary power of the illegal patent in terms of the relevant market for the product involved. Without a definition of that market there would be no way to measure the patentee's ability to lessen or destroy competition.

§ 5. Tax Treatment of Patents

Patents, patent applications, and trade secrets all have the status of "intangible assets" under the tax laws, their acquisition and transfer having tax consequences.

[1] Transfer

The transfer of patent rights may constitute a taxable event which subjects the transferor (assignor or licensor) to income taxation on the revenues that he derives from the transfer. Depending on the circumstances, proceeds from such a transaction are to be treated as ordinary income or as a long-term capital gain. A transfer may qualify for long-term capital gains treatment under the general provisions relating to long-term capital gains or under a section relating specifically to patents.

Sections 1201-1223 of the Internal Revenue Code set forth the general requirements for long-term capital gain treatment. Proceeds from the sale of patent rights may qualify for such treatment if the transaction satisfies the general requirements of these sections:

(1) The asset must be a "capital asset;"
(2) The transaction must be a "sale or exchange;"
(3) The asset must have been held by the seller for more than six months.

A capital asset excludes stock in trade (inventory) of the taxpayer and (depreciable) property used in his trade or business.[55] Applied to patents, this has been construed to preclude taxpayers in the business of inventing (that is, professional inventors) from realizing, under these sections, capital gains treatment on the sale of their inventions.[56]

An assignment or license which divests the transferor of all rights of any substantial value qualifies as a sale or exchange.[57] For a license to be treated as a sale or exchange, it must be an exclusive license.[58] Under Sections 1201-1223 a license or assignment limited to only: (1) a portion of the country may constitute a transfer of "all substantial rights" to a patent; (2) a defined field of use or industry may constitute a transfer all substantial rights to a patent.[63] A license or assignment of a patent for a period of less than its unexpired term does not constitute "all substantial rights" to the patent.[60] The grant of the exclusive right to make and sell has been held to be the equivalent of a sale, where the retained right to use was of no potential value to the licensor.[61] The transfer of an undivided interest in a patent is the equivalent of a sale or exchange.[62] By an undivided interest is meant an interest in the entire bundle of right represented by the patent.[63]

A long-term capital gain is taxed at a much lower rate than is ordinary income.[64] A short-term capital gain is treated as ordinary income. What distinguishes a long-term capital gain (or loss) from a short-term capital gain (or loss) is a six month holding period. An asset which has been held for more than six months is to be treated as a long-term or capital asset in the hands of that holder. The holding period of an issued patent begins when the invention has been actually reduced to practice, if this occurred before the patent issued. Otherwise, it begins when the patent issues.[65]

Section 1235 of the Internal Revenue Code applies only to issued patents. It places amateur and professional inventors on the same footing, by sanctioning long-term capital gain treatment of the proceeds derived from any "transfer (other than by gift, inheritance, or devise) of property consisting of all substantial rights to a patent, or an undivided interest therein which includes a part of all such rights by any holder. . . ." Thus, under Section 1235 it is immaterial whether or not the patent is the stock-in-trade of a professional inventor. Section 1235 also obviates another problem which had confronted even amateur inventors seeking long-term capital gain treatment, namely, the manner of payment. It had been the position of the Internal Revenue Service that only a lump-sum payment could qualify for long-term capital gain treatment and that periodic payments (as royalties) or payments contingent on productivity or use were ineligible for treatment as long-term capital gain.[66] Section 1235 obviates this obstacle by stating that under this section there is to be long-term capital gain treatment even where payment is made in any of the aforementioned ways. It should be noted that subsequent to the enactment of Section 1235, the Internal Revenue Service changed its position, in that it now permits long-term capital gain treatment of periodic payments even for transfers which do not qualify under Section 1235 but which otherwise qualify under Sections 1201-1223. Under Section 1235 there is no minimum holding period to qualify for long-term capital gain treatment. To qualify under Section 1235, a transfer must be of "all substantial rights to a patent, or an undivided interest therein which includes a part of all such rights. . . ." This phrase has been construed as excluding from eligibility, under this section, licenses or assignments of rights to only a part of the United States or to only a defined field of use.[67] Eligibility for availing one's self of Section 1235 is further limited by the restrictive definition of holder, contained in Section 1235(b) and (d). Excluded are the employer of the inventor, all corporations, partnerships, estates, trusts, and the inventor's own relations. In short, Section 1235 was designed to give the benefit of long-term capital gain treatment to: (1) the individual, independent inventor; and (2) any nonrelative, individual financial backers who acquired an interest in his invention prior to the time the invention was reduced to practice.

[2] Acquisition

A patent, patent application, or trade secret may be acquired either by purchase or as the result of research and development. The cost of acquisition by purchase can ordinarily only be depreciated.[68] That is, the cost of acquisition may be capitalized (amortized) over the asset's useful life, which, in the case of a patent, ordinarily coincides with its seventeen-year term. Section 174 of the Internal Revenue Code allows the costs incurred in generating a patent, patent application, or trade secret through research and development to be either depreciated or deducted, at the election of the taxpayer. Expenditures incurred in prosecuting a patent application, including fees, drawings, models, and attorneys' fees, are deemed a part of the cost of acquisition.[69] Accordingly, they may be depreciated over the life of the patent or deducted as a current expense in the year paid or incurred. The expenditures incurred in prosecuting an application which ultimately goes abandoned may be treated as a loss under Section 165(a).

[3] Litigation Expenses

Section 162 of the Internal Revenue Code allows a deduction for litigation expenses that are "ordinary and necessary" for carrying on a trade or business or for the collection of income. Litigation expenses incurred in connection with controversies over title to a patent are, however, deemed a part of the cost of the patent and, therefore, must be capitalized.[70] Damages recovered for patent infringement are generally deemed to be a substitute for lost profits and, consequently, are treated as ordinary income.[71] This is true whether the damages are labelled "compensatory" or "punitive."[72] Damages paid for infringement are deductible as ordinary and necessary business expenses.[73]

Notes

[1] L.L. Brown Paper Co. v. Hydroiloid, Inc., 32 F. Supp. 857, 867-868, 44 U.S.P.Q. 655, 666 (S.D.N.Y. 1941).

[2] See Drake v. Hall, 220 Fed. 95, 96 (7th Cir. 1914). See also, Ferrer v. Columbia Pictures, 149 U.S.P.Q. 236, 237 (N.Y.Sup. Ct. 1966).

[3] Waterman v. Mackenzie, 138 U.S. 252 (1891).

[4] Moberg v. Comm'r, 305 F.2d 800, 128 U.S.P.Q. 500 (5th Cir. 1962); King v. Anthony Pools, Inc., 202 F. Supp. 426, 133 U.S.P.Q. 300 (S.D. Cal. 1962).

[5] See Hapgood v. Hewitt, 119 U.S. 226 (1886).

[6] St. Louis Standard Flushing Mach. Co. v. Sanitary Standard Flushing Mach. Co., 178 Fed. 923 (8th Cir. 1910); Sharples v. Moseley & Stoddard Mfg. Co., 81 Fed. 179 (3d Cir. 1897).

[7] 35 U.S.C. 262. See Talbot v. Quaker State Oil Refining Co., 28 F. Supp. 544, 548, 37 U.S.P.Q. 453, 456 (W.D. Pa. 1938), *aff'd* 104 F.2d 967, 41 U.S.P.Q. 1 (3d Cir. 1939).

[8] Bloomer v. McQuewan, 55 U.S. (14 How.) 539 (1852); Drake v. Hall, 220 Fed. 905, 906 (7th Cir. 1914); Blackledge v. Weir & Craig Mfg. Co., 108 Fed. 71 (7th Cir. 1901).

[9] See Paulus v. M.M. Buck Mfg. Co., 129 Fed. 594 (8th Cir. 1904).

[10] Brulotte v. Thys Co., 379 U.S. 29, 143 U.S.P.Q. 694 (1964).

[11] Adams v. Burke, 84 U.S. (17 Wall.) 700 (1873).

[12] General Talking Pictures Corp. v. Western Elec. Co., 304 U.S. 175, 37 U.S.P.Q. 357, *reargued* 305 U.S. 124, 39 U.S.P.Q. 329 (1938).

[13] Benger Laboratories, Ltd. v. R.K. Laros Co., 209 F. Supp. 639, 124 U.S.P.Q. 45 (E.D. Pa. 1959), *aff'd* 317 F.2d 455, 137 U.S.P.Q. 693 (3d Cir. 1963).

[14] N. 12 *supra*.

[15] See Rubber Co. v. Goodyear, 76 U.S. (9 Wall.) 788 (1869); A.L. Smith Iron Co. v. Dickson, 141 F.2d 3, 60 U.S.P.Q. 475 (2d Cir. 1944); United States v. Parker Rust Proof Co., 61 F. Supp. 805, 65 U.S.P.Q. 563 (E.D. Mich. 1945).

[16] Continental Paper Bag Co. v. Eastern Paper Bag Co., 210 U.S. 405 (1908).

[17] N. 10 *supra*. See also, LaPeyre v. F.T.C., 366 F.2d 117, 151 U.S.P.Q. 79 (5th Cir. 1966).

[18] Brulotte v. Thys Co., 379 U.S. 29, 33, 143 U.S.P.Q. 694 (1964).

[19] LaPeyre v. F.T.C., N. 17 *supra*; Peelers Co. v. Wendt, 260 F. Supp. 193, 151 U.S.P.Q. 378 (W.D. Wash. 1966); Laitram Corp. v. King Crab, Inc., 245 F. Supp. 1019, 146 U.S.P.Q. 640 (D. Alaska 1965).

[20] Automatic Radio Mfg. Co. v. Hazeltine Research, Inc., 339 U.S. 827, 85 U.S.P.Q. 378 (1950).

[21] Zenith Radio Corp. v. Hazeltine Research, Inc., 395 U.S. 100, 161 U.S.P.Q. 577 (1969).

[22] See DeForest Telegraph & Telephone Co. v. Marconi Wireless Telegraph Co., 236 Fed. 942 (S.D.N.Y. 1916), *aff'd* 243 Fed. 560 (2d Cir. 1917). See also, Smith v. Nichols, 88 U.S. (21 Wall.) 112, 118-119 (1874); *In re* Heinle, 342 F.2d 1001, 1005, 145 U.S.P.Q. 131, 135 (C.C.P.A. 1965).

[23] See generally, *Men and Volts: The Story of General Electric* (Lippincott, 1941) p. 377.

[24] See United States v. Line Material Co., 333 U.S. 287, 315, 76 U.S.P.Q. 399, 411 (1948) (cross-licensing). See also, Standard Oil Co. v. United States, 283 U.S. 163, 9 U.S.P.Q. 6 (1931) (pooling).

[25] Morton Salt Co. v. G.S. Suppiger Co., 314 U.S. 488, 52 U.S.P.Q. 30 (1942).

[26] International Business Mach. Corp. v. United States, 298 U.S. 131, 37 U.S.P.Q. 224 (1936).

[27] Brulotte v. Thys Co., 379 U.S. 29, 143 U.S.P.Q. 694 (1964).

[28] N. 21 *supra*.

[29] Transparent-Wrap Mach. Corp. v. Stokes & Smith Co., 329 U.S. 637, 72 U.S.P.Q. 148 (1947).

30 See *The Attorney General's Committee Report* (1955), pp.227-229; Turner, "Antitrust Enforcement Policy," 29 *A.B.A. Antitrust Section Rep.* 187, 188 (1965). See also, General Elec. Lamp Case, 82 F. Supp. 753, 815-816, 80 U.S.P.Q. 195, 242-243 (D.N.J. 1949).

31 N. 25 *supra.*

32 Lear v. Atkins, Inc., 395 U.S. 653, 162 U.S.P.Q. 1 (1969).

33 See Drackett Chem. Co. v. Chamberlain Co., 63 F.2d 853, 17 U.S.P.Q. 114 (6th Cir. 1933) (from exclusive license); Scherr v. Difco Laboratories, Inc., 270 F. Supp. 586, 153 U.S.P.Q. 607 (E. D. Mich. 1967) (from nonexclusive license).

34 Wynne v. Allen, 112 U.S.P.Q. 405 (N.C. Sup. Ct. 1957).

35 Appliance Corp. v. Speed Queen Corp., 186 F.2d 798, 89 U.S.P.Q. 1 (7th Cir. 1951); Johnson v. Brewer-Titchenor Corp., 28 F. Supp. 1002, 42 U.S.P.Q. 437 (N.D.N.Y. 1939); Eno v. Prime Mfg. Co., 58 U.S.P.Q. 681 (Mass. Sup. Ct. 1943).

36 See Kool Vent Metal Awning Corp. v. Bottom, 95 F. Supp. 798, 71 U.S.P.Q. 219 (E.D. Mo. 1951), *aff'd* 205 F.2d 209, 98 U.S.P.Q. 371 (8th Cir. 1953); M. Nirenberg Sons, Inc. v. Trubenizing Process Corp., 49 U.S.P.Q. 464 (N.Y. Sup. Ct. 1941).

37 35 U.S.C. 287.

38 See for example, Technograph Printed Circuits, Ltd. v. Bendix Aviation Corp., 218 F. Supp. 1, 137 U.S.P.Q. 725 (D. Md. 1963), *aff'd per curiam* 327 F.2d 497, 140 U.S.P.Q. 285 (4th Cir. 1964); Cold Metal Process Co. v. McLouth Steel Corp., 170 F.2d 369, 51 U.S.P.Q. 108 (6th Cir. 1948).

39 Keeler v. Standard Folding Bed Co., 157 U.S. 659 (1895); Hobbie v. Jennison, 149 U.S. 355 (1893); Adams v. Burke, 84 U.S. (17 Wall.) 100 (1873).

40 Skee Ball Co. v. Cohen, 286 Fed. 275 (E.D.N.Y. 1922).

41 United States v. General Elec. Co., 272 U.S. 476 (1926).

42 General Talking Pictures Corp. v. Western Elec. Co., 304 U.S. 175, 37 U.S.P.Q. 357, *reargued* 305 U.S. 124, 39 U.S.P.Q. 329 (1938).

43 21 Jac. I, ch. 3.

44 See Scott Paper Co. v. Marcalus Mfg. Co., 326 U.S. 249, 256, 67 U.S.P.Q. 193, 196-197 (1945).

45 F.T.C. v. Cement Institute, 333 U.S. 683 (1948); Fashion Originators Guild v. F.T.C., 312 U.S. 457 (1941); F.T.C. v. Beech-Nut Packing Co., 257 U.S. 441 (1922).

46 See Standard Oil Co. v. United States, 221 U.S. 1 (1911).

47 See generally, United States v. Container Corp., 393 U.S. 333 (1969).

48 See United States v. Trenton Potteries Co., 273 U.S. 393 (1927).

49 Morton Salt Co. v. G.S. Suppiger Co., 314 U.S. 488, 52 U.S.P.Q. 30 (1942).

50 See generally, United States v. Aluminum Co. of Am., 148 F.2d 416 (2d Cir. 1945).

51 Automatic Radio Mfg. Co. v. Hazeltine Research, Inc., 339 U.S. 827, 832, 85 U.S.P.Q. 378, 380 (1950).

52 See generally, Hartford-Empire Co. v. United States, 323 U.S. 386, 64 U.S.P.Q. 18 (1945).

53 Kobe, Inc. v. Dempsey Pump Co., 198 F.2d 416, 94 U.S.P.Q. 43 (10th Cir. 1952).

54 Walker Process Equip., Inc. v. Food Mach. & Chem. Corp., 382 U.S. 172, 147 U.S.P.Q. 404 (1965).

55 I.R.C. 1221(1).

56 Harold T. Avery, 47 B.T.A. 538 (1942). See also, Armco Steel Corp. v. United States, 263 F. Supp. 749 (S.D. Ohio 1966).

57 I.R.C. 1235(a).

58 See generally, Rollman v. Comm'r, 244 F.2d 634, 113 U.S.P.Q. 356 (4th Cir. 1957); Broderick v. Neale, 201 F.2d 621, 96 U.S.P.Q. 82 (10th Cir. 1952).

59 United States v. Carruthers, 219 F.2d 21, 104 U.S.P.Q. 283 (9th Cir. 1955); First Nat'l Bank v. United States, 136 F. Supp. 818, 108 U.S.P.Q. 108 (D.N.J. 1955); Lamar v. Granger, 99 F. Supp. 17, 90 U.S.P.Q. 58 (W.D. Pa. 1951).

60 See Bell Intercontinental Corp. v. United States, 381 F.2d 1004, 154 U.S.P.Q. 373 (Ct. Cl. 1967). But see, Heil Co., 38 T.C. 989 (1962).

61 Carl G. Dreyman, 11 T.C. 153 (1948). See also, Comm'r v. Celanese Corp., 140 F.2d 339, 61 U.S.P.Q. 14 (D.C.C. 1944).

62 Parke-Davis & Co., 31 B.T.A. 427 (T.C. 1934). See also, A.E. Hickman, 29 T.C. 864 (1958).

63 I. R. Reg. 1.1235-2(c). Rev. Rul. 59-175, 1959-1 C.B. 213.

64 I.R.C. 1201, 1202.

65 Samuel E. Diescher, 36 B.T.A. 732, *aff'd* 110 F.2d 90 (3d Cir. 1940).

66 Mim. 6490, 1950-1 C.B.

67 I. R. Reg. 1.1235-2(b), as amended by T.D. 6852, 1965-2 C.B. 289.

68 Poole v. Comm'r, 150 U.S.P.Q. 479, 488 (T.C. 1966).

69 I.R. Reg. 1.174-4(c).

70 See generally, Safety Tube Corp. v. Comm'r, 168 F.2d 787, 78 U.S.P.Q. 312 (6th Cir. 1948); Imm v. Comm'r, 94 U.S.P.Q. 92 (T.C. 1952); Falls v. Comm'r, 69 U.S.P.Q. 557 (T.C. 1946).

71 Mathey v. Comm'r, 77 U.S.P.Q. 671 (T.C. 1948), *aff'd* 177 F.2d 259, 83 U.S.P.Q. 193 (1st Cir. 1949).

72 Glenshaw Glass Co., 348 U.S. 426 (1954).

73 Urquhart v. Comm'r, 215 F.2d 17, 102 U.S.P.Q. 427 (3d Cir. 1954).

Chapter 15

LITIGATION: THE ENFORCEMENT OF PATENT RIGHTS

SYNOPSIS

> If any one of the specified differentia of the claim is missing, the defendant's product does not infringe; if any anticipation includes all the differentia, the claim is bad. To pass between this Scylla and the Charybdis, I think a patentee may fairly be entitled to bend sails upon many yards.
>
> L. Hand, J.
> *Parke-Davis & Co.* v. *H.K. Mulford Co.*,
> 189 Fed. 95, 103 (C.C.S.D.N.Y. 1911)

A patent has been characterized as an invitation to a law suit. There are good reasons for this. Thomas Jefferson once observed:[1]

> If nature has made any one thing less susceptible than all others of exclusive property, it is the action of the thinking power called an idea, which an individual may exclusively possess as long as he keeps it to himself; but the moment it is divulged, it

> forces itself into the possession of every one, and the receiver cannot dispossess of it. Its peculiar character, too, is that no one possesses the less, because every other possesses the whole of mine.

In essence, patents are granted for ideas. Because, as Jefferson noted, ideas once disclosed become, by their very nature, in fact freely available to all, people are disinclined to respect exclusivity in anything based thereon—particularly where money is involved. Consequently, patents tend to invite litigation.

By "litigation" is generally meant an in court contest between parties having adverse interests. Litigation is to be distinguished from the proceedings before the Patent Office by which patents are obtained. Although such proceedings are of a quasi-judicial nature, they are uncontested, that is, they are conducted ex parte. The patent examiner is supposed to act as the friend of the applicant; not as an advocate in opposition.[2] Appeals from the Patent Office's refusal to grant a patent pit the Commissioner of Patents against the applicant. Such appeals must be taken either to the United States District Court for the District of Columbia or to the United States Court of Customs and Patent Appeals, at the election of the applicant.

While an interference is indeed a contest between parties having adverse interests, such proceeding is not generally denominated as "patent litigation," perhaps because most interferences are initially brought before the Patent Office and/or because they are part of the process of procuring a patent. Similarly, the seldom invoked Public Use Proceedings, provided for by Rule 291, though in the nature of an adversary proceeding, is not regarded as patent litigation.

Causes of action which involve patent rights, but which do not directly call into question the scope or integrity of a United States patent are also not generally considered to be encompassed by the term "patent litigation." Moreover, such suits have been held not to raise a federal question, and, therefore, they are usually conducted in a state, rather than in a federal court.[3] Such suits include those concerning the construction of: (1) patent licensing agreements; (2) contracts of employment touching on employee made inventions; and (3) testamentary disposition of patent rights. It should be noted that in such a suit, a state court may properly adjudicate the integrity or validity of any patent involved therein, when such issue is raised by way of defense.

There are three adversary proceedings which call into question the scope and validity of United States patents. These are suits for: (1) cancellation. (2) infringement; and (3) declaratory judgment of invalidity.

§ 1. Cancellation

Suits seeking the cancellation of United States patents may be brought only by and in the name of the United States; they may not be initiated or maintained by an individual acting in his own behalf or on behalf of any private litigant.[4] The ground for seeking to set aside a United States patent has invariably been fraud. Indeed, it has been held by the Supreme Court that even the United States government is without power to set aside a patent on the mere ground of error in judgment on the part of the Patent Office, at least where the United States government has no direct proprietary or pecuniary interest therein.[5] Once issued a United States patent may not be revoked or repealed by the executive department.[6] The only authority competent to set aside, or annul it, is vested in the courts of the United States.[7] A judgment cancelling a United States patent vitiates the same, rendering it null and void ab initio against all the world. Accordingly, the patentee of a cancelled patent may be held liable for any royalties that he had collected thereunder.[8] The instances in which the outright cancellation of a United States patent have been sought are very, very few.[9]

The formal cancellation of a patent is not the only means by which the United States government may deprive a patent of its vitality. Section 5 of the Federal Trade Commission Act empowers the Federal Trade Commission to declare what conduct constitutes unfair methods of competition. Acting pursuant to this provision, the Federal Trade Commission has required a patentee to grant licenses, at a royalty-rate set by the Commission, to anyone desiring to exploit the tetracycline patent, which it had determined was tainted with fraud.[10] In another case, the Commission found that the calculation of rental fees based upon the amount of labor saved by the lessees of patented shrimp peeling machinery violated Section 5 of the Federal Trade Commission Act, where such criteria for determining the rental fees resulted in lessees in one region of the United States being charged a different rental per pound of shrimp peeled than lessees in another region of the country, even though the difference was due to the size of the shrimp caught in each region. The lessor-patentee was required by the Commission to cease and desist from charging discriminatory rentals.[11] While the Federal Trade Commission Act does not invest the Commission with power to invalidate patents, the foregoing cases demonstrate that Commission action may in fact emasculate patents procured and/or exploited in a manner which offend the Federal Trade Commission Act.

The Department of Justice is vested with power to bring suit in the name of the United States. It may sue to cancel a patent on the ground that the same was procured by fraud. It may also sue patentees on the ground that the manner in which they are exploiting their patents constitutes a violation of the antitrust laws that the Department of Justice is empowered to enforce. In such an antitrust suit, the United States may challenge the validity of a patent which is part of the alleged scheme to violate the antitrust laws.[12] In fact, it has recently been held by the Supreme Court that the Government has power to establish the invalidity of a patent in a suit brought under the antitrust laws even where the defendant-patentee is not relying upon such patent as a defense to the suit.[13] Even that Court, however, did not recognize the "unlimited authority in the Government to attack a patent by basing an antitrust claim on the simple assertion that the patent is invalid."

It should be borne in mind that private parties also have power to invoke a panoply of antitrust laws, either as a counterclaim to an action for patent infringement or as planintiff in a separate suit. The substantive aspects of the antitrust implications of patent enforcement are discussed more fully in Chapter 14. The assertion of fraud in the procurement of a patent as a basis for establishing an antitrust violation is discussed in Chapter 13.

§ 2. Patent Infringement

Patent litigation usually refers to suits for patent infringement. The word "infringement" suggests an encroachment. The domain belonging to a patentee is that circumscribed by the claims of his patent. If a patent is analogized to real property, its claims correspond to the metes and bounds recited in a deed. Invasion of the domain circumscribed by the metes and bounds of a landowner's real estate is called a trespass. Invasion of the domain circumscribed by the claims of a patent owner's patent is said to be an infrimgement. Both are civil wrongs or torts.[14] Unlike a trespass to real estate, patent infringement is a statutory wrong and is governed by federal law, infringement being defined by Section 271 of the present Patent Act:

> (a) Except as otherwise provided in this title, whoever without authority makes, uses or sells any patented invention, within the United States during the term of the patent therefor, infringes the patent.
> (b) Whoever actively induces infringement of a patent shall be liable as an infringer.
> (c) Whoever sells a component of a patented machine, apparatus for use in practicing a patented process, constituting a material part of the invention, knowing the same to be especially made or especially adapted for use in an infringement of such patent, and not a staple article or commodity of commerce suitable for substantial noninfringing use, shall be liable as a contributory infringer.
> (d) No patent owner otherwise entitled to relief for infringement or contributory infringement of a patent shall be denied relief or deemed guilty of misuse or illegal extension of the patent right by reason of his having done one or more of the following: (1) derived revenue from acts which if performed by another without his consent would constitute contributory infringement of the patent; (2) licensed or authorized another to perform acts which if performed without his consent would constitute contributory infringement of the patent; (3) sought to enforce his patent rights against infringement or contributory infringement.

From the foregoing statute it should be apparent that United States law recognizes two forms of patent infringement: (1) direct infrigement; and (2) contributory infringement.

One directly infringes a patent when he or his agents personally make, use, or sell in the United States what falls within the scope of any of its claims.

Many patents are directed to a combination of elements which are individually old, the invention residing in a particular manner of combining these elements. Ordinarily, one who makes, uses or sells less than the complete combination, as this has been claimed, is not an infringer. If infringement, however, were limited to the manufacture, sale, or use of the total combination, it would be easy for manufacturers to evade liability for infringement by merely making something less than the entire combination and instructing purchasers thereof how to complete the combination. Attempts to enforce combination patents under such law would almost always be an exercise in futility since a patentee could only bring suit against ultimate users, each of whom would be liable for, at most, a few acts of infringement. The cost of prosecuting suits so directed would far exceed the patentee's damages, and would not cut off the real source of the infringement. A judgment in favor of the patentee against an ultimate user would amount to a pyhrric victory, for a manufacturer could continue to supply, with impunity, the myriad of users not sued. To obviate such situation, the courts developed the doctrine of contributory infringement, which has been codified as Section 271(c) of the present Patent Act. It should be noted that contributory infringement requires:

(1) a sale

(2) of a material component of a patented invention;

(3) with knowledge that such component has been especially made for use in an infringement of such invention.

Only the seller of such component is liable as a contributory infringer. The buyer becomes liable as a direct infringer when he uses the overall patented combination.

That an item, though a component of a patented invention, is a staple article or commodity of commerce suitable for a substantial noninfringing use constitutes a defense, precluding liability for contributory infringement. To form the basis for contributory infringement the item must almost be uniquely suited as a component of the patented invention.

It should be noted that Section 271(b) makes liable as a direct infringer one who actively induces infringement. While one who sells a component of a patented invention with knowledge that the same has been especially made for use in an infringement of such patented invention literally induces infringement, liability under Section 271(b) requires conduct somewhat more egregious, that is, it requires something more than mere knowledge by the seller that an item he sells is a component especially made for use in an infringement of some patented invention. To incur liability under this proviso the seller must, in addition, actively aid or abet direct infringement, as by instructing a purchaser how to use the item he sells in the patented combination.[15]

Direct and contributory infringers enjoy the status of joint tort-feasors.[16] To reach a contributory infringer, however, direct infringement must be first proved and at least one direct infringer must be joined in a suit against a contributory infringer.[17]

To understand the import of Section 271(d) one must appreciate the distinction between contributory infringement and a tying arrangement. Tying arrangements involve the conditioning of a patent license upon the purchase, from the patentee, of goods, which though usable in or with the patented invention, are themselves unpatented. A classic example was an arrangement whereby the patentee of a salt tablet dispenser conditioned a license to use the same upon the purchase from it of the salt tablets (which tablets were unpatented) to be used in such dispensers. Tying arrangements are illegal and constitute patent misuse, a topic discussed at greater length in Chapter 14. It will be noted that both contributory infringement and tying arrangements concern commerce in something which itself is unpatented, but which, nevertheless, is used in connection with things which are patented. The crux of the distinction between the two is that in tying arrangements an attempt is made to create a monopoly in what is not patented.[18]

Overlapping the doctrine of contributory infringement is the repair-reconstruction doctrine. Does the purchaser of an article embodying a patented combination have the right to repair that article when one or more of its components wear out? Can one who sells replacements for such worn out components by liable as a contributory infringer? Although the rule used to answer these questions is simple to state, the factual determinations which must precede its application can be exceedingly complex. The owner of an article, notwithstanding the fact that it embodies one or more subsisting patents, has an unqualified right to repair such article without incurring liablility for infringement, but reconstruction of an article embodying a patented combination would constitute infringement. Replacement of a component as the same wears out amounts merely to repair; only the rebuilding–or second creation of the patented entity as a whole–constitutes reconstruction .[19]

It should be noted, at least with respect to direct infringement, that *knowledge* that what is being made, used, or sold is covered by a substituting patent is not an element necessary in establishing infringement.[20] That is to say, one who makes, uses, or sells whatever is covered by a subsisting United States patent, unless authorized by the patentee, is an infringer thereof, regardless of his state of mind—even if it is in total ignorance of the existence of a patent.

Everyone is conclusively presumed to have notice of the existence of every United States patent. The issuance of a United States patent constitutes constructive notice to the world.

A patentee may appropriately mark patented articles to the effect that the same are patented. In the event of failure so to mark, no damages will be recoverable by the patentee in any action for infringement, except on proof that the infringer had actual knowledge of the infringement and continued to infringe thereafter, in which event damages may be recovered only for infringement occurring after such notice.[21]

Section 271(a) declares the unauthorized making, use, or sale of any patented invention within the United States during the term of a patent therefor to be an infringement of such patent. This provision makes anyone of the three enumerated *acts* an infringement, nothing being said about the actor's *intent* or state of mind. The motive or purpose of one who makes, uses, or sells a patented invention would thus appear to be immaterial. Contrary to widely held belief, the statute does not immunize or exempt personal or noncommercial use. However, infringement suites against such use are impractical. Infringement must first be detected; the cost of prosecuting such suit would far exceed the damages recoverable. While the patent statute is silent about experimental use, it has been held that not every unauthorized construction of a patented article constitutes an infringement and that "the use of a patented machine for experiments for the sole purpose of gratifying a philosophical taste or curiosity or for instruction and amusement" does not constitute an infringing use.[22]

The folly of suing those who make and/or use one, or even several, infringing articles, unless these are of great value, has already been mentioned. Several reasons can be cited for this: the very high cost of patent litigation; the hostility of courts in general to patents, a high percentage of litigated patents being held invalid; the limited extent of recovery to which a patentee who prevails is entitled.

Patent litigation consumes an enormous amount of attorney time.

Consequently, attorney fees for one side in a patent infringement suit may well run into six figures. While Section 285 allows the court, in exceptional cases, to award reasonable attorney fees to the successful party, such awards are relatively rare. Attorney fees will not be awarded under Section 285 except to prevent gross injustice and where fraud and wrong-doing are clearly proved.[23] Section 285 applies to patent owners as well as to infringers. It has been held that: (1) an infringer is not liable for attorney fees unless he infringed a patent known to be valid;[24] (2) a patentee is liable for attorney fees where he used his patent to prosecute vexatious and unjustified litigation.[25] A patentee contemplating suing an infringer should, therefore, not count on being reimbursed for his attorney fees.

The measure of a patentee's monetary award is damages adequate to compensate him for the infringement, that is, for the patentee's lost profits, but in no event less than a reasonable or established royalty. The theory of damages in patent litigation is to deny to the infringer the fruits of his illegal act and to restore to the patentee the benefits which he would have derived form his monopoly had he not been denied the infringing sales. It should be noted that the law draws a distinction between "damages" and "profits." The term "profits," when used without further qualification, refers to what an infringer makes; "damages" signifies what a patentee loses by such infringement.[26]

Under prior law, a patentee was entitled to recover an infringer's profits. The existing statute, except in regard to design patents, makes no reference to the term "profits."[27] Some courts have construed the omission of the term "profits" from the present Patent Act as barring a recovery based upon the same.[28] Other courts have deemed it proper to consider an infringer's profits as evidence of, and perhaps even the measure of, the patentee's damages.[29]

With respect to design patents, the Patent Act[30] does make infringers thereof liable to the patent owner to the extent of the infringers' total profits, but not less than for $250. While this statute precludes a double recovery for profit made from infringement of a design patent, the right of a design patent owner to recover an infringer's total profits or statutory damages ($250) does not prevent him from pursuing those remedies available for infringement of the other kinds of patents.

Where the infringing device is one of many components of a

machine manufactured and sold by an infringer, in order to assess damages, the value of the machine must be apportioned between the infringing and noninfringing components. However, some courts recognize that the patented component may so contribute to the commercial success of the whole as to possess a value far in excess of the unit sale price of the component as a separate article of commerce.[31]

In exceptional circumstance, the court, in its discretion, may treble the damages, in addition to awarding attorney fees.[32] Absent an award of treble damages, however, a patentee's potential monetary recovery is, at best, purely compensatory, and not punitive or exemplary. Consequently, some businessmen would rather infringe than pay royalties, knowing that their liability therefore will likely be limited to a reasonable royalty. Should the patent's validity be upheld, and the odds are that it will not, they will only then have to pay out what amounts to royalties in the form of damages.

Patents issue only after an examination has been conducted by the Patent Office, as to whether the form and content of each application appears to confrom to the applicable laws. Actions taken by agencies of the government are generally endowed with a presumption of administrative correctness.[33] This presumption is written into Section 282 of the Patent Act, which provides in part:

> A patent shall be presumed valid. Each claim of a patent (whether in independent or dependent form) shall be presumed valid independently of the validity of other claims; dependent claims shall be presumed valid even though dependent upon an invalid claim. The burden of establishing invalidity of a patent or any claim thereof shall rest on the party asserting it.

The presumption of validity is rebuttable. Indeed, whenever a patentee sues a putative infringer, the very validity of his patent can be, and almost invariably is, called into question by the accused. In point of fact, a very high proportion of litigated patents is held invalid for lack of compliance with one or more of the statutory requirements. This record, however, should not be taken as an adverse reflection on the Patent Office. Due to the nature of the examination, the Patent Office is ordinarily incapable of detecting much of the prior art. Moreover, it has no facilities for testing, but must rather rely on representations made by applicants and their counsel.

Some courts accord a presumption of validity only with respect to prior art applied, or at least cited, by the examiner.[34] As a rule of thumb, the more extensive was the Patent Office's consideration of a case, the stronger will be the resulting patent's presumption of validity.[35] The quantum of evidence necessary to overcome the presumption of validity has been characterized variously by different courts. To overcome the presumption of validity more than a mere preponderence of the credible evidence is required.[36] What is generally required is "strong, clear, cogent and convincing evidence."[37] On some occasions, evidence beyond a reasonable doubt has been required.[38]

Section 282, the same section which codifies the presumption of validity, allows an infringer to avoid liability therefor, if he can establish any one of the following defenses enumerated therein:

> (1) Noninfringement, absence of liability for infringement, or unenforceability *(which include misuse and license under the patent)*;
> (2) Invalidity of the patent or any claim in suit on any ground in Part II of this title *(35 U.S.C.)* as a condition for patentability *(that is, (a) want of statutory subject matter; (b) lack of novelty; (c) absence of utility; (d) unobviousness);*
> (3) Invalidity of the patent or any claim in suit for failure to comply with any requirement of sections 112 or 251 of this title;
> (4) Any other fact or act made a defense by this title.

The foregoing are affirmative defenses which must be pleaded by those seeking the benefit thereof. Section 286 is a statute of limitations which bars recovery of damages for any infringement committed more than six years prior to the filing of the complaint or counterclaim for infringement in the action.[39] Like statutes of limitation barring other causes of action, that barring liability for patent infringement is an affirmative defense which must be pleaded by the party relying thereon. This statute of limitation applies only to remedies at law, namely, damages, the doctrine of laches applying to the equitable remedy of injunctive relief. The doctrine of laches precludes equitable relief where there has been: (1) an inexcusable delay in instituting suit seeking enforcement of patent rights; and (2) such delay has prejudiced the accused. The time interval which will constitute laches varies with the particular facts involved. In some cases it may be shorter than the statute of limitations; in others, it may be longer.[40]

To the above list of defenses, the courts have added fraud committed in the procurement of the patent.[41]

To establish a prima facie case of patent infringement, the plaintiff need only introduce into evidence: (1) letters patent; (2) evidence of his title to such patent; *and* (3) evidence that the defendant has engaged in any of the activities proscribed by Section 271.

After the plaintiff has presented his case, the defendant may attempt to avoid liability for infringement by offering evidence in rebuttal, including evidence tending to establish any of the defenses enumerated in Section 282 and/or evidence of a defect in the plaintiff's title to the patent or patents in suit.

To avoid liability for infringement, one need only establish any one of the above defenses or defects. It should be noted, however, that an infringer will be liable to the same extent whether it is found that he infringed one or a hundred claims of a patent, except that, where one or more claims of a patent are held invalid, the patentee will recover no costs unless a disclaimer of the invalid claims has been entered at the Patent Office before the commencement of the suit.

The two key issues in every patent infringement suit are: (1) the validity of the patent or patents alleged to have been infringed; and (2) whether the defendant did infringe the claims of the patents in suit. Since the ultimate issue in every patent infringement suit is whether the defendant has infringed, the plaintiff, as in other civil litigation, has the burden of proving the affirmative of the ultimate issue by a fair preponderance of the credible evidence.[42] Where, however, the issue of infringement is contested by the defendant, the presumption of noninfringement has no effect. To give it weight would alter the burden of the plaintiff's proof to one greater than a fair preponderance of the credible testimony.[43] The presumption of patent validity excuses the plaintiff from proving the same in the absence of defendant's allegation and evidence to the contrary. Unlike validity, infringement is a question of fact, its resolution being therefore the province of the trier of fact.[44] Invariably, the validity of the patents in suit will be put in issue by the putative infringer, who will at least attempt to establish their invalidity.

Whether there in fact has been an infringement of a patent in suit is not only the ultimate issue in patent infringement litigation, it is also one of the most technical known to man.

Section 271 defines patent infringement as the unauthorized making, using, or selling of any patented invention. Accordingly, it is necessary to determine just what constitutes the patented invention. One can infringe a patent, only by infringing one or more of its claims. The claims define, and are the measure of, the metes and bounds of the invention disclosed in letters patent.

Thus, to determine whether there has been infringement, it is necessary to construe the claims: segregate out the effective limitations (the wheat) from the verbiage (chaff). How to identify the effective limitations has been extensively treated elsewhere in this text.

Determination of whether or not there has been infringement then becomes essentially a process of comparison: Are the features (that is, the effective limitations) recited in the patent claims to be found in what is alleged to infringe? Stated in the parlance of the trade: Does any claim read on what is alleged to infringe? If at least one claim reads on what is alleged to infringe, then such does infringe.

Although the effect of open and closed language has been discussed elsewhere, it is felt that this is so important that it will be summarized here. If a claim is couched in opened language (e.g., "comprising . . . "), then there will be infringement if what is alleged to infringe possesses the claimed features, it being immaterial whether or not what is alleged to infringe also possesses additional features not recited in the claim. If, however, a claim is couched in closed language (e.g., "consisting of . . ."), then there will be infringement only if there is a complete correspondence of features between the claim and what is alleged to infringe, there being no infringement if what is alleged to infringe possesses *any* features in addition to those recited in the claim.

Whether a claim is couched in open or closed language, it will not be infringed by anything which lacks any of the features recited in the claim.[45]

[1] Doctrine of Equivalents

The foregoing rules for determining patent infringement must be qualified by the judicially created doctrine of equivalents and doctrine of file wrapper estoppel.

Although it is the claims of a patent which are the measure of the invention disclosed therein, these are to be construed in light of the specification.[46] Where an unauthorized device employs substantially the same means, to achieve substantially the same results, in substantially the same way, as that claimed, such unauthorized device may be deemed an infringement of what has been claimed—even though not a single claim of the patent can literally be read on the unauthorized device.[47] The foregoing rubric is a statement of the doctrine of equivalents. It is equitable in nature, invoked by courts to save a meritorious invention from the modesty of its inventor in expressing the fair limits of his contribution. It is not limited to claims drawn to devices, being applicable to all statutory classes of invention.

The doctrine of equivalents had its inception in a Supreme Court opinion of 1853 vintage.[48] The opinion grew out of a suit for the infringement of a patent covering an improvement in railroad cars for carrying coal and like materials. According to its claims, the improvement consisted in "making the body of a car for the transportation of coal, etc., in the form of a frustrum of a cone . . . ."[49] The car alleged to infringe differed from that claimed in that it was pyramidal in form, rather than cylindrical, having a hexagonal base. Both the specification and the claims of the patent taught, in the following words, the principle which dictated the selection of the claimed form: "the force exerted by the weight of the load presses equally in all directions, and does not tend to change the form thereof so that every part resists its equal proportion, and by which, also, the lower part is so reduced as to pass down making the truck frame and between the axles, to lower the center of gravity of the load without diminishing the capacity of the car as described."

The Supreme Court, reversing the trial court, held, over the dissents of four of its justices, that the pyramidal-hexagonal form employed by the defendant embodied the patentee's invention, the Court stating that "to copy the principle or mode of operation described is an infringement, although such copy should be totally unlike the original in form or proportion." Thus, in effect, the Court found that, in the context of the invention, a pyramidal form, having a hexagonal base, was the functional equivalent of a conical form, having a circular base. Railroad cars embodying the principle of the patentee's invention were capable of carrying loads several times heavier than cars of existing design.

It should be noted that, as permitted by the practice of that day, the claim of the patent in suit contained a recitation to the effect the invention was that substantially as described in the claims. While such saving recitations are no longer proper, the courts, not without dissent, have repeatedly reaffirmed and consistently applied the doctrine of equivalents.

In 1950, the Supreme Court found that, in the context of the invention, manganese silicate was the functional equivalent of magnesium silicate, notwithstanding the fact that the two chemical elements magnesium and manganese are not generally regarded as possessing analogous properties. The patent in suit contained claims drawn to a composition of matter, in the form of a mixture of ingredients, that is useful as a welding flux. A representative claim called for:

> (20) A composition for electric welding containing a fluoride and a major proportion of alkaline earth metal silicate, and being substantially free from uncombined iron oxide and from substances capable of evolving gases under welding conditions.

The composition alleged to infringe contained the silicates of calcium and manganese, the latter not an alkaline earth metal (the alkaline earth metals being beryllium, magnesium, calcium, strontium, barium, and radium). Both the prior art and the specification of the patent in suit taught the suitability generally of substituting manganese compounds for those of magnesium in fabricating welding fluxes. Holding that a composition containing the silicates of calcium and manganese infringed the claims in suit, the Court made the following comments on the application of the doctrine of equivalents:[50]

> What constitutes equivalency must be determined against the context of the patent, the prior art, and the particular circumstances of the case. Equivalence, in the patent law, is not the prisoner of a formula and is not an absolute to be considered in a vacuum. It does not require complete identity for every purpose and in every respect. In determining equivalents, things equal to the same thing may not be equal to each other and, by the same token, things for most purposes different may sometimes be equivalents. Consideration must be given to the purpose for which an ingredient is used in a patent, the qualities it

has when combined with other ingredients, and the function which it is intended to perform. An important factor is whether persons reasonably skilled in the art would have known of the interchangeability of an ingredient not contained in the patent with one that was.

A finding of equivalence is a determination of fact. Proof can be made in any form: through testimony of experts or others versed in the technology; by documents, including texts and treatises; and, of course, by the disclosures of the prior art. Like any other issue of fact, final determination requires a balancing of credibility, persuasiveness and weight of evidence.

The doctrine of equivalents has come under fire from many quarters, including the Antitrust Division of the United States Department of Justice. In a recent case, in which a writ of certiorari was granted, that Department filed a brief amicus curiae, urging the Court to abolish the doctrine of equivalents. The justices of the Supreme Court, however, split four to four in their decision, thereby preserving the vitality of the doctrine of equivalents.[51]

[2] Doctrine of File Wrapper Estoppel

The applicability of the doctrine of equivalents is circumscribed by the effect of another doctrine, namely, the doctrine of file wrapper estoppel. The latter is but a specific application to patent claims of a doctrine which, as will presently become apparent, is of wide and general applicability. The word "estoppel" signifies a bar. The doctrine of estoppel bars or precludes one from asserting a fact or truth where he had previously:(1) taken a position inconsistent with his present position; and (2) another has acted in reliance upon his earlier representation.

Applied to patent claims, the doctrine of estoppel precludes a patent owner from recapturing in patent litigation the breadth which was given up in the Patent Office to secure allowance of the application. The manner in which the doctrine of estoppel is applied to patent claims is well illustrated by a case involving a pinball machine, and specifically, a resilient switch which closed an electric circuit when the target pin was hit by the rolling ball. The claims of the patent called for: "conductor means . . . embedded in the table." In the accused device, the conductor means was "carried by the table," but not "embedded in the table." The application, as originally filed, did have claims calling for a conductor means "carried by the table." However, in order to overcome a prior art rejection made by the Patent Office examiner, and thus secure the allowance of his application, the applicant had amended his claims by limiting them to a conductor means "embedded in the table." The patent owner later sued one who made pinball devices wherein the conductor means was "carried by," but not "embedded in the table," alleging that such modification was a functional equivalent of what was covered by his claims. The Supreme Court invoked the doctrine of estoppel, stating that:[52]

> By the amendment he [the inventor] recognized and emphasized the difference between the two phrases and proclaimed his abandonment of all that is embraced in the difference.

The court added that it was immaterial whether or not the examiner's rejection was proper. Mere acquiescence, manifested by amendment, will suffice to constitute an estoppel. This rule is particularly harsh where an applicant, in order to secure a patent, has abandoned more ground that was necessary to overcome an examiner's interpretation of the prior art. Accordingly, it has been held that a reissue patent may be available to obviate the possible effect of file wrapper estoppel.[53] To be entitled to a reissue patent, however, there must be compliance with all the requirements prescribed by the reissue statute, including, where any enlargement of any claim is sought, that filing of application therefor take place within two years from the date of grant of the original patent.[54]

The term "file wrapper" denotes the stiff paper jacket in which all the papers relating to an application are preserved by the Patent Office. The file wrapper connotes the official record of the case within the Patent Office, and includes the amendments and arguments submitted by the applicant. Some lower courts have carried the doctrine of file wrapper so far as to have found that the mere arguments of an applicant or his attorney constituted file wrapper estoppel.[55] Amendment of the claims in response to a rejection not based upon prior art (as one founded on Section 112) is generally held not to involve any element of file wrapper estoppel.[56]

[3] Inverse Doctrine of Equivalents

Before a court will resort to the doctrine of equivalents to enlarge the scope of a claim in order to find an infringement thereof, the literal wording of the claims will receive a liberal construction. However, there will be no infringement, though the claims of a patent literally happen to read on some physical embodiment, where such physical embodiment does not employ substantially the same means, in substantially the same way, to achieve substantially the same results as that claimed. This rule, sometimes referred to as the inverse doctrine of equivalents, says, in effect, that an incidental infringement is no infringement at all.[57]

The policy of construing claims so as to capture a patentee's real contribution is peculiar to patent litigation, being in contrast to the policy prevalent before the Patent Office, where proferred claims are literally construed. The reason behind the latter policy is sound: make an applicant amend his claims so that they will carefully and accurately define his actual invention.[58] The claim language of an issued patent is unalterable. Only by a reissue can it be changed.

It must be borne in mind that a prime purpose of the patent system is the encouragement of early public disclosure of inventions. The public is always at complete liberty, even during the life of a patent, to make whatever use of the information that is contained in the specification so long as such use does not infringe the patentee's claims.[59] Accordingly:[60]

> One may legitimately study the patent and microscopically examine the language of the claim in order to make a product which will serve the same purpose and yet avoid infringement of the patent. Such is the logical, beneficial result which was sought through the adoption of the comprehensive patent system of our government.

And:[61]

> [I]t does not detract from the good faith of a competitor for him to procure and examine a patent and its claims, as well as the subject matter thereof, in order to ascertain what is open to the public.

It has been held that not every unauthorized embodiment of a patented invention constitutes an infringement. Thus, the construction and single use of a patented device for the purpose of advertising defendant's product was held not to infringe plaintiff's patent.[62] Also, the construction of a patented device merely for experimental purposes was held not to constitute an infringement.[63]

§ 3. Declaratory Judgments and Counterclaims

Hitherto, the instant chapter has placed the patent owner, who is involved in patent litigation, in the position of plaintiff, with the alleged infringer cast in the role of defendant. Such indeed is the lineup in many suits for patent infringement. The Declaratory Judgment Act, however, makes it possible, under certain circumstances, for an infringer to take the initiative, by suing a patent owner for a declaratory judgment of patent invalidity and/or noninfringement.[64] Where suit is brought against a patent owner for a declaratory judgment that his patent is invalid and/or not infringed, the patent owner may interpose as a counterclaim a cause of action for patent infringement. A cause of action for a declaratory judgment may also be interposed as a counterclaim. Thus, one sued for patent infringement may seek, as a counterclaim, a declaratory judgment of invalidity and/or noninfringement.

The term "claim," as used in the *Federal Rules of Civil Procedure,* signifies a cause of action set up by a plaintiff in his complaint. A counterclaim is an opposing claim set up by a party being sued, either against the party suing him or against some third party. Because the term "claim" has a very special meaning in patent law, namely, a definition of the invention disclosed in a patent specification, to avoid confusion, its use in this text to signify a cause of action will be curtailed.

While the *Federal Rules of Civil Procedure* allow a defendant to assert, as a counterclaim, *any* cause of action that he may have against the plaintiff, these rules also allow the court to order separate trial of a particular issue, if this in fact is more convenient or desirable. Whether the issues raised in a counterclaim will be tried along with those raised in the complaint will depend on how closely related and interrelated they are, it being of significance whether the issues arose out of the same transaction. It would seem that a strong case could be made out for the common trial of a claim for patent infringement and a counterclaim asserting that the plaintiff used the patent defendant is alleged to have infringed in violation of the antitrust laws. This would seem to be particularly true where a basis for the antitrust counterclaim is fraud alleged to have been committed in the procurement of that patent.

The *Federal Rules of Civil Procedure,* moreover, draw a distinction between "permissive" and "compulsory" counterclaims. Failure to interpose a compulsory counterclaim forecloses forever thereafter the assertion of a cause of action involving the same. A counterclaim is deemed compulsory where it involves the same issues as those raised by the claims set forth in the complaint.[65] Such would certainly seem to be the case when the claim is for a declaratory judgment of patent invalidity and noninfringement and the counterclaim is for patent infringement.[66]

The right of would-be infringers to challenge the validity of patents in federal court is not unlimited or unconditional. United States district courts are only competent to decide justiciable controversies, that is, actual cases or controversies arising under the Constitution or the laws of the United States; they do not give mere advisory opinions.[67] Accordingly, a suit for a declaratory judgment of invalidity and/or noninfringement will not be entertained unless the patent owner has done something to enforce, or to attempt to enforce, his patent, so that a real controversy exists.[68] A mere threat by the patentee to sue a putative infringer will generally suffice to give such latter person grounds for bringing a declaratory judgment action.[69]

§ 4. Some Consequences of Invalidity

In Anglo-American jurisprudence, civil litigation is generally regarded as a purely private affair between the parties thereto, the state being wholly disinterested in the outcome. Moreover, while the facts as found and the law as applied by the court are usually embodied in an opinion which is entitled to deference as precedent in accordance with the principle of stare decisis, in subsequent litigation, the actual judgment rendered binds only the parties to that suit and their successors in interest. Between these parties, however, a final judgment, except in the most exceptional circumstances (viz., fraud, newly discovered material evidence) is conclusive. Where the judgment relied upon and the instant suit are based upon the same cause of action, such prior judgment is said to be res judicata, being conclusive as to not only the issues that were actually determined in the earlier suit, but also as to all the issues that might have been raised there. The legal theory behind res judicata is that the cause of action has become merged in the final judgment. Where the judgment relied upon was based upon a cause of action different from the instant one, such prior judgment is said to constitute collateral estoppel, barring relitigation of those issues—but only those issues—actually litigated in the earlier suit. In either a res judicata or collateral estoppel situation the party seeking the benefit of the prior judgment must have been a party to the earlier suit in which that judgment was rendered. For many years a majority of courts adhered to the view that there could be no estoppel by judgment unless the estoppel was mutual, that is, the party invoking the benefit of a prior judgment as conclusive would have to have been bound by the determination had it been adverse to him. Such, the courts said, was a requirement of due process.[70]

Because of the absence of mutuality, it was possible for a patentee, though his patent had been declared invalid by one or more courts, to sue another, relitigating the validity of his patent.[71] Recently, however, the Supreme Court has held that mutality is not an absolute requirement and that, where a patentee has had a full and fair opportunity to litigate the validity of his patent, a resulting judgment of invalidity may be interposed as a bar even by one who was not a party to that earlier suit.[72] Such a judgment, though it specifically names only the parties to that suit, is in its effect an in rem judgment of invalidity, precluding the patentee from suing anyone ever again for infringement of his patent.

We have just seen how the doctrine of estoppel can now be used against a patentee, whose patent has once been declared invalid. Until fairly recently, another application of estoppel accrued to the benefit of the patentee. For many years, it was the law that a licensee was estopped to challenge the validity of any patents under which he was licensed. The rationale of this doctrine, known as licensee estoppel, was that by taking out a license, the licensee in effect admitted the validity of the licensed patents. To allow a licensee to challenge the validity of his licensor's patent, while the licensee, by virtue of his license, was immune from suit for patent infringement, was felt to be inequitable. In abrogating the doctrine of licensee estoppel, the Supreme Court expressed the opinion that "the equities of the licensor do not weigh very heavily when they are balanced against the important public interest in permitting full and free competition in the use of ideas which are in reality a part of the public domain."[73] For symmetry, it will here be noted that the so-called doctrine of licensor estoppel is still viable. This doctrine holds that a licensor is estopped to assert his nonownership of a patent at the time he granted a license, where the license purported to cover a patent which, in fact, was not acquired by the licensor until after the license was granted.[74]

In its opinion abrogating the doctrine of licensee estoppel, the Supreme Court also observed that licensees may avoid further royalty payments, regardless of the provisions of their license, once a third party proves that the patent is invalid.[75] It has been held that a licensee under a patent which has been declared invalid is not entitled to recoup royalties which he has already paid, a judgment of invalidity, in this regard, operating only prospectively and not retroactively.[76] Where, however, a patent has been cancelled, it is void ab initio, so that the patentee would be liable to his licensees for whatever consideration they paid.[77]

§ 5. The Conduct of Patent Litigation

The conduct of patent litigation, like that of other civil actions in federal courts, is governed by the *Federal Rules of Civil Procedure* and by the applicable provisions of the federal Judiciary Act (28 U.S.C.). The few remaining pages of this chapter are devoted to an outline of the highlights of federal civil procedure of special significance in patent litigation.

[1] Subject Matter Jurisdiction

28 U.S.C. 1338 vests United States District courts with original jurisdiction of civil actions arising under any Act of Congress relating to patents, copyrights, and trademarks. Such jurisdiction, by this section, is made exclusive of the courts of the states in patent and copyright cases. Section 1338(b) empowers the district courts to hear and determine a claim of unfair competition when the same is related to, and joined with, a claim under the copyright, patent or trademark laws. This is an example of the ancillary or pendent jurisdiction of the federal courts, which had been assumed by federal courts even prior to this legislation.[78] In suits against the United States, the forum is the United States Court of Claims, as provided for by 28 U.S.C. 1498.[79]

Jurisdiction over the person of a defendant is acquired by the service of process thereon, as provided for by Rules 4 and 5 of the *Federal Rules of Civil Procedure.* Section 1694 of the Judiciary Act further provides:

> In a patent infringement action commenced in a district where the defendant is not a resident but has a regular and established place of business, service of process, summons or subpoena upon such defendant may be made upon his agent or agents conducting such business.

[2] Venue

The situs of the district court wherein a suit may be brought is subject to 28 U.S.C. 1400(b), which provides:

> Any civil action for patent infringement may be brought in the judicial district where the defendant resides, or where the defendant has committed acts of infringement and has a regular and established place of business.

Where, however, the defendant is an alien, Section 1391(d) controls, and, accordingly, suit may be brought in any district.[80]

[3] Discovery

The *Federal Rules of Civil Procedure* sanction the discovery of "any matter, not privileged, which is relevant to the subject matter involved in the pending action."[81] This has been construed to include such matters as those reasonably calculated to lead to the discovery of admissible evidence and those useful merely for impeaching the credibility of a witness.[82] Rule 26(b) allows for discovery of the"identity and location of persons having knowledge of relevant facts," and this includes the names of a party's own witnesses.[83] Trade secrets are not immune from discovery, merely because they are trade secrets, there being no definite privilege against their disclosure.[84] Moreover, disclosure may be had even of the content of pending patent applications, it having been held that 35 U.S.C. 122 does not render patent applications privileged for judicial purposes.[85] However, it is the policy of the law to protect property in trade secrets against unnecessary and unjustified invasion.[86] Disclosure of trade secrets will be required only where it is relevant and necessary. The burden of showing relevancy and necessity rests on the party seeking disclosure.[87] A court may take appropriate steps to guard against the general disclosure of trade secrets, including the production of documents in camera.[88] While the work product of an attorney is privileged, it has been held that the attorney-client privilege does not extend to the work product of a mere patent agent.[89]

[4] Preliminary Injunction

A court, in its discretion, has the power to grant a temporary injunction, pending the outcome of the law suit.[90] Preliminary injunctions in patent infringement litigation are rarely granted, since a clear showing of irreparable harm and likelihood of success must first be demonstrated to the court's satisfaction. Moreover, a party in whose favor a preliminary injunction is granted must post a bond adequate in amount to compensate the party against whom the injunction is granted for damages suffered by reason of the injunction. Such compensation will be actually awarded only if the party against whom the injunction was granted ultimately prevails in the pending litigation. Only where the invention's commercial life span is demonstrably ephemeral and the validity of the patent is not challenged or validity has been established in an earlier suit is there a probability of securing an injunction against acts of infringement before the disposition of the suit.[91]

[5] Trial

Where only a remedy at law is sought, namely, damages, either party may request that the issues of infringement and validity be tried by a jury.[92] Where equitable relief is sought, namely, an injunction, there is no right to a jury trial. Assessment of damages, following a verdict of validity and infringement, is normally determined by a court-appointed master, who sits without a jury.

Expert witnesses play an important role in patent infringement litigation. Their chief function is to translate the patent specification from the arcane terminology understood by those skilled in the art to which the invention relates into terms comprehendible to courts.[93] Expert testimony may also be received on other matters, such as the state of the prior art, whether the specification of the patent in suit is sufficient to enable one skilled in the art to carry out the claimed invention, and whether the claimed invention is capable of being carried out.[94] Some courts will even allow an expert witness to express an opinion as to whether the claimed invention is unobvious and has been infringed.[95] Such conclusions, of course, are not binding on the court.[96]

[6] Appellate Review

A party dissatisfied with the decision of the district court has a right of appeal to the United States Court of Appeals of the circuit in which the district court is situated.[97] It is the policy of these circuit courts not to disturb primary or evidentiary findings made by the district court unless such are clearly erroneous.[98] However, questions of law, as well as inferences and conclusions based upon primary findings, are fully reviewable by the circuit courts. Access to the Supreme Court for review on the merits is at the discretion of that Court. To obtain such review, application must first be made to it for a writ of certiorari.[99] Such application is, in effect, a screening process. Generally, the Court will select for plenary review only those cases which raise, what it deems to be, significant questions of federal law. In many instances, review will be granted to resolve conflicting circuit court decisions. Review is generally limited to questions of law. It is significant to note here, however, that the Court deems patent validity to be a question of law, appropriate for final determination by itself.[100]

Notes

[1] *Writings of Thomas Jefferson,* Vol. VI, (Washington ed. 1814), p. 180, quoted in Graham v. John Deere Co., 383 U.S. 1, 8-9, 148 U.S.P.Q. 459, 463 (1966).

[2] See Ex parte Donovan, 1888 C.D. 100, 102, 44 O.G. 698, 699 (Comm. Pat. 1888). Compare, Carter-Wallace, Inc. v. Davis-Edwards Pharmacal Corp., 443 F.2d 867, 886, 169 U.S.P.Q. 625, 639 (2d Cir. 1971) (Mansfield, J., dissenting).

[3] See Pratt v. Paris Gas Light & Coke Co., 168 U.S. 255 (1897). See also, Becker v. Contoure Laboratories, Inc., 279 U.S. 388 (1929); Luckett v. Delpark, Inc., 270 U.S. 496 (1928); Unarco Indus., Inc. v. Kelley Co., 465 F.2d 1303, 175 U.S.P.Q. 199 (7th Cir. 1972); Republic Engineering & Mfg. Co. v. Moskowitz, 141 U.S.P.Q. 409 (Mo. Ct. App. 1964); Zemba v. Rodgers, 145 U.S.P.Q. 628 (N.J. Super. 1965).

[4] United States v. Bell Telephone Co., 128 U.S. 315 (1888).

[5] United States v. Bell Telephone Co., 167 U.S. 224, 269 (1897).

[6] United States v. Bell Telephone Co., 128 U.S. 315, 363 (1888).

[7] McCormick Harvesting Mach. Co. v. Aultman, 169 U.S. 606, 609 (1898).

[8] See United States v. Hartford-Empire Co., 73 F. Supp. 979, 981, 75 U.S.P.Q. 118,119 (D. Del. 1947). See also, Mowry v. Whitney, 81 U.S. (14 Wall.) 434 (1871).

[9] See United States v. Saf-T-Boom Corp., 164 U.S.P.Q. 283 (E.D. Ark.), *aff'd* 431 F.2d 737, 167 U.S.P.Q. 195 (8th Cir. 1970). United States v. Colgate, 21 Fed. 318 32 Fed. 624 (C.C.S.D. N.Y.), *appeal dism'd* 127 U.S. 792 (1888); United States v. Frazer, 22 Fed. 106 (N.D. Ill. 1884); Unites States v. Gunning, 18 Fed. 511 (D.N.Y. 1883); Attorney General ex rel. Hecker v. Rumford Chem. Works, 32 Fed. 608 (D.R.I. 1876).

[10] Chas. Pfizer & Co. v. F.T.C., 401 F.2d 574, 159 U.S.P.Q. 193 (6th Cir. 1968), *cert. denied* 394 U.S. 920 (1969).

[11] LaPeyre v. F.T.C., 366 F.2d 117, 151 U.S.P.Q. 79 (5th Cir. 1966).

[12] United States v. U.S. Gypsum Co., 333 U.S. 364, 76 U.S.P.Q. 430 (1948).

[13] United States v. Glaxo Group, Ltd., 410 U.S. 52, 176 U.S.P.Q. 289 (1973).

[14] Railex Corp. v. Joseph Guss & Sons, Inc., 40 F.R.D. 119, 125, 148 U.S.P.Q. 640, 644 (D.C.C. 1966).

[15] Westinghouse Elec. & Mfg. Co. v. Precise Mfg. Corp., 11 F.2d 209 (2d Cir. 1926); Stamicarbon, N.V. v. McNally-Pittsburgh Mfg. Co., 302 F. Supp. 525, 161 U.S.P.Q. 323 (D. Kan. 1969).

[16] Wallace v. Holmes, 29 Fed. Cas. 74 (No. 17,100) (C.C.D. Conn. 1871).

[17] Cold Metal Process Co. v. United Engineering & Foundry Co., 235 F.2d 224, 110 U.S.P.Q. 332 (3d Cir. 1956).

[18] See Morton Salt Co. v. G.S. Suppiger Co., 314 U.S. 488, 52 U.S.P.Q. 30 (1942).

[19] Aro Mfg. Co. v. Convertible Top Replacement Co., 377 U.S. 476, 141 U.S.P.Q. 681 (1964); 365 U.S. 336, 128 U.S.P.Q. 354 (1961).

[20] Wahl v. Carrier Mfg. Co., 358 F.2d 1, 3, 148 U.S.P.Q. 699, 701 (7th Cir. 1966); C.H. Dexter & Sons, Inc. v. Kimberly Clark Corp., 292 F.2d 371, 130 U.S.P.Q. 1 (1st Cir. 1961).

[21] 35 U.S.C. 287.

[22] Gayler v. Wilder, 51 U.S. (10 How.) 477, 497 (1850).

[23] Berry Brothers Corp. v. Sigmon, 317 F.2d 700, 706, 137 U.S.P.Q. 590, 595 (4th Cir. 1963); Mab, Inc. v. Piedmont Shirt Co., 248 F. Supp. 71, 82, 147 U.S.P.Q. 470, 478 (D.S.C. 1965).

[24] Sarkes Tarzian, Inc. v. Philco Corp., 351 F.2d 557, 147 U.S.P.Q. 172 (7th Cir. 1965).

[25] American Chain & Cable Co. v. Rochester Paper Co., 199 F.2d 325, 95 U.S.P.Q. 115 (4th Cir. 1952); Mab, Inc. v. Piedmont Shirt Co., N. 23 *supra*.

[26] Duplate Corp. v. Triplex Safety Glass Co., 298 U.S. 448, 451, 29 U.S.P.Q. 306, 308 (1936).

[27] 35 U.S.C. 284.

[28] Georgia-Pacific Corp. v. U.S. Plywood Corp., 243 F. Supp. 500, 516, 146 U.S.P.Q. 228, 242 (S.D.N.Y. 1965).

[29] Zysset v. Popeil Bros., Inc., 318 F.2d 701, 707, 137 U.S.P.Q. 694, 698 (7th Cir. 1963); Graham v. Jeoffrey Mfg., Inc., 253 F.2d 72, 74, 116 U.S.P.Q. 542, 543 (5th Cir.), *cert. denied* 358 U.S. 817 (1958).

[30] 35 U.S.C. 289.

[31] England v. Deere & Co., 221 F. Supp. 319, 323, 138 U.S.P.Q. 608, 611 (S.D. Ill. 1963). See also, Dowagiac Mfg. Co. v. Minnesota Moline Plow Co., 235 U.S. 641 (1915); Westinghouse Elec. & Mfg. Co. v. Wagner Elec. & Mfg. Co., 225 U.S. 604 (1912).

[32] 35 U.S.C. 284.

[33] See Morgan v. Daniels, 153 U.S. 120, 123-124 (1893).

[34] See for example, Hewlett-Packard Co. v. Tel-Design, Inc., 460 F.2d 625, 174 U.S.P.Q. 140 (9th Cir. 1972).

[35] See Radio Corp. of Am. v. Radio Engineering Laboratories, Inc., 293 U.S. 1, 7, 21 U.S.P.Q. 353, 355 (1934); Gulf Smokeless Coal Co. v. Sutton, Steele & Steele Co., 35 F.2d 433, 437, 3 U.S.P.Q. 82, 85-86 (4th Cir. 1929); U.S. Plywood Corp. v. General Plywood Corp., 230 F. Supp. 831, 837, 141 U.S.P.Q. 134, 137 (W.D. Ky. 1963).

[36] Moon v. Cabot Shops, Inc., 270 F.2d 539, 541, 123 U.S.P.Q. 60, 61 (9th Cir. 1959).

[37] U.S. Gypsum Co. v. Rock Wood Insulating Co., 212 F. Supp. 1, 2, 136 U.S.P.Q. 524, 525 (D. Colo. 1962); Moon v. Cabot Shop, Inc., 270 F.2d 539, 541, 123 U.S.P.Q. 60, 61 (9th Cir. 1959); Sperry Rand Corp. v. Texas Instruments, Inc., 206 F. Supp. 676, 677, 133 U.S.P.Q. 680, 681 (N.D. Tex. 1962).

[38] Mumm v. Decker & Sons, Inc., 301 U.S. 168, 171, 33 U.S.P.Q. 247, 249 (1937).

[39] 28 U.S.C. 2501 is the statute of limitations for suits in the Court of Claims. It requires that suit be filed "within six years after such claim first accrues."

[40] Potash Co. of Am. v. International Mineral & Chem. Corp., 213 F.2d 153, 154, 101 U.S.P.Q. 264, 265 (10th Cir. 1954).

[41] Walker Process Equip., Inc. v. Food Machinery & Chem. Co., 382 U.S. 172, 147 U.S.P.Q. 404 (1965).

[42] Seymour v. Osborne, 78 U.S. (11 Wall.) 516, 538 (1870).

[43] See for example, Corning Glass Works, Inc. v. Federal Glass Co., 239 F.2d 674, 675, lll U.S.P.Q. 451, 452 (6th Cir. 1956).

[44] National Athletic Supply Corp. v. Tone-O-Matic Prod., Inc., 421 F.2d 407, 410, 164 U.S.P.Q. 330, 332 (5th Cir. 1970).

[45] Parke-Davis & Co. v. H.K. Mulford Co., 189 Fed. 95, 103 (C.C.S.D.N.Y. 1911).

[46] See Graver Tank & Mfg. Co. v. Linde Air Prod. Co., 339 U.S. 605, 85 U.S.P.Q. 328 (1950). Compare, Aro Mfg. Co. v. Convertible Top Co., 365 U.S. 336, 339, 128 U.S.P.Q. 354, 356-357 (1961).

[47] Sanitary Refrigerator Co. v. Winters, 280 U.S. 30, 42, 3 U.S.P.Q. 40, 44 (1929); Machine Co. v. Murphy, 97 U.S. (7 Otto) 120, 125 (1877); Hunt v. Armour & Co., 185 F.2d 322, 327, 88 U.S.P.Q. 53, 58 (7th Cir. 1950).

[48] Winans v. Denmead, 56 U.S. (15 How.) 330 (1853).

[49] U.S. Pat. No. 5,175 (1947), See Appendix B for a copy of the specification.

[50] Graver Tank Co. v. Linde Air Prod. Co., N. 46, *supra*.

[51] Tigrett Indus., Inc. v. Standard Indus., Inc., 397 U.S. 586, 165 U.S.P.Q. 289 (1970).

[52] Exhibit Supply Co. v. Ace Patents Corp., 315 U.S. 126, 136, 52 U.S.P.Q. 275, 278 (1941).

[53] *In re* Richman, 409 F.2d 269, 161 U.S.P.Q. 359 (C.C.P.A. 1969).

[54] 35 U.S.C. 251.

[55] See for example, U.S. Pipe & Foundry Co. v. James B. Clow & Sons, Inc., 205 F. Supp. 140, 133 U.S.P.Q. 576 (N.D. Ala. 1962); General Steel Prods., Inc. v. Lorenz, 204 F. Supp. 548, 132 U.S.P.Q. 574 (D. Fla. 1962); Hanks v. Ross, 200 F. Supp. 605, 617, 132 U.S.P.Q. 129, 137 (D. Md. 1961).

[56] See Borg-Warner Corp. v. Paragon Gear Works, Inc., 355 F.2d 400, 406, 148 U.S.P.Q. 1, 6 (1st Cir. 1965).

[57] Westinghouse v. Boyden Power Brake Co., 170 U.S. 537 (1898).

[58] McClain v. Ortmayer, 141 U.S. 419, 425 (1891).

[59] See 1 Op. Att'ys Gen. 171 (1812).

[60] Atkins v. Gordon, 86 F.2d 595, 596, 31 U.S.P.Q. 347, 348 (7th Cir. 1936).

[61] Union Carbide Corp. v. Graver Tank & Mfg. Co., 282 F.2d 653, 660, 127 U.S.P.Q. 3, 8, (7th Cir. 1960), *cert. denied* 365 U.S. 812 (1961).

[62] Kaz Mfg., Inc. v. Chesebrough-Ponds, Inc., 317 F.2d 679, 137 U.S.P.Q. 588 (2d Cir. 1963).

[63] Dugan v. Lear Avia Co., 55 F. Supp. 223, 229, 61 U.S.P.Q. 404, 410 (S.D.N.Y. 1944), *aff'd* 156 F.2d 29, 69 U.S.P.Q. 357 (2d Cir. 1946).

[64] 28 U.S.C. 2201, 2202. Fed. R. Civ. P. 57.

[65] Fed. R. Civ. P. 13(a).

[66] Shubin v. U.S. District Court, 313 F.2d 250, 136 U.S.P.Q. 405 (9th Cir. 1963).

[67] See generally, Hayburn's Case, 2 U.S. (2 Dall.) 409 (1796).

[68] E.W. Bliss Co. v. Cold Metal Process Co., 102 F.2d 105, 41 U.S.P.Q. 342 (6th Cir. 1939).

[69] Federal Telephone & Radio Corp. v. Associated Telephone & Telegraph Co., 169 F.2d 1012, 78 U.S.P.Q. 1 (3d Cir.), *cert. denied* 335 U.S. 859 (1948); Dewey & Almy Chem. Co. v. American Anode, Inc., 137 F.2d 68, 58 U.S.P.Q. 456 (3d Cir.), *cert. denied* 320 U.S. 761 (1943); Japan Gas Lighter Assn. v. Ronson Corp., 257 F. Supp. 219, 150 U.S.P.Q. 589 (D.N.J. 1966).

[70] Triplett v. Lowell, 297 U.S. 638, 19 U.S.P.Q. 1 (1936).

[71] *Ibid.*

[72] Blonder-Tongue Laboratories, Inc. v. University of Illinois Foundation, 402 U.S. 313, 169 U.S.P.Q. 513 (1971). But see, Kaiser Indus. Corp. v. Jones & Laughlin Steel Corp., 181 U.S.P.Q. 193 (W.D.Pa. 1974).

[73] Lear v. Atkins, Inc., 395 U.S. 653, 670, 162 U.S.P.Q. 1, 8 (1969).

[74] Minnesota Mining & Mfg. Co. v. E.I. du Pont de Nemours & Co., 448 F.2d 54, 171 U.S.P.Q. 11 (7th Cir. 1971).

[75] Lear v. Atkins, Inc., 395 U.S. 653, 667, 167 U.S.P.Q. 1, 7 (1969).

[76] Troxel Mfg. Co. v. Schwinn Bicycle Co., 465 F.2d 1253, 175 U.S.P.Q. 65 (6th Cir. 1972), *rev'g* 334 F. Supp. 1269, 172 U.S.P.Q. 292 (W.D. Tenn. 1971).

[77] See United States v. Hartford-Empire Co., 73 F. Supp. 979, 981, 75 U.S.P.Q. 118, 119 (D. Del. 1947). See also Mowry v. Whitney, 81 U.S. (14 Wall.) 434 (1871).

[78] 28 U.S.C. 1338(b), codifying the rule of Hurn v. Oursler, 289 U.S. 238, 17 U.S.P.Q. 195 (1933).

[79] 28 U.S.C. 1506 provides that the Court of Claims can transfer to a proper district court any suit erroneously filed in the Court of Claims, the plaintiff thereby not losing the benefit of his original filing date for purposes of the statute of limitations.

[80] Brunette Mach. Works, Ltd. v. Kockum Indus., Inc., 406 U.S. 706, 174 U.S.P.Q. 1 (1972).

[81] See generally, Hickman v. Taylor, 329 U.S. 495, 500-501 (1947).

[82] See generally, Broadway & Ninety-Sixth St. Realty Co. v. Loew's Inc., 21 F.R.D. 347 (S.D.N.Y. 1956).

[83] McCall v. Overseas Tankship Corp., 16 F.R.D. 467 (S.D.N.Y. 1954).

[84] Hartley Pen Co. v. United States District Court, 287 F.2d 324, 328, 129 U.S.P.Q. 152, 157-158 (9th Cir. 1961).

[85] Crown Mach. & Tool Co. v. KVP-Sutherland Paper Co., 244 F. Supp. 543, 544, 146 U.S.P.Q. 1, 2 (N.D. Cal. 1965).

[86] N. 84 *supra.*

[87] *Ibid.*

[88] Ferment-Acid Corp. v. Miles Laboratories, Inc., 338 F.2d 586, 588, 143 U.S.P.Q. 275, 276 (7th Cir. 1964).

[89] United States v. United Shoe Machinery Corp., 89 F. Supp. 797, 85 U.S.P.Q. 5 (D. Mass. 1950).

[90] Fed. R. Civ. P. 65(a).

[91] Carter-Wallace, Inc. v. Davis-Edwards Pharmacal Corp., 443 F.2d 867, 169 U.S.P.Q. 625 (2d Cir. 1971); Simson Bros., Inc. v. Blancard & Co., 22 F.2d 498 (2d Cir. 1927).

[92] Fed. R. Civ. P. 38.

[93] See generally, Kohn v. Eimer, 265 Fed. 900, 902 (2d Cir. 1920).

[94] *Ibid.*

[95] Marvin Glass & Associates v. Sears, Roebuck & Co., 318 F. Supp. 1089, 167 U.S.P.Q. 33 (S.D. Tex. 1970).

[96] N. 93 *supra*.

[97] Fed. R. Civ. P. 73.

[98] Fed. R. Civ. P. 52(a). See for example, Jiffy Enterprises, Inc. v. Sears, Roebuck & Co., 306 F.2d 240, 243, 134 U.S.P.Q. 158, 160 (3d Cir. 1960), *cert. denied* 371 U.S. 922 (1962). See also, Great Atlantic & Pacific Tea Co. v. Supermarket Equip. Corp., 340 U.S. 147, 153, 87 U.S.P.Q. 303, 306 (1950).

[99] 15 U.S.C. 2102.

[100] Graham v. John Deere Co., 383 U.S. 1, 17, 148 U.S.P.Q. 459, 467 (1966).

–Part VI–

PATENTS IN GLOBAL CONTEXT: OBTAINING AND MAINTAINING RIGHTS ABROAD

> The grant of exclusive licenses and the fixation of prices therein, the grant of patents on trivial and nonpatentable improvements, that are absolutely void, yet capable of use, in belaboring industry, *and the grant of patents to aliens and their assigns, which are far more valuable than are patents granted to our citizens by foreign countries* – these are the evils at which the corrective measures should be aimed. They in no way impeach the wisdom of rewarding those who contribute to the production of heretofore unknown products of great value, such as curative, medicinal, and health-giving discoveries, and cost-lessening inventions which bring luxuries within reach of the many. [Emphasis added].
>
> Evans, J.
> *Chicago Steel Foundry Co. v. Burnside Foundry Co.*,
> 132 F.2d 812, 816
> 56 U.S.P.Q. 283, 288
> (7th Cir. 1943)

It is a common observation that the study of foreign languages not only brings with it an understanding of those languages, but that it also enhances the student's grasp of his native tongue. In the course of learning a different mode of expression, one is forced constantly to relate what is new and strange to what is already known and understood: to compare and contrast; to analyze and place in perspective. One learns by building upon his own prior experiences. In so doing, he reinforces those prior experiences. At every juncture, the student is compelled to re-examine and dissect what he had theretofore taken for granted. The result is a deeper appreciation of potentialities and limitations. An analogous phenomenon accompanies the study of foreign legal systems. Issues, such as the imposition of maintenance fees and compulsory licensing, which for one reason or another lie dormant in United States patent law, become apparent with the study of the foreign patent systems in which these features are more highly developed.

Chapter 16

ELEMENTS OF TRANSNATIONAL PATENT LAW

SYNOPSIS

> To promote the progress of useful art, is the interest and policy of every enlightened government.
>
> J. Marshall, Ch. J.
> *Grant* v. *Raymond,*
> 31 U.S. (6 Pet.) 218, 241 (1832)

As the term "transnational" suggests, the substance of this chapter is concerned with those aspects of patent law which reach across national boundaries. It is concerned with the general legal rights and obligations in regard to patents which the nationals of one state have in other countries. As will become apparent, these rights and obligations, at least when viewed macroscopically, are mutual and reciprocal, being equally applicable to nationals of all countries.

The primary purposes of this chapter are to identify the principal patent problems which accompany commercial intercourse among nations and to demonstrate how these may crystallize into obstacles to obtaining and maintaining patent rights abroad. Where valid, the principles have been couched in general terms without reference to any particular country. In other instances, United States practice has been employed as the frame of reference, both for the edification of those seeking patent rights in this country and in order to present one manner of resolving the problems presented. In large measure, these represent the norms, differing only in degree from the solutions adopted by other nations. In fact, one of the salient characteristics of transnational law, in contradistinction to purely internal or domestic laws, is its universality or at least relative uniformity among nations.

§ 1. A Patent is Effective Only Within the Territory of the Sovereign Which Grants It.

With respect to patents, trademarks, and copyrights, the doctrine of nationality or territoriality prevails.[1] Accordingly, foreign patents can neither grant nor limit patent rights in the United States.[2] Similarly, United States patents confer no rights outside the geographical boundaries of the United States,[3] its territories and possessions.[4] Moreover, the use of an invention covered by a United States patent on any vessel, aircraft or vehicle of any country entering the United States temporarily or accidentally does not constitute an infringement, if the invention is used exclusively for the needs of the vessel, aircraft or vehicle and if that country affords similar privileges to vessels, aircraft and vehicles of the United States.[5]

However, United States citizens may be liable in the United States for acts of infringement committed outside the territorial boundaries of the United States, where the extraterritorial acts adversely affect vested intellectual property rights within the United States. Thus, a United States court has enjoined a United States citizen from stamping in Mexico his watches with the United States registered trademark owned by the plaintiff and then selling them as such in Mexico.[6] Moreover, a United States court has enjoined a patentee, who was a United States citizen, from committing abroad acts which that court deemed to be a misuse of the patentee's United States patents.[7]

§ 2. No Country Can Be Expected to Enforce Rights Granted by Foreign Patents.

Under ordinary circumstances, United States courts will decline to adjudicate claims alleging the infringement of foreign patents, even though the alleged infringers are subject to the jurisdiction of a United States court.[8] The acts constituting the infringement of a foreign patent necessarily occurred beyond the territorial jurisdiction of any United States court. Suit should be brought within the territory of the sovereign which granted the patent. Nevertheless, federal courts are empowered to consider claims arising under foreign patents.[9]

Decisions of a tribunal of one country touching the validity of its patent do not control the validity of foreign patents even where all are directed to the same invention.[10]

A judgment rendered by a United States court, which purported to pass upon foreign patent rights, was held, by a court of the country which granted those patent rights, not to be binding on it.[11]

§ 3. If There Is More Than One Foreign Filing

An inventor must file separate, parallel patent applications in each country in which he seeks patent rights. Each such application must comply, both as to form and content, with the patent law of the country in which it is filed.

Every sovereign state still jealously reserves to itself the right to control its patent system: to determine just what shall be patentable and to define the rights and obligations of its patentees. Thus, an invention unpatentable in the United States may, nevertheless, be patentable in one or more other countries. Patents corresponding to the same invention in different countries are often referred to as corresponding, cognate, or parallel patents. Similarly, the application upon which such patents are based are known as corresponding, cognate, or parallel patent applications. The failure of an inventor to avail himself of patent protection abroad, by obtaining foreign counterparts of his domestic patent, may not only result in immeasurable financial loss to himself but may also adversely affect his country's competitive position in world markets. The patent specification, being available to all, will teach the world how to make and use his invention. However, without parallel foreign patents, foreign industry would be free to exploit the invention and would thereby have a cost advantage over both the inventor and his domestic licensees, since the inventor would be burdened with the cost of development and his licensees with the cost of royalties. Edison's unwillingness to expend about $150 in foreign patent filings for his motion picture camera cost him the British and European markets![12]

On the drawing board are plans for multi-national patent applications and patents.

West European countries have endorsed the European Patent Convention, which, when it comes into force in 1976, will enable an applicant to obtain multi-national patent protection by filing a single European patent application and designating the signatory countries in which protection is sought. The Convention provides for a uniform, supranational law to govern the disposition of all European Applications, which will be administered by a European Patent Office to be established in Munich. Application may be made in either the English, French, or German languages. Even nationals of nonsignatory countries (e.g., Americans) may avail themselves of the European patent application. At least into the foreseeable future, in all but the Common Market countries, subsisting national patent laws will continue in force, and patents granted under national patent laws will coexist with patents granted by the European Patent Office under the Convention. In all but the Common Market countries, a European Patent Application will become a separate national patent in each of the countries in which protection was sought. The Common Market countries propose to replace completely their respective national patents with a single Common Market patent that will be effective throughout the countries of the European Economic Community, thereby removing the trade barrier between them that exists when an invention is covered by separate national patents.

The Patent Cooperation Treaty, which is yet to be ratified by the United States Senate, will establish a procedure that will somewhat facilitate the acquisition of parallel patents in signatory countries. Under the Patent Cooperation Treaty, an application conforming to certain formal requirements is, in effect, an international application. The national patent office with which the application is initially filed, if it has the capability, will conduct a search of the relevant prior art, such search and a report thereof to be completed within eighteen months from filing. The chief benefit of the Patent Cooperation Treaty accruing to Americans is that they will be able to defer until the end of the eighteen-month period designating those additional countries in which to seek patent protection. Under the

Paris Convention, a right of priority exists for at most twelve months from the earliest filing. Also, when at the end of the eighteen month period the applicant must elect in which other countries to seek patent protection, he will have the benefit of an official search report. In those additional countries in which patent protection is sought, the international application will be treated as a national application and be accorded the benefit of its initial filing date. Each country, however, will still be free to conduct its own examination and to make a supplemental search of what it deems to be relevant prior art.

§ 4. The Paris Union

Each country belonging to the Paris Union has undertaken to accord to foreign nationals the same patent rights which it accords to its own nationals.

A multilateral treaty, known as the Paris Convention for the Protection of Industrial Property, has established the Paris Union for the protection of such property. Each member state has obligated itself to accord to applicants domiciled in any state belonging to the Union whatever protection its own patent laws accord to its own nationals. This principle, known as "national treatment" or "assimilation with nationals" is expressed in Article 2 of the Convention.[13] Nearly all sovereign states have adhered to the Convention. The United States first adhered in 1887[14] and has also adhered to the Lisbon Revision in 1962.[15] Thus, at least theoretically, foreign patent protection is as accessible to Americans as it is to nationals of the countries in which it is sought. However, such factors as language barriers and discrepancies between the requirements of United States and foreign laws frequently pose formidable, if not insurmountable, obstacles.

§ 5. Later-Filed Patent Applications

Upon fulfilling certain requirements, a later-filed patent application enjoys the benefit of the filing date of a parallel application filed earlier abroad, provided that such later application is filed within the priority period.

An application for patent filed in the United States may be entitled to the benefit of the filing date of a prior parallel application filed in a foreign country. Such an earlier filing date may benefit an applicant by enabling him to overcome an intervening reference or to establish his priority of invention. Note that the term "priority" is used both to refer to the issue which exists in an interference proceeding (Chapter 9) and to the preservation of a date as against acts which would otherwise bar the grant of a patent. It is used in the latter sense in this chapter.

The priority period is, in effect, a grace period. It gives an applicant time to decide in which other countries to seek patent rights. During the interval which coincides with the operative priority period, the applicant is protected in all countries of the Paris Union from the effect of intervening publications and patent applications.

By Article 4 of the Paris Convention, each member state of the Paris Union has undertaken to accord to any person who has previously filed an application for a patent on the same invention in another country belonging to the Union a right of priority, based upon such earlier filed, foreign application. Each member state, upon the applicant's fulfilling of certain formal requirements, has obligated itself to treat a parallel application filed in its patent office as though such application had been filed on the day the application on which the right of priority is based was filed in the foreign patent office. Such earlier, foreign filing date on which reliance is placed, is also known as the priority or Convention date.

The mere act of filing a patent application in one country of the Union gives rise to a potential right in all other countries of the Union. However, this right of priority with respect to a foreign filing date is contingent, because it is dependent upon actual subsequent filings. No rights vest on behalf of the inventor in any foreign country unless and until application is actually made there and there has been compliance in each country with the requisite formalities. Once priority has been secured in a country, it is not lost by subsequent invalidation of the foreign patent or application on which the right of priority is based.

In the United States, the formalities with which those seeking priority treatment must comply include a written request or claim for priority treatment and the submission of a certified copy of the foreign application, specification, and drawings upon which the claim for priority is based. It has been held[16] that the mere disclosure of the existence of a foreign filed application in the oath of a foreign inventor's parallel United States application does not amount to a claim of right of priority. An express claim for priority treatment must be submitted.[17] A translation of foreign documents may be required if they are not in the English language and the examiner may persist in his rejection, ignoring the claim for priority, until a translation is submitted.

For a United States patent to enjoy the benefit of an earlier, foreign filing date, the claim for priority treatment and all supporting papers must be received by the Patent Office before the patent issues. However, a reissue was granted where the only error urged was the failure to file a certified copy of the original foreign application before the patent issued.[18] Also, it has been held[19] that a divisional application, the parent of which contained a claim for priority treatment, is entitled to such treatment even though the divisional did not itself contain an explicit claim for such treatment. It should be noted that the benefit of an earlier, foreign filing date protects not only the application while it is pending before an examining authority, but also in court after it issues as a patent.

If priority is to be accorded, the content of the specification must conform very closely to the foreign counterpart on which the claim for priority is based. This may raise difficulties in that the disclosure requirements of the foreign country may differ markedly from those that prevail in the United States. Thus, a foreign applicant may find his United States patent application rejected for insufficiency of disclosure, while his parallel foreign application, identical in content, is perfectly acceptable under the law of his own country.

While each country which adheres to the Paris Convention is obliged to accord a right of priority to an application which satisfies the disclosure requirements of the domestic law of the foreign country where the foreign application was filed, a country in which priority treatment is sought may deny patent rights to any application which fails to satisfy its own disclosure requirements.[20]

For a later-filed application to enjoy the beneift of an earlier, foreign filing date, the later one must be filed within the applicable period of priority. For utility patent applications, the period of priority is twelve months from the earliest foreign filing;[21] for design patent applications, it is six months.[22] The right of priority is not dependent upon first filing in the country of which the inventor is a national or in the country in which the invention was made, although national law may impose such a requirement as a condition to receiving domestic patent protection.

Article 4, Section C(4) of the Paris Convention only requires that member states accord a right of priority to the first-filed application describing the invention, unless such first-filed application has been abandoned and has not yet served as a basis for claiming the right of priority. Such first-filed application will endow later-filed applications with the earliest possible filing date, where there has been, with respect to each such later-filed application, compliance with the formalities hereinbefore mentioned.

The term "effective filing date" is generic for whichever date is operative: the actual or Convention filing date. It is the cut-off date, that is, the date after which another disclosure with a later effective filing date cannot affect the applicant's assertion of novelty. One who files an application with the United States Patent Office is required to disclose in his oath or declaration whether or not any application for patent on the same invention has been filed by him in any foreign country, and if so, the countries and the date of filing of the earliest such application.[23]

Though an applicant is entitled to the benefit of his filing date of his earliest filed foreign application for the same invention, such earlier foreign filing date cannot be applied to negate the novelty of another's United States patent application.[24] That is to say, a disclosure contained in a United States patent is effective as a reference only as of the date it was actually filed in the United States Patent Office.[25] Furthermore, the Convention date may not be used to negate novelty, in the sense that the invention had been made in the United States by the author of that reference as of that foreign filing date,[26] even where both the earlier filed, foreign application, bearing the priority date, and the application filed in the United States claim the identical subject matter.[27] Only the actual filing date in the United States or the actual date on which the invention was made in the United States may be applied against a third party.

The following examples illustrate the foregoing principles.

Suppose *A* files a patent application in the United Kingdom on a utility invention on February 22, 1960 and then files a patent application for the same invention in the United States on December 16, 1960, claiming the benefit of his filing date in the United Kingdom. *A*'s United States patent issues on August 2, 1962.

A Files in U.K.	*B Files in U.S.*	*C Publishes (anywhere in world)*	*A Files in U.S.*	*A's Patent issues in U.S.*
2/22/60	3/17/60	4/23/60	12/16/60	8/2/62

(1) Because of *A*'s right of priority, *C*'s disclosure, published on April 23, 1960 is not effective as a reference against *A*.

(2) *B* files a patent application in the United States on March 17, 1960, which claims an invention disclosed, but not claimed in *A*'s specification. The examiner may not reject the claims of *B*'s application on the disclosure contained in *A*'s United States patent, even though *A*'s application has the benefit of *A*'s filing date in the United Kingdom of February 22, 1960. However, if the specification of *A*'s British patent had been published anytime before *B*'s effective filing date, then it would be a good reference against *B's* claims (35 U.S.C. 102(a)). In such case, *B* would probably be able to establish by means of a Rule 131 affidavit that he completed his invention in the United States before the publication of the British patent specification.

A's United States application relates back to his United Kingdom filing date for the purpose of overcoming *C*'s intervening publication made anywhere in the world (35 U.S.C. 119).

A's United States specification after it is published as a patent only relates back to its actual filing date in the United States as a reference against a third person.[28]

(3) Suppose *A*'s patent application filed in the United States on December 16, 1960 claims the same invention claimed in *B*'s United States patent application. Although *B* filed in the United States before *A*, *A* would have the earlier effective filing date, February 22, 1960. An interference would be set up with *A* as the senior party and *B* as the junior party. Assuming that *B* made his invention in the United States, he undoubtedly would be able to establish his priority of invention by recourse to proof of an earlier conception and reduction to practice. Assuming *A* did not make his invention in the United States, he would not be allowed to establish a date of invention earlier than his earliest effective filing date. A provision in the United States Patent Act precludes a party from establishing a date of invention by reference to knowledge, use or other activity in a foreign country apart from a foreign filing.[29] If both *A* and *B* had made their inventions abroad, then the one with the earlier effective filing date would conclusively be presumed to have been the first inventor, as neither would be permitted to prove their inventive activities abroad. Thus, *A* would prevail.

Since in nearly all foreign countries (except Canada and the Philippines) priority of invention is based solely upon filing dates, nationals of foreign countries in which Americans file will not be permitted by their own national patent laws to establish dates for their inventions earlier than their own effective filing dates. Finally, it should be noted that applications filed after the period of priority has elapsed may still possibly mature into valid patents. However, the applicant must rely upon the date on which he actually files the application in the country in which patent rights are sought. Such late applications may be defeated by a disclosure contained in the applicant's very own foreign patents or domestic or foreign publications as well as by intervening patents and publications of others.

Notwithstanding the right of priority, there may be situations in which disclosure contained in the very patent specification on which the claim for priority is sought to be based can be used as a reference to deny patent rights. Consider the following situation.[30] *A*, a United States citizen, files a patent application in the United States Patent Office on September 29, 1950 claiming a utility invention. Thereafter, *A* duly files a Convention application addressed to the same invention in the United Kingdom on August 21, 1951. *A*'s British specification is published on May 13, 1953. While *A* is waiting for the United States Patent Office to reach his application for examination, he decides to seek more extensive rights in the United States. Accordingly, *A* files a continuation-in-part application on May 9, 1955, adding a generic claim and examples of additional species in the specification. When the United States examiner acts on *A*'s continuation-in-part application, he rejects *A*'s generic claim as obvious in view of *A*'s previously published British patent specification. The examiner's position, apparently sanctioned by the Court of Customs and Patent Appeals, was predicated on the following reason. There was insufficient support for the generic claim in the original application; the rejected generic claim of *A's* continuation-in-part application and those of *A*'s original application are addressed to different inventions. Therefore, the continuation-in-part application is not entitled to the filing date of the earlier filed application.[31] Since *A*'s British patent specification was published more than a year before the filing of *A*'s continuation-in-part application, the disclosure contained in the published British patent specification is effective as a reference (under 35 U.S.C. 102(b)) against the new matter added to *A*'s original application and the generic claim supported thereby.

A Files in U.S.	*A Files in U.K.*	*A's Specification Published in U.K.*	*A Files C-I-P in U.S.*
9/29/50	8/21/51	5/13/53	5/9/55

While the preceding situation does not properly involve a question of the right of priority under the protection of the Paris Convention (because the applicant was an American and the examining authority making the rejection was the United States Patent Office),[32] a court arrived at a similar result where the facts involved a foreign national who first filed abroad and then, based on that foreign filing, filed a Convention application in the United States. In that case,[33] a foreign national filed first in Germany and then filed a corresponding application claiming the right of priority in the United States. The latter application was rejected by the United States examiner as being based upon an insufficient disclosure in that it (and its German parallel) lacked an adequate disclosure of how to use the claimed products.

X Files in Germany	*X Files in U.S.*	*X's Specification Published in Germany*	*X Files C-I-P in U.S.*
8/17/59	8/1/60	4/27/61	7/24/64

More than a year before the applicant filed a continuation-in-part application (which did adequately set forth how to use the claimed composition), the German applications were published. As it is settled United States law that there is no effective continuity between applications, the earlier of which lacked a sufficient disclosure, the United States examiner then rejected the claims of the continuation-in-part application as anticipated by the published German applications. Although, of course, the published German application lacked a teaching of how to use the compositions they disclosed, it was held that such disclosure was entirely adequate to anticipate claims to the recited compositions. Thus, the same disclosure may be inadequate to support the allowance of claims and yet be sufficient to sustain a rejection of the same claims!

Where a Convention application, as initially filed in the United States, contained patentable though unclaimed subject matter, it has been held[34] that the right of priority entitled the applicant to claim such patentable subject matter by amendment, even though the parallel foreign application, disclosing that subject matter, was published more than a year before the amendment was submitted.

At this point, it should be noted that some courts have indicated that a foreign patent should be construed more strictly than a domestic patent when applied as a reference against one seeking patent rights in the United States;[35] other courts have indicated that such a distinction is unfounded.[36]

Finally, mention should be made of the fact that the right of priority established by the Paris Convention raises an interesting question of United States constitutional law, namely: Did the right of priority automatically become a part of the internal law of the United States upon the President's proclamation of the treaty or was further action, in the form of enabling legislation, necessary to activate this right? There is more authority for the view that the Paris Convention is not a self-executing treaty[37] and that, therefore, enabling legislation was necessary.[38] The rationale is that the Constitution expressly confers upon the Congress (and not just the Senate) power to promote the progress of science and the useful arts. Thus, enabling legislation would seem to be necessary to activate any treaty relating to intellectual property.

§ 6. Inventions Made in the United States

Applications for patents for inventions made in the United States must be filed first in the United States unless an export license is obtained from the Commissioner of Patents.

Parallel applications may not be filed in foreign countries prior to six months after filing in the United States, unless a license authorizing such foreign filings has been obtained from the Commissioner of Patents. And where the application is a continuation-in-part, the six-month waiting period has been construed as beginning to run from the time that it (and not its parent) is filed in the United States.[39]

The Patent Act[40] expressly empowers the Commissioner of Patents to grant what amounts to an export license[41] authorizing filing abroad prior to the expiration of the six-month waiting period and to do so retroactively where the filing abroad was inadvertent and the application does not disclose an invention vital to national security. To be entitled to such a license, the petitioner must cogently demonstrate to the Patent Office that any unauthorized foreign filings were indeed inadvertent; mere unsupported allegations to that effect are insufficiennt.[42] While the great weight of authority holds that a license, duly granted, even validates an already issued United States patent,[43] one district court has held that a license granted after a patent had issued was ineffective, and consequently the patent void, on the theory that the Commissioner has no jurisdiction over issued patents.[44] That holding, however, was reversed on appeal. The Patent Office has indicated that where the requisite showing is made, the Commissioner will grant a license, even for an already issued patent, leaving to the courts the question of the license's effect.[45] While it has been held that the granting of a license lies within the Commissioner's discretion, a third party having no standing to oppose such grant,[46] the Commissioner has been required to issue such license where the court of appropriate jurisdiction was satisfied that the petitioner had made a satisfactory showing.[47] ,

The consequences of failing to obtain an effective license are loss of patent rights in the United States[48] and, in addition, where the application does in fact disclose an invention vital to national security, possible imposition of criminal sanctions.[49]

§ 7 Problems Arising From Importation and Exportation of Patented Goods

The maintenance of separate and distinct national patent systems may give rise to problems when goods covered by one or more subsisting United States patents are purchased abroad and imported into the United States. Because of the compartmentalization of patents along national lines, the same or different parties may own the different national, but parallel patents. Imported items may be unpatented in their country of origin and yet be patented in the United States. The United States patent may cover only the product or merely the process of making the product or both the product and process of making it. Exported items may themselves be unpatented and yet be manufactured in the United States with the intent that they be assembled abroad according to the claims of a subsisting United States patent directed to a combination of these components. Would assembly of these components abroad avoid infringement of the United States patent? All these and still other factors affect the legal status of imported and exported goods. The relevant United States law is summarized below. The reader should recall that geographical division within the United States of patent rights is permissible.

Mere importation is not infringement; there must be a sale or use within the United States.[50]

Even the sale or use within the United States of goods made abroad according to merely United States process claims is not an infringement of such claims.[51]

United States product claims are not infringed where goods, though they read on those claims and were imported and sold within the United States, were purchased abroad from the holder of the United States patent, who did not as a condition of that sale expressly forbid their importation.[52]

Where goods are purchased abroad from one who is licensed to make and sell abroad and his licensor is also the holder of the United States patent, no power should be imputed to the foreign licensee to affect rights in the United States. Thus, the failure of the foreign licensee to explicitly restrict importation into and sale in the United States should not impair the right of his licensor, the United States patentee, to treat a sale of such goods in the United States as an infringement.[53]

United States product claims are infringed where goods, which read on those claims, are imported and sold in the United States by one who has purchased them abroad from the United States patentee, who as a condition of the sale abroad prohibited their importation into the United States.[54]

United States product claims are infringed where goods, which read on those claims, are imported into and sold in the United States by one who purchased them abroad from one other than the United States patentee.[55]

Mere importation of goods, covered by United States product[56] and/or process[57] claims, may be deemed a violation of the Tariff Act of 1930. Accordingly, the Tariff Commission may, after conducting a hearing, recommend that the President direct the Secretary of the Treasury to instruct customs officers to exclude from entry into the United States such goods where the Commission has found that the importation constituted an unfair method of competition. An advantage of such a proceeding before the Tariff Commission over an infringement suit is that in the former invalidity of the patent may not be raised as a defense.[58]

A patentee may, in licensing others under his United States patent, reserve for himself the exclusive right to make and sell for export or use in foreign countries; not because the United States patent monopoly includes such other countries, but because his actual monopoly does include all making and selling within the United States.[59] The license, moreover, may be so framed that mere exportation by the licensee or his agents will terminate the license, and, thus, any further manufacture would be an infringement.

The Supreme Court recently held that a United States patent, the claims of which were drawn to a combination of components, was not infringed where something less than the entire combination, as claimed, was assembled in the United States. The fact that all the components were manufactured in the United States and were assembled in the United States except in merely minor respects was insufficient to constitute infringement.[60]

Notes

[1] See Aluminum Co. of Am. v. Sperry Prods., Inc., 285 F.2d 911, 925, 127 U.S.P.Q. 394, 406 (6th Cir. 1960) (patents); F. Palicio y Compania, S.A. v. Brush, 256 F. Supp. 481, 490-493, 150 U.S.P.Q. 607, 614-615 (S.D.N.Y. 1966) (trademarks); Sheldon v. Metro-Goldwyn Pictures Corp., 106 F.2d 45, 52, 42 U.S.P.Q. 540, 545 (2d Cir. 1939) (copyrights), *aff'd* 309 U.S. 390, 44 U.S.P.Q. 607 (1940).

[2] G.D. Searle & Co. v. Byron Chem. Co., 223 F. Supp. 172, 173, 139 U.S.P.Q. 337, 338-339 (E.D.N.Y. 1963).

[3] 35 U.S.C. 154.

[4] 35 U.S.C. 100(c).

[5] 35 U.S.C. 272, codifying the rule first enunciated in Brown v. Duchesne, 60 U.S. (19 How.) 183 (1856).

[6] Steele v. Bulova Watch Co., 344 U.S. 280, 92 U.S.P.Q. 266 (1952). See also Branch v. F.T.C. 141 F.2d 31 (7th Cir. 1944).

[7] Zenith Radio Corp. v. Hazeltine Research, Inc., 395 U.S. 100, 104, 161 U.S.P.Q. 577 (1969).

[8] See Ortman v. Stanray, 371 F.2d 154, 157, 152 U.S.P.Q. 163, 165 (7th Cir. 1957); Velsicol Chem. Corp. v. Hooker Chem. Corp., 230 F. Supp. 998, 1016, 142 U.S.P.Q. 131, 145 (N.D. Ill. 1964).

[9] See Distillers Co. v. Standard Oil Co., 150 U.S.P.Q. 42, 47 (N.D. Ohio, 1964).

[10] American Infra-Red Radiant Co. v. Lambert Indus., Inc., 360 F.2d 977, 987, 149 U.S.P.Q. 722, 734 (8th Cir. 1966); Ditto, Inc. v. Minnesota Mining & Mfg. Co., 336 F.2d 67, 70-71, 142 U.S.P.Q. 416, 419 (8th Cir. 1964).

[11] British Nylon Spinners, Ltd. v. Imperial Chem. Indus., Ltd., 1953 Ch. 19 (1952), [1952] 2 All E.R. 780. See also United States v. Imperial Chem. Indus., Ltd., 105 F. Supp. 215, 91 U.S.P.Q. 78 (S.D.N.Y. 1952).

[12] M. Josephson, *Edison* (McGraw-Hill Book Co. 1959), p. 391.

[13] See *In re* Certain Incomplete Trademark Applications, 137 U.S.P.Q. 69 (Comm'r Pats. 1963).

[14] 57 Stat. 1748.

[15] 13 U.S.T. 1. See generally Eli Lilly Co. v. Brenner, 248 F. Supp. 402, 432-434, 147 U.S.P.Q. 442, 467-468 (D.D.C. 1965), *rev'd on other grounds* 375 F.2d 599, 153 U.S.P.Q. 95 (D.C.C. 1967).

[16] Eli Lilly & Co. v. Brenner, 248 F. Supp. 402, 418, 147 U.S.P.Q. 442, 466 (D.D.C. 1965), *rev'd on other grounds* 375 F.2d 599, 153 U.S.P.Q. 95 (D.C.C. 1967).

[17] The required formalities are set forth in detail in the *Manual of Patent Examining Procedure* 201.13-201.14(c).

[18] State of Israel v. Brenner, 273 F. Supp. 714, 155 U.S.P.Q. 486 (D.D.C. 1967), *aff'd* 400 F.2d 789, 158 U.S.P.Q. 584 (D.C.C. 1968).

[19] Deutsche Gold-und-Silber Scheideanstalt v. Comm'r, 251 F. Supp. 624, 626, 148 U.S.P.Q. 412, 413 (D.D.C. 1966), *rev'd on other grounds* 397 F.2d 656, 157 U.S.P.Q. 549 (D.C.C. 1968).

[20] Eli Lilly & Co. v. Brenner, 248 F. Supp. 402, 418-419, 147 U.S.P.Q. 442, 457 (D.D.C. 1965), *rev'd on other grounds,* 375 F.2d 599, 153 U.S.P.Q. 95 (D.C.C. 1967). But see *In re* Smyth, 189 F.2d 982, 986-989, 90 U.S.P.Q. 106, 109-112 (C.C.P.A. 1951).

[21] 35 U.S.C. 119.

[22] 35 U.S.C. 172.

[23] Rule 65.

[24] *In re* Hilmer (I), 359 F.2d 859, 149 U.S.P.Q. 480 (C.C.P.A. 1966). Accord, Eli Lilly v. Brenner, 375 F.2d 599, 153 U.S.P.Q. 95, *rev'g* 248 F. Supp. 402, 147 U.S.P.Q. 442 (D.D.C. 1965); Waterman-Bic Pen Corp. v. W.A. Sheaffer Pen Co., 267 F. Supp. 849, 854, 153 U.S.P.Q. 499 (D. Del. 1967); Ex parte Raspe, 156 U.S.P.Q. 217 (P.O. Bd. App. 1967). Contra, Ex parte Zenila, 142 U.S.P.Q. 499 (P.O. Bd. App. 1964).

[25] 35 U.S.C. 102(e).

[26] *In re* Hilmer (II), 424 F.2d 1108, 165 U.S.P.Q. 255 (C.C.P.A. 1970).

[27] 35 U.S.C. 102(g).

[28] *In re* Hilmer (I), 359 F.2d 859, 149 U.S.P.Q. 480 (C.C.P.A. 1966).

[29] 35 U.S.C. 104.

[30] The facts are essentially those of *In re* Ruscetta, 255 F.2d 687, 118 U.S.P.Q. 101 (C.C.P.A. 1958).

[31] 35 U.S.C. 120.

[32] Cf. G.P. Putnam's Sons v. Lancer Books, Inc., 239 F. Supp. 782, 784, 144 U.S.P.Q. 530, 532 (S.D.N.Y. 1965) (Universal Copyright Convention construed as not protecting in the United States authors who are American citizens who first publish abroad).

[33] *In re* Hafner, 410 F.2d 1403, 161 U.S.P.Q. 783 (C.C.P.A. 1969). But see Merck & Co. v. Commercial Solvents Corp., 225 F. Supp. 318, 322-326, 140 U.S.P.Q. 172, 175-177 (D. Md. 1964).

[34] *In re* Renz, 326 F.2d 792, 799, 140 U.S.P.Q. 256, 261 (C.C.P.A. 1964).

[35] National Latex Prods. Co. v. Sun Rubber Co., 274 F.2d 224, 236, 123 U.S.P.Q. 279, 283 (6th Cir. 1960), citing Seymour v. Osborne, 78 U.S. 516, 557 (1870). See also Brown v. Brock, 240 F.2d 723, 726, 112 U.S.P.Q. 199, 202 (4th Cir. 1957).

[36] *For example,* see Greiser v. Brenner, 253 F. Supp. 906, 909, 149 U.S.P.Q. 115, 117 (D.D.C. 1966).

[37] Ortman v. Stanray, 371 F.2d 154, 157, 152 U.S.P.Q. 163, 165 (7th Cir. 1967), citing 19 Ops. Att'ys Gen. 273 (1889); Eli Lilly Co. v. Brenner, 248 F. Supp. 402, 432-434, 147 U.S.P.Q. 442, 467-468 (D.D.C. 1965), *rev'd on other grounds* 375 F.2d 599, 153 U.S.P.Q. 95 (D.C.C. 1967). See also Cameron Septic Tank Co. v. City of Knoxville, 227 U.S. 39 (1913) (Treaty of Brussels); Robertson v. General Elec. Co., 32 F.2d 495 (4th Cir. 1929) (Treaty of Berlin). Contra, Vanity Fair Mills, Inc. v. T. Eaton Co., 234 F.2d 633 (2d Cir.), *cert. denied* 352 U.S. 871 (1956).

[38] The enabling legislation is 35 U.S.C. 119.

[39] Beckman Instruments, Inc. v. Coleman Instruments, Inc., 338 F.2d 573, 143 U.S.P.Q. 278 (7th Cir. 1964).

[40] 35 U.S.C. 184.

[41] The license referred to in 35 U.S.C. 184 is analogous to the export license mentioned in the Export Control Act of 1949. Such license is required for the exportation of certain specified commodities and certain "technical data or other information." 63 Stat. 7, as amended, 50 U.S.C. App. 2021 *et seq.* (1964) as amended by 79 Stat. 209 (1969).

[42] *In re* Sternau, 149 U.S.P.Q. 70 (Comm'r Pats. 1966).

[43] Barr Rubber Prods. Co. v. Sun Rubber Co., 203 F. Supp. 12, 149 U.S.P.Q. 204 (S.D.N.Y. 1966); Ross v. McQuay, 257 F. Supp. 14, 150 U.S.P.Q. 510 (D. Minn. 1966); Union Carbide Corp. v. Microtron Corp., 254 F. Supp. 299, 149 U.S.P.Q. 827 (W.D.N.C. 1966); Davidson Rubber Co. v. Sheller Mfg. Corp., 248 F. Supp. 842, 147 U.S.P.Q. 511 (S.D.Ia. 1965); Engelhard Indus., Inc., v. Sel-Rex Corp., 255 F. Supp. 620, 145 U.S.P.Q. 319 (D.N.J. 1965); Blake v. Bassick Co., 245 F. Supp. 635, 146 U.S.P.Q. 157 (N.D. Ill. 1963).

[44] Minnesota Mining & Mfg. Co. v. Norton, 240 F. Supp. 150, 145 U.S.P.Q. 81 (N.D. Ohio 1965), *rev'd* 366 F.2d 238, 145 U.S.P.Q. 1 (6th Cir. 1966), *cert. denied* 385 U.S. 1005 (1967).

[45] *In re* Rinker, 145 U.S.P.Q. 156 (Comm'r Pats. 1966) (Corresponds to Engelhard Indus., Inc. v. Sel-Rex Corp., N. 43 *supra*.)

[46] Barr Rubber Prods. Co. v. Sun Rubber Co., 253 F. Supp. 12, 149 U.S.P.Q. 204 (S.D.N.Y. 1966).

[47] The Pillsbury Co. v. Brenner, 146 U.S.P.Q. 99 (D.D.C. 1965); McCormack v. Brenner, 146 U.S.P.Q. 340 (D.D.C. 1965).

[48] 35 U.S.C. 185.

[49] 35 U.S.C. 181, 186.

[50] 35 U.S.C. 154. Boesch v. Graff, 133 U.S. 697 (1890).

[51] *In re* Amtorg Trading Corp., 75 F.2d 826, 832, 24 U.S.P.Q. 315 (C.C.P.A. 1935). *Contra, In re* Northern Pigment Co., 71 F.2d 447, 21 U.S.P.Q. 573 (C.C.P.A. 1934).

[52] Holiday v. Matheson, 24 Fed. 185 (S.D.N.Y. 1885).

[53] See Parke-Davis & Co. v. Centrafarm, CCH Common Market Reporter Par. 8054 (Eur. Ct. J. 1968).

[54] Dickerson v. Matheson, 57 Fed. 524 (2d Cir. 1893).

[55] Dickerson v. Tinling, 84 Fed. 192 (S.D.N.Y. 1885).

[56] 19 U.S.C. 1337.

[57] 19 U.S.C. 1337a.

[58] *In re* von Clemm, 229 F.2d 441, 108 U.S.P.Q. 371 (C.C.P.A. 1955).

[59] Dorsey Revolving Harvester Rake Co. v. Bradley Mfg. Co., 7 F. Cas. 946, 947 (No. 4,015) (N.D.N.Y. 1874).

[60] Laitram Corp. v. Deepsouth Packing Co., 406 U.S. 518, 173 U.S.P.Q. 769 (1972). Cf. Hewitt-Robins, Inc. v. Link Belt Co., 371 F.2d 225, 151 U.S.P.Q. 670 (7th Cir. 1966); Cold Metal Process Co. v. United Engineering & Foundry Co., 235 F.2d 224, 110 U.S.P.Q. 332 (3d Cir. 1956); Radio Corp. of Am. v. Andrea, 79 F.2d 627, 27 U.S.P.Q. 364 (2d Cir. 1935).

Chapter 17

COMPARATIVE PATENT LAW
SURVEY OF PRINCIPAL FOREIGN PATENT SYSTEMS

SYNOPSIS

§ 1. Screening of Patent Applications Prior to Grant of Patent Rig

§ 2. Content of the Description of the Invention and the Extent to Which Such May Be Amended

§ 3. Claiming the Invention

§ 4. Priority of Invention

§ 5. Obligations of the Patentee to the State

§ 6. Nonstatutory Subject Matter

§ 7. Petty Patents

§ 8. A Comparison of the Five Major Patent Systems

The nations, which have made the greatest advance in the last hundred years, are the three countries which have rewarded the inventors through patents.

Evans, J.
Chicago Steel Foundry Co. v.
Burnside Steel Foundry Co.,
132 F.2d 812, 816, 56 U.S.P.Q. 283, 287 (7th Cir. 1943)

Although each country administers its own patent system, the differences in substance among national patent laws is not so great as the uninitiated might fear. The variations, while numerous, are an elaboration of but a limited number of concepts. Once the reader grasps these concepts and the concomitant problems, he should experience but relatively minor difficulty in mastering the particular details incidental to the implimentation of each national system. While it is not the function of this chapter to present all, or even most, of these details, some are included as illustrative of the underlying concepts. There will be an examination of seven features which determine the essential character of a patent system: (1) the extent to which applications are screened prior to grant of patent rights; (2) the content of the description of the invention and the extent to which such may be amended; (3) claiming the invention; (4) priority of invention; (5) obligations of the patentee to the state; (6) nonstatutory subject matter; and (7) petty patents. Many other topics either follow logically from or are included under one of the foregoing. For example, novelty and unobviousness are discussed under (1). The discussion of these topics is followed by capsule summaries (in outline form), which highlight these and other salient points country-by country, for each of the world's prototype patent systems (United States, United Kingdom, Union of Soviet Socialist Republics, West Germany, and France). Most other countries have modelled their own patent law on that of one of these five. On each table, note is made of the other countries whose law most nearly follows that prototype, together with the other countries' significant deviations therefrom. The United States has been included for the sake of comparison and contrast and because the laws of Canada and of the Republic of the Philippines have many features in common with those of the United States.

§ 1. Screening of Applications Prior to Grant of Patent Rights

The problem whose manner of resolution has the most profound influence upon the character of a patent system is the degree of official scrutiny of the contribution prior to the granting of exclusive rights thereon. The official scrutiny, known as the examination, is, in most countries, delegated to an administrative agency of the government, known as its patent office. Those countries whose examination purports to pass upon the novelty of the contributions submitted to their patent offices are said to have an examination system, while those countries which do not make a novelty determination before granting patent rights are said to have a registration system. Even in most countries wherein there is no novelty examination, applications are nevertheless screened for compliance with certain matters of form, and such a screening is sometimes referred to as a formal examination. The latter is usually most superficial. To warrant denial of patent rights by the patent office of a registration country, even one wherein applications are subjected to a formal examination, the irregularity must be apparent on the face of the application papers, as, for example, the claims are not in proper form, or the invention lies outside any of the statutory classes, or the invention is contrary to public morals. Of course, the patent office of countries operating under a true examination system also reject on these formal grounds and many defects (such as inoperativeness and insufficient disclosure) uncovered in the course of a novelty examination require more scrutiny than could be given by the inspection made under a registration system. It is interesting to note that Switzerland, befitting its essentially bilingual character, has a dual system in effect: there is a novelty examination for only two arts (textiles and horology) and a formal examination for all others.

Many examining countries, particularly the technologically more advanced, require something more than bare novelty, that is, something more than a mere colorable variation of the prior art. This something more, which in United States law is called unobviousness, is called inventive heights (*Erfindungshoehe*) in Germany. West German law further requires that the contribution represent an advance in the art, called technical progress (*Technischer Fortscrilt*).

Novelty itself is defined differently in different countries. Some require absolute or worldwide novelty (e.g., U.S.S.R., France, Italy, Netherlands); others require only relative novelty—that is, novelty with respect to the country in which protection is sought, and for some purposes the latter group distinguishes between the source of the knowledge (personal knowledge, printed publication, public use, etc.).

In some countries widely divergent standards of novelty are applied at different stages. For example, in West Germany, the ex parte novelty search is limited to prior publications (anywhere in the world) within the last one hundred years preceding the filing date. In the United Kingdom, the ex parte novelty search is limited to United

Kingdom patent specifications published not more than fifty years prior to the filing of the application. In the United Kingdom, moreover, it is not permissible for an examiner in the ex parte proceeding to combine references, though he may combine a prior publication with common general knowledge. However, in inter partes proceedings, both in the United Kingdom and West Germany, the aforementioned artificial limitations (no doubt imposed as administrative expediencies to conserve precious examining time) are not imposed, the antiquity or number of references being in themselves no bar to their application against a claim. In fact, one of Thomas Edison's German patents was held invalid because "something similar had been used in Egypt in 2000 B.C."

The examination may be broken down into two phases or stages: (1) a search and retrieval of relevant prior art; (2) application of that prior art to the subject matter of the invention, involving an administrative determination of patentability. In some countries these functions are separated, such that different personnel performs each.

The chief virtues of an examination system are that: (1) it endows patents with a modicum of certainty as to their validity and, hence, value. This in turn encourages the investment of risk capital in the exploitation of patented ideas; and (2) it allows an intelligent election to be made between continued secrecy, on one hand, and, on the other, disclosure in exchange for patent rights. This is turn encourages the submission of ideas for consideration for patent protection.

It is interesting to note that most Latin countries have favored a registration system, while the Northern countries have favored an examination system. The registration system is, in fact, a creation of French jurisprudence, being founded upon a well justified fear that administrative discretion will be abused. Consequently, in France, patentability determinations are left exclusively in the hands of the judiciary, the question only arising when a patentee attempts to enforce his patent rights against an infringer. Lest the French public be deluded into deferring to the imprimatur of a patent marking, French law requires that this be accompanied by the disclaimer: *sans guarantie du government.*

There has been, and continues to be, a curious parallel between the vigor of an industrial economy and the rigor of its patent examination, which in turn tends to be reflected in the overall strength of its system of protecting industrial property. Thus, the United

States, West Germany, Japan, and the Netherlands subject patent applications to particularly rigorous scrutiny. The United Kingdom is an examining country, but as already noted, the scope of the examination is significantly limited there. France has, since the Revolution, had a registration system, though she has recently moved toward an examination system, and thus in closer harmony with her Common Market partners in Germany and the Netherlands, by requiring a preliminary search and a search report. However, true to tradition, a French patent will still issue regardless of what prior art the search reveals. On the other hand, West Germany and the Netherlands, in an effort to cut the cost of administering their patent systems while speeding the diffusion of technological information and relieving backlog of pending applications, have modified the procedure by which patent rights are obtained, adopting a system of deferred examination. There is no longer an automatic examination of each and every application in these two countries. Rather, examination on the merits is deferred until a petition for examination is filed. This may be done by the inventor, his assigns, or, indeed, by any member of the public. In Germany a request for both search and examination (accompanied, by the requisite fees, of course) may be filed simultaneously, whereas in the Netherlands the request for search must be filed before the request for examination. If no petition is filed within seven years of the filing date, the rights which come into being upon the publication of the applicant's disclosure lapse. Publication will automatically occur within eighteen months of the earliest effective filing date. In the interim between publication and patent issuance, an infringer cannot be enjoined, though he may be liable for damages, measured by a reasonable compensation standard. Because publication is likely to occur before the patent grant is secured, the applicant who does not immediately request and obtain examination surely risks the loss of secrecy in the event a patent is denied. Thus, those now seeking protection in West Germany and the Netherlands will very likely be compelled to gamble for patent protection, with odds similar to those offered by pure registration countries.

Two significant consequences which flow naturally from a strict registration system should be noted at this point: (1) the early publication of patent specifications; (2) absence of precise definition of the scope of the patented invention when the patent emerges from the Patent Office. Since no time is expended in searching and evaluating the prior art, applications submitted for patents under a registration system are generally processed and published within a year of the filing date. As noted in the preceding chapter, such early disclosure may have a disastrous consequence for one who files first in a registration country and subsequently in an examination country, where it is determined by the examination country that the common disclosure is insufficient to support a patent under its law. The claims which appear at the end of a patent specification not only define the invention for the public, but also serve as a guidepost for the search of relevant prior art. Where there is to be no search and examination, there is no need for written claims. Accordingly, the résumé of the French *Brevets* granted prior to the legislation of 1968 were construed as mere summaries and not as a limitation of the scope of the patentee's rights. However, the recently enacted French law adopts the requirement that there be claims which define and limit the invention.

Many countries earnestly desire to issue patents which truly represent contributions to their technology, and yet either cannot afford to or are unwilling to allocate the complement of technically trained manpower necessary to perform and evaluate adequate prior art searches. Others may want to check the efforts of their own examining staffs. There are two devices to which such countries may turn as a substitute for, or supplement to, their own official searches: (1) imposition of a requirement that applicants furnish particulars of the prior art cited in the official searches made by the examining authorities of other countries against parallel applications. Such is currently required in Canada, the four Scandanavian countries, Eire, Israel, Netherlands, New Zealand, and Czechoslovakia; (2) provide for opposition, nullity, cancellation, and/or revocation proceedings. Of course, the former device merely tends to shift the burden of search to those countries with more extensive examining capabilities. The latter device has been adopted by such technologically sophisticated countries as the United Kingdom and West Germany. Such proceedings have the following special advantages: (1) through them prior public use may be exposed, something which ordinarily cannot be detected by the official ex parte search; and (2) interested members of the public are given the opportunity to participate. However, such proceedings impose a considerable expense and burden upon the inventor, particularly the independent inventor. He must bear the added, and possible ruinous, costs of defending inchoate rights against the assaults of entrenched interests, before they have matured to the point where they are endowed with much economic value. Recall that the mere publication of a disclosure causes whatever rights its author had at common law, by virtue of secrecy, to vanish forever. Ideas, once they enter the public domain, are irretrievably lost by their author. It should be noted that in the United States, the declaratory judgment, though it does not have quite the same effect as does a decree of nullity or revocation, places in the hands of the public many of the safeguards associated with nullity or revocation proceedings. The declaratory judgment remedy, moreover, protects the patentee against harassment by those whom he has not provoked.

§ 2. Content of the Description of the Invention and the Extent to Which Such May Be Amended

American practice is distinct from that prevalent in most other countries, both with respect to the content of the description and the latitude permitted in amending the same after it has first been filed in the Patent Office.

In United States practice, the description (i.e., specification and any drawing) must be virtually complete in itself. Even details of features known to the prior art must be described and graphically illustrated, if they are to be recited in the claims. Incorporation by reference is normally not an acceptable substitute for a full disclosure spelled out within the four corners of the specification. In contradistinction, the patent offices of some other countries, and that of West Germany in particular, will not accept a specification containing lengthy recitations of the prior art.

Another significant difference is the requirement, rigidly adhered to by the patent offices of many other countries, that the claims as allowed must demonstrably fulfill the very objects of the invention which are recited in the introductory paragraphs of the specification. This is particularly true of British practice. There, the title of the invention, which appears at the beginning of the specification, must also be consistent with the objects of the invention. Thus, the title, objects, and claims must all be in complete harmony.

No new matter may be added to a specification once the same is filed in the United States Patent Office. This is a rigid and, except for obvious typographical errors, a virtually inflexible rule. In United States practice the "remedy" for an insufficient disclosure is to submit another application, which if filed before the original is abandoned, will have the status of a continuation- in-part application. In contrast, most other countries are quite liberal in allowing amendment of the disclosure, as by including additional examples or embodiments. Such an amended disclosure may, particularly in the country that permitted it, enjoy the benefit of the original filing date.

In Canada, new matter may be added by way of a supplemental disclosure. This becomes attached to the end of the principal disclosure and becomes part of the patent. However, the supplemental disclosure is effective only as of the time that it, and not the principal disclosure, was filed. A separate set of claims accompanies the supplemental disclosure. Only one supplemental disclosure will be permitted per patent.

A remedial device available in a number of countries is the Patent of Addition. It will protect an improvement conceived even after the application for the main patent has issued, but will expire at the same time as the main patent. There need be no copendency between the applications for the main patent and for the Patent of Addition. Invalidity of the main patent will not automatically vitiate a Patent of Addition. Unlike the reissue patent, known to United States practice, there need be no defect in the original or main patent. The main patent remains in full force along with any Patents of Addition.

§ 3. Claiming the Invention

The manner in which inventions may or must be claimed varies, to some degree, from country to country. There are, however, but two basic systems—perhaps philosophies would be a more appropriate characterization—of claiming. There are, in turn, two aspects to each system: (1) How the invention must be defined before a patent will issue. (2) How closely, in infringement litigation, the patentee will be bound to such definition.

One system is that which prevails in the United States and British Commonwealth nations. In these countries, the outer limits or periphery of the invention must be rather clearly and completely circumscribed before a patent will be granted, and, in infringement litigation, the patentee will be closely held to these metes and bounds. This system will be referred to as "peripheral claiming."

The other system will be referred to as "inventive concept claiming." It includes those countries in which a patent may issue without any claims at all. Such systems are modelled after the French. However, French law has been recently amended to require the inclusion of claims. What all countries following an inventive-concept claiming philosophy have in common is that a patentee, in attempting to enforce his patent, will not be held to a rigid definition of his invention arrived at in a prior administrative proceeding. In countries which require no claims, the entire burden of determining the metes and bounds of the invention is placed upon an infringement court. In those countries which do not require any claims to obtain a patent, one need only describe what has been done–how to make and use the invention. Then, in the course of litigation, the court must attempt to extract, from the patent disclosure, the points of novelty and to formulate therefrom, and for the first time, the scope of the invention. In some countries adhering to such a system, what is thought to be the invention *may* be set forth, at the end of the description, as a résumé.

Other countries which follow an inventive-concept philosophy do require of their patents that they contain claims. These countries include West Germany and others having patent laws modelled thereon. Such claims, however, will not necessarily be construed literally. All embodiments of the *inventive concept* will be deemed an infringement. In West German law, the claims must segregate the old from the new features of the invention, the old features being relegated to the preamble or introductory phrase. The new features follow the transitional phrase "the improvement comprising . . . ." This claim format corresponds closely to what in United States practice is referred to as a Jepson-type claim. Its use in the United States is permissible, even preferrable, but not mandatory.

§ 4. Priority of Invention

That which, more than anything else, distinguishes United States practice from that which prevails in the other major countries of the world is the manner in which priority of invention is resolved.

In all countries, except the United States, Canada, and the Republic of the Philippines, priority of invention is determined solely on the basis of filing dates, that is, the party who was the first to file an application for a patent is conclusively presumed to have been the first to invent. In contrast thereto, the United States is said to have a first-to-invent system, in that factors other than who was the first to file an application for patent will be considered, in an elaborate proceeding known as an "interference."

The words "first-to-invent," however, should not be taken literally, particularly by those who have made inventions abroad. Section 104 of the Patent Act precludes the establishment of a date of invention by reference to knowledge or use thereof, or other activity with respect thereto, in a foreign country, except for a Convention filing in a foreign patent office. Thus, as a general rule, the earliest date of invention which a foreign inventor can establish is that on which he filed an application for patent.

While the patent laws of Canada and of the Republic of the Philippines make provision for inquiry behind filing dates, these proceedings are limited to pending applications. Such an inquiry in Canada is called a "conflict proceeding."

§ 5. Obligations of the Patentee to the State

All countries require of those who would avail themselves of their patent system that they contribute to at least the cost of administering it. The United States imposes a relatively modest application fee, which must be paid upon the filing of the application. If the Patent Office is willing to pass the application to issue, an additional fee, known as the final fee, must be paid. The final fee is based upon the length of the disclosure, and is imposed to defray the cost of printing the same. Patent Office revenues, of which application and final fees make up only a part, fall considerably short of the Patent Office budget. Once a United States patent issues, the owner thereof owes no further financial obligation to the government. Moreover, he is under no obligation to work his invention, and except under very special circumstances, he is under no obligation to allow others to do so.

In contrast to this laissez-faire approach, most other countries impose special fees, not only during the pendency of applications before their patent offices, but throughout the entire life of their patents. These fees, are known as maintenance fees (or taxes), renewal fees, or annuities. They are periodic, falling due at stated intervals, usually beginning with the filing of the patent application. In some countries, the initial fee is relatively low, with the amount gradually escalating as the life of the patent progresses. Failure to make payment on schedule may cause prospective rights in an application or patent to lapse.

While the avowed object of these fees is to reimburse the state for expenses incurred in maintaining its patent system, they also have the effect of harassing, and even deterring, those who would patent useful inventions. Although the spreading out of fees over the life of the patent may enable the state to charge a relatively low initial fee, such approach necessitates the frequent making of decisions as to whether to maintain patents or allow them to lapse. To the large corporation this is a nuisance; it may suffice to discourage the small, independent inventor from even seeking patent protection at all.

Direct financial obligations are not the only burdens which may be imposed upon patentees. In addition, there may be a requirement that the patented invention be commercially exploited or worked within a specified period. Moreover, to satisfy the working requirement of many countries, the "working" or manufacture of the patented invention must be performed within that country. Failure to comply with the working requirement may, in some countries, result in loss of prospective patent rights. In others, a patentee who fails to exploit his invention may be required to license others who wish to do so. This is generally true in regard to inventions in the medical and food arts. Such licenses are referred to as compulsory licenses, and statutes providing therefor may specify the rate of royalty. Some countries link their maintenance fees to a working requirement, by imposing either no maintenance fees or a lower rate upon those patentees who exploit their inventions or who allow others to do so. In some countries an applicant for patent may voluntarily elect to waive the right of exclusivity, endorsing his patent licenses of right. In exchange therefor the state may either wholly waive its maintenance fees or impose a schedule of reduced fees.

Countries justify their working requirements, compulsory licensing, and even their maintenance fees, on the ground that these are ploys to protect their own, domestic industries. Most countries, particularly the less developed, fear that the net effect of their patent systems, without such provisions, would be to stifle the development of indigenous industry. Many patents will be controlled by citizens of more technologically advanced nations; manufacture of patented inventions is likely to occur in those countries; citizens of the underdeveloped countries would be barred from manufacturing these inventions by patents which their own government granted.

§ 6. Nonstatutory Subject Matter

In the United States, with the exception of inventions relating to atomic weapons, no broad field of industrial technology is excluded, by statute, from the pale of patent protection.

In contrast thereto, some countries, as if to make it appear that the public health and welfare would otherwise suffer, deny patent protection to all inventions relating to pharmaceuticals and/or foodstuffs, be they addressed to the product or to the process of making the same. Such countries regard a patent monopoly upon these inventions as a privilege that is inconsistent with the objectives of a socialist society. Other countries do not recognize claims directed to any compositions of matter per se, be they for pharmaceuticals, foodstuffs, or other substances. The motivation for such exclusion may be not only to shelter from exclusive exploitation an area sensitive to the public welfare but to limit the scope of patents to specific methods of making the composition. The approach in West Germany is to protect compositions of matter by claiming a process of making the same. Such claims, though couched in terms of process limitations, may be construed as covering the product made thereby. Accordingly, German law distinguishes between: (1) original processes (*chemisch eigenartige Verfahren*), wherein the invention resides in the process itself; and (2) analogy processes (*Analogieverhahren*), wherein the invention resides in the product made by the process.

In all countries except Belgium, South Africa, and the United States, patent protection for the surgical treatment of man is probably unavailable.

§ 7. Petty Patents

Petty patents, which are also known as utility models, have no real equivalent in United States practice. "Utility model" is a literal translation of the German *Gebrauchsmuster.*

A petty patent, utility model, or *Gebrauchsmuster* is not the equivalent of a design patent (which in German is called a *Geschmacksmuster*). In fact, the former are far more closely akin to utility patents than to design patents. In terms of the protection they give their owners, they are petty only in the sense that their life is of much shorter duration. A German *Gebrauchsmuster* has a life of three years, which is renewable for a second three-year term.

Gebrauchsmuster are much more readily obtainable (usually within a matter of weeks after filing) than are German patents. They were originally intended to provide quick and inexpensive, albeit limited, protection for the small inventor.

Gebrauchsmuster applications, like patent applications, enjoy a twelve-month right of priority. This is in contrast to design patent applications, which are entitled to a right of priority of only six months.

Although West German law requires that its *Gebrauchsmusters*, like its patents, possess novelty and involve a technical advance and inventive height, there is no examination as to these requirements—only formal matters being considered by the patent office. In litigation, the extent of technical advance and of inventive height expected of a *Gebrauchsmuster* may not be so great as that expected of a patent.

Specification of *Gebrauchsmuster* are not printed, but they are available for public inspection. Photocopies thereof may be obtained.

Confusion of *Gebrauchsmuster* with design patents may, at least in part, be attributable to the requirement that the subject matter of *Gebrauchsmuster* possesss *Raumform* (a definite three-dimensional shape). This is not a requirement for German patents, only for *Gebrauchsmuster*. However, *Gebrauchsmuster* do not protect aesthetics. Shape, to be protectible by a *Gebrauchsmuster* must be functional. The *Raumform* requirement has been construed to exclude not only processes and compositions of matter, but *immovable* objects, such as buildings and bridges, as well. Electrical circuits have also been held to lack *Raumform*.

It is important to note that a German patent and a *Gebrauchsmuster* can co-exist in the very same subject matter. Both one and the same invention can be covered by patent and *Gebrauchsmuster*. Application for one does not of itself constitute an election which would bar the other.

In lieu of filing separate patent and *Gebrauchsmuster* applications, one may file a patent application and an application for what is known as a *Hilfs* (auxiliary) *Gebrauchsmuster*. By means of the *Hilfs Gebrauchsmuster*, the patent application may be converted into a *Gebrauchsmuster*, at the option of the applicant, at any time during pendency, provided not more than six years have elapsed from filing.

§ 8. A Comparison of the Five Major Patent Systems

UNITED STATES OF AMERICA

1. TERM: 17 years from the date of grant. No renewals.
2. NOVELTY: relative – only a patent or printed publication from abroad can negate novelty.
3. PRIORITY OF INVENTION: goes to the first to invent, but evidence as to mere acts or knowledge abroad is inadmissible.
4. SCOPE OF EXAMINATION: unlimited.
5. OPPOSITION: none.
6. AMENDMENT OF DISCLOSURE: no new matter may be introduced.
7. METHOD OF CLAIMING: peripheral.
8. NON-STATUTORY SUBJECT MATTER: claims directed to compositions of matter (including pharmaceuticals & foodstuffs) permitted.
9. PETTY PATENTS: no.
10. MAINTENANCE FEES, WORKING REQUIREMENT, LICENSES OF RIGHT, COMPULSORY LICENSING: none.

PECULIARITIES: Importation of an article made according to the claims of a U.S. process claim not deemed an *infringement* thereof.

CANADA: 3. Interferences only between copending applications which are known as "Conflict Proceedings."
6. Supplementary Disclosure permitted.
8. Cannot patent pharmaceuticals as compositions of matter.
10. Compulsory licensing of pharmaceuticals and foodstuffs.

REPUBLIC OF THE PHILLIPINES: 9. Grants petty patents.

UNITED KINGDOM

1. TERM: 16 years from the filing of complete specification.

2. NOVELTY: relative – only knowledge available within the realm can negate novelty. Trial by inventor for up to one year does not negate novelty. Up to 6 months grace for disclosure at Certified Exhibition or disclosure to Learned Society.
3. PRIORITY OF INVENTION: goes to the first to file.
4. SCOPE OF EXAMINATION: limited to prior U.K. patent specifications published within 50 years of filing the application.
5. OPPOSITION: yes, within 3 months of publication or within 1 year of Sealing (latter is known as a Revocation Proceeding).
6. AMENDMENT OF DISCLOSURE: Specification may be filed in two stages; (1) Provisional Specification to be followed by (2) Complete Specifications, within 12 (may be extended to 15) months of the Provisional. Extensive amendment of Complete Specification not permitted.
7. METHOD OF CLAIMING: peripheral.
8. NON-STATUTORY SUBJECT MATTER: patent protection extends to "any manner of new manufacture," which includes pharmaceuticals & foodstuffs.
9. PETTY PATENTS: no.
10. MAINTENANCE FEES: yes. Reduced by one half if patentee voluntarily endorses his patent "Licenses of Right."

    COMPULSORY LICENSES: available for pharmaceuticals & foodstuffs.

PECULIARITIES: Impermissible to combine references in Patent Office Proceedings.

Application may be made in the name of a person or corporate body within U.K. to whom invention has been communicated from abroad.

Acceptance (followed by publication) must occur within a specified period after filing (in U.K. 3 yr. max.).

Must be conformity of title of invention, objects set out in specification, and preamble of claims.

AUSTRALIA: 10. No licenses of right.

ERIE:

NEW ZEALAND:

SOUTH AFRICA: 8. Surgical techniques are patentable.

Patent protection in most Crown Colonies and in most former Crown Colonies is obtained by registering the U.K. patent there.

FRENCH REPUBLIC

1. TERM: 20 years from the date of filing application.
2. NOVELTY: absolute – novelty negated by any kind of disclosure anywhere in the world, except that disclosure by inventor at a Certified Exhibition no more than 6 months preceding filing is excused.
3. PRIORITY OF INVENTION: goes to the first to file.
4. SCOPE OF EXAMINATION: registration, though prior art will be searched and report thereof made of record.
5. OPPOSITION: none, though third parties may cite prior art.
6. AMENDMENT OF DISCLOSURE: patents of addition.
7. METHOD OF CLAIMING: inventive concept.
8. NON-STATUTORY SUBJECT MATTER: claims directed to composition of matter (including pharmaceuticals & foodstuffs) is permitted.
9. PETTY PATENTS: known as certificates of utility (duration 6 years).
10. MAINTENANCE FEE: none.

COMPULSORY LICENSING: yes, if invention not worked within specified period.

PECULIARITIES: Filing in regional "patent offices." Infringement may constitute a crime. No contributory infringement.

BELGIUM: 2. Novelty is relative.
8. Surgical techniques are patentable.
9. No petty patents.

ITALY: 1. 15 years from filing.
8. No patents on pharmaceutical compositions.
9. No petty patents.
10. Provides for licenses of right.

PORTUGAL: 1. 15 years from grant.
8. No patents on any compositions of matter.

SPAIN: 1. 20 years from grant.
8. Oppositions to grant of petty patents.
10. No patents on any compositions of matter.

FEDERAL REPUBLIC OF GERMANY
WEST GERMANY

1. TERM: 18 years from the date of filing the application.
2. NOVELTY: relative – novelty destroyed by printed publication or prior unprinted specification laid open to public inspection anywhere or by domestic prior public use, with grace period of up to 6 months for disclosure at Certified Exhibition.
3. PRIORITY OF INVENTION: goes to the first to file.
4. SCOPE OF EXAMINATION: deferred examination – examination must be requested. Prior printed publication must not be more than 100 years old.
5. OPPOSITION: yes, within 3 months of publication. Nullity and revocation proceedings may be instituted against patent.
6. AMENDMENT OF DISCLOSURE: patents of addition are available.
7. METHOD OF CLAIMING: inventive concept. Novel elements must be segregated from old features. Only a single independent claim is permitted.
8. NON-STATUTORY SUBJECT MATTER: true composition of matter claims are not permitted.
9. PETTY PATENTS: yes, known as *Gebrauchsmuster* (duration 3 yrs., renewable for additional 3 yrs.).
10. MAINTENANCE FEES: yes. Reduced by one half if patentee agrees to licenses of right.

PECULIARITIES: Only industrial use constitutes infringement. Invention must constitute "technical progress." Doctrine of Contributory Infringement applies.

AUSTRIA:
1. 18 years from publication.
2. Prior unprinted specification does not negate novelty.
6. Patents of dependence are available.
9. No petty patents. No contributory infringement.

NETHERLANDS:
1. 20 years from filing application.
2. Absolute novelty required.
9. No petty patents.

JAPAN:
1. 20 years form filing application.
2. Up to 6 months grace for disclosure to learned society. Up to one year grace for trial by inventor.

SCANDINAVIA: (Denmark Finland Norway Sweden)
1. 17 years from filing application.
2. Absolute novelty required.
4. Examination not deferred. Every application is made accessible to public 18 months from its earliest filing date.
6. Application for patent of addition must be filed before application for main patent is made accessible to public.
9. No petty patents.
10. Compulsory licenses available if there has been no working after 3 years from grant.

SWITZERLAND:
1. 18 years from day following filing date.
2. Prior unprinted specification does not negate novelty.
4. Examination on merits only in horology and textiles. Formal examination in all other arts.
5. No opposition proceedings.

UNION OF SOVIET SOCIALIST REPUBLICS

1. TERM: 15 years from the filing of the application.
2. NOVELTY: absolute.
3. PRIORITY OF INVENTION: goes to the first to file.

4. SCOPE OF EXAMINATION: on the merits.
5. OPPOSITION: none.
6. AMENDMENTS OF DISCLOSURE: no patents of addition. Patents of dependence.
7. METHOD OF CLAIMING: peripheral.
8. NON-STATUTORY SUBJECT MATTER: composition of matter claims are not permitted.
9. PETTY PATENTS: none.
10. MAINTENANCE FEES: yes. No penalty for non-working.

PECULIARITIES: Certificates of inventorship available in lieu of a patent. Soviet government thereby gains exclusive right to exploit invention. Inventor gains recognition of inventorship, renumeration based upon use, and certain other benefits.

ALBANIA:

BULGARIA: 6. Patents of addition available.

CZEĆHOSLAVAKIA: 6. Patents of addition available.
Certificates of inventorship available only for new methods of curing or preventing disease.

(EAST) GERMANY: 1. 18 years from the filing of the application.
2. Relative novelty.
6. Patents of addition available.
No certificate of inventorship.

HUNGARY: 1. 20 years from the filing of the application.
No certificates of inventorship.

POLAND: 2. Relative novelty.
6. Patent of addition available.
9. Petty patents available.
No certificate of inventorship.

RUMANIA: No certificate of inventorship.

YUGOSLAVIA: No certificate of inventorship.

Appendix A

CURRENT FORMAT OF UNITED STATES PATENTS

1. Grant and Specification of an Original U.S. Utility Patent (No. 3,826,100)

2. Specification of an Original U.S. Design Patent (Des. 218,335)

3. Specification of a Reissue of a U.S. Utility Patent (Re. 25,558)

Appendix B

Specification of U.S. Patent No. 5,175. (See Chapter 15, footnote 49)

Appendix A

1. Grant and Specification of an Original U.S. Utility Patent (No. 3,826,100)

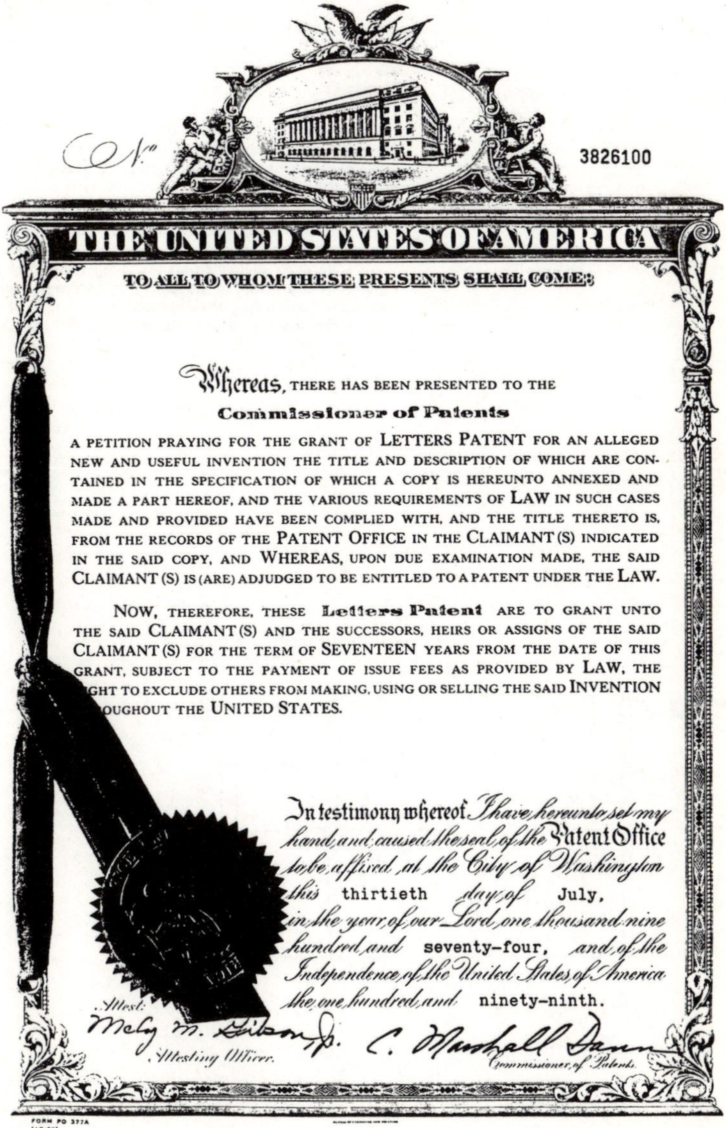
No. 3826100

THE UNITED STATES OF AMERICA

TO ALL TO WHOM THESE PRESENTS SHALL COME:

Whereas, THERE HAS BEEN PRESENTED TO THE

Commissioner of Patents

A PETITION PRAYING FOR THE GRANT OF LETTERS PATENT FOR AN ALLEGED NEW AND USEFUL INVENTION THE TITLE AND DESCRIPTION OF WHICH ARE CONTAINED IN THE SPECIFICATION OF WHICH A COPY IS HEREUNTO ANNEXED AND MADE A PART HEREOF, AND THE VARIOUS REQUIREMENTS OF LAW IN SUCH CASES MADE AND PROVIDED HAVE BEEN COMPLIED WITH, AND THE TITLE THERETO IS, FROM THE RECORDS OF THE PATENT OFFICE IN THE CLAIMANT (S) INDICATED IN THE SAID COPY, AND WHEREAS, UPON DUE EXAMINATION MADE, THE SAID CLAIMANT (S) IS (ARE) ADJUDGED TO BE ENTITLED TO A PATENT UNDER THE LAW.

NOW, THEREFORE, THESE **Letters Patent** ARE TO GRANT UNTO THE SAID CLAIMANT (S) AND THE SUCCESSORS, HEIRS OR ASSIGNS OF THE SAID CLAIMANT (S) FOR THE TERM OF SEVENTEEN YEARS FROM THE DATE OF THIS GRANT, SUBJECT TO THE PAYMENT OF ISSUE FEES AS PROVIDED BY LAW, THE [illegible]GHT TO EXCLUDE OTHERS FROM MAKING, USING OR SELLING THE SAID INVENTION [illegible]OUGHOUT THE UNITED STATES.

In testimony whereof I have hereunto set my hand and caused the seal of the Patent Office to be affixed at the City of Washington this thirtieth day of July, in the year of our Lord one thousand nine hundred and seventy-four, and of the Independence of the United States of America the one hundred and ninety-ninth.

Attest:

Mely M. Gibson Jr.
Attesting Officer.

C. Marshall Dann
Commissioner of Patents.

FORM PO 377A
(10-65)

United States Patent [19]

Vahl

[11] **3,826,100**

[45] **July 30, 1974**

[54] **METHOD AND APPARATUS FOR CONTROLLING FREEZING APPARATUS**

[76] Inventor: **Laszlo Vahl,** Charlotte de Bourbonstraat 22, Delft, Netherlands

[22] Filed: **May 19, 1972**

[21] Appl. No.: **255,071**

[30] **Foreign Application Priority Data**

May 21, 1971 Netherlands..................7106997

[52] **U.S. Cl.**......................... **62/63,** 62/140, 62/375

[51] **Int. Cl.**.. **F25d 13/06**

[58] **Field of Search**....... 62/63, 140, 374, 375, 376, 62/380

[56] **References Cited**

UNITED STATES PATENTS

3,121,999	2/1964	Kasbohm et al.	62/50 X
3,720,072	3/1973	Berta et al.	62/54
3,733,847	5/1973	Powell	62/54 X

Primary Examiner—Meyer Perlin
Assistant Examiner—Ronald C. Capossela
Attorney, Agent, or Firm—Sherman & Shalloway

[57] **ABSTRACT**

Method and apparatus for optimum recovery of an evaporating coolant in a direct contact type of freezing apparatus, such method including measuring the differential pressure in the supply or discharge duct to or from the freezing chamber and the pressure of the air in the space in which the apparatus is located resulting from the diffusion of coolant and air within the apparatus and using the pressure difference to control the discharge of air from the apparatus.

12 Claims, 2 Drawing Figures

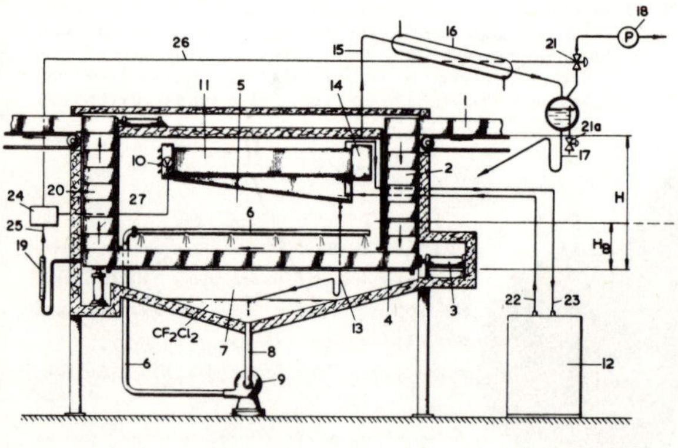

PATENTED JUL 30 1974 3,826,100

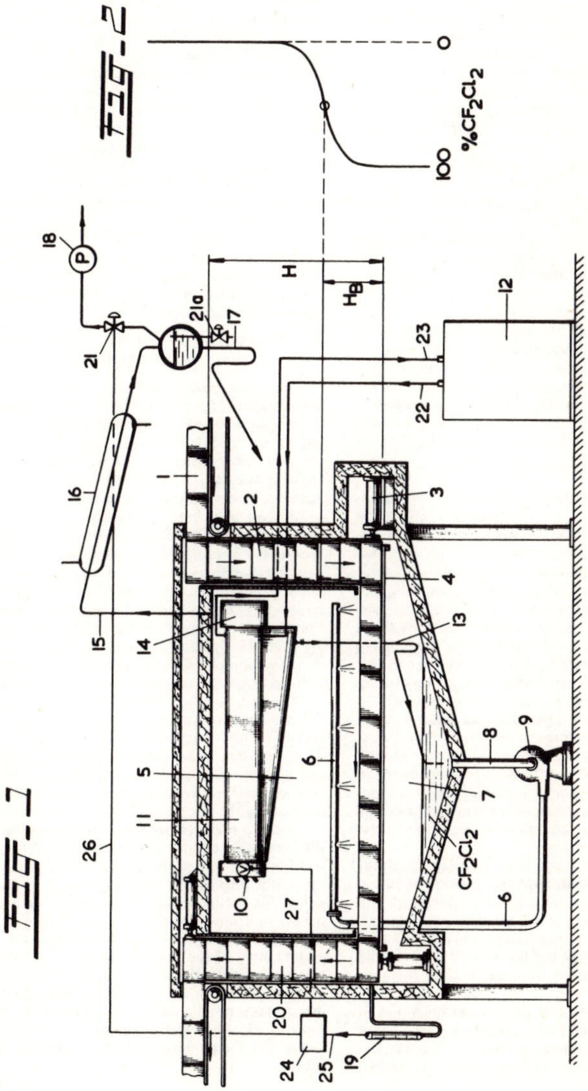

3,826,100

1

METHOD AND APPARATUS FOR CONTROLLING FREEZING APPARATUS

BACKGROUND OF THE INVENTION

1. Field of the Invention

The invention relates to a method and apparatus for controlling freezing apparatus.

2. Description of the Prior Art

Apparatus are known for freezing food and other water containing substances, wherein the removal of heat from the object to be frozen takes place by means of a medium, for example, cooled air, or by direct contact with cooled surfaces. Classified under the first category are freezing apparatus in which the heat removing medium is not gas but an evaporating liquid.

Recent attention in this area has centered on the application of liquid nitrogen as an evaporating heat removing medium as well as to the application of difluorodichloromethanol CF_2Cl_2, and similar coolants that evaporate in direct contact with the food in the freezing apparatus. While applying evaporating liquid nitrogen as a coolant, the gas developed during evaporation is blown into the atmosphere without being recovered (so that liquid nitrogen has to be supplied for each cycle). When applying CF_2Cl_2 as a coolant in the freezing apparatus, high recovery is required because of the high cost of this medium, which is much more expensive than liquid nitrogen. Recovery of the CF_2Cl_2 coolant takes place by condensation on surfaces cooled by cooling machines, but this method using presently available apparatus results in losses of 4 to 5 percent calculated based on the amount of frozen food.

SUMMARY OF THE PRESENT INVENTION

The present invention involves the use of freezing apparatus including a freezing chamber in which the evaporation of the coolant takes place is in open communication with the atmosphere via supply and discharge dicts. The improvement of the method and apparatus of the present invention results from using the difference between the pressure in a supply or discharge duct chamber and the ambient air pressure as a signal for the control of the removal from the freezing apparatus of a gas mixture consisting of air and coolant. A considerable part of the coolant fraction can then be recovered from this gas mixture by condensation.

The present invention is based on the understanding that a difference of pressure due to diffusion must exist between certain places in the freezing chamber and the atmosphere and that this difference of pressure at an appropriately chosen geometry of the channels communicating with the atmosphere is a function of the air contents of supply and discharge ducts, respectively, for the products to be frozen.

The invention can be used in all freezing apparatus which operate at nearly atmospheric pressure by bringing evaporating coolant into direct contact with the material to be frozen and which are in open communication with the ambient atmosphere, whereby the supply into the freezing chamber takes place downwardly and the discharge of supply from the freezing chamber takes place upwardly.

It is therefore an object of the present invention to significantly reduce losses of evaporating coolant in a freezing apparatus operating with direct contact between evaporating coolant and the products to be frozen, e.g. food or food packages, using a more or less continuous supply and discharge of the product by controlling the freezing apparatus in a convenient and economical method.

2

It is a further object of the present invention to significantly improve the recovery of CF_2Cl_2 or other relatively expensive evaporating coolants in freezing apparatus operating with direct contact between the evaporating coolant and products to be frozen using simple and inexpensive sensing and control means.

It is still a further object of the present invention to recover a significantly higher percentage of CF_2Cl_2 or other relatively expensive evaporating coolant than possible using currently available techniques without requiring any major changes in the presently available freezing apparatus by using a differential pressure gauge to control the amount of air in the apparatus.

The foregoing and other objects of the present invention will be described more fully in the following more detailed description of the present invention.

BRIEF DESCRIPTION OF THE DRAWINGS

FIG. **1** is a schematic view of the freezing apparatus of the present invention.

FIG. **2** is a concentration curve of coolant-air mixture within the freezing apparatus.

DESCRIPTION OF THE PREFERRED EMBODIMENTS

The environment within which the improved method and apparatus for controlling freezing apparatus were developed involves a method and apparatus for freezing foods and other water containing substances wherein the freezing method is of the type in which freezing takes place by directly contacting the food or other water containing substance with a coolant which evaporates in a freezing chamber, the food or other water containing substance to be frozen entering and leaving the freezing chamber through duct means. The freezing chamber is in open communication with the ambient atmosphere through such duct means and the freezing apparatus within the general environment of the present invention includes means for discharging air from the freezing chamber and means including a condensation chamber for recovering and recycling excess coolant and condensed evaporated coolant.

The improvement in accordance with the method of the present invention involves the steps of measuring the difference in pressure resulting from the diffusion of the coolant and air between the freezing chamber and duct means, thereby producing a control signal in response and relative to such difference in pressure and controlling the operation of the freezing apparatus in response to such control signal. In one embodiment of the present invention, the control signal is used to control the discharge of the amount of air in the freezing apparatus through the discharge means, preferably an adjustable suction pump. Alternatively, such discharge means in a downcomer filled with a cold air-coolant mixture. Still further, the control signal may in a further embodiment of the present invention operate on control means to control the rate of condensation of coolant evaporating in the freezing chamber. Such control means may be a control valve located between the freezing chamber and condensation chamber or between the condensation chamber and air discharge means.

In accordance with the present invention, the improved apparatus for freezing foods and other water containing substances includes, in addition to those means set forth in the preamble above, measuring means for measuring the difference of pressure resulting from diffusion of coolant and air between the freezing chamber and duct means so as to produce a control signal based upon such difference in pressure with control means to control the operation of the freezing apparatus in response to the control signal. Hereagain, the control means may be a control valve located between the freezing chamber and condensation chamber or between the condensation chamber and air discharge means.

The foregoing characteristics of the improved method and apparatus of the present invention will be described in more detail by reference to the attached drawings.

As shown in FIG. 1, the products to be frozen are supplied in baskets 1 with a sieve bottom with the aid of a conveyor. The baskets are piled up in a perpendicular supply duct 2. At the bottom of the duct 2 the lowest basket of the stack is pushed by means of a hydraulic cylinder 3 onto the horizontal guide surface 4 of a freezing chamber 5 and is pushed through the freezing chamber to the discharge duct 20 by the subsequent baskets. During this horizontal transport, the products to be frozen are sprayed by a liquid coolant via nozzles in supply and distributing line 6. A part of this coolant evaporates on the surface of the product to be frozen. As the coolant evaporates, it removes the necessary heat of evaporation from the material, thereby lowering the temperature to the freezing point. The evaporation temperature of the coolant, i.g. CF_2Cl_2, corresponding to the pressure in the freezing chamber, is almost the boiling temperature thereof (−29° for CF_2Cl_2). The surplus of nonevaporated coolant which flows downwardly through baskets 1 and horizontal guide surface 4 with a surplus is gathered in a collector 7 and is supplied via a discharge pipe 8 to a circulation pump 9, from which it is repumped to the supply and distributing line 6. The evaporated coolant flows via a control valve 10 to a condenser 11. The control valve 10 is located between the freezing chamber 5 and the condensing chamber 11. The cooling of the condenser 11 is obtained, for example, by evaporating coolant CHF_2Cl_2 from a cooling apparatus 12 through supply line 22 and discharge line 23.

The amount of air entering with the product via the supply duct 2 into the freezing apparatus, plus the air penetrating by diffusion via the supply duct 2, is mixed with the evaporating medium in the freezing chamber and flows with this medium via the control valve 10 to the condenser 11. The greater part of the coolant is liquefied by cooling in the condenser 11 and flows via a discharge line 13 to the collector 7. The air with the noncondensed part of the coolant collects in a chamber 14 cooled after the condenser 11 and is guided from this point through a line 15 to an after-condenser 16 where the greater part of the coolant is condensed by cooling with a cooling liquid of a temperature of −80° to −100°, for example, and the condensate, discharged via pipe 17, also flows to the collector 7. The air substantially freed from coolant is removed via a pump 18 or via a downcomer (not shown) operating according to the principle that cold air is heavier than the ambient air.

According to the present invention, the control of the discharge of air takes place by using the difference of pressure, measured by a differential pressure gauge 19, connected to the bottom of the supply duct 2 or the discharge duct 20 and the ambient air, as a pressure impulse-sender. The difference of pressure indicated by the gauge 19 is the result of the average composition of the mixture of air and coolant in the supply duct 2 or the discharge duct 20 and the ambient air. In each duct, the gas contents of the upper part will, during optimum conditions in the freezing apparatus, mainly consist of air and traces of coolant, whereas the gas contents of the lower part will mainly consist of the much heavier coolant with traces of air. As a result of the diffusion of the air and the coolant gas in each other somewhere in the supply duct a more or less sharp change of the gas concentration will occur (see FIG. 2 for the principal change of the concentration). There is a bending point B in the concentration change represented by the point of inflection in the concentration curve shown in FIG. 2. The difference of pressure indicated by the gauge 19 is dependent on the location of this bending point B, i.e., the height H_B. According to the present invention, the discharge of air from the freezing apparatus is controlled by means of the signal from gauge 19, the signal can, for example, be used to adjust the control valve 21 in such a way that the bending point of the gas concentration in the supply duct differs only in a small way from the predetermined value, e.g. 1/3 of the duct length calculated from the horizontal guide surface 4. This is reached by adjusting gauge to a value of

$$\Delta p = (\tfrac{2}{3}\,\rho\text{ air} + \tfrac{1}{3}\,\rho\, CF_2Cl_2)H - \rho\text{ air } H.$$

wherein H represents the length of supply duct 2 or the discharge duct 20, ρ air represent the density of air, and $\rho\ CF_2Cl_2$ represents the density of CF_2Cl_2 and Δp represents the predetermined difference of pressure.

When the pressure gauge reads above this value of Δp, the control valve 21 is opened further, below this value it is throttled. Instead of using the control valve 21 it is, for example, also possible to obtain the same results by adjusting control valve 10 between the freezing chamber and the condenser chamber.

The signal from the gauge 19 can be applied to a controller 24 over a line 25. The controller 24 activates the control valve 21 in a conventional way through the line or link 26, or in the alternative, may operate the control valve 10 over the line or through the link 27. In the illustrated embodiment, therefore, either valve 21 may be controlled or valve 10 may be controlled. Controller 24 is illustrative of any conventional device responsive to signals from the gauge 19 to control either valve.

Having described in detail the improved method and apparatus of the present invention, it is again pointed out that through the use of such method and apparatus it is possible to control freezing apparatus in a manner not heretofore possible prior to the development of the present invention. In this regard, the employment of the improved method and apparatus of the present invention allow for the effective freezing of foods and other water containing substances by controlling the freezing apparatus in a convenient and economical manner through the employment of sensing and control means based upon a difference in pressure, the method and apparatus of the present invention allowing the employment of currently available techniques without requiring major changes in the presently available freezing apparatue. In this regard, it is possible in accordance with the present invention to significantly improve the recovery of CF_2Cl_2 and other relatively expensive evaporating coolants operating with direct contact between the evaporating coolant and the products to be frozen. In this respect, while the foregoing are presented basically in connection with the employment of CF_2Cl_2 as the coolant medium, it is obvious that any conventional coolant utilized in the type of method and apparatus described can be advantageously employed in the present invention.

Inasmuch as the present invention is subject to many variations, modifications and changes in detail, it is intended that all matter described above or shown in the accompanying drawings be interpreted as illustrative and not in a limiting sense.

What is claimed is:

1. A method for controlling apparatus for freezing water-containing substances, such as food, by contacting the substances directly with an evaporating coolant, wherein said apparatus includes a freezing chamber in which said evaporation takes place, duct means into which the substances enter and leave the freezing chamber and by which the freezing chamber is directly opened to the atmosphere, a condensation chamber for recovering and recycling excess coolant and condensed evaporated coolant, and means for discharging air cooled by the condensation chamber from the freezing chamber to the atmosphere, the improvement comprising the steps of:

- measuring the difference in pressure between the ambient atmosphere and one of the duct means due to diffusion of coolant and air in the freezing chamber;
- producing a control signal indicative of said difference in pressure; and
- controlling the operation of the freezing apparatus in response to said control signal to improve recovery of the coolant.

2. The method of claim **1** wherein said control signal is used to control the discharge, through said discharge means, of the amount of air in said freezing apparatus.

3. The method of claim **2**, wherein the discharge through said discharge means is accomplished by an adjustable suction pump.

4. The method of claim **2**, wherein the discharge through said discharge means is accomplished by a downcomer which is filled with a cold air-coolant mixture and allows the cold air to gravitationally escape into the ambient atmosphere.

5. The method of claim **1** wherein said control signal operates on control means for controlling the rate of condensation of coolant evaporating in said freezing chamber.

6. The method of claim **5** wherein said control means is a control valve located between said freezing chamber and said condensation chamber, said control valve opening further as said difference of pressure exceeds a predetermined value and said control valve throttling when said difference of pressure falls below said predetermined value.

7. The method of claim **5**, wherein operation of said control means is accomplished by operating a control valve located between said condensation chamber and said air discharge means.

8. An apparatus for freezing water-containing substances, such as food, wherein the apparatus includes a freezing chamber in which freezing occurs by directly contacting the substances to be frozen with an evaporating coolant, duct means through which the water-containing substances enter and leave the freezing chamber and through which the freezing chamber is opened to the atmosphere, a condensation chamber for recovering and recycling excess coolant and means for discharging air cooled by said condensation chamber from the freezing chamber to the atmosphere, wherein the improvement comprises:

- means for measuring the difference in pressure between the ambient atmosphere and one of the duct means resulting from diffusion of coolant and air;
- means for producing a control signal indicative of the difference in pressure; and
- means for controlling operation of the freezing apparatus in response to said control signal to thereby improve recovery of the coolant.

9. The freezing apparatus of claim **8** wherein said discharge means is an adjustable suction pump.

10. The freezing apparatus of claim **8** wherein said discharge means is a downcomer filled with a cold air-coolant mixture.

11. The freezing apparatus of claim **8** wherein said control means is a control valve located between said freezing chamber and said condensation chamber, said control valve opening further as said difference of pressure exceeds a predetermined value and said control valve throttling when said difference of pressure falls below said predetermined value.

12. The freezing apparatus of claim **8** wherein said control means is a control valve located between said condensation chamber and said air discharge means, said control valve closing when said difference of pressure exceeds a predetermined value.

* * * * *

Specification of an Original U.S. Design Patent (Des. 218, 335)

United States Patent Office

Des. 218,335
Patented Aug. 11, 1970

218,335

RAG DOLL

**Cecelia Jeannette Cummings, 3033 S. D St.,
Oxnard, Calif. 93030**

Filed May 26, 1969, Ser. No. 17,353
Term of patent 14 years
Int. Cl. D21—*02*
U.S. Cl. D34—4

FIG. 3

FIG. 2

FIG. 1

FIG. 4

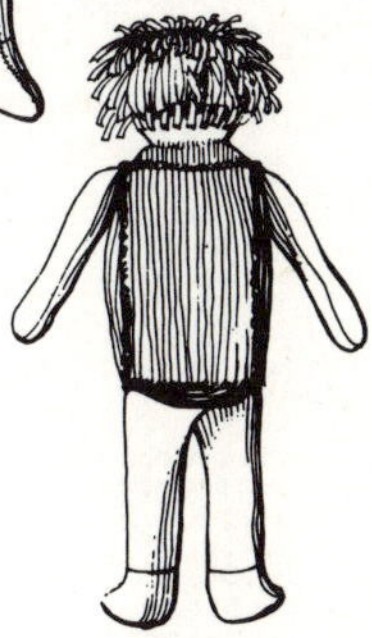

FIG. 5

FIG. 1 is a perspective view of a rag doll showing my new design;
FIG. 2 is a top plan view thereof;
FIG. 3 is a side elevational view thereof, showing the side not shown in FIG. 1;
FIG. 4 is a front elevational view thereof; and,
FIG. 5 is a rear elevational view thereof.
I claim:
The ornamental design for a rag doll, substantially as shown.

References Cited

UNITED STATES PATENTS

D. 57,489	4/1921	Baum	D34—4
D. 84,191	5/1931	Hebert	D34—4
1,498,950	6/1924	Chinn.	

MELVIN B. FEIFER, Primary Examiner

3. Specification of a Reissue of a U.S. Utility Patent (Re. 25,558)

United States Patent Office

Re. 25,558
Reissued Apr. 21, 1964

1

25,558

PYROPHORIC ALLOYS WITHOUT IRON

Walter Bungardt, Essen-Bredeney, Germany, assignor to Ronson Metals Corporation, Newark, N.J.

No Drawing. Original No. 2,978,322, dated Apr. 4, 1961, Ser. No. 712,307, Jan. 31, 1958. Application for reissue Mar. 20, 1963, Ser. No. 267,884
Claims priority, application Germany Feb. 8, 1957
2 Claims. (Cl. 75—152)

Matter enclosed in heavy brackets [ ] appears in the original patent but forms no part of this reissue specification; matter printed in italics indicates the additions made by reissue.

This invention refers to the manufacture of pyrophoric [mass] *material* in rod and like formation for use in connection with lighters, safety lamps and for other industrial purposes.

It is well known that alloys containing [cerium-misch metal] *cerium mischmetal* with zinc when cast, may be employed for pyrophoric purposes, for example, as flints in safety lamps to be operated by miners as well as in the mining industry. Alloys of this type were heretofore manufactured exclusively by casting.

[However, the operational manufacturing conditions and the finished flint rod thereby obtained did not comply with economical and practical requirements, so that all attempts to make use of aforesaid alloy failed.]

New attempts have shown that a most economical and safe process can be carried out by means of extrusion if ingots of alloys of the aforesaid type of predetermined composition are subjected to such special process. It has now been surprisingly found that very desirable practical requirements can be realized and fulfilled and that none of the heretofore encountered difficulties will occur, if alloys are selected which are composed of [cerium-misch metal] *cerium mischmetal* with additions of zinc of predetermined range from 5% up to 25% by weight of the total alloy and more specifically from 12% to 17% by weight.

It is therefore one of the primary objects of the invention to provide means affording the manufacture of flint rods and like shapes of pyrophoric material with improved sparking and other desirable properties [, thereby contributing to increased and varied technically useful alloys].

It is another object of the present invention to provide means conducive to an economical and continuous novel process for obtaining finished extruded flint shapes in conformity with the apparatus in which said flint shapes are employed.

It has been further found that considerable improvements of the pyrophoric properties of extruded flint rods are attained if in the above mentioned alloys which are substantially completely devoid of iron, additional elements are incorporated, such as copper, cadmium, antimony, bismuth and manganese, ranging within certain limits from .5% to 8% by weight and preferably between [2% to 6%] *about 0.5% to about 8%* by weight.

Furthermore, other additions such as magnesium, have been found to be of great advantage in making up the alloy for the ingot to be subjected to extrusion, the magnesium amounting to about .5% to 5% by weight, from which in particular dense spark formation will result.

It is therefore still another object of the present invention to provide means rendering the possibility of influencing crystal formation in the finished flint product, so that on the one hand, the pyrophoric metal will offer great resistance to corrosion and wear during normal use, while on the other hand, its sparking and pyrophoric effect will be considerably increased and may be controlled within a relatively large range.

The invention will be more fully and comprehensively

2

understood from a consideration of the following detailed description with the understanding, that the improvement is capable of extended application and is not confined to the precise disclosure, suggested changes and modifications may be made herein which do not affect the spirit of the invention nor exceed the scope thereof as expressed in the appended claims.

The following examples demonstrate the mode and preferred compounds according to which the present invention may be carried into effect.

EXAMPLE I

An alloy containing about 16% by weight of zinc, about 2% by weight of cadmium and about 1.5% of copper, with the remainder [cerium-misch metal] *cerium mischmetal* of commercial purity, is melted and [made up] *cast* into ingots [cast at about 150° to 500° C.]. After cooling down such ingot may then be subjected to extrusion at a temperature ranging from 380° C. to 400° C. The extrusion pressure applied amounts to about 4,100 kg./cm.².

EXAMPLE II

An alloy containing about 14% of zinc, about 4% of cadmium, approximately 2% of manganese and about 1.5% by weight of copper, is obtained having as a remaining constituent [cerium-misch metal] *cerium mischmetal* of commercial purity. Such alloy is [converted] *cast* into [an] ingot *form* [at about 150° to 500° C.] and after cooling down may then be subjected to extrusion at an extrusion temperature of 380° to 400° C. with an applied extrusion pressure of about 4,200 kg./cm.².

EXAMPLE III

A mixture containing about 15% by weight of zinc, about 3% by weight of cadmium and about 2.5% by weight of magnesium, is alloyed with about 1.5% of copper, the remainder being [cerium-misch metal] *cerium mischmetal* of commercial purity. This alloy is cast [at a temperature ranging from between 150° C. and 500° C. to obtain ingots, which are allowed to cool down. The ingot is] *into ingots which are* then extruded at a temperature of about 380° to 400° C. with an extrusion pressure applied to the ingots and extrusion press die of about 4,800 kg./cm.².

EXAMPLE IV

An alloy is made up containing about 15% by weight of zinc, about 3% by weight of cadmium, about 2% by weight of antimony and 1.5% by weight [by] *of* copper, the remainder being [cerium-misch metal] *cerium mischmetal* of commercial purity. This alloy is cast into [suitably sized] ingots [at a temperature of 150° to 500° C. and after cooling down the ingot may then be] *which are then* subjected to extrusion at 380° to 400° C. at a pressure of about 4,400 kg. /cm.².

EXAMPLE V

An alloy is employed consisting of about 15% by weight of zinc, about 3% by weight of cadmium, about 2% by weight of bismuth with approximately 1.5% by weight of copper, the remainder being [cerium-misch metal] *cerium mischmetal* of commercial purity. The alloy is melted and then cast into ingots [at 150° to 500° C. and may thereafter be] *which are* extruded at 380° to 400° C. at an extrusion pressure of about 4,500 kg./cm.².

The aforesaid [cerium (misch metal)] *cerium mischmetal*-zinc alloys may contain between 14% and 16% by weight of zinc and between 2% and 4% by weight of cadmium, with the addition of [trace] amounts of copper of about 1.5% by weight.

[It ensues from the aforesaid examples that the extrusion pressure may be easily regulated by certain additions of manganese, preferably ranging between .5% to 8% by weight and preferably ranging from 2% to 6% by weight. A further increase of the extrusion pressure was obtainable through the addition of magnesium ranging between .5% to 5% by weight. A particularly useful alloy having an addition of magnesium of approximately 2.5% by weight requires a considerably increased extrusion pressure. Other additions to regulate the extrusion pressure may be additions of antimony of 2% by weight or bismuth of about 2% by weight, in the latter cases, the extrusion pressure being markedly reduced in comparison with the extrusion pressure obtained when magnesium was added to the basic constituents of cerium (misch metal)-zinc-cadmium-copper alloy.**]**

It has been found that the extrusion process may be advantageously carried out at a required extrusion pressure ranging from about 4,000 kg./cm.^{2} to about less than 5,000 kg./cm.^{2}. To this end an ingot is produced by adding to **[**cerium (misch metal)**]** *cerium mischmetal* a zinc content ranging between 5% and 25% by weight with the additions of at least one of the elements selected from the group comprising copper, magnesium, cadmium, antimony, bismuth and manganese.

Although preferred embodiments of the invention have been described, it will be understood that modifications may be made within the spirit and scope of the appended claims. It will, however, be understood that there is no intention to include unmentioned ingredients other than minor impurities.

Having thus described, the invention, what is claimed as new and desired to be secured by Letters Patent, is:

1. A pyrophoric mass suitable for extrusion to produce finished flints in rod formation; consisting essentially of **[**cerium (misch metal)**]** *cerium mischmetal* with zinc ranging from 5% to 25% by weight, and having an addition of at least one of the elements selected from the group consisting of copper, cadmium, antimony, bismuth and manganese, said addition ranging from **[**2% to 6%**]** *about 0.5% to about 8%* by weight, and a further addition of magnesium amounting to about .5% to 5% by weight **[**to adjust the extrusion pressure to at least 4,100 kg./cm.^{2}**]**, the balance being cerium **[**(misch metal)**]** *mischmetal.*

2. A pyrophoric mass suitable for extrusion to produce finished flints in rod formation; consisting essentially of cerium **[**(misch metal)**]** *mischmetal* with zinc of about 14% by weight, and further additions of copper, manganese and cadmium, the amount of copper being about 1.5% by weight, that of manganese being about 2% by weight, and that of cadmium being about 4% by weight.

References Cited in the file of this patent or the original patent

UNITED STATES PATENTS

1,102,575	Faehr	July 7, 1914
1,118,138	Kratky	Nov. 24, 1914

FOREIGN PATENTS

15,507	Great Britain	Oct. 27, 1910
3,350	Great Britain	Nov. 14, 1912

Appendix B

Specification of U.S. Patent No. 5, 175

3 Sheets—Sheet 1.

R. WINANS.

Dumping Car.

No. 5,175. Patented June 26, 1847.

Fig. 1.

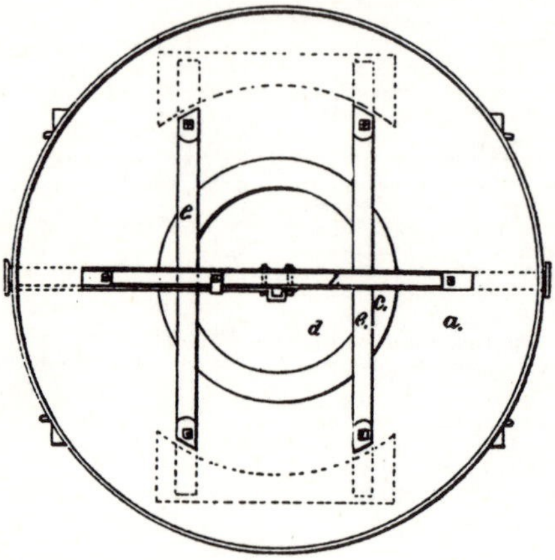

Fig. 2.

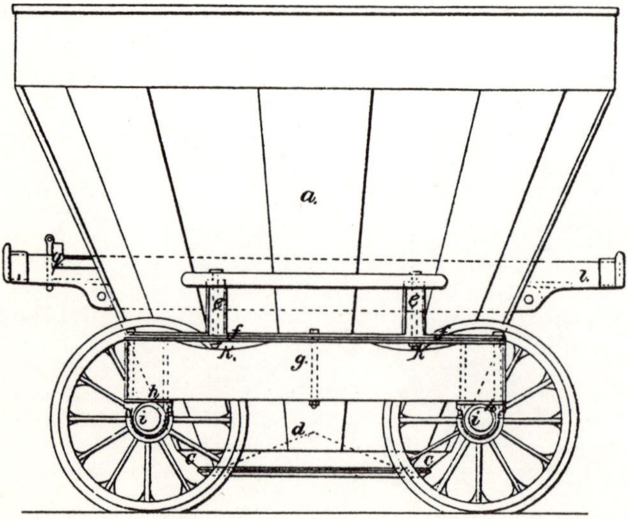

3 Sheets—Sheet 2.

R. WINANS.

Dumping Car.

No. 5,175.

Patented June 26, 1847.

Fig. 3.

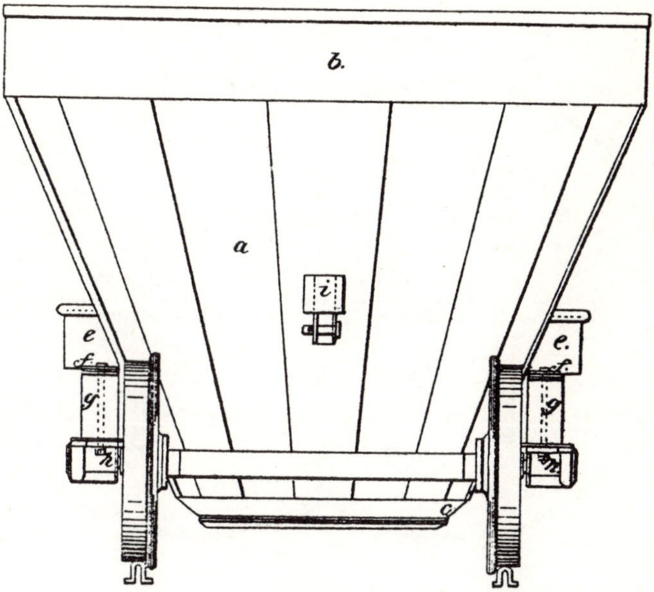

Fig. 4.

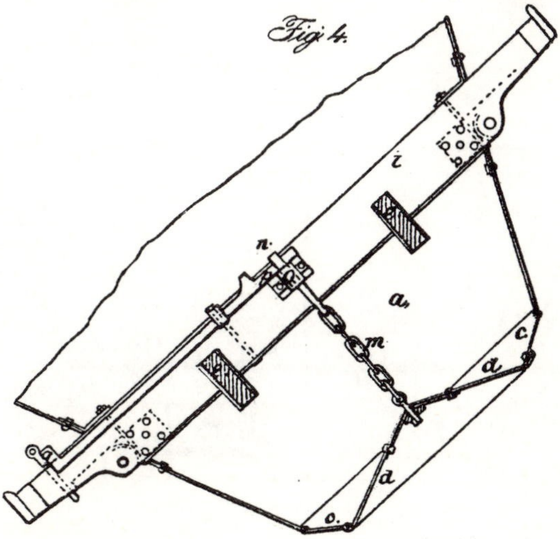

3 Sheets—Sheet 3.

R. WINANS.

Dumping Car.

No. 5,175. Patented June 26, 1847.

Fig. 6.

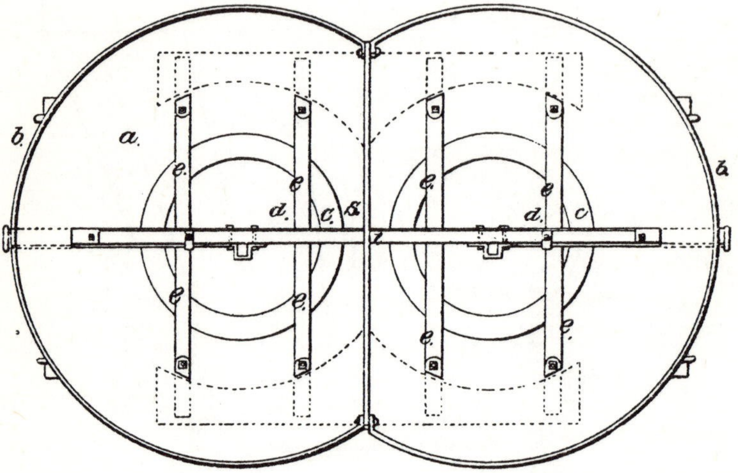

Fig. 5.

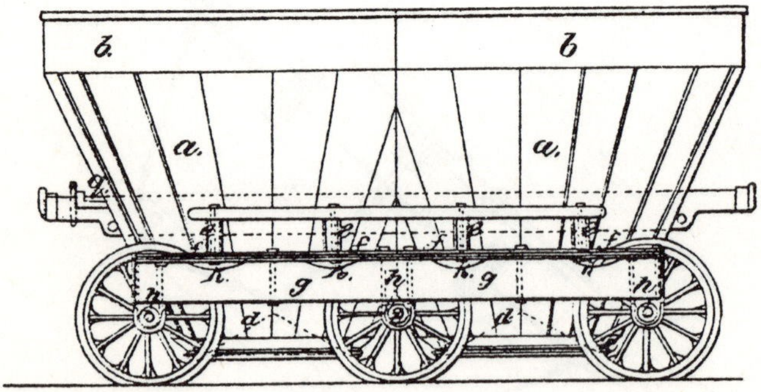

UNITED STATES PATENT OFFICE.

ROSS WINANS, OF BALTIMORE, MARYLAND.

CAR FOR TRANSPORTATION OF COAL, &c.

Specification of Letters Patent No. 5,175, dated June 26, 1847.

To all whom it may concern:

Be it known that I, Ross Winans, of the city of Baltimore and State of Maryland, have invented new and useful Improvements in Railroad-Cars, and that the following is a full, clear, and exact description of the principle or character which distinguishes it from all other things before known and of the manner of making, constructing, and using the same, reference being had to the accompanying drawings, making part of this specification, in which—

Figure 1 is a plan of a car on my improved plan; Fig. 2, a side elevation thereof; Fig. 3, an end elevation of the same; and Fig. 4, a section of the body removed from the truck.

The same letters indicate like parts in all the figures.

The transportation of coal and all other heavy articles in lumps has been attended with great injury to the cars—requiring the bodies to be constructed with great strength to resist the outward pressure on the sides as well as the vertical pressure on the bottom, due, not only to the weight of the mass, but the mobility of the lumps among each other, tending to "pack," as it is technically termed. Experience has shown that cars on the old mode of construction cannot be made to carry a load greater than its own weight, but by my improvement I am enabled to make cars of greater durability than those heretofore made which will transport double their own weight of coal &c.

The principle of my invention by which I am enabled to attain this important end consists in making the body, or a portion thereof, conical, by which the area of the bottom is reduced and the load exerts an equal strain on all parts, and which does not tend to change the form but to exert an equal strain in the direction of the circle. At the same time this form presents the important advantage by the reduced size of the lower part thereof to extend down within the truck and between the axles, thereby lowering the center of gravity of the load.

In the accompanying drawings (*a*) represents the body of the car made of sheet iron in the form of a frustum of a hollow cone, with the upper part (*b*) cylindrical. To the lower edge of this is secured a flange (*c*) which forms part of the bottom and against which the movable bottom (*d*) closes, as will be described hereafter. The body of the car is connected with the truck by means of two cross bars (*e, e*) that pass horizontally through the conical part of it, with their ends resting on bar springs (*f, f*) on the top of the side pieces (*g, g*) of the truck, these being provided with boxes (*h, h*) of any desired construction in which run the journals of the wheel axles (*i, i*) the lower end of the conical part of the body passing down between the side pieces and the axles of the truck. The springs (*f, f*) are plates of steel secured at the ends and middle to the upper surface of the side pieces of the truck, and the bars (*e, e*) that pass through the body of the car are secured to the springs at points midway between their attachment to the side pieces of the truck, the upper surface of these being cut out as at (*k, k*) to give the requisite play to the springs. The draft bar (*l*) which forms the connection between the different cars of a train passes through the conical part of the body above the bars (*e, e*) and is firmly secured to them so as to relieve the body of the strain due to the draft. To this bar is also secured the movable bottom of the car which is provided with a chain (*m*) to the end of which is secured a latch piece (*n*) that passes through a staple (*o*) attached to the draft bar and is there secured by a bolt (*p*) that slides on the bar, the head or handle of the bolt being extended outside of the body, as at (*q*), so that when the car is to be emptied of its contents the bolt (*p*) is drawn which liberates the latch bolt and permits the movable bottom to fall by the weight of the coal, &c., resting on it.

When desired the principle of my invention can be modified to make the car double as represented in the plan Fig. 6 and elevation Fig. 5, plate 2. In this modification the circles of the two bodies intersect each other, and the union is formed between the two by the cord plate (*s*). In this construction there is space enough left between the two cones at the lower end for the middle pair of wheels, such cars being made with six wheels instead of the four used in the first example.

It will be obvious that car bodies constructed on the principle of my invention may be connected with, and supported on the truck without the bars passing through the body by having the supports bolted or otherwise secured to the outside or to hoops embracing the whole circumference; but by these modifications a greater strain will be given to the body than by the arrangement above described.

What I claim as my invention and desire to secure by Letters Patent is—

1. Making the body of a car for the transportation of coal, &c., in the form of a frustum of a cone, substantially as herein described, whereby the force exerted by the weight of the load presses equally in all directions and does not tend to change the form thereof, so that every part resists its equal proportion, and by which also the lower part is so reduced as to pass down within the truck frame and between the axles to lower the center of gravity of the load without diminishing the capacity of the car, as described.

2. I also claim extending the body of the car below the connecting pieces of the truck frame, and the line of draft, by passing the connecting bars of the truck frame and the draft bar through the body of the car, substantially as described.

ROSS WINANS.

Witnesses:
GEORGE W. WHISTLER, Jr.,
JOHN B. EASTER.

TABLE OF CASES

[References are to pages]

B

[References are to pages]

E

F

[References are to pages]

G

H

F.2d 225, 151 U.S.P.Q. 670 (7th Cir. 1966), 334
Hewlett-Packard Co. v. Tel-Design, Inc., 460 F.2d 625, 174 U.S.P.Q. 140 (9th Cir. 1972), 311
A.E. Hickman, 29 T.C. 864 (1958), 284
Hickman v. Taylor, 329 U.S. 495 (1947), 312
Hilmer (I), *In re*, 359 F.2d 859, 149 U.S. P.Q. 480 (C.C.P.A. 1966), 332, 333
Hilmer (II), *In re*, 424 F.2d 1108, 165 U.S. P.Q. 255 (C.C.P.A. 1970), 333
Hobbie v. Jennison, 149 U.S. 355 (1893), 283
Hobbs v. Wisconsin Power & Light Co., 250 F.2d 100, 115 U.S.P.Q. 371 (7th Cir. 1957), 114
Hofstetter, *In re*, 362 F.2d 293, 150 U.S. P.Q. 105 (C.C.P.A. 1966), *cert. granted* 386 U.S. 990 (1967), *app. dism'd* 155 U.S.P.Q. 515 (1967), 255
Holiday v. Matheson, 57 Fed. 524 (2d Cir. 1893), 334
Hollingsworth, *In re*, 278 F.2d 753, 126 U.S.P.Q. 56 (C.C.P.A. 1960), 256
Holstensson v. Webcor, 150 F.Supp. 441, 112 U.S.P.Q. 463 (N.D.Ill. 1957), 165
Honn, *In re*, 364 F.2d 454, 150 U.S.P.Q. 652 (C.C.P.A. 1966), 204
Honnig, *In re*, 193 F.2d 191, 92 U.S.P.Q. 134 (C.C.P.A. 1951), 114, 256
Hotchkiss v. Greenwood, 52 U.S. (11 How.) 248 (1850), 65, 131
Hotel Security Checking Co. v. Lorraine Co., 160 Fed.467 (2d Cir. 1908), 88
Hot Pouncing Mach. Co. v. Hedden, 148 U.S. 482 (1892), 131
Howard v. Detroit Works, 150 U.S. 164 (1893), 131
Hruby, *In re*, 373 F.2d 997, 153 U.S.P.Q. 61 (C.C.P.A. 1967), 87
Huellmantel, *In re*, 324 F.2d 998, 139 U.S. P.Q. 496 (C.C.P.A. 1963), 106
Hull v. Davenport, 90 F.2d 103, 33 U.S.P.Q. 506 (C.C.P.A. 1937), 154
Hummer, *In re*, 241 F.2d 742, 113 U.S.P.Q. 66 (C.C.P.A. 1957), 256
Hunt v. Armour & Co., 185 F.2d 322, 88 U.S.P.Q. 53 (7th Cir. 1950), 311
Hunt v. Mallinckrodt Chem. Works, 177 F.2d 583, 83 U.S.P.Q. 277 (2d Cir. 1949), 253, 256
Hurn v. Oursler, 289 U.S. 238, 17 U.S.P.Q. 195 (1933), 312
Hygenic Specialties Co. v. H.G. Salzman, Inc., 320 F.2d 614, 133 U.S.P.Q. 96 (2d Cir. 1962), 87

I

I.C.E. Corp. v. Armco Steel Co., 250 F.Supp. 738, 148 U.S.P.Q. 537 (S.D.N.Y. 1966), 106
International Business Mach. Corp. v. United States, 298 U.S. 131, 37 U.S.P.Q. 224 (1936), 282
Imm v. Comm'r, 94 U.S.P.Q. 92 (T.C. 1952), 284
Isenstead v. Watson, 157 F.Supp. 7, 115 U.S.P.Q. 408 (D.D.C. 1957), 65

J

Jacobs v. Baker, 74 U.S.(7 Wall.) 297 (1868), 86
Jacobs v. Beecham, 221 U.S. 263 (1910), 65
Jacoby, *In re*, 309 F.2d 509, 135 U.S.P.Q. 317 (C.C.P.A. 1962), 86
Jamesbury Corp. v. Worcester Valve Co., 443 F.2d 205, 170 U.S.P.Q. 177 (1st Cir. 1971), 165
Japan Gas Lighter Assn. v. Ronson Corp., 257 F.Supp. 219, 150 U.S.P.Q. 589 (D.N.J. 1966), 312
Jennings v. Brenner, 255 F.Supp. 410, 150 U.S.P.Q. 167 (D.D.C. 1966), 20, 256
Jepson, Ex parte, 1917 C.D. 62, 243 O.G. 525 (Comm.Pat. 1925), 52
Jepson v. Egly, 231 F.2d 947, 109 U.S.P.Q. 354 (C.C.P.A. 1956), 154
Jiffy Enterprises, Inc. v. Sears, Roebuck & Co., 306 F.2d 240, 134 U.S.P.Q. 158 (3d Cir. 1960), *cert. denied* 371 U.S. 922 (1962)
Johnson v. Brewer-Tichenor Corp., 28 F.Supp. 1002, 42 U.S.P.Q. 437 (N.D.N.Y. 1939), 283

K

Kaiser Indus. Corp. v. Jones & Laughlin Steel Corp., 181 U.S.P.Q. 193 (W.D.Pa. 1974), 20, 312
Katz Drug Co. v. Katz, 188 F.2d 696, 89

L

N

[References are to pages]

O

P

Q

R

[References are to pages]

S

[References are to pages]

F.Supp. 270 83 U.S.P.Q. 153 (S.D.Cal. 1945), 32, 87
Scott Paper Co. v. Marcalus Mfg. Co., 326 U.S. 249, 67 U.S.P.Q. 193 (1945), 88, 106, 283
Scudder, Ex parte, 169 U.S.P.Q. 814 (P.O. Bd.App. 1971), 257
Seaborg, *In re*, 328 F.2d 993, 140 U.S.P.Q. 659 (C.C.P.A. 1964), 53, 86
Sears, Roebuck Co. v. Stiffel Co., 376 U.S. 225, 140 U.S.P.Q. 524 (1964), 19, 32
Seavy, Ex parte, 125 U.S.P.Q. 454 (P.O.Bd. App. 1960), 53
Sel-O-Rak v. The Henry Hanger & Display Fixture Corp., 232 F.2d 176, 109 U.S. P.Q. 179 (5th Cir. 1956), 86
Seymour v. Osborne, 78 U.S. (11 Wall.) 516 (1870), 5, 19, 86, 311, 312
Shaffer, *In re,* 229 F.2d 476, 108 U.S.P.Q. 326 (C.C.P.A. 1956), 256
Sharples v. Moseley & Stoddard Mfg. Co., 81 Fed. 179 (3d Cir. 1897), 282
Shaw v. Cooper, 32 (7 Pet.) 292 (1833), 106
Shaw v. E.B. & A.C. Whiting Co., 417 F.2d 1097, 163 U.S.P.Q. 580 (2d Cir. 1969), *cert. denied* 398 U.S. 954 (1970), 52
Sheldon v. Metro-Goldwyn Pictures Corp., 106 F.2d 45, 42 U.S.P.Q. 540 (2d Cir. 1939), *aff'd* 309 U.S. 390, 44 U.S.P.Q. 607 (1940), 19, 332
Shellmar Prod. Co. v. Allen-Qualley Co., 87 F.2d 104, 32 U.S.P.Q. 24 (7th Cir.), *cert. denied* 301 U.S. 695 (1936), 165
Sherrer, Ex parte, 103 U.S.P.Q. 107 (P.O. Bd.App. 1954), 86
Shubin v. U.S. District Court, 313 F.2d 250, 136 U.S.P.Q. 405 (9th Cir. 1963), 312
Sid W. Richardson, Inc. v. Bryan, 144 F.Supp. 916, 110 U.S.P.Q. 424 (S.D.Tex. 1956), 52
Silverstein, Ex parte, 125 U.S.P.Q. 238 (P.O.Bd.App. 1959), 86, 256
Simson Bros., Inc. v. Blancard & Co., 22 F.2d 498 (2d Cir. 1927), 313
Singer Mfg. Co. v. June Mfg. Co., 163 U.S. 169 (1896), 88
Skee Ball Co. v. Cohen, 286 Fed. 275 (E.D. N.Y. 1922), 283
Skrivan, *In re*, 427 F.2d 801, 166 U.S.P.Q. 85 (C.C.P.A. 1970), 205
Smith v. Dental Vulcanite Co., 93 U.S.(3 Otto) 486 (1877), 154
Smith v. Dravo Corp., 203 F.2d 369, 97 U.S.P.Q. 98 (7th Cir. 1953), 20, 106
Smith v. Nichols, 88 U.S.(21 Wall.) 112 (1875), 20, 65, 131, 282
Smyth, *In re,* 189 F.2d 982, 90 U.S.P.Q. 106 (C.C.P.A. 1951), 257, 332
Smythe, Ex parte, 139 U.S.P.Q. 529 (P.O. Bd.App. 1963), 106
Soundscriber Corp. v. United States, 360 F.2d 954, 148 U.S.P.Q. 298 (Ct.Cl. 1966), 255
Space Aero Prod. Co. v. R.E. Darling Co., 145 U.S.P.Q. 356 (Md.Ct.App. 1965), 165
Special Equip. Co. v. Coe, 324 U.S. 370, 64 U.S.P.Q. 525 (1945), 19, 52
Sperry v. Ex rel. Florida Bar, 373 U.S. 379, 137 U.S.P.Q. 578 (1963), 253
Sperry Rand Corp. v. Bell Telephone Laboratories, 208 F.Supp. 598, 135 U.S.P.Q. 254 (S.D.N.Y. 1962), 106
Sperry Rand Corp. v. Texas Instruments, Inc., 206 F.Supp. 676, 133 U.S.P.Q. 680 (N.D.Tex. 1962), 311
Squires, Ex parte, 133 U.S.P.Q. 598 (P.O. Bd.App. 1961), 65
Stamicarbon, N.V. v. McNally-Pittsburgh Mfg. Co., 302 F.Supp. 525, 161 U.S.P.Q. 323 (D.Kan. 1969), 310
Standard Oil Co. v. United States, 221 U.S. 1 (1911), 282, 283
Steele v. Bulova Watch Co., 344 U.S. 280, 92 U.S.P.Q. 266 (1952), 332
Sterling Drug. Inc. v. Brenner, 256 F.Supp. 1000, 150 U.S.P.Q. 584 (D.D.C. 1966), 65, 132
Sternau, *In re,* 149 U.S.P.Q. 70 (Comm.Pat. 1966), 333
State of Israel v. Brenner, 273 F.Supp. 714, 155 U.S.P.Q. 486 (D.D.C. 1967), *aff'd* 400 F.2d 789, 158 U.S.P.Q. 584 (D.D.C. 1968), 332
Stevens, *In re*, 173 F.2d 1015, 81 U.S.P.Q. 362 (C.C.P.A. 1949), 87
Sticker Indus. Supply Corp. v. Blaw-Knox Co., 321 F.Supp. 876, 167 U.S.P.Q. 442 (N.D.Ill. 1970), 257

[References are to pages]

127 U.S. 792 (1888), 310
United States v. Container Corp., 393 U.S. 333 (1969), 283
United States v. Dubilier Condenser Corp., 289 U.S. 178, 17 U.S.P.Q. 154 (1933), 19, 20, 165, 180
United States v. Frazer, 22 Fed. 104 (N.D. Ill. 1884), 310
United States v. General Elec. Co., 272 U.S. 476 (1926), 283
United States v. Glaxo, Ltd., 410 U.S. 52, 176 U.S.P.Q. 289 (1973), 310
United States v. Gunning, 18 Fed. 511 (D.N.Y. 1883), 310
United States v. Hartford-Empire Co., 73 F.Supp. 979, 75 U.S.P.Q. 118 (D.Del. 1947), 310, 312
United States v. Imperial Chem. Indus., Ltd., 105 F.Supp. 215, 91 U.S.P.Q. 78 (S.D.N.Y. 1952), 332
United States v. Line Material Co., 333 U.S. 287, 76 U.S.P.Q. 399 (1948), 20, 282
United States v. National Gypsum Co., 352 U.S. 457, 112 U.S.P.Q. 340 (1957), 180
United States v. National Lead Co., 332 U.S. 319, 73 U.S.P.Q. 498 (1947), 180
United States v. Parker Rust Proof Co., 61 F.Supp. 805, 65 U.S.P.Q. 563 (E.D. Mich. 1945), 282
United States v. Saf-T-Boom Corp., 164 U.S.P.Q. 283 (E.D.Ark.), *aff'd* 431 F.2d 737, 167 U.S.P.A. 195 (8th Cir. 1970), 310
United States v. Singer Mfg. Co., 374 U.S. 174, 137 U.S.P.Q. 808 (1963), 132
United States v. Stone, 69 U.S.(2 Wall.) 525 (1864), 19
United States v. Trenton Potteries, 273 U.S. 393 (1927), 283
United States v. United Shoe Machinery Corp., 89 F.Supp. 797, 85 U.S.P.Q. 5 (D.Mass. 1950), 253, 313
United States v. U.S. Gypsum Co., 333 U.S. 364, 76 U.S.P.Q. 430 (1948), 310
U.S. Gypsum Co. v. Rock Wood Insulating Co., 212 F.Supp. 1, 136 U.S.P.Q. 524 (D.Colo. 1962), 311
U.S. Pipe & Foundry Co. v. James B. Clow & Sons, Inc., 205 F.Supp. 831, 141 U.S.P.Q. 576 (N.D.Ala. 1962), 311
U.S. Plywood Corp. v. General Plywood Corp., 230 F.Supp. 831, 141 U.S.P.Q. 134 (W.D.Ky. 1963), 311
Union Carbide Co. v. American Carbide Co., 181 Fed. 104 (2d Cir. 1910), 86
Union Carbide Co. v. American Carbolite Co., 188 Fed. 334 (N.D.Ill. 1911), 86
Union Carbide Corp. v. Filtrol Corp., 170 U.S.P.Q. 482 (C.D.Cal. 1971), 257
Union Carbide Corp. v. Graver Tank & Mfg. Co., 282 F.2d 653, 127 U.S.P.Q. 3 (7th Cir. 1960), *cert. denied* 365 U.S. 812 (1961), 312
Union Carbide Corp. v. Microtron Corp., 254 F.Supp. 299, 149 U.S.P.Q. 827 (W.D.N.C. 1966), 333
Union Paper Bag Mach. Co. v. Murphy, 97 U.S.(7 Otto) 120 (1877), 311
Union Stone Co. v. Allen, 14 Fed.353 (C.C.E.D.Pa. 1882), 20
Universal Oil Prod. Co. v. Globe Oil & Refining Co., 322 U.S. 471, 61 U.S.P.Q. 382 (1944), 253
Ulfstedt, Ex parte, 122 U.S.P.Q. 392 (P.O. Bd.App. 1958), 204
Urbanic, *In re,* 319 F.2d 267, 138 U.S.P.Q. 224 (C.C.P.A. 1963), 131
Urguhart v. Comm'r, 215 F.2d 17, 102 U.S. P.Q. 427 (3d Cir. 1954), 284
Utshig, Ex parte, 156 U.S.P.Q. 157 (P.O.Bd. App. 1967), 165

V

Vanity Fair Mills, Inc. v. T. Eaton Co., 234 F.2d 633 (2d Cir.), *cert. denied* 352 U.S. 871 (1956), 333
Velsicol Chem. Corp. v. Hooker Chem. Corp., 230 F.Supp. 998, 142 U.S.P.Q. 131 (N.D.Ill. 1964), 332
Victor Talking Mach. Co. v. The Fair, 123 Fed. 424 (7th Cir. 1903), 262
Von Clemm, *In re*, 229 F.2d 441, 108 U.S. P.Q. 371 (C.C.P.A. 1955), 334
Van Otteren v. Hafner, 278 F.2d 738, 126 U.S.P.Q. 151 (C.C.P.A. 1960), 165

W

Wahl v. Carrier Mfg. Co., 358 F.2d 1, 148 U.S.P.Q. 699 (7th Cir. 1966), 310
Wahl Clipper Corp. v. Andis Clipper Co., 66 F.2d 162, 18 U.S.P.Q. 179 (7th Cir. 1933), 132
Wakefield, *In re* 422 F.2d 897, 164 U.S.P.Q. 636 (C.C.P.A. 1970), 205, 206

[References are to pages]

Y

Z

INDEX

[References are to pages]

[References are to pages]

D

[References are to pages]

E

J

K

L

[References are to pages]

[References are to pages]